D1506996

Persons
What Philosophers Say About You

Warren Bourgeois

Wilfrid Laurier University Press

Canadian Cataloguing in Publication Data

Bourgeois, Verne Warren, 1947-
Persons : what philosophers say about you

Includes bibliographical references and index.
ISBN 0-88920-251-6

1. Persons. 2. Persons – History. I. Title.

BD331.B68 1995   128   C95-930300-6

Copyright © 1995
WILFRID LAURIER UNIVERSITY PRESS
Waterloo, Ontario, Canada N2L 3C5

Cover design by Janet Kimantas using an illustration by Sandra Woolfrey.

Printed in Canada

Persons: What Philosophers Say About You has been produced from a manuscript supplied in camera-ready form by the author.

For My Family

Table of Contents

Acknowledgements

I am grateful to Kwantlen College for awarding me an educational leave in 1989-90 during which the first draft of this book was written. I am also grateful to the University of British Columbia for making me a Research Associate in the Department of Philosophy during my leave. I have benefited greatly from discussions with members of the Philosophy Department, in particular, Professors Richard Sikora, Samuel Coval, Michael Phillips, and Donald Brown. Leonard Angel at Douglas College, Michael Stack at the University of Manitoba, and Ray Jennings at Simon Fraser University offered insightful suggestions about persons. Papers adumbrating the theory developed here were read to two colloquia of the Departments of Philosophy of the University of British Columbia and Simon Fraser University. Sandra Woolfrey's many comments made this a much more accessible book, and I benefited from the criticisms of unnamed reviewers. I would like to have responded to all my colleagues' questions, but I have come to appreciate the saying that one never completes a book but just stops writing. In any case, I have reached the natural limits of my first volume on this subject.

This book has been published with the help of a grant from the Canada Council.

Introduction
Where I Am Coming From

Daphne's tragedy: Radical, personal change

My topics, the nature of persons and personal identity, are for Daphne shot through with significance. At the beginning of the last decade Daphne was teaching at the University of British Columbia where I was on a post-doctoral fellowship. She was a brilliant philosopher. We became an inseparable couple. In the next five years we came to know each other's hearts and minds so well that we could often dispense with spoken communication. We were married in August of 1985. In October of that year, Daphne suffered a massive attack of multiple sclerosis. After nearly a year of attacks and remissions, in August 1986 Daphne passed for the last time beneath the dark archway that separates those who can intelligibly express their wishes from those who cannot.

What people are and what changes a person can survive had long been metaphysical concerns of mine. They suddenly appeared to me as practical questions of great moral import. All too brief expositions of some of the great philosophers of the Western philosophical tradition, including some of our contemporaries, are offered here to reveal some of the sources of our cultural heritage for dealing with what I witnessed and what Daphne suffered. No attempt is made here, however, to deal with the rich traditions of the Orient. My own answers to the questions which forced themselves so roughly to the first place in my philosophical thought are rooted in the past, but, I hope, grow beyond it to become applicable to our current deeds.

On my theory of persons, it is at least possible that one might suffer radical change and still be a person, though not the same person one once was. It is also possible that one might be still a human being but no longer a person at all. Before I work through other's theories of persons, and my own, however, I will explain in further detail what happened to Daphne. This is what I am trying, through my thought, to take up into my life.

The disease had caused massive scarring of the brain resulting in dementia. Daphne, who had been capable of deep philosophical thought and discussion, after the onset of dementia at her most vocal would repeat things by rote, as when she sang with me a few words of simple songs she had known in her girlhood. With heavy-handed irony, fate had written a script in which the only things Daphne could say without prompting were, "I don't know," "Yeah," "No," and "O.K." She would repeat such phrases as many as fifty

1

times in a row as she lay smiling in her hospital bed. Even this limited verbal ability is gone now.

Daphne would have agreed that to merely live through tragedy, to learn nothing from it and to pass nothing on, is to compound the tragedy. In Daphne's own opinion, which she expressed before becoming ill, people in her present circumstances should be counted as the same sentient beings but not the same persons they once were in the crucial sense of "person." Daphne, I believe, can no longer learn from her decline, but we can.

Initially, Daphne was beset by peculiar bodily changes and total exhaustion. She was unable to carry on her life in a normal way. At the beginning, however, neither she nor I could quite believe that this condition would continue. Even though she had already lost the pitch of her intellectual abilities, we did not know this and assumed that she would return to what for her was normal and for most of us would be an exceptional mental clarity. I would say of Daphne at the beginning of her illness, "She is not herself today," in the faith that tomorrow would see the familiar traits return. Intelligence, energy, curiosity, hope, and their allies would surely revive in full measure, I supposed. They did not.

The disease gave Daphne very strange sensations. The myelin sheath, a protective covering on the nerves, was being attacked in Daphne's body by her own immune system. She spoke of inappropriate sensations from familiar stimuli, as, for instance, a warm shower feeling normal on half her body and cold on the other half. Half her tongue was numb. Strange tingling and buzzing sensations came from no observable stimulus at all. With quite good reason, but very uncharacteristically, Daphne became highly irritable, fearful, and depressed. The thought that her body would always undergo such intensely strange sensations was literally driving her mad.

Eventually, after the first massive attack was in remission, hope did return to Daphne, though in a muted form. She began to think that she might have periods of being like her old self. In the past she had worked with great enthusiasm at every task, from putting down inlay in a hardwood floor to the most abstract of intellectual investigations. She was as clever at crafting physical objects as at constructing theories. Although she suspected that she would never regain her former impressive ability to craft material things, since she knew that her eyesight and physical dexterity were permanently impaired, she nonetheless hoped to return to her philosophical work as an outlet for her immense creative impulse. A flame still flickered in those eyes which had burned with a zeal for philosophical understanding. For the time being, however, all our energies were directed at improving Daphne's health. During the period I describe there was no time for reflection. The struggle with the disease consumed us.

Multiple sclerosis is a disease which can take many forms. Some suffer attacks infrequently with long periods of remission. At another extreme, some steadily and quickly worsen, losing physical or mental abilities, perhaps both. At first it was not clear how Daphne's case would progress. From the very beginning, however, she was very different from the way she had been just prior to that massive attack in October 1985.

Daphne had had a keen, incisive mind and a powerful memory. Her mind was immediately somewhat dulled, and her memory, in the short term, was less certain. I remember her lying down with some philosophical books gathered around her, making a valiant effort to be what she had been. She realized that she could not only not understand the text she was reading, but also failed to understand her own marginalia explicating the text. This was not the first time since becoming ill that she had tried unsuccessfully to work. She picked up something else while I returned to a task which distracted me for a moment. What she had picked up fell from her hands. I looked up. It was her own doctoral thesis. She could not understand a word of it. In this moment the realization rushed upon her that she would not recover the abilities in which she had invested so much of her life. She looked up at me as if from a great depth.

In the past she had worked with blazing intensity. She had needed to be reminded to eat and sleep when she became engrossed in philosophical work. Now she could neither concentrate nor work at all, and after many attempts had come to believe she never would work again. Are we what we are able to do? Daphne was inconsolable. For a while she seemed convinced that she had observed her own death.

It is impossible to convey in a few paragraphs, or really at any length, the long droning suffering which was punctuated by dramatic events like Daphne's realization that she could no longer do the work by which she had defined herself. The day to day was not dramatic; rather, her quotidian was a terrible tedium of struggle against an unseen enemy which dragged Daphne by infinitesimal degrees into a dark pit.

There was, however, no way to clearly measure the downward slide. While some characteristics which had seemed necessary to Daphne—her passionate intellectual intensity, her great critical acumen, her immense intelligence—were waning, others seemed to remain unscathed. Daphne, even in such desperate straits, was more concerned for others than for herself and extremely sensitive to the plight of any being which could suffer, whether or not that being could think. Ironically, she had, at times, cursed the intensity of her passion for philosophy which drove her like a whip. She had longed on occasion to be an unthinking sentient being like our pet cats on which she lavished affection. This is the sort of choking irony which inspired the proverb, "The gods grant the wishes of those whom they wish to condemn." In any case, under stress which might have made her totally bitter, Daphne retained love, empathic understanding, and pity for a long time. It was only much later when she was like one possessed that the deeply ingrained sweetness of her character was, at least temporarily, displaced.

After a long period of deep depression about the loss of her mental abilities—a depression which lasted through some attacks and remissions—Daphne began to have trouble remembering her passion for philosophy. I remember distinctly, in a year replete with poignant moments, the moment at which she first said aloud that she no longer felt horror at losing her ability as a philosopher. Why, she asked, could she not be happy as a home-maker without the strange need to ask immense questions? Of course I encouraged this line of thought, but the strangeness of its coming from Daphne chilled me deeply. Who was saying such things to me?

Formerly unthinkable changes had taken place in Daphne, but it still seemed to me that she had to some degree survived these changes, though I did not know her nearly so well as I had supposed. Until she became completely demented, there was usually enough of Daphne's former character to make her recognizable as a continuation of her former self. The changes were quite varied. While some characteristics flew away, others remained as always. There were some things about Daphne which seemed not so much lost as muted or redirected. She had been served well as a theorist by an extraordinary independence of mind and a pertinacity in the pursuit of ideas. Her defence of her considered views sometimes bordered on intellectual ferocity. Once she was unable to understand philosophy, her love of theorizing was directed at surveying the literature on the causes of multiple sclerosis and seeking to discover the nature of the demon with which she struggled. Without the critical ability she once had, she fell prey to many false hopes and tried, partly through desperation, a number of "cures" which she would have dismissed had she had her former abilities and had she lacked a motive so strong as to crush any reasons. Daphne's pertinacity and independence now served her less ably than they had in her earlier life. The pure intellectual passion became a passion to escape from a terrible fate. The horror of the roller-coaster ride downward directed her energy and creativity into fantasies about curing her ailment and delusions about the abilities and motives of the neurologists who delivered the bad and ever-worsening news.

There were times just prior to Daphne's final descent into dementia when I had to ask myself to what extent paternalism was justified in my care of Daphne. This was a question which would have made no sense prior to her illness. Then she always knew what she was doing and clearly had the right to decide for herself what actions she would take. When I heard her say in response to my doubts about some particularly irrational and harmful sort of "cure," "But my brain is being eaten away!" I could hardly respond with an argument. On the other hand, I had to protect her from making her condition worse. There was still some chance of remission of the disease if she could be protected from other serious harms. The immense respect which Daphne had earned had to be tempered with the knowledge that she was, in some important sense, no longer herself, no longer the person who had earned complete autonomy. Whereas in the past I would never have treated Daphne as a child, now I was sometimes forced to do just that, but it put me very ill at ease. Fortunately, she did not seem to be aware, by that time, that I was distracting her from some of her ill-considered attempts at curing the disease.

To describe her as Plato might have done, Daphne was a very spirited person, but one in whom reason clearly ruled. As reason weakened, spirit took the upper hand, with disastrous consequences at times. Whatever the physical mechanisms in terms of loss of cells in the nervous system, the results of multiple sclerosis in this case can be accurately described as the loss of the inhibiting force of reason and the release of violent emotions with a consequent marked change in personality. Those to whom Daphne had always been forbearing felt the full brunt of an anger which had formerly been reserved for those she had good reason to believe to be unjust. Once the disease had an insuperable grip on her mind, she lost the power to distinguish a crime from a minor fault, and the blast of her anger blew at random. What before would have been seen as a change from greatness of heart to meanness, could not, of course, be seen that way when Daphne's mind was unravelling. Perhaps it makes no sense to speak of personality changes or character changes when the mind is so embattled.

In any case, everything remaining that was familiar to me in Daphne's character began to fade in and out. As the ability to reason and communicate —whether verbally or by other signs—diminished, the things I thought of as character or personality traits became harder to assess. When, eventually, she became crippled as well as demented, the opportunity for self-expression was as limited as it is for a babe in arms. This is not to deny that such an infant, or Daphne as she is now, may have and display a personality. I just wish to point out how severely limited this personality is in comparison with that dizzyingly complex personality which Daphne once had.

Some traits may survive even such dread changes as a total loss of intelligence. Sweetness of temper, for instance, is a trait which we can now, once again, attribute to Daphne with very minimal action on her part. One can also have such sweetness as an underlying characteristic and yet be a fierce debater on the side of what is just, as Daphne was before her illness. Daphne had a fine sense of humour as well. In a way, it never left her. The wide range of things which amused her narrowed to the humour of the pit, but she could still laugh in the face of an unimaginably wretched fate. Now she sometimes smiles still, though it is apparently the tone of voice rather than the content of what is said which amuses her. Week to week I now hardly notice the changes, but as I reflect on longer periods I see the gradual ebbing away of even what little is left to Daphne. The complex personality which includes such traits as considered gentleness, subtle whimsicality, intellectual pertinacity, and highly developed empathic understanding cannot survive the simplifying effects of the loss of all reasoning ability.

Daphne suffered a diabolical torture in going into and out of states of some lucidity before she descended finally and utterly into dementia. In lucid moments she begged for euthanasia but was too weak to take her own life. This wish to die seemed to be the considered and rational wish of someone who did not want her body to live on after the death of her mind and personality. It was, however, uncertain whether remissions might not still occur and give Daphne a life worth living. Once she had passed beyond the horror of watching her mind ebb away, once she could no longer understand what was happening to her, her foremost source of misery had ceased. Should Daphne's wishes still be considered for this new Daphne who seems like a sometimes happy infant? Is this really Daphne or rather a human being only as closely related to her as a retarded daughter would have been? What rights did Daphne have to specify what was to be done with her body when she no longer could control it? The questions spring up like weeds. Answers are rare, delicate blossoms indeed and will have to be carefully cultivated in what follows.

In spite of the terrible inspiration for this book, it is not a book cloaked in mourning. Mourning is something I have come through. My tone may even seem flippant to those who think philosophy must never smile. Philosophical ideas are not forbidding things. They are meant to be lived. I refuse to dress them in armour.

How to read this book

The intended audience

This is a broad survey, not a book for professional philosophers specializing in the area of concepts of a person. I have tried to make it accessible to anyone who cares deeply about people and is willing to think hard. My aim is to provide a map of a large and strange territory. Professional philosophers usually take some part of that territory and explore it very thoroughly, but there is not space for such intense investigation in a work of this scope. This book covers a huge range of ideas about persons and points out many pathways which may invite you to explore further. There are numerous sketches of historical developments concerning the concepts of a person. For the lay reader or philosophy student these sketches provide choices between varied philosophical traditions within Western philosophy. At the end there is a quick look at where my own explorations have led me. You may wonder, though, as you view the sweep of Western thought on persons, how to compare the many views which are adumbrated here.

A framework for comparing views about persons

One question to keep in mind is how these views are related to common sense about persons. Philosophers are fond of the old saying that common sense is not all that common and seldom sensible, but I am more sanguine about common sense and believe it is a good way to categorize views on persons. Some of the philosophers mentioned in these pages are, indeed, partly the source of today's common sense. What was once philosophical invention has filtered down. Of course these are Western philosophers, and it is a culturally relative Western common sense that we use. As long as we apply the concept with this in mind, common sense helps. Even prior to any analysis of common sense, for instance, one can say that a philosopher whose theory implies that each human body is associated with a series of about a dozen different persons or one who says there are no persons at all is departing considerably from common sense. Since a concept of a person is fundamental to much of our thinking, it would be nice to stick as close to common sense as we can.

To elaborate it is necessary to anticipate, somewhat, the second-to-last chapter of this book to say a little about some common ideas about persons in the history of Western philosophy and to prepare you for these ideas as they crop up between here and the distant end of this book. Here, then, are some beliefs that many of us have about ourselves. To begin with, we are *complex* creatures. Any view which characterizes persons as so simple as to have no parts or internal divisions would not be about us. On the other hand, we are *not reducible* simply to a set of parts in a certain configuration. You cannot take a person apart and put her back together in the way that you can, say, a computer. Each of us is, moreover, a unique *individual*. People seem to be, as well, *continuous* during the life of their bodies with more or less *determinate* beginnings and endings. In some sense, a person is an *indivisible* whole. Persons as individuals, and perhaps even as a class, *cannot be defined*. Finally, persons have *freedom* of the will.

The picture of persons I have just drawn is one that many philosophers reject in one or more of its aspects. You can watch for the sources of these ideas as they emerge through the history of the concepts of a person and use them as ways of comparing views. I will eventually defend some form of each in what I take to be a defence of common sense.

Another way to compare views is to look at their applications. Daphne's story is one which will come up again and again as I ask what various philosophers would say about it. You may have cases of your own to which these theories can be applied. Ask of each philosopher's theory: is it speaking of real people and what difference would the theory make to your life if you believed it.

ONE
The Nature of Persons

Philosophical answers and irritants

The context dependency of the question

If you have had any dealings with philosophers, you are probably aware of their devilish habit of giving out questions in response to questions. Contrary to an opinion popular among students who have done poorly on their first exam, this philosophical questioning of the question is not usually motivated by the desire to be irritating and evasive. What philosophers generally try to do is to find out precisely what the question is before they attempt an answer. Philosophers, whenever they undertake to answer a question, are acutely aware that what the question really means depends on the context in which it is asked.

Here we are asking maddeningly difficult questions: "What are persons?" and "What makes this person now identical to that person in the past?" "What marks the beginning and the end of a person?" Of course we have to be very careful about what we are asking. That depends in part on whom we ask. If, for instance, you ask a lawyer what persons are, she will probably tell you that they are individuals, corporations, or other organizations satisfying a certain list of juridical requirements. If you do not stop her there, she will probably rattle off that list. While we may be vitally interested in what the law says about persons, we have some prior work to do on the concept of a person to answer some of the questions which arise whenever someone undergoes radical change.

Another example of context dependency shows us that we might get sidetracked regarding the related question, "What makes this person identified in one way identical to that person identified in another way?" Suppose that I inquire at a government office whether Jane and Mary Smith are two persons, identical twins perhaps, or just one person with two names. I am told by a clerk that they must be one person because they have the same social insurance number. Jane and Mary show up later, looking as alike as two peas in a pod, and gently dispute the clerk's opinion. The clerk refuses to revise her opinion. Jane and Mary then have a not unheard of bureaucratic headache, but that has nothing to do with the real question I wanted to ask. Seeing them together, I know they are not the same person. They are identical for the clerk's bureaucratic purposes until they get their records revised, but we should not let this quaint fact about the bureaucracy discourage us from treating them as different persons.

This example of Jane and Mary underlines our tendency to accept a difference of bodies, however similar, as a knock-down, drag-out argument in favour of the conclusion that there is a difference between two persons. As was pointed out above, this difference of bodies is rather limited as a criterion of difference. It seems to work at a given time but not over time. None of us has the same body that we had when we were rocked in our mother's arms. It will become evident that much of the puzzling we do about persons depends on prior assumptions about time. We will have to stop and ask in some of the debates about who's who whether we are talking about persons through complete lifetimes, persons through a large segment of a life, or persons in a brief period of time. You may have no difficulty thinking you are the same person who began reading this paragraph, but are you the same person you were when you were two? Will you be the same person if you become senile in later life? If you say "yes," is some sort of continuity other than the mere continuity of your body the underlying reason? You will see what your answers are as you read critically the answers of the philosophers in what follows. First, I will issue some warnings about our methods.

Defining terms

In the miasma of unclear intellectual discussion, the oft-heard cry of the great bull philosopher, "Define your terms!" reverberates like a fog-horn. Often, however, it makes little sense to try to define a term. It may be perfectly well understood in a context of use. It may be poorly understood, but the resources for a precise definition may not be at hand. In some cases, it may not even be in principle definable, though its meaning is understood. For instance, Moore pointed out[1] that we know what "pleasure" means but cannot define it. Similarly, Strawson[2] treats "person" as a primitive term, that is, as a term at the base of our vocabulary, a term which is used to define others but is not itself defined in a non-circular way. He is treating the term "person" as Moore treats "pleasure." Perhaps there are some contexts in which it is reasonable to treat "persons" in this fashion, but there are others where definition is worthwhile.

Amelie Rorty's list of person-candidates

Just considering a list of terms sometimes used in place of "person" can be enlightening. Consider these comments on terms from literature offered by the philosopher Amelie Rorty: "'Heroes,' 'characters,' 'protagonists,' 'actors,' 'agents,' 'persons,' 'souls,' 'selves,' 'figures,' 'individuals,' are all distinguishable. Each inhabits a different space in fiction and in society."[3] With the possible exceptions of "heroes," "protagonists," and "figures," these terms all function in some contexts outside of literary criticism as synonyms of "person." Note the strangeness, however, of debating the possibility of most of these terms describing a fetus, a corporation, or God. As soon as one notices the variety of concepts of a person, many of the debates about what beings fall within the category of a person become harder to understand.

The history of the term "person"

Concerning oneself with various definitions of "person" may seem to be a totally ivory-tower pursuit to those who think that we know well enough what persons are. That it is not so is evident from the weight people put on the term "person" in debates concerning abortion and euthanasia. Nor is this seriousness about definition a new phenomenon. The definition of "person" was a matter of life and death long ago as well. In the late Middle Ages, for instance, Servetus, a physician and polemicist, wrote an essay on the mistakes in the doctrine of the Trinity. This is the puzzling Christian doctrine that God is three persons in one. Servetus used one of the possible derivations of *persona*, the Latin term for "person." He was assuming that *persona* came from words referring to an actor's mask. This suggested to him that "person" in this religious context meant "role" like the role that the actor would play. He then gave a very reasonable explanation of the puzzling doctrine of the Trinity. There was only one God, but God played three roles or performed three functions. Servetus was burned to death at the stake as a heretic on Calvin's accusation.[4] Define your terms, but carefully.

Although there are people on both sides of the abortion issue who talk as if they would like to burn their opponents at the stake, the more likely causes of death of human beings are from abortion itself on the one hand, and radical, fringe pro-life groups blowing up abortion clinics on the other. Much of the difference between the pro-life and pro-choice groups hinges on the question of whether all human beings, including fetuses, are persons. Murder is unjustifiably taking the life of a *person*. Using an abortion for, say, birth control, would be murder if the fetus is a person. Pro-choice groups deny that the fetus is a person. Neither side denies that the fetus is a human being. This may seem strange to someone who thinks that all and only human beings are persons, a standard assumption among pro-lifers. What the pro-choice groups are saying, though, is that it is wrong to think of all human beings as persons. Obviously, we are badly in need of some definitions from both sides to begin to clarify the heated debate between them.

Why can we not just look at a dictionary and find out who is right? For one thing, you will find many definitions of "person" in any good dictionary, some on one side of the issue, some on the other, some favouring neither, and some irrelevant. It turns out that our choice of a meaning for "person" in such contexts as the abortion debate is a moral choice. On this choice hang important decisions about what we should do.

One response, then, to the problems we are having with the concept of a person and the definition of "person" is to decide what we should do, and then choose the concept of a person which suits that decision. This is in effect what often happens in debates about abortion and euthanasia. But while there are philosophers who would agree with this policy, there are many who think that reflection on the concept of a person should be a precursor to or at least a concomitant of the ethical decisions. In fact, our contemporary concepts of a person include some that developed as innovations in ethics.

Trendelenberg goes so far as to say that the development of the concept of a person as an end is an indication of moral progress in a society.[5] The distinctly moral use of the concept is, however, a relatively recent invention in our culture. The watershed in this development is Kant, who tells us, "Rational beings are called persons because their nature distinguishes them as an end unto themselves; that is, as something that may not be used simply as a means, and consequently in so far limits all caprice and is an object of esteem."[6] This introduces the idea that persons cannot, like tools or animals, be treated simply as a way of achieving some result and also the idea that rationality is a necessary feature of persons. The special place this conception accords to persons has been the foundation of much of our thinking about rights and duties which are conceived of as only applying to persons. Recently this has been challenged by animal rights activists, who accuse the traditional ethicists of speciesism. Perhaps animals do have rights, but I will argue that persons' rights are stronger. We should treat both animals and people better than we do.

The concept of persons as ends, not means, as those for whom things are done rather than that which is used to accomplish purposes, is linked to rationality. Rationality is itself a contested concept, but it is often taken to include not merely the capacity for logical thought but also the capacity to express thought in language. Rational beings of any sort are worthy of esteem, on this view, but, as it happens, the only beings we know of who are indisputably rational are human beings. Other beings may behave as if they understand reasons for doing things, but we are the only beings who can boast about it. Now some would claim that some chimpanzees, like Washoe, who has learned many signs in the American Sign Language for the Deaf, have demonstrated that non-human beings are rational. There is also much speculation of late that the ancient dream of machines that can really think will be realized. Does this make them worthy of the esteem we accord to persons? Perhaps rationality is irrelevant, as Bentham thought, and merely the ability to suffer and feel pleasure is what should give us cause for concern about a being. There is, then, a debate about whether being a person as defined in terms of rationality or mere sentience is the mark of a member of the moral community.

If we accept "person" into our moral vocabulary, either as a defined term or a primitive one, the question remains whether it is descriptive of something which is the source of moral value or is merely honorific. Do we first value something and then confer on it the title of person? To some extent this is what is happening when environmentalists use talk appropriate to persons to speak of ecosystems or the whole planet. They have not suddenly turned into animists. They are trying to persuade us to value and treat well the planet on which we live. If we say that the earth has rights or that she is our mother, these are honorific, extended uses of terms. They are evocative and poetic. There may be a use of "person" applied to the fetus which is similar. We want our society to be especially careful of the future interests of fetuses, and we achieve this by speaking of their "rights." This talk is almost totally indistinguishable from the differently motivated claims that there are genuine rights of the fetus and that the fetus is a person in more than this extended sense. If fetuses are to be classed as genuine persons with full rights, then clearly the sense of "person" being used is not that sense discussed earlier which requires developed rationality. To avoid taking the seemingly irrelevant criterion of mere species membership as determining whether a being is a person, one might look at an idea of ancient origin, that of the soul.

Those who believe that a soul inhabits the body at conception and that this soul is the source of the esteem in which we hold the person or that this soul just is the person would say literally the things that others might say as a figure of speech in speaking of the fetus. To call it an unborn person is to make a strong claim. The debate over how to best use this term is a fight over the tools of moral persuasion.

Whatever one may think of the religiously inspired sense of the term, "person" is a powerfully evocative moral term. Consider, for instance, its importance in the feminist movement. The group that can persuade others to adopt its usage is the group which will sway hearts and minds to its moral position. We will, then, have to examine closely the concept of a person and the cluster of related concepts like rationality, soul, self, and rights. Before we proceed, another warning is in order: there are some philosophers who would nip this investigation in the bud. They do not believe we can ask or answer any sensible questions about persons at all.

Pseudo-questions

One philosophical tack to take when one sails into a troublesome question is to dismiss the question as not a real question at all, as a pseudo-question. The question "What is a person?" or the question "What makes this person identical to that person?" may be said to ask nothing at all. One reason which might be given is that the general criteria sought are not to be had. What answers the question will get will always be relative to the particular usage and context. They are real questions when limited to such contexts, but as general questions are meaningless.

On the other hand, one might think there is a generally accepted use of "person" but no answer to the question merely because the term is primitive. Other terms of importance like "duty" or "moral" are to be defined in terms of "person." In that case to ask, "What is a person?" is not to ask a genuine question for there can be no answer. The only answer would be a definition, and that is just what cannot be given if the term is genuinely primitive.

The term "person" may be said to be so ambiguous that the question of personal identity and survival, unqualified, is no question at all. This, in fact, is my view, but I want to qualify the question in various ways to make it various clear questions rather than to merely dismiss it. I do not want to say that the term must be used to name mere fictions and phantasms.

Paradoxes of conflicting intuitions

When I see Daphne lying in a hospital bed who seems recognizable as the woman with whom I spent years prior to her illness, I may say to myself that this is the person I knew, but she is much changed in personality and abilities. It seems equally intuitively plausible to say that the person whom I once knew could not survive such changes. There is so little psychological continuity, and so much of the brain of this woman has been destroyed, that by the psychological or bodily criteria of sameness of persons, this woman is a different person from the one I knew. Dictionaries reflect the different usages of "person" which correspond to these conflicting intuitions about what a person is. Outward resemblance and some kind of continuity of body are, however, the most weighty considerations in our society. The police would have no hesitation, for example, in identifying this woman as my wife and the same person who, in far better health, was a brilliant philosopher and teacher. The strength of this outward-resemblance criterion is probably dependent on our religious heritage, on the doctrine of the immortal soul which enters the body at conception and, whatever the changes to the mind, leaves the body only at death.

Even in a largely secular society, we retain the doctrine of the soul, or some vestige of it through the outward-resemblance doctrine of the person, as a safety. We do not want to give up on people too soon. Whenever anything can be done to revive them we must try. Doctrines like these help us to make incredible efforts to preserve life and health in others. If we see them as persons—indeed as the same persons they were—after a catastrophe, then we will treat them very differently than we would if we were to see them as mere bodies from whom the person has fled or as new persons in familiar bodies. We are more likely to honour promises made to the person prior to the catastrophe. We are able to steel ourselves, with the help of gratitude, to the task of seeing to their medical care and comfort.

It seems a good idea then, as a social insurance policy, to think of people as the same even after a mental catastrophe. Sometimes, however, it leads to unreasonable expectations of those who have directly suffered the catastrophe and of those who care for them. We may, when things get bad enough, wish to adopt the view that calling the one who remains after the catastrophe the "same person" may be a fiction which has outlived its usefulness. Nonetheless, it is often difficult to do so. The power of our conflicting intuitions on this score can pull us apart. For this reason alone, it is best to look for whatever clarity we can muster.

Puzzles concerning related concepts

When we ask about the nature of persons or, for many purposes the same question, about what makes a person the same through change, ancient puzzles about identity and time raise their grizzled heads. Many philosophers are in rough agreement about how to define "is identical to," but we should be aware of the complications that arise from the roughness. Here is a standard way of defining identity called Leibniz' Law:

> whatever x and y are, x is identical to y if and only if x and y have all their properties in common.

To say that x and y have all their properties in common means that they are totally alike. In other words, it means that x is red if and only if y is red, and x is shorter than the Eiffel Tower if and only if y is as well, and so on for anything you might want to say about these things x and y. Now Leibniz' Law has two parts, one controversial and one not much disputed. I will begin, however, with the controversial part, which is called "the identity of indiscernibles," and goes roughly like this: if x and y are totally alike, they are identical. Being indiscernible means being totally alike.

Could there be two people who are totally alike? I am not talking about mere similarity of the sort one gets with "identical" twins. Could there be two people who were alike in *every* respect? To answer that question we have to know whether a radially symmetric universe described by Max Black[7] is possible, and that is a very long story. To make the story short, I hold[8] that on the interesting interpretations of Leibniz' Law, it is logically possible for there to be two people at one time who are indiscernible, totally alike. Such people would exist on opposite sides of a point of symmetry in the centre of a radially symmetric universe. Such considerations are, however, interesting as limits on possibility, not my major concern here. I am concerned now with the survival of persons over time in possible worlds like our own in their physical aspects.

The relatively uncontroversial part of Leibniz' Law is the indiscernibility of identicals. It says that if x and y are identical then they are totally alike or indiscernible. This works, of course, for a person, or anything else, at a given time. You do not expect to be exactly the same in ten years time as you are now. Indeed, you will change in some respects second by second. If x is a person from birth to death, the whole life, and y is too, then again we will have no trouble with applying the indiscernibility of identicals. If x really is y, all of the events in x's life will be in y's life. The problem with the principle is in its application to one person at different times of her life.

(1) Identity over time

Since what primarily interests me is the survival of persons through changes, I need to know a little about identity of individuals (persons or not) over time. While both parts of Leibniz' Law are false if x and y are one individual at different times, some restricted version of one or both parts of Leibniz' Law might be true in such cases. To see that they are false if unrestricted, we just have to notice that we change properties as we live; so we do not have all the properties we once had. My hair is longer than it was yesterday, so I am not totally like myself yesterday. A naive application of Leibniz' Law assures me that I am not the same person as I was yesterday. The reply that jumps to many a philosopher's lips is: "Properties like hair length are not essential to the person." Now we see how we might restrict our principles, namely, to talk not of having all properties in common but of having the essential properties in common.

What on earth is an essential property? The idea is that it is a property a thing has to have to exist. If you take an ordinary chair and remove its back and legs, it is no longer a chair but a disconnected collection of chair parts. Are there any properties which persons must have to be persons, in general, or are there properties which certain persons must have to be themselves? Suppose that a person permanently loses consciousness. Does that person cease to exist? The body and, perhaps, the subconscious remain. This is, for many of us, one of those kinds of case where we want to say both "Yes" and "No." Similarly, a brilliant person like Daphne who becomes demented provides us with a difficult example. The only kind of answer which will be adequate to our intuitions is likely to be that for some purposes we say the person remains and for others we do not. There are, it appears, various concepts of a person.

(2) Other relations called "identity" by the hoi polloi

Another way of approaching the problem which harks back to the business of pseudo-questions is to claim that identity is a concept which does not apply to persons. Persons are changeable things. The number two is identical to the sum of one plus one, but these are unchanging abstract objects. A person at one time is never identical to a person at another time, it may be claimed, since there are always changes over time. What the *hoi polloi* take to be identity is only similarity. This claim is something of an irritant. We know perfectly well that we are in some important sense of "identical" identical with ourselves in earlier periods of our personal histories. I am not just like the person who started writing this book; I am that person. To get rid of the irritant, we will have to find a way to speak about identity of objects over time in ways that preserve more than mere similarity of the various stages of the objects.

(3) Objects

The problems with identity are exacerbated by our tendency to treat as primary such examples of identity as involve unchanging objects or objects that change relatively little in comparison to persons. Almost none of us doubt that the number two today will still be the number two a thousand years from now. One might explain this in a way congenial to Plato and friends by saying that two is an unchanging abstract object. The moon is also going to be the same moon it was, despite minor changes. We generally accept as objects things which do not change or which do not change in ways that are very noticeable or pertinent to our practical concerns. Persons, however, change from.moment to moment, and, whether or not they appear stable to their friends and loved ones, over the years they change their bodies and many of the characteristics by which we know them. The young lovers who gazed at the moon become the old couple who, I hope, still gaze at the apparently unchanging moon. Perhaps their love survives (oh fortunates!) and they say that they are still the people they knew back then on a warm summer night. But even their love is very different now. Persons sometimes seem to be much more like the things we call "processes" than like the things we tend to call "objects," much more like a sunrise than like the relatively stable moon, though they are importantly unlike either sort of thing. On the other hand, when we think of persons as souls or selves unchanging within the body and mind, persons seem more like objects and less like processes.

(4) Processes

Processes are notoriously hard to deal with simply because they are a stream of changes. Heraclitus' old saying, "You could not step twice in the same river; for other and yet other waters are ever flowing on,"[9] is an ancient expression of the puzzles which the identity of processes affords. Of course, if we consider the matter carefully, we see that, if Heraclitus is right about rivers, we would have to admit that one cannot step on the same rock twice. Some properties of the rock will have changed from one moment to the next. In fact, though, we want to answer Heraclitus by saying that being totally unchanging is not necessary for remaining. Rocks, rivers, and persons retain their identity through change. For practical purposes outward similarity is sufficient to guarantee that we have the same ones from moment to moment. When the rock is worn down by the river over time or the person ages, we lose similarity between the beginning and end of the process, but neighbouring stages of the process are similar, and that is enough for us to count the rock or the person as a single thing.

If you have a brother, Al, who goes away on a long journey and comes home remarkably changed in appearance and character, you might not admit that he is the same person at first. If he shows you that he knows where your pet cat was buried dozens of years ago and comes up with enough such detail about your earlier lives together, you may accept him, guardedly, as Al. It would not be so difficult to accept if you had seen him go through the changes day by day. As it is, you use memory as an assurance that such a process took place. Memory as a criterion of personal identity comes in for a lot of discussion by philosophers. We shall have occasion, if I remember, to talk much of memory later on.

Generally speaking, we are fairly confident about how to decide whether brother Al is one with this apparent stranger who comes to the door. We are prepared for great change when it happens over time and at a distance. What is harder to deal with is great change which comes suddenly and which does not fit the expected or hoped-for pattern of life. Daphne's change from a brilliant scholar, a complex personality, and a physically strong person to someone who is physically and mentally infantile all came about within ten months. A part of the pattern of life which is accepted at the beginning or the end is suddenly forced upon the middle period. The process does not take its expected course like a river that is forced out of its banks and into another bed by some cataclysm. Is it the same river? Our understanding of sameness, objects, and processes will be stretched as we look at what philosophers have to say on these topics.

(5) Reduction

Another way to deal with the difficulty of the concept of a person is to trade it in on something more tractable. "Reductionism" is the term for theories which reduce the concept of a person to some other manageable concept like that of a repertoire of behaviour or that of a a brain. From the behaviourist point of view, the highly skilled woman who becomes demented has simply lost a complex repertoire of behaviour, much of it linguistic. To say that she is a new person is to say that certain stimuli no longer elicit the former responses. To say that the woman is a different person from the one formerly inhabiting that body is just quaint shorthand, according to the behaviourist, for talking of this complex change in stimulus-response patterns. For those who accept the motto, "same-brain-same-person," the woman would be the same person given that the brain has remained largely unchanged, but in cases of dementia from organic causes the brain does change radically; hence the person is a different one. That the behaviour indicating dementia is the same even given different causes of dementia is of no importance to the same-brain-same-person theorist. Evidently, then, reductionism is a broad category into which we can fit various conflicting theories about persons. The main thing reductionists have in common is that they attempt to boil persons down to something they think they can understand.

Reductionism, especially for a rich concept like that of a person, seems to rely on the principle of the drunkard's search. Kaplan tells us, "There is the story of a drunkard searching under a street lamp for his house key, which he had dropped some distance away. Asked why he didn't look where he had dropped it, he replied, 'It's lighter here!'"[10] Reductionists tend to restrict attention to whatever is well lit by our understanding; thus they may ignore that which really makes up persons. Not all are so motivated, but those who look at one aspect of persons like their brains, their psychological continuity, or their behaviour are illuminating their investigation without due regard for the likely location of the solution to problems concerning concepts of a person.

(6) Thought experiments

Philosophers frequently dream up weird examples to test their understanding of concepts. With respect to persons they talk about machines that can duplicate human behaviour and appearance, brain transplants, mind interchanges, teletransportation, and various other supposedly logically possible kinds of event which need not be medically or even physically possible. This tends to alienate people in other fields who wonder what philosophers have been smoking. The justification given is usually that philosophers are torturing the concepts to see just what they are made of. Just as the metallurgist stretches metals until they break to find their tensile strength, philosophers try out our ordinary concepts in situations designed to see what their limits are. Unlike the tensile strength of a metal, however, the limits of a concept are not definite and quantifiable. The testing procedure is, by consequence, not a single, clear, rule-governed one.

For example, a philosopher may speculate on what we would want to say about personal identity if we had a machine that could record all the data in a person's body and duplicate the person.[11] No sooner has this speculation been put forth than another philosopher will say that it is not even clearly a logically possible example until we are shown in detail the background assumptions concerning this process of replication. Wilkes, for example, would argue[12] that we have no reason to take this example seriously since it is not clear that there could, even in principle, be an exact replica produced. Lots of things seem possible only because we have not spelled out the details.

Another kind of attack on such thought experiments comes from a philosopher who objects to the presupposition of materialism. The duplication is, by hypothesis, a duplication of the structure of the matter of the original person. There is no guarantee, the anti-materialist would argue, that such a duplication produces a person at all. It is, moreover, bound to be an imperfect replica since selves, or souls or whatever the non-materialist thinks we are in addition to bodies, are not replicable.

While reductionism is very popular in philosophy now—especially the materialist kind of reductionism—it is often put forward with insufficient attention to the kinds of objections adumbrated here.

A grand system to ground the question

One of the ways to avoid having your philosophical theory nipped in the bud is to be systematic. If, instead of just focussing on the concept of a person in isolation, you develop a unified theory of existence, knowledge, and morality in which your concept of a person fits, then you are better prepared for all the slings and arrows of outraged objectors you are likely to call down upon your head. There are three main kinds of metaphysical view—that is views about existence in general—which are used in the discussion of the concepts of a person.

(1) Materialism: Never mind

Materialism is the view that everything that exists is matter. There are no minds or souls or spirits or selves which are non-material persons or parts of persons. This is considered by its defenders to be a no-nonsense, what-you-see-is-what-you-get sort of theory. They may even say that it would be nice if all this romantic bull about spirits were true, but, sorry Virginia, there is no Santa Claus. Their opponents accuse them of feigning anesthesia.[13]

(2) Dualism: Mind and matter

Dualism is the view that both material and non-material things exist. Non-material things like thoughts and minds are every bit as real as material things like brains and electro-chemical impulses at the neuron-synaptic connections. Most non-philosophers whom I have questioned about this are dualists. They believe, for instance, that their memories are different in kind from whatever physical things are going on in their heads when they have these memories. Their opponents ask them, with a smirk, how the material and non-material worlds interact.

(3) Idealism: No matter

Idealism is the view that there is no matter, just minds, ideas and perhaps other things like spirit which give rise to the illusion of a material world. Millions of people in India think this is just common sense, but on this side of the world people tend to take a step away if you spout this view. Their opponents accuse them of ignoring the obvious.

(4) Neutral monism: Never mind it doesn't matter

Some philosophers, like Bertrand Russell, have held that there is only one kind of stuff that dreams and rocks are made of. Mind and matter are built from the same building blocks. This view is called "neutral monism." Materialists think the neutral monists are closet idealists, while idealists think they are closet materialists. Dualists think they are missing something.

This metaphysical starting point concerning what kind of stuff there is usually influences our views about how we know things about this stuff. Ethical views tend to be influenced as well. Dualists and idealists can make a place for spirit, for example, which generally carries with it views about human dignity and worth. These views are harder to defend on the other metaphysical ground.

Wittgensteinian ladder-heaving

There are philosophers who abhor systems of the sort just discussed. For the early Wittgenstein, a noteworthy example of system abhorrence, his own system was a mere ladder to be climbed to a better understanding of the world.[14] Once one had this understanding, the ladder could be heaved away. The system, then, is not the truth, but a mere means to seeing the truth. He seems to conclude that the truth about persons is that there are none. On his account of persons, the concept of a self or person pretty well disappears.[15]

Reaction to philosophical interpretation

After this day-trip through the territories of philosophy, you may have some strong reactions. To be fair, none of the views or methods adumbrated above has really been given a run for its money. Still, you may as well know what some of the anti-philosophic reaction is. Like Wittgenstein's reaction mentioned earlier, this other reaction is more likely than not to be absorbed into philosophy where it is taken seriously by philosophers. Intelligent anti-philosophy is often a kind of philosophy.

Irritation with the exaltation of language

One of the strong contemporary winds on the borderlands of philosophy is great irritation with the philosopher's exaltation of language. The twentieth-century philosophical trend to reduce questions about persons, existence, morals, or whatever to questions about language was itself once a reaction to what was seen as an excess of ungrounded speculation. The pendulum swings. Now we are exhorted to talk about persons rather than merely about the word "persons." It seems to me for reasons already given that we cannot just talk about persons without examining the language we use to do so. If I am right, we are talking about many different things. This does not mean that we should merely speak about things having to do with usage. This is properly the realm of the scientific linguist. Maybe we should farm some of the work out. Ultimately we have to get down to the questions about what there is, how we know it, and what to do. If we get hung up in the linguist's enterprise and never get to these questions, then we have abdicated our ancient role as philosophers. Some philosophers are quite willing to give it up as a bad job. I am not.

Rejecting the vocabulary and method of Analytic philosophy

Continental philosophy

Readers should be aware that philosophers in the West are roughly divided into the British/North American and Continental schools which are separated by a grand gulf of method. The Britons and North Americans are largely fond of the fine detailed analysis of concepts with a heavy concentration on the insights to be gained by examining language. They are sometimes called the "Analytic School." The Continentals, by contrast, are fonder of large system building and larger pictures in general. They think of the Analytic School as lacking profundity. The Analytic philosophers sometimes deride what they see as the imprecision or vacuity of the Continentals, as Berlinski did when he spoke of the great soupy volumes which pour off the European presses with the inevitability of death.[16] There are, however, other good philosophers, on both sides of this wide methodological gulf, who find work to value on the farther shore.

The Analytic School is the place where I was brought up, and I will try to analyze the concepts of a person and perhaps add to those concepts. The continental style of philosophizing, however, which tends to be systematic and more poetic than I am used to, has influenced me. But one can only study so much. The influence of the Continentals on what you read here is mainly indirect, through philosophers who write in a way accessible to the Analytically minded.

Survival is what counts

While I have some larger systematic opinions, I will not always be working from the top down. Trying to settle on the most general philosophical views without at the same time working on the middle and lower levels makes for the danger of becoming separated from life and bound within the walls of a coherent but inapplicable system. This approach from all levels at once sometimes makes for a spaghetti of ideas, but I hope that a larger pattern will emerge for you. If not that, then may you enjoy the sauce.

What is crucial to me in keeping the connection with life is that puzzles about, for example, duplication of persons, not lead us too far astray from the real work at hand. We have only academic concerns about duplication at this stage in our technical history, but we have some very real and present worries about what constitutes survival of a person. That is the focus.

Legal problems

As I was writing the first draft of this book, the Parliament of Canada was attempting to put a new law concerning abortion into the Criminal Code. The Supreme Court of this country is still wrestling with the definition of "person" as it has done in the past. As the legal proverb goes, hard cases make bad law, and, I wish to add, intractable concepts do as well. Fortunately, we currently have no law on abortion.

According to the polls[17] reported on the news, a large majority of people in this country side with the pro-choice movement. This is some indication that the majority's attitudes to the fetus are consistent with the idea that a fetus is not a person in the sense that confers rights and duties. Some philosophers hold that the fundamental right is the right to be treated as a person and that all other rights flow from this.[18] It makes, for them, a huge difference what you count as a person. If for example, a fetus is not a person but merely a potential person, then it may have something like what lawyers call a "future interest" in life and being a person which is a much weaker entitlement than a full-fledged right. This is a concept I will try to clarify after looking at the history of the concept of a person.

The way the answers miss the point

Our new-world version of Western European culture is in the throes of giving birth. Birth may have its beauty, but it is not a sight for the faint of heart. The infant, if it survives, will be a new and coherent view of what we are as individual persons and how we fit into our world and society. We desperately need some answers. The old religious world order is no longer capable of motivating the majority. The answers that are offered by pundits of the present are necessarily anachronistic. Either they cling to a dead order or they wait for a new one in which they might inhere.

I will not try to avoid anachronism. What emerges here is a series of proposals for a way to think, and, as a consequence, a way to live. I may advise living to some extent in the past, to some extent in the future. What I will try to avoid is the giving of answers which miss the point of such questions about personal identity as are asked by those in the front lines. The couple contemplating abortion or the family wondering whether to commit a beloved parent to an institution want to know where persons begin and end. There are lots of answers like, "All and only human beings are persons," which do not address their difficulties. That answer may underlie one concept of a person, but it is not one which helps them make a decision. If it is forced into that role, as it frequently is, then it creates only a hollow illusion of a solution. Instead of this, I intend to explore the many concepts of a person to see how they are motivated and what, if anything, each can do to help us live and make choices.

TWO
So Who Cares?

What really matters about people?

Kinds of mattering

What matters seems relative to cultures, countries, or individuals. There is, nonetheless, a degree of objectivity, even cross-cultural objectivity, in assessments of what matters.[1] People everywhere tend to care about people, for instance. That does not mean we all think of people in the same way. Some cultures seem not to have a concept of a person. Who or what gets counted as a person may also vary from place to place and time to time, with results in one culture or period that another considers abominable. Sometimes individuals or even large groups seem to care deeply about things which, from other points of view, it is irrational to care about. Hitler's caring about astrology but not about millions of lives is a paradigm of an irrational scheme of what matters, but no less an evil for being absurd. While there is always debate on what matters, there is also widespread agreement within cultures on particular cases.

Often when there is disagreement, as between a Nazi and almost everyone else, the disagreement is not over principles. Most everyone in the West admits that we ought to respect persons. The disagreement is over what a person is. The absurd idea that only "Aryans" are real persons, once the Nazi takes it to heart, allows the Nazi to commit horrific atrocities with less emotional trauma and fewer moral qualms than could be managed with the admission that Jews, Slavs, and the other victims are persons. In general, we agree on what matters, but we disagree about the facts or willfully ignore some of the facts where persons are concerned.

What matters about people includes, moreover, much that goes beyond whatever moral principles we may adopt. Few of us are exclusively concerned with morality. Frankfurt even claims that those of us who take morality seriously may still not, in some circumstances, find moral considerations pre-emptive.[2] This seems to me to be false. Frankfurt's example is of someone who finds it too costly to explore various alternatives to find the best one: "he might plausibly judge it more important to himself to reserve for other uses the time and the effort which a conscientious exploration of the relevant moral features of his situation would require."[3] In this kind of case,

---

Notes to Chapter Two are on pp. 315-16.

one is right to forgo the investigation only if the moral obligation to seek the knowledge is weak enough. If people's lives depend on the investigation, and I fail to investigate on the grounds that it might bankrupt me, I will remain culpably ignorant of the best thing to do. If it is a small matter of which of two actions might be more fair, and I fail to investigate on the grounds that it might bankrupt me, I would remain ignorant of the best thing to do, but not culpably so. I have a moral justification or at least a morally valid excuse for not investigating. It seems to me, that although there are many other things that matter about people, the ones which matter from a moral point of view must always be given first consideration. Only when there is a morally sufficient reason for leaving aside further moral considerations can we go on to the other things—practical, aesthetic, or whatever they may be—which move us.

We have to be wary about oversimplifying the point of the pre-emptive strength of our moral attitudes towards persons. We should not permit, for example, the sort of slavish adherence to principle evident in the following example. A Nazi knocks at my door looking for Anne Frank in order to send her to a concentration camp. I say, "I cannot tell a lie. She's in the closet." This is mindless adherence to the principle that we should be honest, if there is no reason to tell the truth in this case other than honesty. Sometimes we are morally obligated to lie. Not only the facts of the situation but our decisions concerning what matters about people will strongly influence our application of principles of morality. The process of carefully weighing and balancing principles, facts, and what matters to us is one which taxes even a saint. There is no simple way to decide how to treat other persons. It would, however, help if we could agree on what counts as a person.

There was once, in our culture, a somewhat easier answer to the question of what matters. The idea that what matters to me might not matter to you was accepted for a limited number of cases, but many societies of the past believed that what ultimately mattered was what mattered to God. Even then, it wasn't so easy, after all, as there were many differences of opinion about what mattered to God or the gods even within a given religion, much more across religions. One could, however, look to the religious leadership of a society to get a fairly definite answer concerning what mattered. In Europe, Britain, and North America, at least, this leadership no longer holds sway. We are cast upon secular devices to get congruence of opinion on what matters.

To whom?

If God is dead, to you and your group

Now we can always ask a question after the question, "What matters about people?" We can ask, "To whom?" If one answers, "To God," that will no longer win the day. Many think that, in Nietzsche's famous phrase, God is dead. Some think He is just resting. In any case, if something matters to God, then He must have a good reason for caring about it. The religious believer will only be able to persuade the non-believer that something matters by appealing to those reasons. "Many and mysterious are the ways of the Lord," is not a reply which will impress those who think there is no Lord to have any ways.

"Matters to whom?" can, however, often be answered, "To you," or "To your group." That will usually elicit, "Show me." If, for example, I say to Ms. Phobe, "You ought to care about the people in the third world," she may find my remark foolish until I can prove to her that their suffering can lead to harm to her country and herself. Ms. Phobe might be persuaded, for instance, that her country's using up the forests of the third world will ultimately have deleterious effects on her own country's environment by threatening the earth's atmosphere. Or, I might even be fortunate enough to persuade her that people should matter to her even if their suffering does not impinge on her country. A person's suffering matters, no matter who, no matter when, no matter where. This latter principle, however, is so fundamental to most Western moral systems, that it is that from which other principles are deduced rather than itself admitting of deduction.

God substitutes

Secular absolute moral standards

This brings us to the standards by which we judge what matters. These include our own proclivities, but they also include moral standards which we have accepted for whatever reason. The religious believer will say there is nothing like the real thing and cite God's will. The whole idea of substituting something else for God in the discussion is upsetting for the believer. The idea of including God is equally anathema for the non-believer. If they are going to talk to each other, they will have to consider what matters to them about people independently, to some extent, of why it matters. There are various creeds other than the religious ones which bear examination.

For example, Judith Shklar defines "liberals" as persons for whom "cruelty is the worst thing they do."[4] It is unlikely that Ms. Phobe adopts such a standard, but if she does we need merely persuade her that many of our actions are thoughtlessly cruel to people in the third world whose lives are made grim by our consumption of their resources. This grim tenure of life is crucially important on the liberal standard since that standard makes what matters about people their capacity to be cruel and to suffer cruelty. The dictates of liberalism were, in the past, founded on religious dogma. The abolition of slavery by Europeans and North Americans depended largely on the Judeo-Christian tradition. Liberalism remains, while the source of it is secularized.

Having such a standard as Shklar's liberalism is not necessarily a matter of believing that the standard is, or is grounded in, some absolute. Rorty invites us[5] to adopt it even though he admits that there are no absolutes, but he is careful not to defend this liberalism as if there were standards for its defence to which he could appeal. This would be to expose liberalism to the doubts to which those standards are bound to be subject. If we simply choose to affirm liberalism without deriving it from anything, we are, by an act of will, caring about people. Rorty's method is radical; he tries to change the vocabulary in which we speak of liberalism and thereby to support liberalism through making its opponents' vocabulary look bad. Rorty's rhetorical persuasiveness notwithstanding, his choice of liberalism cannot escape criticism merely by avoiding absolutes or making the vocabulary in which these absolutes are expressed look bad.[6] The refusal to accept absolute standards does not entail that any standard is acceptable.

Most of us want to say that there are, relative to a given context, things it is rational to care about and others which are not proper objects for our concern. If I choose to care deeply and exclusively about the pattern on my wallpaper, I will probably end up in a padded cell. Those of us who choose liberalism would, moreover, be willing to criticize Ms. Phobe if she chose to be concerned only about people in her own country. Whether or not they are absolute, we will use our standards to criticize choices of what to care about. Even if we believe there is no God to back up our choices and even if we admit that they are unfounded, chosen with an absurdist's belief that there can be no foundation, we tend to act as if God were on our side. What our side is, morally, depends, usually, on the context in which we find ourselves and, in Western societies, on our concept of a person.

The relationship between the concept of a person and morality is a vexed one in contemporary philosophy. Findlay claims that separateness of persons is the basic fact for morals.[7] Williams denies this utterly:

> The category of person, though a lot has been made of it in some moral philosophy, is a poor foundation for ethical thought, in particular because it looks like a sortal or classificatory notion while in fact it signals characteristics that almost all come in degrees—responsibility, self-consciousness, capacity for reflection, and so on.[8]

It becomes clear enough that philosophers are working with a number of different concepts of a person. We will look at a slate of these to see which might help us with our problems, moral and other kinds. An initial taxonomy of concepts of a person will emerge.

Aesthetic standards

Even more than moral standards, aesthetic standards are contentious. Curiously, even more than moral standards, aesthetic standards tend to be treated as God-given. Judging people's choices by aesthetic standards is, moreover, in my experience, even more likely to arouse hostile reaction than is doing so on moral grounds. It seems that we tend to forgive others if they are morally sincere in their differences with us, but let them but be what we consider low in taste! Dear reader, admit that you can respect the cannibal who sincerely believes it is his moral duty to feast on human flesh, but that you have more trouble respecting those whose choice of interior decor makes you nauseous. No? Well, you are probably a rare one.

The moot nature of aesthetic standards and our intolerance of difference in these may cause us no direct ill effects in trying to ascertain what a person is. There is, of course, an aesthetics of theory which might affect us if there were any possibility of achieving an elegant theory about the nature of persons. We seem so far from such a blissful state of theorizing that I believe that these aesthetic standards ought to come into play hardly at all in our choice of concepts. This is an area where we have not the luxury of choosing a pretty idea. We need one that works, even if it is as ugly as home-made sin.

Where aesthetic standards may be relevant is in the general battery of tests we have for being a person. One might suppose that having some kind of aesthetic sense is a distinguishing quality of persons. Other animals and some machines may be rational, but only persons have the capacity for aesthetic awareness, it may be claimed. This is at least an interesting claim. There is, however, a considerable debate about what it is to have some kind of aesthetic sense. Still, some take solace in believing that, while God is dead, Art lives. From their point of view, what matters about people is their ability to have the aesthetic experience.

Most of us, however, put aesthetic judgments lower on the mattering list, at least second to moral judgments. It is not unheard of, however, that an artist be out of step with the majority on this point. Artists have been known to put art above, for example, human and animal suffering—not just their own. It is, in fact, part of the traditional role of the artist to challenge the values of society, and this, together with the elevation of aesthetics to the pinnacle of what matters, may bring about moral monstrosity, including a profound disrespect for persons. Ironically, the use of the aesthetic sense as the defining characteristic of persons may lead to the undermining of the worth of persons.

For the majority, in any case, there is another sense in which aesthetics typically comes into what matters about persons. We are attracted to those we consider beautiful, sometimes in spite of their lack of moral character. We are attracted also to those who produce beauty around them or who can reveal it to us in nature. It seems, then, useful to reflect on the aesthetic experience in order to see a little more clearly what it is we care about in people. According to W.D. Ross, aesthetic enjoyment is "a blend of pleasure with insight into the nature of the object which inspires it."[9] This view explains why it is easier to appreciate the appearance of beautiful people than of non-representational works of art. As persons we have insights into people ready-made. Art, however, requires an understanding which does not come free. The necessary insight is hard-won.

There seems, in addition, to be another explanatory feature of Ross' view of art. Since the aesthetic experience includes pleasure, those who can evoke or help to evoke this experience would naturally be valued. One never has to seek an explanation for people caring about pleasure. I, for one, have never stopped in the middle of an orgasm to ask whether it is worthwhile. Nor are more subtle pleasurable experiences usually questioned except when they are bought at great cost morally or financially. Then it is not the goodness of the experience in itself which we question but the means to achieving it. People, therefore, who can bring out the aesthetic experience through their personal appearance or their work are people we tend to care about. In general, the capacity of persons to evoke and experience the aesthetic is a large though often unrecognized part of what matters about them. Aesthetic value is one of the commonest but least recognized sources of absolutes in a society which no longer relies on religion to supply those absolutes.

Solidarity of persons

God's death, moreover, makes people huddle together. Without someone to protect us and to want us to get along, we are all we've got. That may make us value one another more. One who misguidedly thinks himself the instrument of God's wrath can push the button to start a nuclear conflagration. So the world ends in fire; well isn't that what it is supposed to do? This world is not what counts. When that fire-and-brimstone attitude dies, the importance of the here and now and those who populate it becomes paramount. The vitality of the Shklar-Rorty liberalism alluded to earlier is, perhaps, an effect of the secularization of the world for all that it had its original source in religion. The liberal can take no joy in seeing herself as the avenging angel armed with the fiery sword.

This liberalism is a close relative of a movement which has been steadily gaining ground since nineteenth-century authors like Butler, Mill, and Bentham clarified it, some would say "created it"—I mean Utilitarianism, the doctrine that what we ought morally to do is to create the greatest pleasure and least suffering for the greatest number of people. In short, we ought to maximize pleasure. Bentham would prefer to maximize the pleasure of all sentient beings though, not just people. Some versions of Utilitarianism are, apparently, able to dispense with the concept of a person as morally funda-mental. Instead of saying, "We persons are all we have got," one might say, "We sentient beings are all we have got."

This move to sentient beings, however, does not obviate the moral diffi-culties which we have already seen to be entangled with the concept of a per-son. As soon as one defends a doctrine in which the interests of sentient beings other than persons might supersede those of persons, the problems emerge in another form. Perhaps the best way to maximize pleasure on this planet would be to eliminate persons. After all, people are destroying the planet. That there could be a justification for killing everyone—say by creat-ing and releasing an incurable viral ailment specific to human beings—seems to be an odd result at best in what purports to be a moral theory. To stop it, one would have to argue that there is more pleasure to be had by keeping us persons around. To do that, one might argue that persons are capable of more pleasure than mere sentient beings; so the pleasure of the person having an aesthetic experience through listening to music should not be equated with the pleasure of the mosquito taking a sip of a person.

Of course this business of weighing our pleasures against those of other sentient beings brings us back to the problem of what we are and why we should care so much about us. The general answer in terms of solidarity of persons is that we are all we have. Animal welfare activists and environmen-talists will blanch at this claim. They think too much emphasis has been placed on this new god of human solidarity. By elevating people to a position of ultimate value, we may ignore the other inhabitants of the earth and the earth itself. Not only people, but other animals—indeed, whole ecosystems—are all we have.

I, for one, am not about to make the world safe for mosquitoes by killing off persons, no matter how numerous mosquitoes and their little pleasures might be. Almost all utilitarians would agree with me on this point. It may nonetheless be true that we do care too much about persons and too little about other sentient beings. Perhaps we should care more about the planet on which we live. However we may change our attitudes in these respects, we ought not to return to caring too little about people. The ideal is to expand the circle of solidarity to include non-persons and their interests in our con-sideration of what we ought to do.

Spirituality

Not all who want to give up the idea of a deity want to give up the idea of spirituality. Some maintain that this is the essential characteristic of persons. Saying just what spirit might be, however, is not at all easy to do. Spirit is often held to be ineffable or expressible only indirectly as, for example, through the poetry of the Romantics. Nonetheless, some have attempted definitions.

For example, Steven G. Smith, after an interesting historical survey of definitions of the term "spirit" defines it as "the intentional togetherness of beings who are for themselves 'I' and for others 'You,' that is, other to each other."[10] Now a fetus cannot make the distinction between I and You and cannot participate in intentional togetherness. Nor it seems can some severely brain-damaged adults, but these are only the most extreme cases. There are many whose minds are terribly limited who would be able to join in this intentional togetherness. Thus the resulting concept of person, when we take persons to be those beings with spirit, takes the emphasis off mind and intellect, thereby including many more human beings as persons. Nonetheless, it still distinguishes the babe-in-arms from the two-year-old, since the babe does not have spirit.

There are, of course, many competing notions of spirit which would not have the consequences just noted. In any case, thinking of persons in terms of spirit gives us a set of definitions of "person" corresponding to those of "spirit." This particular example from Smith serves to show that taking spirit as the God-substitute may have important consequences for the distinction of some human beings from persons. Furthermore, doctrines of spirit bring with them views about what matters; often spirit itself is a the top of a hierarchy of what matters where God used to be. What matters about people, on this view, is their spirit.

Love

"Love is everything," is one of those expressions summing up what some people care most about, namely the foremost kind of caring. Although romantic love is the first kind of love that springs to mind, the love of the parent for the child, love of friends, of country, of humanity, of natural objects, and of artifacts are all familiar. When love is the God-substitute and so is placed at the top of the hierarchy of mattering we may have any or all of these kinds of love being glorified. People may matter on this kind of view since they are the objects of love or since they are the ones who love. The capacity to love at least has a chance of being a capacity that picks out persons while merely being an object of love does not. It seems, then, that being able to love is what matters about people when love is the God-substitute.

"Mutual love seems to be a blend of virtuous disposition of two minds towards each other, with the knowledge which each has of the character and disposition of the other, and with the pleasure which arises from such disposition and knowledge."[11] Definitions of love are passing rare, but this is one of the better ones. Notice that the kind of love here defined is person-to-person love, and the conception of a person necessary to support such love is quite complex. While an expectant mother could love a fetus, that would not be mutual love as here defined. Only highly developed human beings could be the sort of persons to have the emotional and intellectual means to experience this kind of love. Even very young children and adults with the intellectual or emotional maturity of young children cannot love in this way, though they may well love in other ways.

If capacity to love is, as I have speculated, one of the things that matter about persons, then we ought to look closely at love. As reflection on Ross' definition reveals, there are various things in this category of love which we might have in mind when we think of the capacity to love. The capacity for what Ross calls "mutual love" is, I believe, a defining characteristic of persons in a narrow but very important sense. It is, in fact, part of a common ideal. When we consider what persons should be, we include this capacity. When we praise someone as "a real *Mensch*" (a real person) for example, a large part of what matters so much to us about this person is the capacity for engaging with others in mutual love.

Assuming what?

When we ask what matters about people, we have to consider, as for all questions, the background assumptions. One such assumption is that there is something that matters. Pity the person who does not share this minimal assumption. Another is that something about people in particular matters. Most of us, save the very depressed, have few doubts on either score. We are assuming, though, that nihilism with respect to values has been defeated. It is never completely defeated. It raises its ugly head from time to time. We put it down largely by an act of pure will. We create our own values, not in the sense that we dream them up, but we ally ourselves to standards and views about what matters which tend to be shared by all people.

There are, unfortunately, persons for whom other persons do not matter. Some of these are egoists. For an egoist, only she herself matters. Some are concerned not so much with themselves as with things outside the realm of persons. The scientist, for instance, is praised for being cold, dispassionate, and fascinated with items quite beyond the personal. I think of this praise as an evil. The world is becoming uninhabitable for persons, and scientists need to be passionately involved with people to help overcome this tragedy. I am no more enamoured of the totally dispassionate scientist than of the artist who elevates aesthetics above persons. In any case, in contradistinction to those who reject this basic assumption, I, and I hope with you, am assuming that, somehow, people matter.

One more assumption that only a philosopher is likely to consider is whether there are persons in the world at all. Perhaps all of the concepts of person which we use are defective. In that case, there might be no such things. Once we thought there was phlogiston—a mysterious substance that was thought to be transferred from one object to another when heat was transferred. Now we think that supposition was based on a misconception of what heat is. What if all of our informative and value-laden conceptions of person turn out like that? Certainly I am assuming that there is something to talk about under the general heading of "persons." The proof is in the pudding. If, at the end of this investigation, we find that we have no clearer conception, then perhaps we will be willing to take a leaf from Rorty's book and to try to develop a vocabulary in which we no longer have terms like "person."[12] This would overcome by evasion the intractable questions of our current enterprise. Sidestepping is not such a bad thing if it gets us out of a blind alley and into one that leads somewhere. We must, however, explore this alley thoroughly before taking that out, and I think we will find the alley is not blind after all.

Mystical and religious importance

Mystics, religious believers, Platonists, and many others think that what is important about any person is the immortal part. Trapped within our physical being or temporarily residing voluntarily in, on, or through us in this mortal coil is the real person. This is a very strange idea when you think it through. Consider the ever-popular transmigration of souls doctrine, for instance. If you were a buccaneer in a former life, but you have nothing in common with that buccaneer now (that you can remember), in what sense was that you? If you become totally demented, at least there is the continuation of a body connecting the earlier and later self. If we imagine being buccaneers in earlier lives, do we imagine being continuous egos who are conscious in now one body, now another, with no memory of what happened in earlier bodies? With continuity like that, who needs discontinuity? This bare Ego that flits from body to body may not really be something we can consistently work into a plausible theory of persons. It is worth a try, though. Undeniably, the bare Ego has a strong intuitive appeal as the popularity of the transmigration myth testifies.

Problems like the identification of such featureless egos or souls led Aristotle and St. Thomas Aquinas to demand that the body go along with the soul as an inseparable unit, the soul being the form of the body. Although the relationship between the soul and the body is more complex, one can think of their inseparability as comparable to the inseparability of a body and its health. It would no more make sense to speak of the soul leaving the body and yet still existing than it would to speak of the health leaving the body behind and still existing out there somewhere: "I've lost my health but it's around here somewhere." Much less does a doctrine of transmigration stand up under the light of Aristotle's concept of the self or soul:[13] "Sam lost his health. Now my brother Harry has Sam's health." Of course we can talk sensibly of people having the same *type* of health but not have the very same *token* of health.

By the way, the Christian doctrine of the resurrection was necessitated by this Aristotelian view of the soul. You cannot go to heaven without your body; so you have to be reconstituted when that trumpet sounds. While this doctrine is a little less problematic than that of the featureless soul that could transmigrate, it has its problems. For instance, which body should be resurrected on that day, your two-year-old body, your body in its prime, or your then-current remains? We have had occasion to remark that the body is a process. Different stages of this process may be more different than two different bodies at the same time. If the soul is the form of the body, it too must be a continuing process. All the difficulties of identifying persons through time which arise when we focus on our mortal changing bodies will arise for this kind of soul. One wants something unchanging, incorruptible, and immortal to serve as an identifier through the changes of all the other parts of the person. This soul doctrine does not, at first glance, look promising. Suspend judgment on it, though, until we have given it a good run.

Being yourself (who else?)

It is not only the philosophers and mystics who claim to be aware of some continuing soul, self, Ego, or inner person which underlies the changes in the visible person. Most of us have been exhorted to "be ourselves," for instance by parents who did not want us to run with the gang and be moved by stronger personalities or groups to do what is not "true to ourselves." Well, who else can you be but yourself? Sartre's message in the play *Huis Clos* is that you are what you do, not what you say or imagine yourself to be but the sum total of your actions. But then who is performing these actions, a series of subtotals? Most of us think that when we choose to act in a certain way, consistently with our character, or even in a bootstrapping operation to change our character, *we* choose. There is a choosing self which precedes and survives the choice. Such is the dictate of common sense. We have to ask whether this common view is really sensible. Some of the philosophers discussed below challenge it, though I myself am rather partial to common sense.

Promises and the question of "who's who?"

That was then this is now

If you are lucky enough to have a friend whom you would describe with such well-worn phrases as, "steady as a rock," then you seem to have some concept of a dependable person. Such a person does not say, when you invoke her promises, "That was then, this is now." You know what to expect from her. This is not necessarily the kind of persistence through change which is sought by those who put forward ideas of an immortal soul, but this continuity of personality and character is much of what we normally refer to when we use the words, "the same person."

That was her, this is me

If remembering and living up to promises made, not under duress, is an example of the sort of thing we can ideally expect when we are met with the same person over time, then how far can this expectation be disappointed without damaging that sameness? Even posing this question will seem to some to conflate metaphysical and ethical issues, but many of the concepts of a person which are most useful are not easily confined within the boundaries of one philosophical field. We have terms like "psychopath" to single out those at one extreme with respect to what can be expected given their promises. At this extreme, there is genuine doubt about classifying human beings who are truly psychopathic as persons. At least there is the tendency to classify them as incomplete persons since they are mentally deformed. The total lack of the moral dimension is just as serious as the total loss of the intellectual capacity when it comes to being a person. A woman who is always content to answer, "That was then, this is now," when confronted with a promise might as well answer, "That was her, this is me." Or is that far too strong? The connectedness of the parts of a person's life is, at least partly, a moral matter. We will have to look into the extent to which abiding by certain moral rules is necessary to being a unified person throughout the life of the body of that person.

Loneliness and person surrogates

Being alone is being without the company of persons. On the proverbial desert island, one may have the company of coconuts and wild pigs, but neither can play chess or music, discuss philosophy or sympathize. Reflecting on what would make me feel less alone on a desert island, I discover some of the features of persons that I value, not all of which are inseparable from persons. Chess-playing ability, for example, can be hived off and assigned to a machine, but it is a poor substitute for playing with a person. It is the total package that makes the difference. Playing whatever you play with what some silicon worshipper has called "liveware," namely a person, introduces important changes which are hard to name. Playing music with a band and doing all the parts oneself on a sequencer are very different experiences. Part of the difference comes out in a remark of Pascal's concerning not cooperative activities like these but hostility of a sort. He notes that the universe can easily crush a man, but

> of the advantage which the universe possesses over him the universe knows nothing. Thus all our dignity consists in thought. It is that upon which we must take our stand, not upon space and duration. Let us, then, labor to think well; that is the principle of morals.[14]

A person's thought, unlike a machine's processing, is grounded in self-knowledge.

Many would suppose that the chess-playing computer does know that it possesses an advantage over me when it beeps hideously and flashes "Checkmate!" on the screen with unnecessary repetition. In an impoverished behavioural sense of "know" it may be said to know of its advantage, but Pascal would be unlikely to accept this as knowledge of the sort he has in mind. When a real person says, without beeping or flashing, "Check and mate," she conveys so much more to me than does the computer. She really knows she has won. There is a mystery to be penetrated in distinguishing the sense in which persons know, feel, and even detect things from the sense in which, to date, computers, their peripheral devices, and their programs can know, feel, or detect things.

Do not suppose that I am setting up the barricades in such a way as to defend carbon-chemistry chauvinism, the view that persons must be housed in flesh-and-blood. It is not clear to me that computers could not possibly be persons in some useful sense. They are a long way from being so now. Not to put too fine a point on it, they mimic some specific tasks of persons very well, but are narrow to the point of being laughable compared with even a limited person. It is unlikely that we will ever value them much like persons unless they can be made to look somewhat like and act and feel very like us. One should not suppose, however, that a huggable body is, in general, necessary to being a valuable person. Consider the Elephant Man, a famous example of a grossly deformed human being who was a person of merit.

Certainly as we explore the idea that machines might be person surrogates, or even persons plain and simple, we will see that, as with persons and morality, the concepts of a person and the concepts of a computer when rubbed together generate much heat and little light. On one side are contemporary philosophers like Dennett who see the difference between computers and persons, or persons and thermostats for that matter, as a difference in degree, at least with regard to belief attribution.[15] Opposed to this view are those who would agree with Thomas Nagel's prediction, "Eventually, I believe, current attempts to understand the mind by analogy with man-made computers that can perform superbly some of the same external tasks as conscious beings will be recognized as a gigantic waste of time."[16] Here, too, there arises the question of the limit on the variety of concepts of a person.

The usefulness of the computer model in conjunction with some concepts of a person may contrast sharply with its usefulness with others.

Continuity of an individual's projects

Can you imagine Einstein giving up physics to become a janitor? Some people become so identified with their projects that we can just barely envisage them in other projects. Some people sacrifice their lives for the continuation of something they have worked for: democracy, the family, the progress of science, the health of the environment, or a country. Many are even more willing to sacrifice the lives of others. Whatever matters about people, it is not always taken to be pre-emptive. Consideration for the individual person may become submerged in the pursuit of a goal even when this goal has to do with the betterment of people generally.

Indeed, there is an opinion which still has some currency in this age of individualism that persons count not so much as individuals but as parts of the whole. It is the ongoing history of the species, the striving for perfection of the human race, which gives meaning and purpose to the individual project, and hence, to the individual person. Yet the artist in a prison cell whose works are never seen is a tragic figure just for being cut off from the people who might appreciate her art. There is no art in isolation. On this view, projects have meaning only insofar as they are at least potentially connected to the great fabric of interpersonal connection. What matters about persons is that they are the warp and woof of this fabric. This wide view of what matters has had tragic effects in the hands of, for instance, the Nazis, some of whom may really have believed in a utopian goal to which they sacrificed individuals.

Continuity of the species' projects

Adopting this wide view of what matters, in which the value of the individual depends on that of the species, we come quickly to the question, "Well what matters about the species then?" Is there some huge, overarching project of the species which gives meaning to our beetling little efforts as individuals? One way back to individuals is through the suggested perfection of individual persons through the striving of the species. Each contributes something to the wisdom of the whole which is then passed on until persons evolve who are as good as they can be within the limits of the flux of the quotidian. This hope usually rides under some such banner as "The Perfectibility of Humankind."

There are some unattractive features of this sort of species project. It crushes incentives provided by our Western individualism. Most Western religions have provided for the survival of the individual person in their theology. It is you yourself who will get to heaven if you do what the religious leaders tell you. Working selflessly for some species perfection is less than attractive for most people. Another wrinkle is that the species has not been getting clearly better. A candid look at history does not encourage the adoption of this perfectibility view. Nonetheless, there is some truth in it. Part of what we usually think is important about people is their connection to the great ongoing river of persons through time. Few of us can conceive of our work as important in itself without that connection. The unattractive features of thinking in terms of large projects are not far to seek. Consider the humane goal of Marxism to make all people cooperative and its outcome in Stalinism. Our understanding of persons should, ideally, help to balance the projects of individual persons with the grand projects in aid of all humanity. Only then can the continuity of some grand project truly help us to improve what matters at the level of individuals.

Persons for persons' sake

The individualist's response to finding what matters in grand projects is partly to value persons for their own sake as intrinsically worthwhile. Persons just matter. They do not have to be part of something bigger. Often the debate between the individualist and the promoter of the species is pursued at the level of mottoes. "No man is an island," says one. "Nothing of value was ever achieved by a committee" is the response. This is the strategy recommended by Rorty[17] of making the opponent's vocabulary look bad. Perhaps it would be better to admit, as an individualist, the importance of our connections to the whole while striving to understand what it is about the concept of a person which serves as a moral barrier to the excesses of Stalin and of the Nazis. Often, however, rather than justification of a satisfying sort we simply hear the motto that persons are intrinsically valuable.

There is another facet to this move away from justification of our valuing persons by saying they just matter. This facet has to do with the apparent absurdity of the lives of persons. Nagel speaks of "the collision between the seriousness with which we take our lives and the perpetual possibility of regarding everything about which we are serious as arbitrary, or open to doubt."[18] If we are always creating our own values, including our valuing other persons, we are always in danger of seeing the whole of our lives from a point of view outside that system of values. Our ability to take such points of view may be part of some of the important concepts of a person. This ability, however, lets us pull the rug out from under our own feet. If we accept Nagel's view, we see that we simply choose to value persons, not because of some reason or absolute moral standard, but just because we choose. What matters about persons, like what matters about anything, is up for grabs.

To pursue this and other leads discovered in this chapter, we need to try to develop some of the various concepts of a person which have begun to emerge as we tried to notice why people matter to us. The kind of mattering may correspond to the kind of concept of a person which is a background condition of the mattering. The first place to look for enlightenment concerning all the questions which have been raised is in the record of what great minds have produced on this topic. The history of the concept of a person collects for us the wisdom of our culture with respect to persons. Within this history are the contributions of the great philosophers to whom I now turn.

THREE
Persons in Ancient Greece and Rome

What the great thinkers had to say
This you call great? Sources of the obvious

Philosophical insights of yesteryear are the commonplaces of today. Over the centuries, the novelty of thinking in a way that was once a great discovery wears off. What we now take for granted was once controversial. Take, for example, the idea that it is inconsistent with the dignity and worth of persons that any person be made a slave. While this idea is of ancient origin, the concept of the person did not, in ancient times, include all human beings. Aristotle, for example, thought some human beings were slaves by nature.[1] The success of contrary opinions is relatively recent and sometimes seems to have a tenuous grip on the minds of our contemporaries. Although it is widely regarded as common sense now, prior to the Civil War in America there were frequent public denunciations of the more inclusive notion of persons. The impression that many of us have, then, that this claim, "No human being ought to be made a slave," is self-evidently true is an impression which has been established recently with much bloodshed. Many of the things which we look at in the quick tour through the history of philosophical contributions will have this feature of being today's common sense and yesterday's controversy.

Recycling

Another thing that is strange about philosophical investigation as opposed to most other fields is the reissuing of former systems. Kathleen Wilkes at Oxford, for example, is a defender of Aristotle's views about human beings (though she does not defend slavery).[2] Old ideas in a new historical context become new ideas. It is not that there is no progress, but that the progress in philosophy is not linear. In the enormous spaghetti of ideas which philosophy presents, one may follow a single noodle—like the concepts of a person—through many twists and turns. The structure of the whole may appear elusive in such an investigation. Nonetheless, there is an overall structure and development to the discipline which makes the dish palatable to those with a taste for strong spice. As in cuisine, there are many kinds and measures of progress in philosophy. Ideas are sometimes lost and recovered or recre-

---

Notes to Chapter Three are on pp. 316-17.

ated. The old and the new mingle in surprising ways. The thoughts of the great philosophers of the past may seem odd to us now, or too obvious, but what we now think often depends on their work in subtle ways.

A way of proceeding

To spark ideas about persons, I will give an impressionistic tour through the history of Western philosophy from the ancient Greeks to the present on the topic of persons. I accept in advance the penalty for offering opinions on the thought of the great philosophers—some aficionados of each philosopher will say I have got that philosopher wrong. The issue is even more complicated than interpretation usually is since the word from which our word "person" is derived, the Greek *prosopon* is not used in any of our senses of "person" until the Stoics;[3] so the things I say about Plato and Aristotle's views on persons will be deemed by some to be anachronistic. I maintain that they were talking about persons in some of our senses of "persons" whatever words they used. However I may be pilloried or praised by those who take the history of language and ideas seriously, I will be satisfied if this historical survey proves to be a useful heuristic in our coming to understand the many concepts of a person now current.

The ancients

Prior to the invention of persons

Trendelenberg begins a scholarly treatise on the history of the word "person" by speaking of a Kantian sense of "person." Persons are rational decision-makers who are ends unto themselves; that is, they may not rightly be used as a mere means to achieve some purpose. Then he tells us,

> We would be at a loss to translate this concept back into Greek, the noble mother of our scientific ethical terms. Plato and Aristotle have no adequate expression for it. They talked about the man, not the person, when they wished to designate what was peculiar to man. A concept like that of Kant cannot develop where there are slaves, at any rate not out of the general moral consciousness. It denotes progress in scientific concepts when a later period is able to define such a concept as person.[4]

Slaves are used as tools or as beasts of burden. This is an unthinkable thing to do to a person, or as we would say today, contrary to *human* rights or the rights of *man*. The Greeks of that day had no word for person in the very narrow sense of which Trendelenberg speaks, but there are concepts of a person that we now use which are of course translatable. In almost any English dictionary one can find, for instance, "a human being" as one of the synonyms of "person." The Sophists, moreover, challenged the institution of slavery.

Aristotle considered arguments that it was an unjust institution.[5] Perhaps they didn't have a word like the one Trendelenberg is using, but it seems safe to say that they probably had some of the concepts of person which we use today. The way to understand what Trendelenberg is saying or ought to say, then, is that the concept of a person as an end but never a means and, thereby, as fundamental to morals was not among the concepts of a person which were popular enough to generate jargon in ancient Greece.

To go this far with Trendelenberg does not mean, of course, admitting that the problems we have noticed thus far in our investigation have not come in for comment by the Hellenic philosophers of antiquity. One might say, nonetheless, that there tends to be a light emphasis on the personal in the philosophy of that time. Those philosophers saw puzzles about persons as merely a special case of more general problems to do with the cosmos or at least the state. Prior to the time when Socrates and the Sophists debated ethical matters at length, most of the philosophical inquiry had to do with the nature of things, human beings among them. The Pythagoreans developed a concept of form or limit as a means of differentiating matter into separate entities.[6] Persons, like other things, were considered to be matter together with form. This prefigures later concepts of the person as body plus soul which was originally body plus form.

Before we try to make sense of the notion of form which was so important in the development of Western civilization, we should, while dallying with the pre-Socratics, consider some other concepts and problems which have influenced the evolution of the concepts of a person.

Heraclitus: Identity through change—the same river

Heraclitus is often quoted as saying that you cannot step twice into the same river, drawing our attention to the problem of identity through change.[7] Just as a single river is a constantly evolving process, all things are in this state of change. The river constantly changes its waters, its banks, and its bed. Heraclitus was interested in the general concept of the identity of a process. What makes one river remain through all the changes? Heraclitus did, after all, admit that there was a sense in which the river was the same even though new waters were always flowing through it, for he also says, "In the same rivers we step and we do not step. We are and are not."[8] One can make many things of a paradoxical fragment preserved by chance through the centuries. I read it as saying that we should attend to different kinds of identity for both rivers and people. A person, a river, or any process is made up of many temporal segments or stages. If one seeks an unchanging person, one finds nothing: we are not. If one looks at the whole process one finds something to identify: we are. There is one process, but each stage of it is different from every other stage. "The sun is new every day."[9]

What stays the same through change, according to Heraclitus, is that which underlies all existing things, what he called "fire." It is anachronistic, but gives contemporary readers a fair idea of his thought, to say that he envisaged a kind of matter/energy out of which all things are formed and which is conserved through change: "all things are an exchange for Fire, and Fire for all things."[10]

It would be too great an anachronism to attribute to the ancient Greeks a distinction between mind or soul and matter. Souls, minds, and spirits were conceived as simply a more rarefied version of the stuff of which all things are made.[11] Heraclitus, then, like those who followed in this period, did not think of a continually existing soul or mind as preserving the unity of the person. Like any existing thing, a person was just a quantity of Fire, an individual blaze within the great conflagration of the universe which burned for a time and then went out. There are those today who would think of persons as a particular system of matter/energy which develops through a part of space-time before entropy sets in. This kind of physicalist account, though it can provide much more detail than the theory of Heraclitus put forth in 504-501 BC,[12] can claim that ancient speculation as its great-granddad.

Although both Heraclitus' speculation and current physicalist doctrines are suggestive of a way of understanding persistence through change, neither tells us what we mean by a person until we know how to distinguish persons as blazes from the whole big Fire and persons from other little blazes like trees, cows, and computers. Since physicalists do not permit themselves the explanatory uses of soul, mind, or spirit, they will have to say how to get along without these. They may wish to delete such categories as that of persons in the end, but they have a lot of explaining to do which talk of little blazes or localized systems of matter/energy does not accomplish.

Although the non-materialist options did not appear in the explanation of what we are, not back in those days, there was a move in that direction which was sparked by a concern with what we should do. Socrates and the Sophists gave rise to Plato.

Man as the measure: Protagoras vs. Socrates

Socrates is the model of the philosopher for most people who have any conception of what a philosopher is. Once one gets into a philosophy department at a college or university, one finds that, while Socrates is admired, he is hardly the current model. It is hard to follow someone who thought we ought not to write books. The Socratic method of leading questions works as a teaching tool and a heuristic, but that is not where most of us want to stop. Unlike Socrates, we cannot influence our society by going down to the marketplace to discuss the true and the good with our countrymen. Just try getting a philosophical discussion going in your local supermarket or at the stock exchange. I suppose that shopping malls have some possibilities, but be careful.[13] Socrates was put to death for practising philosophy in public. As for me, I will write books and discuss philosophy in colleges and universities for now. Space is too expensive in the mall.

Socrates spent a lot of his time in ancient Athens in intellectual combat with some intellectuals of the day called "Sophists," men who taught practical logic and rhetoric but who also purveyed a philosophy of relativism and skepticism. Knowledge, truth, and value were thought by these teachers to be either unattainable or fictions. Socrates studied with some Sophists at the rather informal equivalent of today's university and then turned their skills to the pursuit of absolute knowledge, value, and truth.

The foremost of the Sophists, Protagoras, said, "man is the measure of all things, of the things that are, that they are, and of the things that are not, that they are not."[14] In other words, what is real is relative to the observer. On the one hand Protagoras is putting people at the centre of the universe and making them the lords of reality. On the other hand, the universe shrinks to the size of the individual.

Maintaining a kind of dignity of persons in the face of this relativism, Socrates sought to find a route for them through this observer-dependent reality to something more real beyond the reality we make up. Even at this early stage in philosophical discussion, however, there appears the tension between relativist views which tend to devalue persons and absolutist views which exalt them. Naturally the absolutist views tended to be more popular from that day to the near past. Ultimately, they were a bit hard to believe in the face of the evidence of contemporary anthropology to the effect that what is taken as absolute varies from culture to culture. In our own age, relativism has been a driving force, and, in academic circles, the winner, though not the clear winner, of this ancient debate. To see how absolutism won back then and for most of the intervening history of Western culture, we should start with Plato's views about what we are.

Plato: Participating in the form of person

Plato's solution to Heraclitus' problem of unity in diversity and Plato's response to Protagoras' relativism come by way of a development of the Pythagorean concept of form. By the time Plato wrote the *Republic*[15] he had fully developed a unified theory of reality, knowledge, and value—the theory of the Forms. Like all the theories we will look at in this quick trip through history, we will see the theory mainly in its application to understanding what we are, though that was not its primary focus. According to this theory, persons, like all things in the flux of the quotidian, had a degree of reality, knowability, and value according to the degree to which they participated in certain Forms which were beyond, in a realm of absolute and unchanging reality, knowability, and value.

A red ball was red and round, according to Plato, because it participated in the Forms of redness and roundness. The more it participated, the redder and rounder it got. One can get a very rough grasp of what this participation is by thinking of copying or imitation of a pattern. I imitate a role model, perhaps, and so become a pale imitation of that model. If that model were perfect, even a pale imitation might not be so bad at all.

Persons participated in Forms. A good person was one who participated in the Form of goodness. In fact, anything which existed did so by participating in the Form of goodness; so everything was to some degree good. Our current saying that there is a little goodness in everyone was thought by Plato to be necessarily true. Being evil was being spiritually deformed, but a total loss of Form was a loss of existence. A person could not be totally bad any more than a statue could be totally shapeless or a musical composition totally unstructured. It is tempting to think of the Forms as abstract universals, like some contemporary conceptions of redness, roundness, goodness, and the like, but it is not clear that the distinction of the abstract from the concrete was the same in Plato's mind as it commonly is in ours today. Like the distinction of the material from the non-material world, this is probably a distinction which evolved from later reflection on Plato's theories. In any case, the Forms were postulated to provide an explanation of why things are the way they are. A person endured through change, moreover, because an unchanging and eternal part of the person maintained some Form. This self or soul had been, prior to being born into the chains of mortality, directly acquainted with that other world, the realm of the Forms. In this way, Plato answered both Heraclitus' question about change and Protagoras' question about value.

The good qualities that a person had were a reflection of these eternal forms in that person's soul. Bad qualities were to be thought of as mere deprivations of such a reflection. Forms were wholly positive in value. The well-ordered soul, the soul of the just person, was a soul in which the three main parts, Reason, Spirit, and Appetite, were in their appropriate roles. The just person was one in whom Reason ruled both Spirit and Appetite. Spirit was that part of the person from which courage and anger, for instance, sprang. Appetite can be thought of as a collection of such drives as those to seek shelter, comfort, food, and the bodily pleasures, especially sexual satisfaction. Reason was to direct us as to the priority of Spirit and Appetite. Courage might lead us, for instance, to try to cross a desert, while Appetite would try to keep us nearer comfort and sustenance. Reason would rule in favour of Appetite if there was good evidence that crossing the desert would be fatal and to no great purpose. Appetite, on the other hand, might keep us away from battle when Courage would draw us in. Reason would give courage the nod if doing battle was necessary to preserve the city-state which made one's life worthwhile. The ideal person, then, to put it in somewhat modern terms, would not be immune to the tug of emotions and drives, but would think through the best course of action rather than simply submitting to emotions or drives. The ability to see what is best, moreover, corresponds to the ability to see the Forms.

I have not gone into Plato's reasons for believing in the Forms or the tri-partite soul composed of Reason, Spirit, and Appetite. Ultimately his reason for adopting both is that they give us a coherent picture of the world and our place in it. I will not argue further for the theory of Forms here but I would like to put forward one of Plato's arguments for the tripartite soul. This soul or self which directs the body is rather unlike the Christian idea of soul or the Cartesian notion of the self which we will come to later. These later kinds of soul or self are simple things, not divided into parts. Plato, however, sees a need for complexity in persons simply because persons are themselves often divided concerning what to do. If I am extremely thirsty, but I have reason to think that the water hole I have crawled up to is poisoned, I am drawn to drink and repulsed from drinking at the same time. Plato reasons that one, simple, indivisible thing could not be in two opposite states at the same time. There must, therefore, be at least two things within me, one attracted to the water and one repulsed from it. The self must be complex, not simple.

This idea, that there are different decision-making faculties within us, is not hard to accept today because of the blanketing influence of Freud. It has not always been so. A divisible self or soul may still sound strange to some contemporary ears. On the other hand, we still have expressions like "sounds strange to my ears" which hark back to the era of Plato and earlier. The he-roes of Homer's *Iliad* speak as if their hands, feet, hearts, minds, and various other bits are all decision-makers. A person was thought of as a complex collection of things, a committee of decision-makers.[16] The triadic structure which Plato gives to this collection is reflected in Freud's division of our selves into the Ego, the Super Ego, and the Id.[17] If you think of your inner self as one, single, continuing, indivisible thing, then you must come up with some other explanation of the phenomenon of the divided self at the poisoned water hole. Plato's explanation, which was a natural in the ancient world, will not suit you at all. The many thinkers who have argued for the simplicity of the soul will appeal to you more. As usual, I wish you to consider that there may be two different concepts of a person here rather than a disagreement about the characteristics of a single thing. Alternatively, we may be looking at different parts of a person under the single title of "soul" or of "self." Perhaps we have an indivisible self as well as a committee of decision-makers within.

The conception which we often meet today of a person as an essentially social being is very much a part of Plato's theory. It is an anti-individualist stance that Plato takes, since he believes that the Form of goodness is a clear and perfect guide which should be followed despite individual ideas about what is good. The perfect state is one which has the same Form as the perfect person. Reason rules. This means that a class of those who are themselves ruled by Reason in their own souls should have complete autocratic control of the society. This was the class of Guardians. Below them would be a military and policing group, the Assistants, who were ruled by Spirit. The base of society would be formed by those who produced goods and services and had personal souls driven mainly by Appetite. This was the class of Craftsmen. Plato would think our own societies in the Western democracies wicked because they are ill-formed. The Craftsmen are allowed to rule. Similarly, military dictatorships are evil in so far as the dictator or oligarchy is from the class of Assistants. To be a truly capable ruler is to be a truly capable person, physically, morally, and intellectually at the height of human ability. A state that participates in the Form of goodness is one whose rulers do as well. The ideas of the individual and individual freedoms must be severely limited, according to Plato, in order to enforce the participation of the state in goodness.

At the beginning of this all too brief exploration of Plato's theory I intimated that persons were not the main focus of that theory. The reason is that, with respect to valuing persons as individuals, Plato stands midway between Christ and the Buddha. Buddha teaches that the ultimate attainment for an individual person is the annihilation of individuality, absorption into the cosmos, getting off the wheel of becoming. Christ, on the other hand, teaches that individuals will be rewarded for their merit by eternal life. The individual is not merely absorbed, but survives to enjoy the fruits of moral rectitude in this vale of tears. Following Aristotle, who comes up next in this historical jaunt, Christians before Protestantism believed the soul to be the form of the body; so even the body had to survive by resurrection. Plato, however, offered us a very limited form of survival. If I think of myself as a body governed by Reason, Spirit, and Appetite, it is clear that Appetite and the body get left behind, perhaps Spirit too. Only my intellectual component, perhaps conceived of as some rarefied, airy matter, is released at death. The distinction between the full-bodied survival that Christ offered and the absorption that Buddha welcomed is blurred. It is unlikely that the survival of our immortal souls, as understood by Plato, would appeal to any of our contempo-raries who are concerned with survival of bodily death.

Such a brief presentation of bits of Plato without much defence must make Plato sound rather quaint. If you think about the way you talk and think about things, though, you may find that Plato's influence is everywhere in your own worldview. We speak of Platonic relationships, meaning a relationship which is not driven by sexual desire from that part of ourselves called Appetite but which is the result of Spirit governed by Reason. Another example; one who knows something is *informed*. The intervening centuries have not prevented us from thinking often in terms of something like Forms. The enormous appeal of a world of the Forms where things are as they ought to be, a world of which our own is a pale imitation, a world that can be attained by a struggle of the soul to perfect itself in morals and intellect, is an appeal that will not let Plato's Forms go the way of phlogiston and other concepts which are just quaint antiques. There are serious criticisms of the theory, some brought by Plato himself,[18] so we must proceed cautiously with anything we gain from it.

Application to Daphne's Case

What does the theory of Forms do to help us with our topic? Consider Daphne, whom I spoke of in the introduction. She has lost most of the physical and mental abilities by which we knew her, but her body remains, to outward appearance, much as it was. Daphne can be seen from Plato's vantage point as someone who has changed Form. She no longer participates in the Forms to the degree she once did. This deformation of the self is an evil, a privation of the Form of the Good, which eradicates the natural gifts which Daphne had, thereby placing her in a different position in society. Once she had a soul in which Reason was foremost, governing Spirit and Appetite. Plato would have considered Daphne an example of the sort of person fit to be among the rulers of the state, someone who could see the Forms.

But how are we to think of Daphne's survival, and how should we act towards her? In Plato's time, Daphne could not have stayed alive as she does now with heroic medical care. Probably Plato would have considered Daphne a deformed instance of the same person as the former Daphne, but whoever survives in a deformed state survives only to a degree. But then how are we to act towards such people? Justice, for Plato, is achieved by giving each person in the society the role to which that person is suited by natural gifts, and there is no longer any role for Daphne in Plato's scheme of things. There is no further guidance to be had from Plato in such cases, but it would be anachronistic to expect it. All Plato can do is to underline the extremity of the tragedy of such a complete deformation of a soul so finely wrought.

For others, however, who are not in Daphne's state, Plato's conception of the person as an inner self composed of Reason, Spirit, and Appetite may have some appeal. To order one's soul well with Reason ruling, Spirit second and Appetite firmly under their control is a task well worth undertaking whether one understands it literally or figuratively. Rather than giving us a view about what persons, in general, are, Plato has given us an ideal. He tells us what, given certain natural gifts, we should be.

What I like about Plato

Plato tells us something of the inner complexity of people: the way we fight with ourselves is picturesquely captured in the doctrine of the tripartite soul. He also holds up an ideal of personal development towards greater goodness, greater participation in the Form of the Good. It seems like a good idea to subjugate one's spirit and appetite to one's reason. Whether or not we swallow the theory of Forms holus bolus, we can still adopt the concept of an ideal towards which human beings must strive to become the best persons which their natural gifts allow. He reminds us as well that people achieve their development in the context of a society, not as totally independent agents. Some of these themes are carried on in the work of Plato's most famous student.

Aristotle: Down-to-earth souls

Plato's student, Aristotle, gives us a lot to think about with respect to persons just as his teacher did. There are many differences in their views, but perhaps the main one is that Aristotle concentrates on the here and now, on what we would think of as the real world. Plato thought our world was an illusion, low in value, knowability, and reality, the muck of change and hence of corruption. Aristotle, by contrast, shows no desire to escape from this world to a world of Forms; instead, he brings the Forms back to this world and reduces their godlike stature. For him, form, or structure, loses its capital F.

Even less than for Plato is there any ground for making a distinction of material from non-material things in Aristotle's worldview. Form and matter are not really separable. We have already seen that in Aristotle's down to-earth-approach, the soul is the form of the body. You cannot have one without the other. This seems to simplify the problem of reidentifying people over time. To see if the same person is there, one might think you merely have to see if the same body is there, for the person is an embodied soul in the sense of materialized form or formed matter.

There are some difficult cases of identification of bodies of living organisms just as there are difficult cases for any thing. The difference between a wax statue and a puddle of melted wax is clear enough, but there are some stages in the melting process where it is hard to say if the statue is gone yet or not. A statue's form is just its shape. With more complex forms, like the soul of a person, identification gets even more difficult. As if that were not enough, persons' souls are special, because they include the capacity for reason. This means that, after all, even when we can apparently identify the body as the same, if the abilities have changed enough, the person is gone. Actually, Aristotle would not count the body as the same body if the person could no longer reason. The person, the embodied soul, is a substance in which properties like being able to reason inhere. If the soul itself is changed, then something necessary to the existence of the person, the essence, is changed rather than just an accidental property like having black hair. You still exist when you go grey, but not when you become totally senile. To see, given Aristotle's views, how we might test for sameness of a person, let us look a bit more closely at the Aristotelian notion of a soul.[19]

"*Psuche*" was Aristotle's term for soul, self, or organizing principle of a living organism. It was not what the soul became in later Christian thought but, rather, a group of capacities. The *psuchai* or souls of living things constituted an ordered hierarchy from the *psuchai* of the simplest vegetables through those of the various animals up to the *psuchai* of persons at the top.[20] Just as the capacity for locomotion distinguishes animals from plants, the capacity for rational thought distinguishes human beings from lower animals. This capacity is a part of a person's *psuche*, but so is the capacity to eat.[21] In fact, the *psuche* has an indefinite number of parts.[22] This is much more complex and interesting than the tripartite soul Plato proposed. To understand a person, in Aristotle's way of looking at things, you need to understand her biology as well as her psychology. That is not all.

As with Plato, the social and political aspects of a person's life are crucial. Aristotle looks at the whole universe the way we would look at a person. If you want to know why a person does something, you ask about that person's intentions. If you want to know why an acorn is made the way it is, for Aristotle, you look for an explanation in terms of what it intends to become or what its purpose is. You look at adult specimens of any organism to see what the end or purpose of their earlier developmental stages were. Since the end of human social development is a state, people are political animals.[23] Somewhat as acorns were meant to produce oaks, people were meant to produce societies. A hermit, I suppose, is malformed, missing something in her *psuche*.

Just as Aristotle saw the soul as a more complex entity than it was in Plato's theory, so the state is not just divided into thee classes of person. Our varied *psuchai* allow for many types of persons. He holds, nonetheless, to Plato's idea that a good state is one made up of good people. The rules for being good, hence the rules for politics, are not so limited for Aristotle. Nonetheless, within a community it was important for everyone to abide by the same laws to prevent discord. People are by nature sociable and an olive tree by nature bears fruit, but the tree may not bear fruit if conditions are poor, and people may be unsociable unless the state is carefully regulated.

With people, as with everything in nature, the antecedent purpose determines the eventual outcome, *given the right conditions*.[24] As Voltaire said much later in *Candide*, "We must cultivate our garden."

Because all of Aristotle's explanations are couched ultimately in terms of the purpose things have by nature (their *telos* or end) he is concerned with the way things turn out in the end. A fetus or a child is not yet a full person but merely a potential person. The fully and normally developed adult is the model we must look at to understand his conception of a person as an embodied soul. This is often what we do in contemporary debates when we think about what persons are, but we forget this normal adult model and then try to apply our results to children or adults who have lost certain essential capacities. For some of our purposes, children are full persons, not just potential persons, but saying this requires a different concept of a person to the one Aristotle is employing, and such a different concept entails a very different sort of moral view to Aristotle's. To get an appreciation for Aristotle's view we must look at his notion of a person's soul.

The core idea in the notion of the *psuche* or soul is that of ability. Once one loses the essential abilities which one must have to be a certain kind of substance, then one no longer is in the same class of substances. Take a simple case first. Suppose I use an oblong piece of sandstone as my door step in front of my house. It weathers and crumbles. It is now not a deformed door step, it is not a door step at all. It is just a heap of rubble. Similarly, Aristotle, seeing that a human being has lost the capacity to reason which he takes as the crucial capacity for separating persons from animals with lower orders of *psuchai*, would not count this human being as the same person, nor as a person at all.

Aristotle had, because of his emphasis on ability, what would seem to us today to be a rather harsh moral and political outlook. He was happy with viewing some human beings as slaves by nature and with keeping women totally out of politics. He failed to take up Plato's view, unbelievably radical for its time, that women could be in any position for which they had the ability, even Guardianship of the Republic.[25] While Aristotle has much to say to us that may be useful, we probably will not be able to make do with his concept of a person on its own.

Application to Daphne's case

Given the theory I have adumbrated here, Aristotle would have thought that Daphne had gone out of existence. Something of the matter that made up Daphne remains, but with a different form. The woman we now call "Daphne" is not a person in the sense that Daphne of old was; for rationality, the foremost part of her *psuche*, is gone.

What I like about Aristotle

What is particularly useful in Aristotle's conception is the great complexity which he sees in the soul or self, its inseparability from the body, and the integration of people into a taxonomy of living things. People are part of nature. The concept of a soul as not something which is out of this world but to be found only in the world is a concept which merits further investigation. The *psuche*, soul, or self can only be had by "a natural body of a particular kind, viz. one having *in itself* the power of setting itself in movement and arresting itself."[26] The difference between animals and people on this account is not in having a soul but in its degree of complexity. We are all part of one fabric.

It may well be objected, for reasons alluded to earlier, that the use of "soul" or "person" in our discussion of Aristotle is anachronistic. Certainly, whatever he was talking about, he was not talking exactly about what most speakers of English have in mind when they use these English terms. There is reason to think, however, that his remarks are pertinent to our present concerns about our souls, selves, or persons. For now, we will see what the ancients following Aristotle had to say.

Rome and the invention of "persons"

In an exceptionally Teutonic offering in the *Monist* back in 1910, "A Contribution to the History of the Word Person: A Posthumous Treatise by Adolf Trendelenberg," one finds some clues as to current dictionary definitions and philosophical predilections. A person may be thought of as a role or a part played, and this is associated with the possible origins of the word "person" in the Latin *persona*, meaning "an actor's mask."[27] What is behind the mask? Perhaps the human being puts on this role, and since one may have different roles from time to time, there may be different people associated with a single human being. Playing one's role well and consistently was the ethical desideratum of the Stoics, so even this minimal sense of "person" has a moral use. This use of the term flows into that in Roman law where the legal drama had its *dramatis personae* and *persona* indicates those who bear characteristic legal relations, such as the plaintiff and defendant (346). It is also related to such uses as "first person" in grammar (349). Trendelenberg believes that the grammatical and legal uses "helped each other along in the course of the generalization in which finally *persona* and *homo* became synonymous" (351). In early Roman law, all human beings, even slaves, were distinguished from mere things and included among persons (348). The ideas that persons are necessarily human and that they have moral and legal importance are part of the early evolution of the concept of a person. Philosophers who call this carbon-chemistry chauvinism and see no moral import in the concept of a person fly in the face of Western European common sense. That is the philosopher's job, to some extent, but gadflies can sting themselves.

In Justinian's time, relatively late in the history of ancient Rome, slaves began to be conceived as mere things, not persons, because the concept of freedom became closely linked with that of a person. Freedom, in this body of law, was the "natural power to do what you please unless you are prevented by force or law" (356). This, too, it seems to me, is clearly related to the dignity of persons which sometimes gets glossed over, passed off, ignored, or denied in the contemporary debate on personal identity. We do not want to mess up our metaphysics with such messy, fuzzy stuff as freedom.

One must not get too carried away with the advent of the word *persona*. I have been speaking of the views of philosophers in classical antiquity on persons. Even following the introduction of *persona*. however, they did not have a word with all the connotations of "person" that we find in contemporary European languages. The words and phrases the Greeks were using could be translated by "human being" or, in political contexts, possibly even "free, adult, male human being." Slaves and women were only considered persons by the enlightened few. The heritage of our word "person" does, however, reach back to classical antiquity where it even has some moral force. Much of its current moral force, however, dates back only to Kant in the eighteenth century.

The equivalent of the word *persona* in Latin is the Greek *prosopon*. These words both refer to the mask that actors wore on stage. The mask became associated with the role the actor played. We still use person in the sense of "role" sometimes in English. This sense of the role or character played is a very important one, morally, for the ancient philosophers in Greece and Rome known as Stoics (342, 344).

Stoicism

The Stoics thought that what we ought to do is to play the person or role we have been given by providence. This role is totally beyond our control to choose. In the grand theatre of the universe, we should accept our parts and play them well. That is the only scope for human choice and self-betterment. One can choose to rankle at the person one must play or one can accept this role and play it well. In a world where everything is determined by providence, it is odd that we nonetheless have, on this deterministic Stoic view, the freedom to choose to accept or rail against our roles.[28] We are, in any case, determined to play those roles however we choose to feel about them.

This Stoic philosophy was already established in the third century BC and still going strong when Epictetus wrote in the first century AD:

Remember that you are an actor in a play, the character of which is determined by the Playwright: if He wishes the play to be short, it is short; if long, it is long; if he wishes you to play the part of a beggar, remember to act even this role adroitly; and so if your role be that of a cripple, an official, or a layman. For this is your business, to play admirably the role assigned you; but the selection of that role is Anothers.[29]

This limited view of what a person is stifles the striving to change one's conditions. It is, consequently, a means of maintaining the status quo. People bear pain and injustice stoically because it is their lot in life to act the good sufferers. In this case, however, the interest of the individual is not, as with Plato and Aristotle, subjugated to the interests of the state. The focus, at least, has shifted to concern about individual lives. The Stoics, however, assume that individual lives are best served by the recognition that we are only acting out roles given to us by providence. This is the way to happiness. If one is a miserably treated slave, one becomes happy with being just that. Like the Epicureans before them, the Stoics thought not of satisfying desires for power or pleasure but of overcoming desires. In this subjugation of desire there is a superficial resemblance to Buddhism, but, unlike the Oriental views in which the individual is ideally absorbed into something larger, the Stoic philosophy puts the individual in the spotlight.

While the Stoics gave us a rather limited concept of a person—the person as a role—they did develop the concept of a person beyond mere species membership. The satisfaction, moreover, in the quiet life of acceptance which they promoted was personal satisfaction, not satisfaction in serving the state. Personal freedom, though limited by Stoicism to the choice between acting one's role or railing against it, was also tied at this early stage of its development to the concept of a person.

Application to Daphne's case

The Stoic's idea that it is part of the nature of persons that persons have the ability to choose and are responsible for the way they feel about their lot in life is one which, however limited the freedom, rules out a severely mentally handicapped human being as a person. Daphne cannot choose to accept or reject her role, so far as we can tell. When she was last able to choose, she utterly rejected her approaching role as a demented cripple and chose death, demanding euthanasia. The Stoic development of the concept of a person does not help us with the questions raised earlier about respecting the choices of a person when those choices were made prior to radical changes. Some may find comfort in Stoicism as a means of bearing their own suffering, but it gives us too limited a concept of a person to rule on our conflicting intuitions where Daphne is concerned. We can only say that Daphne is not a person in the sense of the term introduced by the Stoics who invented, if not the concept, the word.

Plotinus and later Roman developments

While its limitations for our present purposes are evident, Stoic forbearance was much admired in ages which followed the classical period of Greece and Rome. The idea that we should apathetically play whatever role we discover is our lot in life was to be modified, however, to permit a kind of striving for self-improvement within the role. The religious thinking that dominated the Middle Ages was responsible for the movement away from the limited concept of a person which the Stoics had bequeathed. The Christian concepts of persons, moreover, were presaged in Roman times by Plotinus' revision of Plato.[30]

Consider first the development of the concept of a person in the law. The courtroom was seen, by the Romans, as a kind of drama, and the roles in this play, for instance of the plaintiff and the defendant, were naturally called *persona*, persons. As only human beings can have legal rights and stand in juridical relations to one another, this legal usage moved the term in the direction of being synonymous with "human being."[31] Assuming that the use of language has a lot, though not everything, to do with concept-formation, the concept of a person which is our heritage from the Stoics, person as character or role, was being enriched to include our juridical relations and our humanity. At the same time, spiritual dimensions were being thrown into the mix.

The spiritual input came from a dramatic revision of Plato by the Roman philosopher Plotinus. Plotinus revived the notion of an immortal soul as the crucial part of the person, but he moved this concept more in the direction of the non-material. Throughout ancient Greek philosophy, spirit was thought of in terms of some material but rarefied thing, like breath. The immortal soul that Plotinus sees as the true reality, as opposed to our bodily, earthly, existence, resembles fairly closely the Christian notion of a soul which is of a different order entirely from the body. The soul is responsible for its actions, although Plotinus, like the Stoics paradoxically maintained as well that all events are determined. This soul then seeks to perfect itself morally and intellectually, thereby achieving a mystical union with God.[32]

This sort of view is radically different from that of the Stoics in that it gives the person the chance for self-improvement. Unfortunately, it reverts to the other-worldly conception of reality. The healthy here-and-now emphasis of Aristotle and his successors is lost. This has the decidedly unfortunate effect of making the world and persons' bodies merely disposable packaging. As the events of the Middle Ages show, such a view of the person can lead to incredible atrocities. It is not an evil to torture a heretic into recanting her heresy then to kill her quickly once she has confessed. Her soul can then go to heaven in a state of grace. If the here and now is of no value, human suffering in this temporal world can always be justified by an appeal to the eternal bliss to come.

Respect for persons becomes respect for their immortal souls, and the devil take their poor, suffering bodies. Although it is misleading in many respects, and well out of fashion with historians, there are reasons for the epithet the "dark ages." Respect for the whole person is kept in abeyance while concepts of the non-material side are developed. People are expected to accept their suffering stoically and play the roles they have been given, but they are expected to perfect themselves spiritually. The intellectual perfection that Plotinus strove for is sometimes dropped from the picture as a hindrance to faith. The mortification of the intellect and the flesh in favour of the spirit is a new twist. Another concept of a person is emerging in the Middle Ages. We will see how this comes about through looking at some major figures in the philosophy of those wonderful and terrible times.

The Roman idea of persons under law has been developed in such a way that we now treat Daphne as a person for juridical purposes, though as one who must be in the guardianship of others. This reflects a concern for persons in some sense broader than that which we have seen developing in ancient Rome. Certainly it goes beyond the picture of persons as beings struggling for their betterment through spiritual development. Perhaps the subjugation of the intellect to faith has had a beneficial side-effect in making us realize the worth of features of persons which are outside of the realm of reason. Intellectual ability had been the primary distinguishing feature of persons according to Aristotle. The Stoics, Roman law, and Plotinus helped to broaden the concept so that a person could have legal or spiritual worth of importance equal to or greater than intellectual ability. The battle to distinguish persons from the cosmos or the state—a battle against absorption in larger units—was also vigorously engaged in Roman times. We will see this struggle continue in the Middle Ages.

FOUR
The Mediaevals

The Soul and the Intellect

St. Augustine adopted a worldview similar to that of Plotinus, making it the standard view of the Middle Ages. The world was arranged in a hierarchical form with God at the top, somewhat like the Form of Goodness in Plato's system. God, of course, is mysterious and unknowable. Love of God and faith are substituted for knowledge in this worldview. Although Augustine strives to make Christianity intellectually acceptable, reason is not given the first place among man's abilities. Nonetheless, persons gain a new importance with the advent of Christianity since they are made in the image of God and are closer to God than other things in creation except angels. Plotinus had bequeathed a hierarchy with God at the top and unanimated matter at the bottom.[1] Augustine adds human dignity to the picture. Each person is worthy of the love of others unless, by choice, that person makes herself less than worthy by being insufficiently loving.

Augustine assures us that God cares about us as individuals. That love is the source of our worth, and he assures us that we can strive as individuals to be worthy of love. Still, a person cannot achieve a state of grace by effort alone, but only by God's gift of grace. We can be damned on our own steam, but we need God's help to be saved. This gives some scope, at least, for freedom of the will as an important feature of persons.

The ability of persons to love is, however, the most notable feature which is given new importance in Augustine's conception of a person. We inevitably love, and we may love things, other people, and ourselves. When we expect too much from the object of our love, our love is disordered; hence we become restless and miserable. Of course, Augustine claims that our ultimate spiritual need can only be satisfied by love of God (144-45). It is love of God, according to Augustine, which makes us a member of a society, the City of God, which is at war with the City of the World. The latter is composed of those who love themselves and the world (149). What or whom we love and how we love turn out to be the most important features of persons, bar none. In spite of the heavy apparent debt to the classical period, Augustine ushers in a new way of thinking about persons and a new importance for them in the old hierarchy. Persons still do not count because they

Notes to Chapter Four are on p. 317.

are ends in themselves, but they have dignity and value since God has a purpose for them and cares about them.

Unfortunately, the enlightenment of some of Augustine's views does not carry through in practice. He is writing as the Roman Empire is in its death throes, and with it goes much of the civilization necessary to provide a context for the humane pursuit of Augustinian ideas. Instead of the emphasis on individuals as exalted by God's love and worthy of love, one sees in this period the idea of the hierarchy burned into human society. In imitation of the divine hierarchy there is a social hierarchy in which the King is at the top, then come the nobles arranged in a subordinate hierarchy of their own, followed by the free men at the next level, and—near the position of inanimate matter—the poor suffering serfs are at the bottom. Rigidity of the social structure prevents the pursuit of justice as Augustine conceived of it, justice based on mutual love (148). The serfs were told by religious leaders to stay in their social place and wait for the reward in the next life.

Augustine may have said that justice is the habit of the soul which imparts to every man the dignity due him (148), but that habit would not be in anything remotely approaching general circulation until the repressive economic and cultural forces of the Middle Ages relented. Neither Christian doctrine nor the religious philosophers like Augustine or Plotinus gave credence to the politically expedient view of persons as immortal souls in largely expendable packaging. The mortification of the flesh is not required by those teachings but only by repressive political forces.

The nod in the direction of gender equality which we saw in Plato's *Republic*[2] is certainly nowhere to be seen in this period. In a strictly hierarchical society in which persons get varying degrees of respect, women are in a relatively poor position with respect to men. The queen is less than the king. The noblewoman is less than the nobleman. So it goes until one finds at the bottom of the hierarchy the female child of a serf. On the plus side, there are women in such a society, like the queen, who are treated with great respect for their persons.

Other groups who are slowly gaining the status of persons in our society have, perhaps, benefited from the changes wrought by Augustine. Those who are handicapped, mentally or physically, provide an example. Although the Augustinian contribution to the concept of a person is dependent on the acceptance of a particular brand of theism in which the worth of individuals is conferred by a loving God, the influence of this view on secular opinion is considerable. One does not have to be a religious thinker in our times to accept the general principle that persons have worth and dignity independently of their abilities and usefulness to society. In particular, intellectual ability is not the essence of persons. At least while our times remain less harsh, in Europe and North America, than Augustine's era, we find room to value people who require the support of society but do not have the wherewithal to continue to contribute to society. In extreme cases, the very defencelessness of the person is taken as a ground for special protection as a member of the class of persons rather than as a ground for ejection from that class.

Another feature of Augustine's work on our topic is the increase in individualism. The Oriental ideal of absorption of the individual in the state or in the cosmos is fended off with the doctrine of individual excellence through the striving to be worthy of God's love. This emphasis on the person as opposed to a larger entity is continued by some of the subsequent major figures in philosophy during the Middle Ages.

Application to Daphne's case

The emphasis on love is interesting from two vantage points. On the one hand, taking the capacity for mutual love as a defining ability of persons may count against treating Daphne as a full person. Daphne's capacity for mutual love is very much diminished, if it remains at all. One must have some sense of self and other for love. One must be able to remember other people to some degree. On the other hand, since Augustine makes the dignity and value of persons dependent simply on their being loved by God, rather than on their possession of abilities, Daphne would be a person to whom we have strong moral obligations although she could not be a person in the sense of one who bears responsibilities.

What I like about Augustine

The emphasis on mutual love and on worth being independent of ability are strong strains in secular humanist as well as religious thinking. Perhaps they need not strain against one another as long as we characterize the capacity for mutual love as a defining capacity of persons while being loved or at least being an appropriate object of love as a moral feature of human beings whether persons or not. Appropriately secularized, the idea that being a person is partly an affair of the heart is an idea with great appeal.

The Arab-Christian dispute over individualism

While Plato, through Augustine, exerted a strong influence on the thought of the early Middle Ages, the works of Aristotle were temporarily lost to scholars of that time. Through Arabian philosophical communities, however, where Aristotle's works were still read there came some of the opposition to Plato which we have already noticed. Avicenna, a Persian writing in the tenth and eleventh centuries, was hotly discussed in Europe. His view of persons was like that of Aristotle. Persons were formed matter, the soul being the form of the body. Avicenna, however, threw in a dash of Plato in that the soul, or some intellectual part of it, somehow survived the death of the body to be absorbed into a kind of mass soul or mind.

As with the Greeks generally, intellect was considered by Avicenna to be the most important feature of the person. It included perception of objects external to the person, memory, and the power to discover the essence of things through abstraction, although the ability to abstract was not a human ability but something done for us from the outside by the somewhat mysterious Agent Intellect. This disturbed St. Bonaventura since this idea of an Agent Intellect—somewhat like a super-conscious mind—"threatened the notion of the discrete individuality of each soul, since each returned to its source, the Agent Intellect."[3] Maimonides, the great Jewish philosopher of the fourteenth century, developed a similar view to Avicenna's. Here we have again the Eastern idea of absorption of the individual into the mass soul.

It is interesting that it is Christianity which seriously opposes this absorption doctrine while retaining the idea of a reality beyond this world. After all, the other-worldly aspect of Christianity is used during those times for political purposes inimical to individualism. Conceptually, however, Christianity drew to itself all that was useful in promoting the importance of the individual soul. The older Greek ideas which gave less importance than Christianity to the individual, though more to the intellect, succeeded only in eventually improving the reputation of the intellect. St. Anselm, for instance, thought that reason together with faith and divine guidance would reveal rational proofs of articles of faith. But no major Christian thinker returned to the idea of the absorption of souls into something larger without personal distinctions in the souls remaining. Individualism was here to stay as long as Christianity was. The dogma which supported the worth of individual souls eventually supported the political power of the individual, but only in later ages after long evolution of the concept of a person.

Another philosopher from the Arabic world was the Spaniard Averroes, writing in the then-Moslem culture of Cordova in the twelfth century. In his famous commentaries on Aristotle his version of the Aristotelian doctrine about persons was true to the original. The soul was the form of the body and was itself material; hence, the soul died with the body.[4] This down-to-earth, secular philosophy could not have survived in the parts of Europe controlled by Christians. Opposition to the Platonic doctrine of the immortal soul was, of course, anathema to Christianity. Even more than Avicenna, Averroes undermined the separateness of individual intellects, putting all of our intellectual abilities at the doorstep of the Agent Intellect, that impersonal rational force in the universe. While this secularizing force had its impact diverted by the great thinkers of Christian Europe, they benefited from and adapted the Aristotelianism of Averroes. In particular, the greatest systematic philosopher of the Middle Ages, St. Thomas Aquinas, found a place for Aristotle at the heart of Catholicism.

St. Thomas Aquinas

By the thirteenth century when Aquinas was writing, the influence of Aristotle was rising and threatening the philosophical ground on which Christianity had taken its stand. It is easy to maintain a doctrine of the immortality of the soul against the backdrop of Platonic metaphysics since Plato himself had put forth such a doctrine of the soul. Mind you, we have seen that the soul which Plato conceived was a rather wispy thing by comparison with the full-blooded person that was needed to make Christian doctrine work. If I were to be concerned about my personal survival in an afterlife, I would not be motivated to follow a religion which promised me only that some intellectual part of me would survive. It is not just my reasoning capacity that I would want to defeat death.

Here then is the dilemma which inspired so much of the subtle metaphysics of Aquinas' era: immortality of the soul requires something unchanging and incorruptible as the soul, while full-blooded personal survival requires that we take along our corruptible, changeable old bodies. Recall that the soul Aristotle conceives of is a part of the person which dies with the body, as that soul is just the form of the body. Survival without the body makes no sense, for the body is an essential part of the person.

Intellect is, for Aquinas as for Plato, Aristotle, and the Aristotelians of Aquinas' day, the distinguishing characteristic of human beings. We need intellect to come to know God and thereby to come to love God.[5] The idea that to know Him is to love Him is reminiscent of Plato's view that to know the Form of Goodness is to do good things since Goodness is irresistible to the soul that sees it. Aquinas, however, emphasizes another feature of persons which is not clearly compatible with such a doctrine of irresistibility, namely that we are free to choose sin or devotion.

The restrictions of theology forced Aquinas to be very creative in fashioning a system which, while it emphasized Aristotle, did not leave Plato behind. Since Aristotle had designed his own system to supplant Plato's this proved to be a task which Aquinas, for all his skill, did not quite manage. In the process of his magnificent failure, however, he had a profound influence on what we think we are. Since theology demands that persons be able to commune with God, Aquinas was driven to try to retain the other-worldly features of the soul while not overthrowing Aristotle's insight that our bodies are essential to us. But how can the corruptible, changeable, and finite commune with the incorruptible, unchangeable, and infinite? Plato's answer, that the immortal part of us escapes from the body, just is not compatible with Aristotle's insight.

Aquinas asserts, then, that our incorruptible, free, intelligent, individual souls are not merely housed in our bodies, but must be unified with those bodies if we are to be whole persons. He does not, of course, accept Aristotle's claim that such a soul cannot exist without the body. The soul, however, is radically incomplete without the body. Now think of what most people are imagining, in Christian culture, when they think of themselves going to heaven. It is not the decrepit body from the grave that gets dragged along. It is not merely a disembodied intellect without memory or attachment to the earthly body that is absorbed into another reality. It is probably the body in the adult stage of life made perfectly healthy and beautified, free of pain and all the defects to which matter is prone, that soars off into the blue. Aquinas merely extends the Platonic conception of rarefied matter, which was the Platonic soul, to include not just something like the breath but the whole body in a reformed, purified, glorified state. Just as the soul, purified of the evil that was in it, is renewed, so the body is made better than it ever was with this renovated form to structure and limit it properly. In our life on earth we are always to some degree malformed. Our bodies will be perfectly formed in the hereafter, according to this doctrine.

Aquinas is often thought of as replacing the Platonic metaphysics, by and large, with Aristotelian metaphysics within the church. While this is true in some sense, it can be misleading if we overlook the victory of Plato in the fundamental areas of the doctrine of the immortality of the soul and the existence of a greater, better reality beyond this vale of tears. Aristotle told us that what you see is what you get. It is, furthermore, wrong to see in Aquinas a return to Aristotelian materialism and a retreat from Platonic dualism in Aquinas. It is wrong because the distinction between materialism—the view that all is matter—and dualism—the view that both material and non-material things exist—cannot be foisted on the ancient world without anachronism. Plato, like Aristotle, thought in terms of one kind of stuff out of which both souls and bodies are made. Souls were much more subtle, as breath is more subtle than flesh. Our current dualism with respect to persons had still not clearly formed in Aquinas' time. He was simply extending the Platonic doctrine of the soul to include more of what makes up the person on earth.

It should be apparent now, how I disagree with statements like this from Stevenson, "It is a common and recurrent misinterpretation of Christian doctrine that it asserts a dualism between the material body and an immaterial soul or mind. Such a dualism is a Greek idea."[6] I would say, rather, that the Christian doctrine through a large part of its history incorporates the Greek monistic view that there is just one kind of thing. For persons, in particular, there is not a distinction to be made between material and non-material parts of ourselves. In the many streams of current Christianity, of course, there are dualist factions. This dualism is, however, the outcome of a long process of evolution of ideas through Plato and Aquinas to Descartes, and it does not become a robust part of Christianity until the seventeenth century. Aquinas' philosophy is even today the theoretical underpinning of a major player in the Christian community, Roman Catholicism. The battle between dualists and monists (who believe that there is just one kind of stuff) still goes on within the Christian community. Aquinas contributed to this debate the claim that we can have immortality and keep our bodies. The body is reconstituted for judgment day.

Like any have-your-cake-and-it-it-too sort of theory, Aquinas' runs into some difficulties. From an Aristotelian vantage point and from many modern viewpoints concerning persons, some of Aquinas' problems seem quaint. For example, Aquinas has trouble with cannibalism. When two human bodies are intermingled in this grisly way, what gets resurrected and how?[7] Although there is a certain black comedy in these concerns, the theory that makes them important to Aquinas has been enormously influential in our conception of ourselves. After all, Aquinas gets himself into these fixes by insisting on both Aristotle's idea that we are one, single, unified thing, body and soul, while wanting to claim that we are more than the corruptible temporal stuff of this life.

Most of us believe that we are something more than intricately organized chunks of matter capable of locomotion. Those who accept and those who deny this belief both get into difficulties that are reminiscent of the debate between Aquinas and his Aristotelian contemporaries. We need to know how to identify and reidentify bodies; we need to know what else there is to us, and we need to know how to identify and reidentify that something else. We need to know whether our personalities can be expressed through different bodies or in other ways. Aquinas' problem of survival of the person in the afterlife is very similar to many of our contemporary concerns about survival within this life. Many of the questions we might ask have answers in Aquinas' adaptation of the classical Greek literature on persons.

A fetus, for example, is not a person by these lights, no more than an acorn is an oak. As Aristotle would have it, the fetus is merely a potential, not an actual, person. But, for Aquinas, the fetus has, after some weeks of development, an immortal soul, but not from conception onwards. Both the soul and the body develop and change. What keeps them the same through change is the underlying substance which remains through all changes of properties to that substance. There are properties which the substance cannot lose while remaining in existence, necessary properties, and properties which it may change, accidental properties.

While the person is the fully formed adult, there is a continuity of substance through the changes from the potential person to the person. The soul, or form of the body, becomes more fully actualized over time, but is never perfectly actualized in this life. The soul which chooses evil over good deforms itself and loses the chance of perfect actualization in the next life. Nonetheless, to make sure the right person is rewarded or punished in the next life, we must have a way of seeing this deformed person or this glorified person as the same person who walked this earth. The substance is the same. That is why, for Aquinas, and for Catholics today, the body had to be resurrected—not some ghostly apparition of the body but the real thing from the grave. This gruesome solution to the problem of survival of persons is the strange result of trying to wed incompatible systems, Plato's and Aristotle's. Aristotelians would say that one cannot separate the form and the matter temporarily prior to resurrection the way that Aquinas was forced to do. Formless matter is not a particular thing, and matterless form cannot exist.

Whether or not one takes the problems surrounding resurrection seriously, the idea that there is an essential me which exists through all my changes is one which appeals to *me*. What this underlying substance is that remains through the changes is to be found, according to Aristotle and Aquinas, by looking for my necessary or essential properties. What is there about me which could not change while I remain in existence? Notice, however, that their answers have to do with my existence as a human being rather than as a person. The person is not actualized at the beginning of the life of the human being. The underlying substance does not initially have, for instance, the personality which is unique to the later person. The question naturally arises for Aquinas, as it does for many of us, whether different persons could be in one body. After all, if the Aristotelian inseparability of body and soul is denied, how do we keep our physical and spiritual parts properly paired up? Aquinas can always appeal to God's benevolence to overcome such problems. A benevolent and omnipotent god would not allow and could prevent mix-ups.

There are other difficult questions which arise in the context of Aquinas' theories. When does the potential person develop enough to be the actual person? The adult human being in the prime of life is the person by Aristotle's lights. But for both Aristotle and Aquinas, there is the problem of what the person is through change. Since the distinction between person and human being is only nascent in the works of Aristotle, like the distinction between material and non-material, it would be anachronistic to pull out too definite an answer to such questions. By Aquinas' time, however, the problem of the three persons of the Trinity, which will be discussed later, had placed the question of the concept of a person at front and centre. The particular part of that problem, though, which arises for Aquinas is that a person choosing a personality by training herself to respond in certain situations with a certain kind of action is deliberately changing some of her properties. While these may be accidental properties of the human being, they appear to be necessary properties of the individual person, at least if a particular personality is essential to being an individual person.

In Aquinas this survival through radical change becomes particularly difficult since the beatified soul and body make up a person who is vastly different from the earthly original. Even within our earthly lives, however, we may change from sinners to saints. To say that one remains the same substance, or the same human being, while changing the personality only points to further difficulties. What is the continuing person who is responsible for the old sinful acts, the new saintly ones and, indeed, for changing from a sinner to a saint? What is essential to the person if one can go through such radical change? These sorts of questions are left largely for later philosophers to explore.

Applications to Daphne's case

The notion of radical change brings us to Daphne's case again, that is the case of a fully developed adult who becomes severely demented. As long as it is possible to be a person when the intellect and control of the body are destroyed, Daphne would still remain in the class of persons and merit the treatment due all persons. This does not, in and of itself, entail that the person we are confronted with after the radical changes is the same person who we once knew. Survival requires that the special characteristics which singled her out within the class of persons are also sufficiently represented after the change. The problem for Aquinas is to say how the soul, now devoid of intellect and character necessary for being responsible for actions, is the same soul that was once well-formed or deformed depending on the choice of good or of evil that Daphne might have made. Daphne can no longer, for example, exercise the good character she developed. She cannot prove her merit by responding to situations. Perhaps Aquinas would say that the soul in such a demented human being is like the soul in one who is dead. On resurrection of the body it will resume its abilities. One wonders, however, what the soul is, over and above the intellect and its abilities.

What I like about Aquinas

With all its problems, the picture of the person that emerges in the work of Aquinas reinforces the conception that we are individuals. The intellectual part of us which survives bodily death and awaits reunion with the perfected body is distinct from other intellects. No super-conscious mind absorbs the individual.[8] Intellect is crucial in distinguishing us from the other animals. From this point of view, the demented human being is, perhaps, no longer a person in the same way that a fetus or an infant is not yet a person. Unlike the Aristotelian system, that of Aquinas does not make a great deal of the value of persons depend on intellect. Those who are intellectually impoverished in this world, as long as they choose, within their limited capacity, good over evil, will be reformed and able to know God in the next world. Nonetheless, there is enough of an emphasis on intellect and its capacity to distinguish us as individuals to disturb some of those who followed Aquinas. The mystic and anti-intellectual tendency within Christianity is still at war with Aquinas' intellectual faction within Christianity.

In any case, Aquinas' adaptation of Greek thought importantly advances individualism and the conception of persons as free and self-determining. We move further in the Western tradition away from the fatalistic and anti-individualistic doctrines associated with the Orient. The idea of personality becomes crucial as well. Our intellect and freedom are properly used to choose certain habits which will guide us through sticky patches in our moral lives. In the course of development as persons then, we perform this paradoxical bootstrapping operation of making ourselves the persons we eventually become. The person—perhaps even the potential person—chooses a personality or set of habits that will make the future person what she becomes. The guide is not some Aristotelian *telos* (end or purpose) which makes this development inevitable. We are our own guides. I must train myself to automatically do the right thing when the occasion of a sin arises.[9]

In some ways, the contemporary view of Sartre, that existence precedes essence, that we first exist and later create what is necessary to our being the persons we are, is anticipated in Aquinas' view of persons. This boot-strapping doctrine of self-creation and the denial of a limiting, pre-existing nature of persons is also to be found in the humanists, especially in Pico Della Mirandolo's *Oration on the Dignity of Man.*[10] All of these authors need to grapple with the distinction between two questions: "What must something be like to be a person?" and "In what does the survival of an individual person consist?" The individual would have to keep the general characteristics necessary to be a person at all, and retain as well certain characteristics which made that person different from other persons. A class essence and an individual essence are both needed for survival.

We have to see where we have been to see where we are going in philosophy. I hope that it is evident by now that contemporary secular concerns are guided in part by Aquinas' hand. In any case, I am going to tax you further by looking at some other mediaeval religious developments which carry the concepts of a person forward into the later Middle Ages. They do so with great drama.

God is everywhere

Philosophy as the handmaiden of religion

In the Middle Ages, philosophy played second fiddle to religion. Since religion was such a powerful part of the culture, second fiddle was a pretty good position. In any case, the doctrine of the trinity, and theology generally, coloured the concepts of person. One astonishing example of questions concerning persons causing an immense stir occurred in 362 AD when a church council was held solely for the purpose of investigating and determining the meaning of the word "person."[11] Imagine what was required to draw bishops from around the Christian world to Alexandria for a meeting with one item on the agenda. In those days when travel was arduous and dangerous, only a topic of the utmost importance could produce such a remarkable meeting.

The religious doctrine which required this philosophical discussion at the highest levels of the church was the doctrine of the holy trinity. According to this doctrine, there is but one God; however, God is three persons, the Father, the Son, and the Holy Ghost. The question of the meaning of "persons" which the bishops went to such enormous trouble to decide was crucial because it determined the orthodox interpretation of the doctrine of the trinity. If all this leaves you cold, remember that in the Middle Ages people died for being unorthodox, that is, heretical. People take the definition of the concept of a person to be a matter of life and death today as extremists among pro-lifers use the rhetoric of civil war and condone shooting doctors. In 1532 it was no different. Recall from chapter two that Servetus declared that the three persons in the Godhead were three functions in the same sense as three roles. They burned Servetus at the stake. It was his bad luck that the bishops did not agree on what they meant by the term "person" back in 362 AD

There were three positions. The Greek bishops thought that God had three hypostases (substances) but one essence. The Roman bishops thought this would lead them away from monotheism. They demanded that the word "person" be used instead of the word "hypostasis." A third group thought the whole debate was a quibble over words. All agreed that the three persons of God were not merely roles that God was playing. The third group seems ultimately to have carried the day since the words "hypostasis" and "person" became synonyms in the theology of the Middle Ages. There were, however, genuine philosophical differences which were patched up by this linguistic plaster of diplomatic synonymy.[12]

The position of the Greek church seems incoherent in terms of the Aristotelian philosophy from which it sprang. If God is three substances or hypostases, then God cannot have one essence, since individual substances are defined by and inseparable from their essences. The concepts of a person which had been used up to the time of the bishops' council did not help. They did not want to use "person" to mean "role" or "human being." They could not use it in such a way as to imply that God was not really one being, but they could not use it so as to say that it was a mere manner of speaking to say that he was three of something. History had boxed them into loading onto the concept of a person the full weight of a mysterious doctrine. Anyone who, like Servetus, tried to take a perfectly legitimate meaning of the word "person" and demystify the doctrine of the trinity was likely to pay the highest price for such perfidy.

On the one hand this is not a propitious turn of events for the discussion of a concept or concepts. Things got worse before they got better. Even such civility as Aquinas had accorded to intellectual knowledge was viewed with suspicion by some later religious leaders. Mysticism was seen as a safer road to knowledge of God, since reason tended to unseat faith rather than to shore it up.

On the other hand, out of the theological wrangling came the use of the Latin term *persona* to mean "an individual, intransmissible (incommunicable), rational essence which is self-existent." A thing is self-existent if and only if it is not a part, nor a quality of another thing.[13] This moves the concept of a person from that of a mere role which cloaks the living human body to something independent of the body and, perhaps, something of greater dignity and moral significance. A general warming trend in the political life of Europe coinciding with a waning of the power of the church was still needed before the public, philosophical discussion of persons could be undertaken without grave danger. This thaw began in the late Middle Ages and was accelerated in the Renaissance.

FIVE
The Renaissance and the Early Moderns

Mechanism versus humanism

Erasmus' humanist tradition

As it is in our own age, particularly in philosophy, so it was in the Middle Ages: the devotees of logic, precision, and clarity turn out to be the most difficult to read. Montaigne wrote, "I can't recognize most of my daily doings when they appear in Aristotle. They are decked out or hidden in another cloak for the benefit of the schoolmen."[1] Part of the problem was the corruption of Aristotle's texts that were used by the scholars of the Middle Ages. Even with better translations, closer to the original, most of you would still agree with Montaigne. Still, reading good translations is much to be preferred to reading bad or stilted ones. Erasmus, the greatest promoter of humanism in the Renaissance, set about providing translations in which the elegance of the language was preserved and the stilted, ritualized language of some scholars was avoided. The democratization of things intellectual that was the result of Erasmus' efforts had a great effect on concepts of a person both by creating new avenues for discussion of the topic and by making acceptable the idea that those at the bottom of society's hierarchy were also worthy and capable. As learning spread downward, through this democratization, the idea that the value of persons was determined by their place in the social hierarchy became harder to maintain:.

Erasmus also attacked the view of the person as distinguished essentially by intellect, the view inherited from the Greeks and from Aquinas. The attack on the overweening importance of intellect was part of Erasmus' attempt to democratize religion. Faith was something one could pursue with the heart, Erasmus thought. He did not think heaven would be populated by intellectuals only. He did not deride reason by any means, but he thought there was more to the person than Aquinas and some of his predecessors had noticed or, at least, emphasized. Humanism is, partly, a return to the richer view of Augustine in which such things as the capacity to love are important features of persons. This helped to establish the atmosphere in which the idea of the dignity of persons, no matter what their station in life, could emerge. The humanist tradition is essential to the contemporary moral force of the term "person."

Notes to Chapter Five are on pp. 317-18.

Protestantism

At the same time there emerged a criticism of the old order much stronger than the criticisms from Erasmus. Arguing that both the corrupted mediaeval doctrines and the Protestant Reformation were driven by vast exaggerations, Erasmus tried to steer a middle course. "The whole world," he said, "is now shaken by the thunder and lightning born of the collision of such exaggerations."[2] On the one hand Erasmus opposed the clergy who magnified the importance of the papacy and, thereby of their own role. Some were making a tidy profit selling salvation in the form of plenary indulgences and such. On the other hand, Erasmus found the cure for this corruption as bad as the disease. Of the Protestants he said, "They liquidate the freedom of the will and teach that man is driven by the Spirit of Christ" (107). The dignity of persons was undermined both by those who said that heaven could be earned by fattening up the priests and by those who said that it could not be earned at all. One side reduced the spirit to commerce. The other negated the freedom which is essential to persons.

Taking aim particularly at Luther, Erasmus asks, "What's the good of the entire man, if God treats him like the potter his clay, or as he can deal with a pebble?" (109) This shows the importance, to humanists like Erasmus, of free will as a characteristic of a person. Although it elevates people from the role of plaything of the deity, it does exclude people like Daphne from the essential source of dignity. Daphne would have agreed. That is why she chose death over a life of dementia. Luther, by contrast, while lashing out at Erasmus, leaves open the possibility of the worth of any person through God's grace. Unfortunately, this worth is entirely reflected from God; there is no real personal worth. The most meritorious of saints, however, cannot be · saved without God's beneficence, by Luther's lights. Nothing one does is ever good enough to merit salvation.

Not only was Luther unmoved by human freedom as a value, he also preached diatribes against intellect. Luther took the primacy of faith even further than his predecessors so as to actually exclude the usefulness of reason in supporting religious belief. Erasmus' emphasis on the positive features of people and their capacity for moral improvement was dashed by Luther's return to the mediaeval view that man is by nature corrupt.[3] The worth of the individual person is utterly denied. Intellect and achievement are derogated in favour of subjugation of oneself through faith. Whatever its achievements in rooting out the corruption of the church, the Protestant Reformation tended to promote a backward-looking idea of persons.

Montaigne

Erasmus was not, however, alone in the revival of the humanism of classical antiquity. We have already noted Pico Della Mirandola's *Oration On The Dignity of Man* with its praise of human freedom.[4] Erasmus' friend Thomas More wrote of the near perfectibility, through reason, of people and their government in his *Utopia*. The humanist movement put forward freedom and reason as the essentials of a person. Though they did not neglect the emotions, it was usually reason on which the dignity of persons depended. This attitude is nicely summed up by Paracelcus:, "He who knows nothing loves nothing. He who can do nothing understands nothing. He who understands nothing is worthless. But he who understands also loves, notices, sees" (125).

Another admirer of the classical period of Greece and Rome was Michel de Montaigne, sometimes called "the French Socrates." He was influenced by the Skeptics of the ancient period. Their method, quite opposed to that of Socrates by the way, was to hold tightly to no doctrine, submitting all to doubt so as to live to the full. A life hemmed in by preconceptions about the way things are is not likely to be a happy one. Montaigne wanted to break down the strict, ritualized worldview of the Middle Ages in favour of one more flexible. One should not, on Montaigne's view, adopt final answers to very subtle, variable questions. Dogmatism is not the way to truth. We might do well to heed this advice as we debate abortion. Notice the final answers both sides have adopted concerning the nature of persons prior to engaging in the debate on abortion.

Montaigne, like Erasmus, tended to promote the idea of the dignity of persons. He asserted the humanist idea of our interconnection: "Every man carries within himself the whole condition of humanity."[5] He exalted our judgment as opposed to faith or intellect. To be a real person is to make conscious choices based on experience (215). Montaigne, however, did not wish to overthrow the political system and customs which provided some stability within which one could pursue philosophical wisdom, at least if one was a nobleman like Montaigne (216). This conservative attitude, as a result of doubt about absolute ends to which society should move, is very similar to that of the Sophists with whom Socrates contended. It comes too from an emphasis on personal rather than political development. It is, however, folly to think that the two can be separated. Montaigne's own development depended on his privileged position in society.

As to our present concern, the nature of persons, Montaigne the skeptic would have warned us that constant change denies us access to this or any other nature:

And if by chance you fix your thought on trying to grasp its essence, it will be neither more nor less than if someone tried to grasp water: for the more he squeezes and presses what by its nature flows all over, the more he will lose what he was trying to hold and grasp.[6]

Like the humanists before him, Montaigne was amazed by the variability of people. Nonetheless, Montaigne spent his life in personal development and advice to others on this difficult subject. One must know in some sense what a person is to do this. The impressive variability of persons is, in fact, one of the things about us which makes us what we are, and that, in turn, is dependent on our freedom.

Galileo and the new science

Generally opposed to the new focus on personal issues was the development of a new kind of objectivity in science which was accompanied by a mechanistic materialism as the underlying philosophy and a successful use of mathematics in prediction and control. Discussing Galileo, who was one of the pre-eminent practitioners of the new science, Stumpf[7] draws a clear opposition between the attitude towards persons promoted by science and the humanist notion of the dignity of persons. Galileo thought of reality in terms of primary (objective) qualities like motion, size, position, and density which can be quantified and dealt with mathematically. Opposed to these are secondary (subjective) qualities like colour, taste, emotion, and sound. We can talk about human beings in terms of primary qualities. Personal characteristics, Stumpf asserts, are usually represented by secondary qualities. These secondary qualities are either fictional or are to be reduced to the mathematically manipulable reality of primary qualities, according to Galileo's philosophy. "In either case, the unique dignity, value, or special status of human beings in the nature of things is severely diminished" (218). As Leonard Cohen said, "We are so small between the stars, so large against the sky."[8]

Application to Daphne's case

Without the ability to freely choose her own actions, Daphne really is reduced to the potter's clay from Erasmus' point of view. Since she has no free will, the main feature he holds out against the Protestants and the new science, she seems to be stripped of her dignity. Daphne herself saw matters this way when she anticipated being reduced by dementia to a mere mechanism. She demanded euthanasia as a protection from this fate.

Picks and pans from the Renaissance

The Renaissance, then, provided an atmosphere in which one could begin to think of persons as having dignity and moral worth by virtue of their own achievements, not just in the reflection of a deity. Individual freedom begins to assume more importance in conceptions of a person. At the same time, there were opposing views of the person presented by the severe Protestantism of the Reformation and the mechanistic, materialist philosophy underlying the new science. Protestantism made people out to be evil while mechanism reduced them to material things and thereby reduced their dignity and worth.

The oldest moderns

Hobbes: The emerging modern worldview

The success of empirical science in the prediction and control of events in the natural world gave philosophers pause. The mediaeval idea that pure intellect could find the truth was giving way to the modern recognition of the need to use the five senses in observation as well as the intellect to gain knowledge. Thomas Hobbes, best known for his political philosophy, ushered in the modern era by accepting completely the scientific method and its underlying assumptions. He believed in the need to observe and gather facts prior to erecting a theory. Actually, this is impossible. Facts are dependent on theories. Hobbes also accepted empiricism; that is, he believed that our knowledge comes from information we get through our five senses. Distinguishing himself from Descartes and his followers on the continent, Hobbes, in Britain, was a materialist. Recall that materialists believe everything is made of matter. Minds and spirits, if they exist at all, must be material. Hobbes' moral theory, moreover, was a precursor of a giant in this field, utilitarianism. Utilitarians believe that the right thing to do is the action which will bring about the most happiness for the greatest number of people. While Hobbes held all these views in a form which was to be refined by later thinkers, he set the tone for much of later philosophy, especially in Britain.

Living as he did in chaotic times, he wished for security more than anything else. This political aim dovetailed with his materialistic philosophy. He believed that he could understand the way persons behave in terms of mathematical laws governing bodies in motion.[9] If a person is a physical system whose behaviour can be predicted and controlled just as the course of a billiard ball on a table can be controlled by a master player, then the key to security is to understand the physical principles of human behaviour well enough to fashion a political system which will banish chaos and uncertainty. The political system turns out to be complete totalitarianism, and the value and dignity of the individual person is largely ignored. This is not terribly surprising, given the view that persons are merely elaborate mechanisms. Although Hobbes did not accomplish anything like the aim of finding the mechanical principles needed to predict and control persons, he bequeathed this aim and his view of the person to his philosophical heirs.

It was the success of mechanics in Hobbes' day which misled him into his vastly oversimplified view of persons as mechanical systems. The success of computer science today has the same effect on his heirs, who also try to reduce mind and persons in general to matter. Some wish, for instance, to treat the brain as a computer and the rest of the person as a program. Hobbes' concept of a person as an elaborate mechanism has merely been updated with currently fashionable scientistic jargon. Hobbes wished to reduce mind and spirit to material bodies in motion. Current reductionist theories differ from Hobbes' mainly in the complexity of the thing to which they wish to reduce these features of a person. In their degree of overconfidence, these theorists are Hobbes' equals. On the other hand, Hobbes and later empiricists reestablished the healthy attitude of Aristotle that takes our sense experience seriously. Attention to the here-and-now and lip service to common sense marks the work of Hobbes and his descendants. Wild speculation about persons untrammeled by the limits of experience is supposedly anathema among empiricists. One cannot help but smile, however, when asking how well founded, empirically, are their materialistic conceptions of persons. Such theories tend to go well beyond the evidence available from the senses, and in true empiricist fashion, they ignore equally strong evidence from other sources.

Application to Daphne's Case

On the one hand, Hobbes would see Daphne as merely a defective machine, which seems to diminish the importance of Daphne as an individual. There is no harm in thinking of her as a person or as the same person as the woman prior to the onset of the disease, so long as one does not suppose that the machine which is this person still functions normally. On the other hand, nobody has importance as an individual in Hobbes' philosophy. It is the state as a whole which must be well-ordered by fitting the individuals into their proper places. The utilitarian moral view which Hobbes prefigured would take Daphne's happiness as seriously as anyone else's in the calculation of the happiness. Whatever actions one contemplates which affect Daphne would have to be judged according to their total impact on all people affected. Thus Daphne's happiness may have considerable importance in comforting those who worry about what would happen to themselves if they were so reduced and also to those who cannot accept the reality of Daphne's current limitations.

Cartesian egos

While to many Hobbes' view of the person seems to be not a propitious beginning to the life of that concept in the modern era, this era began in cultural schizophrenia. As view opposite to Hobbes' and equally extreme was proposed at the same time by the renowned philosopher and mathematician René Descartes. Descartes and his school in philosophy are the archrivals of Hobbes and his. Hobbes' empiricism is countered with their rationalism. Rationalists not only deny the empiricist claim that sense experience is the source of all knowledge, they assert that reason alone is a much better source of knowledge than experience. Anything we get by experience must be filtered through our rational critical faculties before being accepted. The empiricist says that we should believe our eyes and ears. The rationalist tells us that we should not trust these unless reason supports the information they give us. The mind is glorified as Hobbes glorified the body. Descartes, however, does not wish to reduce the body to the mind. He is a dualist, one who believes that both mind and matter exist. Mind is just a lot more clearly known than matter.

The person, according to Descartes, is an amalgam of mind and body. This is a view which, today, is still often taken as common sense. Prior to Descartes, however, the distinction of mind and body was not at all clear. The ancient Greeks made no such distinction, although it is sometimes incorrectly attributed to Plato.

The distinction of mind from body seems undeniable to many of us. As is often the case, what was once a contentious theory has seeped down into the general consciousness to become obvious common sense. We no longer think with the ancients that thought and mind are merely subtle forms of matter like air. Most of us, outside of philosophy departments, suppose that mental events are quite different from physical or material events. If I have a pain in my nose after witnessing my dog get stung on the nose by a bee, for instance, you might tell me it is all in my head. You might say the pain has a mental cause rather than the physical or material kind of cause which my dog's pain has. We are often very unclear about the exact nature of the distinction, but most of us staunchly affirm that mental and physical events are different. Descartes has had a profound effect on the way we think about what it is to be a person.

Perhaps the most famous saying concerning persons is Descartes' reply to the skeptics who think we should doubt every claim since there is nothing we can know for certain. The first thing Descartes thinks we can be sure of is the self. He asserts confidently, "I think; hence I am."[10] Descartes means that he cannot think and at the same time doubt that he exists. What would be doing the doubting if he did not exist? Here, Descartes seems to return to the Greek and early mediaeval emphasis on intellect as the essential feature of persons. Actually, thinking, in Descartes' terms, is much more than mere intellectual thought. When he defines a self as a thinking thing, he packs a lot into the word "thinking": "But what, then, am I? A thinking thing, it has been said. But what is a thinking thing? It is a thing that doubts, understands

(conceives), affirms, denies, wills, refuses, that imagines also, and per-
ceives."[11] The interior self which directs the body and does this thinking is
often referred to as the Cartesian Ego. Descartes thinks it is independent of
the body and would exist even should the body cease to exist.[12] While many
think that nothing could be more certain than the existence of such a Cartesian Ego, others claim that there is no such thing. Since Descartes still has a
corner on common sense in our era, the philosophers who claim there are no
Cartesian egos really have their work cut out for them. While dualism can still
claim to be common sense, it may nonetheless be in danger of losing that
status. Problems arise. Is this thinking thing, the Ego, a thing which must be
thinking to exist? What happens when we are asleep? Perhaps we must say
with Unger that Descartes thinks the Cartesian Ego is always conscious, but
sleep is a kind of forgetting of what was consciously thought during the
night.[13] This seems rather desperate. Why can the body not preserve our
continuity instead of some mysterious Ego?

Descartes, in any case, does not leave Cartesian egos unhoused. Like
Plato's intellectual soul or self, Cartesian egos have a body to direct. Unlike
the Platonic soul which is made of a subtler form of the same stuff as the
body, the Cartesian Ego is different in kind from the body. This gives rise to
the interaction problem: how can a non-material self interact with a material
body? If I want to walk to the store, I do it. But my wanting goes on in my
mind which does not exist in space as my body does. How do the two of
them get together? The mystery of how a mental event, like wanting, can
cause a physical event like walking is just not solved by Descartes. In fact, I
do not think it is solved at all. The common sense view of persons has, to this
day, this completely paradoxical feature. We think of persons as minds with
bodies, but we do not know how the mind makes the body do the simplest
thing, nor do we know how physical events, passionate kisses for example,
are associated with their complex mental concomitants, doubts for example.

Descartes was not too concerned with this problem. In a religious age
like his, it was still possible to argue, as his follower Geulincx did, that when I
exert my will to make my body do something, my mind has no direct effect
on my body. God intervenes to make my body do what I want it to do.[14]
Some of you may wish to accept this solution. Many more will wonder why
we have the problem. Perhaps common sense is not so sensible in this instance.

Descartes was much more concerned, with respect to persons, about the
problem of how we know what we are. We think we have bodies of a certain
sort, but the skeptics argued effectively that we could be mistaken. I might be
dreaming that I have an ordinary human body, but when I wake up it may
turn out that I have three orange eyes and green feelers. Perhaps I have no
body. Could it be that I am just a disembodied mind? If such oddities seem

too strange to contemplate, perhaps I might wake up and find that I have a body like a dolphin's and that I was just dreaming that I was a human being. Descartes wanted to show that we are justified in dismissing such speculations. He thought he could prove that we are what we seem to be.

His proof is structured like this. Once I accept the indubitable claim that I exist, as a thinking thing, I can examine some of my thoughts. I conceive of God. Descartes argues that I could not conceive of a being such as God without there being a God. Descartes thinks he has established that God must exist. God, however, would not deceive us all of the time. Consequently Descartes thinks he can know not only that he is a thinking thing, but that this thinking thing or Cartesian Ego is housed in the body it seems to have. He will not wake up one day and realize that he had three orange eyes and green feelers all along.

Unfortunately, Descartes' certainty that we persons are minds in bodies is not really underwritten by his argument. Part of Descartes' method is to try to doubt everything and to accept only what we clearly and distinctly conceive to be true. He admits, moreover, that we could be systematically deceived. Even our basic reasoning processes which we rely on to do simple arithmetic might be faulty.[15] But if all this is so, the complicated reasoning Descartes gives for his belief in God must surely be doubted. We are left thinking that we are just thinking things until we move over to Hobbes' camp a little and accept some of the evidence of our senses without rational proof.

In any case, Descartes has given us good rational grounds for believing that we are thinking things in his wide sense of "thinking," and Hobbes is right to accept the evidence of his senses and to say that we have bodies which are prone to act when caused to do so. Much modern and contemporary philosophy has set itself the task of figuring out the nature of the thinking and bodily parts of the person and the means of their interaction, if indeed they are separate. Descartes left us also the closely related problem of understanding how our freedom of will operates. The picture of the person which emerges from Descartes is of a Cartesian Ego which supports a conscious mind operating a body, a free individual being responsible for all her own actions.

Application to Daphne's Case

Daphne seems barely able to understand what is going on around her, as an infant would be. Descartes might think that the Ego is trapped within a body which no longer responds to its commands. The Ego is what is essential to Daphne; hence, she has survived. The same person may, indeed, survive changes no matter how harsh, since the Ego is indivisible and hence indestructible. The thinking thing which is the essential Daphne no longer thinks as a philosopher but only as an infant. This is rather like the religious view from which Descartes took his lead. Christians would say that the soul remains the same while the mind and body have deteriorated; hence the same person exists. The difficulty of course is that there is no way to tell whether the same Ego or soul persists in a person, since all outward show is irrelevant to that determination.

Spinoza: The unity of all persons in God

Not all rationalists took this Cartesian approach to persons. Spinoza believed that God was the whole universe and that a person is just a mode of God's being. He thought he could establish this by the use of reason and a higher means to knowledge called "intuition."[16] Although persons have both minds and bodies, both are just attributes of a single substance, namely, God. There is, then, no interaction problem. There is, however, no free will either. Speaking against Descartes and others, Spinoza reminds us that we are part of the natural order and, as such, subject to its laws:

> Most writers on the emotions and on human conduct seem to be treating rather of matters outside nature than of natural phenomena following nature's general laws. They appear to conceive man to be situated in nature as a kingdom within a kingdom.[17]

Spinoza, like Aristotle, sees the universe as unified. Every human action and every event whatsoever is determined, and there is no purpose or final cause, in Aristotle's sense, for individual persons, the human species, or the universe. God just is. A person can be thought of as merely a way in which God contemplates Itself, not as a separate free agent.[18] Spinoza, it seems, moves us away from individualism to the oriental idea of absorption of the individual in the greater whole.

Since Descartes and not Spinoza holds sway in the popular conceptions of a person, few of us find what Spinoza has to say immediately plausible. It is a view which opposes the individualism and belief in freedom that is a part of our main Western cultural doctrines. Spinoza's belief in the necessity of all our actions leads, as it did with the Stoics, to resignation and acquiescence (253). The predominant Western concepts of a person are of beings who control, to some extent, their own actions and the events in the world around them, beings who ought to strive to get it right rather than simply accepting whatever happens.

Application to Daphne's Case

Spinoza gets by a very different route to Hobbes' estimation of Daphne's importance. She is to be valued as everyone else. After all, Daphne is just one more way in which God contemplates God, like the rest of us. There is no harm in saying that Daphne has survived the immense changes wrought by dementia. An event of Self-contemplation has changed in character. Since all is God, the importance of individuals in themselves is diminished as it was for Hobbes through their absorption into the state.

Locke's neutral ground

Locke may be the most important philosopher in history with respect to determining current Western concepts of a person within philosophy. So many philosophers are now either furthering his way of thinking of persons or objecting to that way of thinking.[19] One who currently wants to improve on Locke's account is Derek Parfit[20] at Oxford, whose views we will discuss later. The opposition from Thomas Nagel,[21] for example, revivifies some elements of the Cartesian understanding of the subject of experiences.

While Locke is an empiricist elaborating the tradition ushered in by Hobbes, he attempts to find some neutral ground between Hobbes' materialism and Descartes' dualism. Locke is very much concerned about what changes a person can undergo while remaining the same person. His reason was the religious one we have discussed before, the resurrection of the dead.[22] One wants, of course, to have the person being rewarded or punished on Judgment Day to be the same one who did the deeds being judged. He asserts that neither the same material substance nor the same non-material substance preserves the sameness of the person. For example, neither having the same soul or Cartesian Ego on the one hand nor having the same body on the other hand will preserve the sameness of the person.[23] It is, rather, sameness of consciousness that makes sameness of persons.

Locke's reason for this view about identity of persons is his understanding of a person as a self. "Self is that conscious thinking thing (whatever substance made up of, whether spiritual or material, simple or compounded, it matters not) which is sensible or conscious of pleasure and pain, capable of happiness or misery, and so is concerned for *itself* as far as that consciousness extends" (II. xxvii.17). It is consciousness which is crucial to Locke, and apparently consciousness might be had by a Cartesian Ego or by a mere living body. Locke also says,

> to find wherein *personal identity* consists, we must consider what person stands for; which, I think, is a thinking intelligent being that has reason and reflection and can consider itself as itself, the same thinking thing in different times and places; which it does only by that consciousness which is inseparable from thinking and, as it seems to me, essential to it: it being impossible for anyone to perceive without perceiving that he does perceive (II. xxvii.9).

The person, self, or thinking thing is like an eye with a mirror which always sees itself as well as any object seen. This idea of the person as self-conscious consciousness pushes the problem of persons one step back. Now we must ask what consciousness is and why one can only have consciousness along with self-consciousness.

Now we have seen that persons had been explicitly a subject of philosophical conversation since the Stoics used the Greek term *prosopon* to mean "person" in the sense of "role." The term "consciousness," however, comes on the scene about the same time as Locke, if Wilkes is correct.[24] Locke's view apparently marks an important departure where concepts of a person are concerned. To understand Locke's concept of consciousness we must, unfortunately, also look into the mysterious concept of substance. We need to distinguish continuity of consciousness from continuity of a thinking substance, since Locke says persons are not thinking substances even though they are thinking things.[25]

For Locke, a substance whether it is material, mental, or something else, is the thing which has qualities but is not itself a quality. The things we can know through our five senses are qualities. For example that a thing is round, red, and made of wax can be known through the senses; therefore, roundness, redness, and being wax are qualities. What has these qualities is a substance, the thing that lies beneath the qualities. That is almost all we know about substances, that they have qualities.[26] Perry, however, reads a little more than this into Locke: "The concept of substance is of the ultimate things in a causal sense: those things whose properties and relationships explain (or would explain, if known) the properties and relationships of the larger composite entities we deal with as human beings."[27] Substances may be material or immaterial. Persons are composed of bodies which seem to be based on material substances, and minds, which may be based on immaterial substances, but Locke is not committed to their immateriality. Importantly, the substance which thinks, possibly an immaterial substance, is not identified with the person as it was for Descartes. "The sense in which immaterial substances are said to think is analogous to the sense in which our hands can be said to grasp things"(21-22). Now, if it is being grasped which is important, not which hand is doing the grasping, then one hand will do as well as another. Being conscious is what is important for persons, by Locke's lights, and it is unimportant which things, body, mind, or combination of these, support the consciousness. The person is the thinking thing in the sense of the continuing consciousness, no matter which substance is used to continue that consciousness.

Consciousness is, if anything, even more mysterious than substance as explained by Locke. Consciousness includes memory and knowledge of past events and current happenings as well as anticipation of the future. It is the source, according to Locke, not only of our identity but of our concern for ourselves.[28]

Consider, first, a common understanding of consciousness today: awareness of what is going on in oneself, particularly in one's mind. If I am unconscious, then my return to consciousness is a return to knowing what is happening to me now, or at least how I perceive what is happening, and knowing what I am thinking. It is as well a return to the knowledge of what I have done and am likely to do—in short, a knowledge of who I am. As Noonan[29] reads Locke, in addition to this weak kind of consciousness as a kind of knowing one's own current states, there is a stronger type of consciousness frequently presupposed by Locke, namely that of knowing together with someone:

> To be conscious of one's acts is to share, *qua* witness, knowledge of their occurrence with oneself, *qua* agent. And having been witness in this way to one's own acts one can retain the knowledge of them thus gained. It is such shared knowledge had by a present self of a past self's actions which Locke thinks of as constituting personal identity. (53)

Both the weak and the strong sense of "consciousness" as used by Locke are senses in which we are not always conscious even during our waking hours. A severely demented human being may never be conscious in these senses, and most of us are not so during our unreflective waking moments. Perhaps the correct notion of such consciousness as we have most of the day is a dispositional one. If I were to reflect, during my waking hours, I would know who I am and thus be conscious in Locke's strong sense.

"Consciousness" is, moreover, closely related to "conscience." The Oxford English Dictionary tells us that "consciousness," in the sense of internal knowledge or conviction, is especially of one's own innocence, guilt, or deficiencies. Locke is, of course, using the term with this connotation of self-accusation since he is motivated by concerns about the resurrection of the dead and Judgment Day. He is thinking of the person who is conscious of former actions as punishable for those actions. Our current use of "consciousness" often drops this connotation of blame, but we carry along as a primary concept of a person the one Locke fashioned using consciousness. That is why it is often said that a person must have the capacity for self-awareness. This rules out infants, the senile, and many other human beings from the category of persons.

Because Locke is fixated on the Judgment Day when he speaks of persons and their continuation through time and change, he introduces some features into his theory which have been widely criticized. The main implausibility is that the theory claims that we have only done what we are conscious of having done.[30] If I go through a period of amnesia during which I remember nothing of my past life, I am, on Locke's view, not the same person. Some might agree with this, but Locke actually thinks that we cannot rightly be punished for anything which we do not remember. If I should commit some heinous crime when drunk and not recall it at all, then I have not done it and cannot rightly be punished, according to Locke. He admits, of course, that people will be punished for things they do not remember in our merely human justice system, "But in the Great Day, wherein the secrets of all hearts shall be laid open,...no one shall be made to answer for what he knows nothing of" (II. xxvii.22).

This is morally obtuse whatever we want to say about my being the same person drunk as sober. Either we should say I am the same person, and Locke's criterion of continuous consciousness is not the correct analysis of a person, or we can agree with Locke but point out that I chose to temporarily lose myself in drink. This choice makes me culpable for any evils which result from my "absence." Most of us think that drunk and sober I am the same person, but you can well imagine someone saying that I am a different person when drunk, meaning that my personality changes radically.

Putting together Locke's concepts of substance and consciousness, it appears that Locke thinks of a person as a complex thing formed out of more basic substances. As my body develops, the changes happen to an underlying substance which persists. My consciousness too, may be made up of a series of changes to a thinking substance whether material or immaterial. Thus the person or self is a continuing consciousness making use of substances to live and think. The man that I am came into being at conception, and, by all report, has continued uninterrupted to this day. The person who I am, however, goes out of existence when I sleep. It flickered into being about the age of two. That is when the earliest events of my life of which I am conscious took place.

Locke is not too concerned about this patchy picture of a person that his theory gives. He is quite happy to have gaps in persons because of sleep or drunkenness. The religious person accepting Locke's theory could still find a way to provide for punishment of a person's drunken rage. On Judgment Day, perhaps, our memories will be improved. Hell or heaven, I suppose, might well be perfect memory. Which of these two memory gives us would depend on how we had lived, but Locke does not engage in such speculation. We should not try to force Locke into a more sensible moral view about punishment than he wished to hold. We should be careful, moreover, in the contemporary secular uses we make of the Lockean concept of a person. We must make do with our memories as they are in real life, and we cannot appeal to divine goodness to get us out of difficulties with our concepts. Even those who agree on the existence of a personal deity disagree on what His, Her, or Its goodness comes to. The extensive use of Locke's concepts today does not always make sense, given the wider audience and the loss of the background assumptions concerning resurrection and final judgment.

God in His goodness, Locke tells us (II. xxvii.13) would not allow us to have memories of things we did not actually do and, hence, to receive undeserved punishment or reward. Outside of the religious picture, however, we must concern ourselves with this continuity-of-consciousness criterion for persons because it is not at all evident that we very accurately remember the things we have done or have done the things we seem to remember. Is there something else in consciousness, as conceived by Locke, besides memory that may provide a more adequate picture of persons? One of Locke's early critics, Reid, claims that by "consciousness" Locke must just mean "memory."[31] Later critics have by and large accepted that account of Locke, but while memory is a crucial part of consciousness, consciousness is broader. I may be conscious of a feeling of guilt when I awake from a drunken rampage even if I cannot remember what I have done. Locke's insistence on our knowledge of past actions, however, bars him from access to this broader concept of consciousness and leaves him open to Reid's interpretation that consciousness in this context is memory. Locke's account is therefore open to objections which follow from that interpretation.

Even before we get into the traditional objections about the nature of the narrower concept of memory, the problem of telling what a person is and telling when one has the same person by appeal to consciousness is this: we are not entirely clear what consciousness is nor when we have the same consciousness. This is especially difficult since consciousness may be interrupted by sleep, for instance. Why can it not, then, be interrupted by bodily death? Would it not be strange to say that Socrates, Pilate, and Caesar Borgia were all the same person? As long as they each were conscious of the actions of the one before, then this is what we would say by Locke's lights. Locke could reply, it seems, that while this is logically possible, God in His goodness would not let this happen.

Yet Locke cannot make this reply, given the rules he plays by. He criticizes, for instance, those who would reject his idea that the identity of a human being, as opposed to a person, is dependent on "one fitly organized body, continued under one organization of life."[32] Those who reject this criterion, Locke tells us, will not be able to say that there is one person through all life's developments unless they also admit that Seth, Israel, Socrates, Pilate, St. Austin, and Caesar Borgia could be one man. (II. xxvii.6). He objects that this is a strange way of speaking. I submit that the same argument which disallows such odd possibilities for men, that is humans, also inveighs against Locke's use of "person."

Even if one is willing to accept the strangeness of Locke's concept of a person and to say that it is nonetheless one useful concept of a person, there may be problems which undermine it entirely. What kind of a thing is consciousness? Not a substance, apparently. It seems then that consciousness is a property of humans; hence, being a person is a property of a substance or substances. Locke handles identity conditions in terms of special properties called "modes." More precisely, a mode is an aspect, that is, a fully instantiated property, a particular not a universal. But it is not at all clear how we identify modes; hence, it is not clear what the identity criteria are for persons. Locke's solution is, officially, through spatio-temporal continuity and, unofficially and illegitimately, through reference to the particulars that have the modes.[33] Neither the official nor the unofficial account could explain how it is that Socrates and Caesar Borgia could be the same person, given one consciousness. Perhaps Locke's problem of identifying modes (and, hence, persons) over time could be solved in terms of higher-order essential properties. We might assert that two modes are identical if they share all their essential higher-order properties in common, where "essential" would be defined so as to exclude space-time location and "higher order" would exclude the modes themselves. Pursuing such an account does not, however, look promising. If, on this account, two simultaneously existing human beings have exactly the same memories, are they not the same person? The fact that the theory cannot rule this out except by appeal to God's goodness is, according to the rules Locke plays by when objecting to his opponents, ground enough to reject the theory of persons Locke presents.[34] In some cases, I think, we can refuse to play by those rules which require us to stick to common usage of the term "person," and we can find a use for Locke's concept of a person, sufficiently modified to survive in the more secular contemporary debate.

Application to Daphne's Case

We have to be careful to note what human beings Locke excludes from being persons. Of Daphne, Locke would say she is the same human being but not the same person as we knew prior to the dementia. Indeed, it seems that, on his account, she would not be a person at all now, assuming that she has no self-knowledge nor sufficient memory to see herself as existing through time. Certainly I would go so far with Locke as to say that Daphne does not bear responsibility for the things she has done while in a demented state. To deny, however, the status of a person to all who lose their memory and the ability to know themselves leaves us in a bit of a quandary about how to treat such human beings. We shall have to look to later developments of the concept of a person for enlightenment.

What I like about the early moderns

Even though Locke's concept should not satisfy Locke, it has, historically, been extremely influential in the separation of the concepts of human being and person. Locke's is also one of the first theories of persons to rest the whole weight of morality on the concept of a person, to the applause of some and the chagrin of others. Probably we should settle on a view between the extremes, saying that there are rights of persons which include the rights of human beings, while the rights of human beings do not include the rights of persons.

Locke's influence extends, however, much further than the moral sphere. Even Locke's style of argument, using thought experiments and emphasizing common usage, set the tone for British and North American philosophical debate on this topic up to the present day. Locke must, therefore, be treated as a watershed. It will be difficult to retain whatever insights we may glean from prior philosophers simply because their contributions are not in the style of Locke and do not share his emphasis. We must be watchful lest these insights are locked out.

The importance of memory may not be as great as Locke supposed, but we must take it seriously. It is also a good idea to focus on abilities like consciousness independently of their causes or the substance underlying them. We need not settle the debate between the materialists and the dualists to talk sensibly about people.

Responsibility, which was much on Locke's mind, seems to be a key concept in our understanding of persons and the distinction of persons as a group within that of human beings.

I also approve of the general approach which rules out of court the appeal to God to get us out of trouble when puzzles arise regarding identity or the nature of persons. Spinoza's approach is, from my perspective, too otherworldly. Cartesian Egos are a bit too much like souls for me. Much of what Descartes has to say about people as thinking things may be reworked without the baggage of religious metaphysics. In particular, we should focus on the subject of the experiences, not just the experiences themselves. This strains against Locke's neutral position between materialism and dualism, but can be brought inside its fold. From Hobbes we should retain the general idea of the importance of the body. Putting all this together will be an interesting cobbler's job.

SIX
More Moderns

Berkeley: The outer limits of empiricism

If one takes seriously the idea that all of our knowledge is the result of sensations of sight, hearing, taste, touch, and smell, then one can, paradoxically but consistently, deny the existence of the human body or any material thing. A smell or a vision or a feel of something is a mental event. As long as one has the right mental events in the right order, then it will be as if there is an entire material world causing such mental events in material bodies. But matter is an unnecessary hypothesis. There might just be a natural world of minds and ideas, including sensations. Natural laws, like that of gravity, would really be shorthand predictions about what perceptions would follow what perceptions. For example, if I perceive as if I drop a small object near the surface of the earth, even though there are no such things as material objects, then I will perceive as if that apparent object falls. The whole of the material world would be a kind of virtual reality. This world of ideas could, then, have a regularity just like the one which our laws of physics describe. This, in fact, was the view adopted by the eighteenth-century philosopher Bishop Berkeley.[1] Berkeley's idealism has a corollary relevant to our topic. The idea of a person as an embodied mind or soul is incorrect. Persons are just minds or souls. Minds perceive as if they had bodies.

This idealist view of Berkeley's sounds strange to a materialist audience, but, in a country like India where it is widely believed that the material world is an illusion, Berkeley's philosophy would be almost a commonplace. In some ways, it should not make any difference whether we think we are all matter or all mind, so long as we are made of only one kind of thing. In practice, however, idealists like Berkeley tend to be more interested in the spiritual side of persons, and materialists tend to discount spirit. Reducing spirit to a material phenomenon seems in practice to deprive it of some of its grandeur and moral force though it need not be so in theory.

Materialists, on the other hand, tend to be less able than Berkeley was to deny the importance of bodily suffering. While these are tendencies rather than generalizations which hold for all idealists and materialists, the metaphysical views about what people are do tend to have a profound effect on moral views about the treatment of persons. It is interesting, in any case, that the empiricism and materialism which are so influential in our current con-

---

Notes to Chapter Six are on pp. 318-19.

cepts of a person can be replaced without loss by empiricism plus idealism. In a society in which metaphysical materialism is accompanied by the crass, commercial variety of materialism, perhaps a switch to Berkeley's strange view that we are minds without bodies is not so crazy.

Leibniz against the drunks

On the continent, a theory in some ways similar to Locke's was developed by Leibniz and then revised in the light of Locke's contribution. Leibniz' work has been less influential than Locke's because the metaphysical system in which it is housed is much less tied to common sense than Locke's own metaphysics. Like Descartes, Leibniz was a rationalist, and rationalism has taken a beating at the hands of empiricism in British and North American philosophy since Locke. Leibniz was, in any case, a philosopher and mathematician of genius whose ideas on identity in general have had a considerable impact on later thought. Noonan points out, moreover, that Leibniz' work on our topic anticipated some arguments of great importance in contemporary philosophy.[2]

Leibniz originally put out a theory of persons in his *Discourse On Metaphysics* prior to reading Locke. The two main similarities of Leibniz' theory to Locke's theory are in its being influenced by religious belief in a way uncommon today and in the treatment of memory and knowledge of the past self as necessary for continuation of the person (60). With God in the background, Leibniz' theory has to be adapted with care to the contemporary secular debate, but—in spite of Locke's reputation for a philosophy tied to common sense and Leibniz' reputation for weaving a metaphysical tapestry that only a philosopher could believe—Leibniz' views on persons run afoul of fewer of the dictates of common sense than do Locke's.

Because Locke thinks that only the same consciousness is needed to keep the same person, one could change bodies and still be the same person. This is not so for Leibniz. Not only is the same consciousness, or at least memory, needed but the same substance is also necessary to retain the person, and a substance cannot possibly be emptied of one person to later house another as Locke would think possible, albeit unlikely. Thus Leibniz could freely maintain against Locke, what most of us would accept, that a person does not become another person when drunk just because later that person does not remember the period of drunkenness. Even more remarkable is Locke's claim that the sober person should not be punished for what the drunk—who is another person according to Locke—has done. Leibniz' way out of this, if he has one in his earlier work on persons, would be to appeal to divine intervention. God does not let a single person go out of existence (59-60). There are no persons popping into and out of bodies. This preserves both our immortality and our moral responsibility. It does not work, of course, without the background religious doctrine. That is what contemporary theories will have to replace outside of theology. Leibniz gives us some clues about how to do this with his later work.

In spite of the antiquated language and the strength of the religious background, parts of Leibniz' writings have a remarkably contemporary ring. This is particularly true in the *New Essays Concerning Understanding* which he wrote in response to Locke.[3] Here Leibniz responds with revisions to the theory aimed at preventing such odd consequences as the innocence of the sober person for the actions of the blind-drunk. What he says is in fact an appeal to an incipient theory of the unconscious. Since Freud we take it as a commonplace that there is much to the person beneath the tip of the iceberg, consciousness. According to Ralph Walker "Leibniz was the first to introduce the idea of the *unconscious*."[4] Instead of requiring actual memories of our past life, Leibniz switches to requiring only a psychological continuity of the person based partly on perceptions of the past of which we may be insensible.[5] "He points out that one can often recall having perceived something—some detail of a familiar scene, perhaps—although one did not notice it at the time: clearly one must have perceived it without being aware of doing so."[6] Further in aid of this drive to take the non-conscious part of the person seriously, note that even an amnesiac does not lose all memory. Elements of the personality, abilities, and other features may remain. These are outside of what Locke would call "consciousness." These phenomena are some evidence that Leibniz is right to deny that one can be stripped of all perception of one's past existence. Everything that happens to us leaves some impression on us though we might not be aware of it. As Noonan puts it, "It is this continuity and interconnection of perceptions which makes someone really the same individual."[7] Our unconscious "memory" of our lives suffices to make us the same persons we were during periods of our lives which we have forgotten.

It may be that this subtle kind of continuity through the subconscious is available to people even in severe dementia. Without the surface of conscious self-awareness, one may be the same person underneath in the poorly understood areas of the subconscious or non-conscious. These areas of the person's mind, as well as the conscious, may be threatened by brain damage, of course, but it is at least not necessarily true that the loss of conscious self-awareness is the loss of what underlies it as well. It seems to me, in any case, that common sense would agree with Leibniz in saying that people are, though greatly reduced in ability, still the same persons due to other sorts of continuity, the continuity of the body and the non-conscious mind.

Now, while Leibniz seems to me more in line with contemporary common sense than is Locke, perhaps he carries his concept of person a bit too far in the other direction. Locke gives the sober man no responsibility for the drunk's actions and Leibniz gives him full responsibility. While, in my neck of the woods, we are becoming less tolerant of drunkenness, full responsibility still seems too much to most of my contemporaries. Often, today, we might consider drunkenness as a legal and a moral mitigation—an argument for lessening responsibility and punishment—though not an excuse. If one kills while drunk, one is guilty of getting drunk and creating the circumstances for the tragedy. This is not, perhaps, as great a guilt as one bears for killing while sober in full knowledge of what one is doing, although Mothers Against Drunk Drivers and Leibniz may not see it this way. The controversial idea is that drunkenness is a mitigating but not excusing factor where punishment is concerned. The culprit did not have the appropriate mental attitude to be said to have done the act completely intentionally. There is a problem that one may intend things while drunk that one would never intend while sober, but we only take sober intentions as the prerequisite for full culpability. It is as if we think that a person has temporarily, though willfully, suspended her good character by deliberately becoming drunk. One can be punished for the de-liberate suspension, but one cannot be punished fully for the acts while the suspension is in effect.

Consider now another kind of case, the case of a mental patient who has a genuine fugue state (dissociation of the personality), supposing there are any such states. Such a person temporarily acquires a different personality and memories. The temporary personality and the normal personality do not influence one another. During the period away from the normal personality and memories the patient has committed murder. Should we punish the per-son who, cured of the mental illness, remembers nothing of the murder? In a recent case a woman was exonerated in court of murdering her mother be-cause she was temporarily in such a state as a result of taking prescription sleeping pills. She took them as prescribed. Leibniz would have counted her guilty. The testimony of others that she did such a thing is enough to maintain what Leibniz called her "moral identity," which entails personal identity.[8]

Whether in fact Leibniz is going too far in such cases depends, in part, on how much we think we are responsible for programming ourselves with our tendencies to act in certain ways when our minds are absent. If such chosen tendencies really are operative when our minds are absent, or our memories are not recording what we do, then perhaps our actions at such times flow freely from choices of which we were conscious. There are documented cases of automatic behaviour such as a doctor taking detailed notes in a thorough examination of a patient but remembering nothing afterwards.[9] If a criminal were to automatically commit a crime and remember nothing after the com-mission, then, even if we believed that the memory lapse were genuine, we might wish to place some blame. We might, in similar fashion, wish to praise the doctor for being so practiced in good routines as to care adequately for the patient even though normal memory processes were suspended. On the other hand, if the doctor made an error under these conditions, we might be less ready to blame the doctor. Our intuitions are over-taxed in such cases because our concept of a person is fuzzy. Leibniz, at least, knows what he would say about these. Part of his confidence in his concepts, however, is based on his views about what a benevolent God would permit to happen. Those who do not believe in such a God or in the same workings of His benevolence will want to tidy up the concept of a person to deal with fugue states and epileptic automatism.

Wilkes suggests that we simply ought to deny the extreme importance of consciousness, our inheritance from Locke. Fugue states and other dramatic aberrations in our lives are really no more a threat to our continuity than sleep, on her view.

> Longer-lasting fugues interrupt the unity and continuity of consciousness more dramatically and drastically; but, if they do not seem to disrupt our intuition that we have, unproblematically, one and the same person here, that must be because the unity or continuity of consciousness, or perhaps even consciousness itself, are not quite as important as one might at first think. (106)

The problem, of course, is to say what really is important for continuity, that is survival, of persons. Leibniz has given us a start.

Leibniz also anticipates an important contemporary criticism of Locke's account given by Williams and known as the Reduplication Argument. Consciousness is the only thing which distinguishes one person from another, on Locke's view. Leibniz points out that, however unlikely it may be, there is no logical impossibility, according to Locke, in there being a human being whose consciousness is indistinguishable from that of another concurrently existing human being. There is then nothing to prevent us from saying that two human beings are one person in such a case. Since it is absurd to think that two human beings are one person, the theory which says this could be so must itself be absurd.

In the face of this objection, the Lockean is faced with biting the rather hard bullet of admitting that two human beings could be one person or adding something to the theory to prevent this consequence. Remarkably, until Williams came up with another version of Leibniz' objection in 1956, this untoward consequence of Locke's theory went unnoticed.[10] This rather belated attention to Leibniz' objection demonstrates the need to pay attention to the history of philosophy.

A Lockean might reply that this thought experiment about two people with the same consciousness—or each with a consciousness indiscernible from the others—is not to the point after all. It will not happen in the real world. This is a hard tack for the Lockean to take. Locke himself is fond of thought experiments as ways of testing the limits of our concepts. The Lockean could do this, however, if she is willing to come up with a whole new slate of arguments for Locke's position, arguments which do not make essential use of such thought experiments. It is much simpler to accept Leibniz' recommendations in some modified form. Few would accept his particular construal of continuing substance, but some acceptance of the body, or at least the brain, as crucial to the person is motivated by Leibniz' objections. The cure, however, is not simple, as we will see when we look at contemporary Lockeans like Derek Parfit later on.

Before we bid adieu to Leibniz, for the time being, we should look at his contribution to the concept of identity, since the concept of a person is often understood, especially since Locke, in terms of personal identity. The reason for the close association between the topics of the nature of persons and personal identity is this: one knows the nature of a kind of thing if and only if one knows how to distinguish and identify particular things of that kind. I will know what persons are, for instance, if and only if I know, in principle, how to tell persons apart and to tell when I am met with the same person twice. Many philosophers believe that there is something essential to persons, something without which a being would not be a person. For Locke, for instance, consciousness was this essence; so person A and person B would turn out to be one and the same by virtue of having the same consciousness. Leibniz thought this was necessary but not sufficient for identity of persons. He has, moreover, a general answer to the question of whether A and B, be they persons or whatever, are identical.

A is identical to B, Leibniz asserts, if and only if A and B have all their properties in common. This principle, called "Leibniz' Law" is not at all a simple principle, depending as it does on what we mean by "property." On most meanings of "property," however, half of the principle is uncontroversial: if A is identical to B, then A has a property if and only if B has that property. If Andrew is identical to Bob, for example, then Andrew is intelligent if and only if Bob is intelligent. But look at the other half: if A and B have all their properties in common, then A is identical to B. This principle is called "the identity of indiscernibles." Is it necessarily true? Is it possible for A to be totally indiscernible from B without their being identical? Philosophers have been arguing about that for some time, ever since Leibniz said it, in fact. It turns out that there are many different things that one could mean by this principle, some of which are necessarily true without much doubt. The interesting versions, however, are still being debated.[11]

With respect to Leibniz' objection to Locke, the problem boils down to roughly this. Suppose that A is a consciousness and B is a consciousness. Suppose further that there is no property which A has that B lacks, or vice versa. According to the identity of indiscernibles, A and B are the same consciousness. If, however, A has the property of being associated with the body of Andrew and B has the property of being associated with the body of Bob, then we can distinguish A from B, given that we can distinguish their bodies. But this is not the kind of distinction between one consciousness and another that Locke wants to use. Bodies are supposed to be non-essential to persons. We ought not refer to anything but some feature within the consciousness itself, whatever that means, to distinguish that consciousness. Consciousness itself, moreover, is all there is to persons. If, however, it is possible that Andrew and Bob could have indiscernible consciousnesses, then we have to admit that it is possible that they are one and the same person with two different bodies. This seems to Leibniz to be absurd.

Whether this objection really succeeds depends, however, on some very complex issues. Not only does one have to clarify the real meaning of "property" in this context, but one has to complicate the appropriate principles, like the identity of indiscernibles, so as to take into account changes in an object across time which are not to be understood in the same way as differences between two objects at a given time. Such complexities will have to await discussion of the contemporary debate about persons.

Butler and Reid reacting

If we leave Leibniz and cross both the channel separating Europe from Britain and the gulf between the rationalists and the empiricists we find that there were other and more famous objections to Locke's criterion of personal identity coming from within the ranks of British philosophers. Butler and Reid make the peculiarly Cartesian claim that persons are indivisible, unchanging things. They are thinking of identity in terms of Leibniz' Law or something like it. Any change of properties over time would constitute difference. When we talk about the same tree, for example, at an earlier time and a later time, we really mean, according to Butler, two very similar trees.[12] A person, however, is unchanging and indivisible; so she is the same at earlier and later times. Butler and Reid are concerned to found moral claims on the concept of person; so they return to something like the immortal, unchanging soul of the religious tradition and reject the developing, changing consciousness that Locke has used as the essence of the person.

Their views about identity are confused. In trying to say that any change makes for a difference of the earlier from the later thing, they conflate identity across time with identity at a time. Even if we accept the idea that a thing must be unchanging to be self-identical over time, persons as conceived by Butler and Reid would not fill the bill. After all, persons have bodies, and those bodies change. We could then say that the earlier person has the property of having a young body which the later person lacks; so the two persons must be distinct. If Butler and Reid object that only properties of the persons themselves, not properties which relate them to other things are relevant, then they are appealing to what have been called "purely qualitative properties" as distinct from "relational properties." In fact, however, properties which seem to be purely qualitative all turn out to be relational. Being red, for example, may mean appearing red to an observer within a certain frame of reference, or it may mean reflecting light at so many Angstrom units of wavelength. There is no precise definition of "purely qualitative property" that gets around the problem.[13]

Reid has, however, an objection which at least requires fans of Locke's memory criterion of identity to revise the criterion. Perry puts the criterion this way: "Person-stages belong to the same person, if and only if the later could contain an experience which is a memory of a reflective awareness of an experience contained in the earlier."[14] Roughly, if I remember something someone experienced from the inside as that person would have experienced it, then I am that person. Memory is taken to be veridical in this context. Merely seeming to remember guarantees nothing. To have a genuine memory, I must be the person who witnessed the event remembered.

Reid imagines[15] a case in which this criterion leads to paradox. He imagines a boy who is flogged and who later becomes an officer who performs a brave deed. The officer eventually becomes a general. The officer remembers the flogging; so he and the boy are one. The general remembers the brave deed; so he and the officer are one. The general, however, fails to remember the flogging; so he and the boy are two. This is, of course, absurd. If both the boy and the general are identical to the officer, then they must be identical to one another. Much of the contemporary work on personal identity is an attempt to improve upon Locke's criterion to make it immune to such objections.

Butler has, moreover, another objection of note, namely that Locke's account is circular. A problem arises when we consider how we identify memories, or consciousness. Butler considers it self-evident that consciousness of personal identity presupposes, and therefore cannot constitute, personal identity (68). One way to interpret what he is saying is this: to say that consciousness A is identical to consciousness B is to say that they are the consciousness of the same person. We can hardly, therefore, define without circularity "same person" in terms of "same consciousness," since "same consciousness" has already been defined in terms of "same person." Noonan says that Locke can respond to this charge of circularity since he distinguishes between persons and thinking substances. Roughly, Noonan would say that "consciousness A is identical to consciousness B" means that they are the consciousness of the same thinking substance. "Same consciousness" is, therefore, not defined in terms of "same person" after all (75-76).

Butler and Reid, however, attack the distinction between thinking substance and person. On Locke's view the person is an evolving changing sort of thing. The consciousness develops over time as it gains new perceptions and has new thoughts; so the person as a thinking thing changes. Underlying this change is the mysterious, unchanging thinking substance in which properties, like the property of being conscious, inhere. This substance is what some philosophers have called a bare particular. All we know about the bare particular is that it is whatever has the properties. Butler says that if a person is, as Locke says, a thinking intelligent being, then that person just is a substance, and Reid says about the same (71). This puts Locke in hot water. He wanted to get away from worrying about mysterious things like substances and to be neutral with respect to whether material or non-material substance underlies consciousness. Only consciousness itself was to be essential to persons.

There are a number of ways for Lockeans to respond. Noonan suggests Locke might just bite the bullet and say that thinking things are not thinking substances. This apparently raises the odd question whether, as Chisholm puts it, "If I want my dinner, does it follow that two of us want my dinner?" Do the thinking thing and the thinking substance both want my dinner? According to Noonan (76), to remain consistent Locke must say that the thinking substance wants me, the thinking thing, to have my dinner and must think that strange thought by thinking, "I want my dinner." Once again, Locke seems to be a long way from common sense. He can buy logical consistency only by multiplying the entities which make up a person. Each of us begins to look like a crowd. Perry, however, has suggested (as we saw earlier in the section on Locke) that I think through the thinking substance as I grasp things with my hand. I do not have to say that both my hand and I pick up my fork to eat my dinner. Similarly, I do not have to say that two of us want my dinner. My wanting is done with my thinking substance as my grasping is done with my hand.

This still looks distant from common sense, but not so distant. Common sense is, in any case, not always the most sensible view, but if we accept the mysterious underlying substance and the rest of Locke's concept of a person, then we do so only because we are driven to this mystery-laden doctrine. The empiricists, after all, wanted to demystify our concepts, which they saw being routed into fantasy by the rationalists like Descartes and Leibniz. As their views are pushed to the limit, we see the empiricist tradition garnering more mysteries. Hume's famous disappearing self is not the last but is the next of these to be considered.

Hume and our disappearance

Hume is almost out of place among the moderns. He is too contemporary in his motivation for his theory and in his kind of theory of persons. As you have noticed, no doubt, God is still everywhere in the modern period, as He was in the mediaeval period. Locke and Leibniz, for instance, are motivated by religious concerns. Hume not only drops the concern to explain such doctrines as that of the Judgment Day, he plays by a tough new rule: when one's theory implies the possibility of some absurdity, one may not call upon God to rescue the theory. One cannot, for instance, say that God's goodness would prevent duplication of people or getting the memory of an action; hence, the responsibility for that action, associated with the wrong consciousness. What is new, then, about Hume is that he tries to give arguments that will appeal to intellect only, not even indirectly to faith. He was not a big hit with the clergy.

Hume, like Locke, is an empiricist. He observes that we have a concept of a person, and spends his efforts trying to explain how we could come to have this fiction via ideas produced ultimately from sensory input. That's right; he does not think there are persons in Locke's sense. There is just a powerful fiction that persons exist. The metaphysical problems about persons and personal identity which we have been investigating reduce to psychological problems about how we could possibly be so deceived as to think that persons exist and endure through time. It is hard to beat Hume for sheer iconoclasm, but we contemporary philosophers have been doing our best. The modern period has a lot of kick left in it following Hume, but ultimately his secular, ferocious style of thinking wins out. Philosophers demand that our concepts defend themselves now, and concepts are given no quarter. If a sanctified concept like that of a person appears to be contradictory, it gets the boot.

At the outset of his discussion of personal identity[16] Hume sets up the concept he is about to attack:

> There are some philosophers, who imagine we are every moment intimately conscious of what we call our SELF; that we feel its existence and its continuance in existence; and are certain, beyond the evidence of a demonstration, both of its perfect identity and simplicity.

Hume says that those of us who think we are aware of our selves are imagining things. There is no self or person continuing through time. Once people believed in the existence of unicorns, fabled horses with a single horn growing from the middle of the forehead. One could explain such a belief in unicorns by pointing, perhaps, to the remains of narwhals which might have been the source of the idea of the unicorn. Hume takes his task to be finding some cause of our believing in another fiction, that of the self.

No doubt you are about to say, "Hold on a minute Hume! Although I do not expect to ever see a unicorn, I am intimately acquainted with a self, mine." "For my part," Hume responds, "when I enter most intimately into what I call *myself*, I always stumble on some particular perception or other....I never can catch *myself* at any time without a perception, and never can observe any thing but the perception." From this Hume concludes that we are "nothing but a bundle or collection of different perceptions, which succeed each other with an inconceivable rapidity, and are in a perpetual flux and movement" (252). Persons or selves are reduced to vortices in the great stream of perceptions.

What Hume has jettisoned is what he would consider metaphysical and religious baggage that merely encumbers our thought. Plato's doctrine of an immortal soul which is carried on through the Christian philosophers is given the old heave-ho. Not since Aristotle had there been such an influential secular philosopher as Hume, and while Aristotle just got rid of immortality, Hume wanted to get completely rid of the soul or substance underlying consciousness. Look inside, and what you see is what you get. "The mind is a kind of theatre, where several perceptions successively make their appearance; pass, re-pass, glide away, and mingle in an infinite variety of postures and situations. There is properly no *simplicity* in it at one time, nor *identity* in different" (253). Once he gets rid of the religious need for an immortal soul or substance which remains through change, Hume finds only a constantly changing river of consciousness, and he takes Heraclitus' dictum literally— one cannot step into the same river twice.

Like Butler and Reid, Hume takes the simplistic concept of identity—which led to the concept of substance in the first place—and objects to the identity through time of anything like Locke's concept of a person. More than this, however, he realizes that the concept of an immortal, simple substance of the sort Butler and Reid would substitute is not possible. Nothing can endure through time without changing some of its properties. As long as a change of properties guarantees a loss of identity, this entails that nothing can endure through time (256). Objects we think of as enduring are really just a series of very similar things. We ourselves are such series (259). We take similarity to be identity just as the ignorant once took a narwhal's tusk to be the horn of a unicorn.

Hume has other things to say about his predecessors, things which are less than complimentary. Memory as a criterion of identity—which is in effect Locke's criterion—comes in for some criticism. Even those who favour Locke's criterion would have to admit that "memory does not so much *produce* as *discover* personal identity, by shewing us the relation of cause and effect among our different perceptions" (262). Since we do not remember our entire lives, memory just helps us to see how we are each a chain of causes and effects, a stream of causally related perceptions. With memory to show us parts of the stream, we extrapolate to fill in the rest and thereby come to our concept of ourselves. What Hume is pointing out here is that our concept of personal identity—he does not really accept it as identity—is of much more than an intellect with a memory. Emotions, imagination, sensations and other events in this stream of perceptions are seen as part of the self with the aid of memory as we fill in the blanks in our causal story. "Twill be incumbent on those, who affirm that memory produces entirely our personal identity, to give a reason why we can thus extend our identity beyond our memory" (262). Since Hume's critique, followers of Locke have, by and large, extended the description of psychological phenomena which they appeal to in producing a concept of a person.

Another feature of Hume's account which has a decidedly contemporary ring to it is his claim that many questions regarding personal identity have no answer or must be settled by semantic fiat rather than philosophical investigation. When we ask whether, in principle, a person can survive such and such changes, we may stretch the concept of a person beyond its limits. Because we have not genuine identity, according to Hume, but degrees of similarity, there are bound to be cases where, because similarity varies by subtle degrees, we enter a grey area in the meaning of "same person." Disputes in such cases are, by Hume's lights, merely verbal. We simply have to make a legislative definition of "same person" to decide how much difference will be tolerated before we give up our fiction of personal identity (272).

Since Hume's time, many philosophers have tried to defeat his skeptical arguments about persons, and many have tried to develop and refine them. This debate is still very vigorous, and it is generally carried on using Hume's methods. Reducing apparent questions of metaphysics to verbal disputes, for example, is a very popular contemporary gambit which Hume anticipated.

Hume did a great deal, as well, to contribute to the current fashion of keeping philosophy and theology independent. But Hume was much ahead of the fashions, and later philosophers returned to the religious fold. They did so, however, as much more knowing sheep than their forebears. The chains of church dogma which had long been loosened were now borne only voluntarily.

As the religious doctrine of the soul loses its grip on our concept of a person, the danger arises that human beings with severe dementia and other kinds of mental incompetence will be treated as unworthy of concern. Taking Hume seriously, however, we can determine the extension of the concept of a person in a conventional fashion. Our conventions can be tailored to match our pre-existing moral concerns. If we want to include the demented in the moral community, then, given the power of the term "person" in our moral discourse, we should arrange our conventions so as to call demented human beings "persons" both before and after a tragic decline into dementia. This does not presuppose that sameness of persons is preserved through such a decline. Suppose your mother, through Alzheimer's disease, becomes severely mentally disabled. She is still, under such tragic circumstances, a person. We might adopt conventions so as to ensure that although she is not the same person who raised you, she is the same human being.

Another way of looking at the situation through Hume's spectacles would show us that one who suffers a decline into dementia has not lost status, metaphysically speaking, as a result of her great loss. We should not concern ourselves with the question of whether she is the same person she once was, since none of us is. Her life took an unexpected course like a river whose bed is upturned by an earthquake. We, most of us, hope for a less dramatic course. In any case, the kind of survival we ask about with Locke hovering in the background does not take place for any of us, if Hume is right. There is no enduring self to survive. In Locke's terms, using the distinction between human beings and persons, there are no persons, just human beings who have, at any given time, a fiction about being persons who have survived from an earlier time. By Hume's standards, you cannot meet the same person twice, not even in the mirror.

Application to Daphne's Case

If, as Berkeley supposes, persons are just minds, their bodies mere illusions, then Daphne is more severely reduced than would appear. Her body is almost all that remains. Leibniz would tell us that, even though her conscious mind is all but gone, there may remain non-conscious features of Daphne's mind which preserve continuity. So strong are such features as preservatives that Daphne would even be considered morally responsible, on this view, for things she did as she was descending into dementia. Her disease, multiple sclerosis, causes personality changes as it attacks the brain. Daphne said and did hurtful things in her downward slide for which I and others did not hold her responsible. After all, her inhibitions were removed by the disease and inhibitions are things we cultivate in keeping up our own characters and personalities. Leibniz seems to go too far.

On the other hand, Leibniz' solutions seem preferable to Butler and Reid's mysterious underlying substance or to Locke's memory criterion of identity. The non-conscious part of ourselves is not to be neglected. Indeed, Hume's disappearing act is premised on there being nothing to us but what is on the surface of the mind. He would say that Daphne is a stream of ideas, sensations, and perceptions which has narrowed from a torrent to a trickle. He solves the problem by destroying the concept of a person, or attempting to do so. Daphne is in no worse state than any of us by Hume's lights.

What I like about these moderns

Leibniz' emphasis on things other than consciousness to preserve continuity of persons is a healthy emphasis. The body and the non-conscious mind must be kept in view. Memory should not be put above all else, given the problems to which Locke is heir. Hume points out the need for a much clearer understanding of what it is we are looking for when we ask about identity. He is also right to point out the conventional nature of the concept of a person, though I think we can take his point without his iconoclasm.

It is time to swim the channel again, if only to escape from hard-nosed British philosophers like Hume. We will see what comfort we can find among the elegant continental philosophers.

SEVEN
Yet More Moderns

The continental emphasis on morality

Rousseau

Rousseau makes a passionate attempt to give philosophy a human face. In the age of the Enlightenment the glorification of the intellect over the heart had furthered the concept of a person as an intellect with whatever else is needed to keep that intellect going. This was sometimes a tendency in the Middle Ages as well, as we have seen with Aquinas. Yet the tendency was moderated by the emphasis on faith in mediaeval times. As faith gave way to reason in the Enlightenment, admiration for the intellect knew no bounds. Rousseau dug in his heels.

Rousseau opposed equally the religious doctrine of original sin and the Enlightenment doctrine of the betterment of persons through intellect. People were, on his view, naturally good. Education and civilization, however, destroyed this natural goodness. There was a native morality common to simple folk, on his view, that belied the theological doctrine of the evil inherent in people and was evidence against the efficacy of education. Education achieved its ill effect by suppressing the individual personality and making us all conform in manners and dress.[1] This makes it difficult to read people's hearts and minds; thus, deception and other vices are made easier.

Rousseau is, then, among those who promote the view of persons as individuals. His thought is important in the long tradition of the West moving away from the Oriental attraction to absorption of the individual into the universe or at least into some larger social group. At the same time, Rousseau is concerned to prevent the egoism that comes from overemphasizing the individual. It is, rather, the preservation of the native morality in us through the furthering of individual character that he seeks to achieve.

What I like about Rousseau

Rousseau champions the individual which, within certain limits, I approve. The idea that people are naturally good is also attractive, though sometimes it seems daft. When, however, I see the wicked world as peopled by a species most motivated by greed and fear, I remind myself that the opportunities for evil are far greater than those of which people take ad-

---

Notes to Chapter Seven are on pp. 319-20.

vantage. That slavery, for example, is widely shunned though not totally abolished, cannot be explained by base motives alone.

Kant

Although Kant admired and was strongly influenced by Rousseau, Kant wished to take morality out of the affective realm and back to that of the intellect. His view of persons as moral beings depends on their being quintessentially rational. Kant, however, like Rousseau, champions the individual. Kant advises us to "Act in such a way that you always treat humanity, whether in your own person or in the person of any other, never simply as a means, but always at the same time as an end." He further clarifies, "Only rational agents or *persons* can be ends in themselves. As they alone can have an unconditioned and absolute value, it is wrong to use them simply as means to an end whose value is only relative."[2] Here we have two of the themes we have noted in earlier developments of the concept of a person: the heavy emphasis on rationality as essential to persons and their being valued above all else. Kant is telling us that we may not use persons to achieve goals; rather, all our goals must be subject to the betterment of people.

Kant sees as the enemy not merely the herding effects of education which Rousseau decried, but utilitarianism. Utilitarianism takes the happiness of the greatest number of people to be the moral guide. Kant thinks that one may not trample on the rights of the individual in order to achieve this mass happiness. The terms in which I have put this may be somewhat anachronistic, but later philosophers who defended utilitarianism found in Kant their major opponent.

The emphasis on metaphysics, the theory of reality, and epistemology, the theory of knowledge, in the British empiricist tradition of Locke, Berkeley, and Hume finds its place in Kant's work as well, but always in balance with ethics, the theory of moral value. As the concept of a person is central to Kantian moral theory, Kant must reject the Humean skepticism about persons. The empiricists who began with a return to common sense ended with the Berkeleyan view that persons are mere disembodied minds or the Humean view that there are no persons.

Kant believes, contrary to Hume, that perceptions must occur in a perceiver. The mere fact that we have knowledge and experience in a unified way necessarily implies that there is a unified self having the experience, but this is no guarantee that there is a single subject of experience over time.[3] Something has to hold memory, imagination, sensation, and the various faculties of the mind together during a given period of consciousness. Persons, however, if they exist over a longer time than just a brief period of self-consciousness, cannot be proven to do so. "For since the only permanent appearance which we encounter in the soul is the representation "I" that accompanies and connects them all, we are unable to prove that this "I," a mere thought, may not be in the same state of flux as the other thoughts which, by means of it, are linked up with one another" (343, A364). We could, given the evidence of introspection, be nothing more than a series of persons each of which is deceived into thinking that she is one with the earlier ones. This is only a mild improvement on Hume's doctrine that we do not exist as continuing selves at all. Kant does, however, believe in our continuity, for moral rather than metaphysical reasons. Indeed, as we shall see below, he believes in our immortality.

Contrary to Berkeley, Kant believes that perceptions of objects are caused by objects outside the mind. Kant, however, distinguishes the things as we see them, phenomena, from the things as they are, noumena. Persons, too, are apprehended by us in the phenomenal world, though they have noumenal existence which we cannot know.[4] We cannot even know our noumenal selves, though we can know that we exist. Without the person, there would be no experience, but the person as noumenon is beyond her own realm of knowledge. Hume was right to think he could not know himself, but wrong to suppose there was nothing to know.

This qualified denial of what, from a Kantian point of view, are the excesses of the empiricists is crucial to Kant's moral theory as well. By limiting our knowledge to the phenomenal world, he is able to explain how there can be personal freedom. While my every action seems to be an event caused by other events in the phenomenal realm, for me to be morally responsible for my actions is for me to be free to have done otherwise. This antinomy of caused actions being free is, on Kant's view, explained by making freedom a feature of the mysterious, unknowable noumenal realm. We are empirically causally determined but transcendentally free. In other words, we are caused as phenomena, but we are free as noumena. Although we cannot understand our freedom as it lies in the noumenal realm which is beyond our knowledge, we can, nonetheless, exercise our freedom.[5] To do so rightly, we must obey a moral law, the categorical imperative, which can be known by reason alone.

One of Kant's formulations of this law encapsulates Kant's famous doctrine noted above that persons must be treated as ends not as means; that is, persons are not to be used as tools to achieve goals, rather valuing persons must be central to our goals. Because no person can be discounted as a mere means to achieving the goals of others, we are all required, according to Kant, to act only on rules that we could, without contradiction, universalize. For us to universalize a rule is to accept it as rule for all people who find themselves in a situation similar to the one in which we are acting. Kant believes that reason alone will tell us which rules can be universalized. Those that cannot be rationally universalized will lead us to logical contradictions when we try to universalize them. This Kantian view of persons, reason, and morals is an extreme case of the emphasis of the intellectual component in persons. We are, for Kant, essentially rational beings. In this lies our value. We must recognize the same value in all other persons.[6]

Kant does not, of course, deny our affective features. He believes, however, that the emotions have absolutely no place in moral decision-making. His is a stern view of duty understood by reason alone. Most people, he knows, will be guided by moral sentiments. In truth, however, the real reason that what they do is right is that it conforms to the moral law, the categorical imperative.[7]

Kant affirms, moreover, that nothing is good in itself except a good will (17). It is not the consequences of our actions which make the actions right, but the intentions we have when we do them. The imperfection of this world is such, however, that the consequences of the exercise of a good will may not lead to happiness. Virtue is not often rewarded. Our reason tells us that virtue and happiness ought to coincide, which leads us inevitably to postulate our immortality; otherwise there would not be enough time for us to achieve the moral perfection and consequent happiness for which we strive.[8] So, like Locke, Kant thinks that persons do not go out of existence, but while Locke took that as a starting point and tried to explain how we could survive our bodily death with our responsibility intact, Kant takes responsibility and perfectibility of persons as given and deduces our immortality. We are rational beings striving for moral perfection; so we need the time to achieve the goal, but our immortality cannot be proven (113).

While Kant's views on immortality have not, perhaps, penetrated popular morality, his view of persons as beings of intrinsic moral worth is quite often taken to be common sense now. To some extent it coincides with the long development of the idea of individual worth which is central to the Western theological and philosophical traditions, but Kant focuses that idea through a systematic philosophy. He joins it, as well, with the Aristotelian view that rationality is crucial to what we are. The principle that all persons, as rational beings, have dignity and must be taken into account when our actions affect them is an idea that has permeated the contemporary world. This principle may be honoured more in the breach, but it is so generally accepted that we feel we must rationalize each breach. For example, when bigots mistreat a particular group of human beings they feel constrained to deny that those in the group are "real persons" of the sort they perceive themselves to be. Kant's influence has seeped deeply into our culture.

On the other hand, the centrality of rationality in what we are and what we ought to do is often challenged. Kant's influence on contemporary views of persons is moderated by a Rousseauesque appreciation of the native moral sentiments. A psychopath, for instance, may be perfectly rational in the sense of logically pursuing egoistic goals. One might well say that the psychopath is, nonetheless, not a complete person for lacking the native moral sentiments of compassion and guilt. This is probably a more common contemporary response than the Kantian approach of trying to show that the psychopath is actually irrational since she universalizes contradictory rules.

Application to Daphne's case

While Daphne appears to be absent from her body, which remains, Kantians could believe that her unknowable self exists yet in the noumenal realm. Her lack of ability to benefit others is, from a Kantian point of view, irrelevant to the treatment she should get. Her value as a person does not depend, as it does for Hobbes, on her place in the state or on her capacity to improve the general welfare. Perhaps a Kantian could argue also, as Kant does for our immortality, that Daphne's continuity is morally necessary though unknowable and unprovable.

What I like about Kant

One rather general contribution Kant has made to the debate concerning persons is the demonstration that one can powerfully link three approaches to the person: metaphysical, epistemological, and ethical. These three pursue the questions of what we are, how we know ourselves and other persons, and what we ought to do. Where Kant has been unable to provide metaphysical proofs to his satisfaction concerning the permanence of persons, he relies on the necessity of our permanence for moral needs. Some would consider this a weakness. Many philosophical discussions today of the popular topic of personal identity narrow the approach to metaphysical questions alone. The motivation, however, to pursue the metaphysical questions and those of epistemology is often a moral one. This should be taken to heart, and the three approaches through metaphysics, epistemology, and ethics should provide checks and balances for one another.

Hegel: God is still almost everywhere

There was a strong reaction to Kant from a school of philosophy known as "German Idealism" or "Absolute Idealism." British and North American philosophers tend to look on this school with the same fondness that they display for German measles. Sallying forth into this territory will no doubt earn me the wrath of the dyed-in-the-wool subset of the Analytic philosophers of Britain and North America as well as the equal ire of their implacable enemies on the continent. That is a price I am prepared to pay for whatever insights about persons we might glean from either the Absolute Idealists or my interpretation of them. Most philosophers on both sides of the great schism are at least willing to listen.

The main proponent of Absolute Idealism was Hegel. Like Kant and un-like most Analytic philosophers, Hegel was a system builder. His main tool of construction was a method, dialectic, in which two contradictory proposi-tions, the thesis and the antithesis, are resolved by a third, the synthesis. Ap-plying this method to the concept of Being, Hegel ultimately concludes that the universe is a Mind.[9] Aristotle had earlier thought of the universe as a ma-terial organism with purposes realized in its parts, but Hegel is denying the existence of matter, as Berkeley had done. Hegel is also denying the separa-tion of minds that Berkeley admitted. All things in the universe are part of one Mind, the Absolute. The universe is a person. Individual persons are merely part of this larger person.

Stated baldly like that, the conclusion Hegel approaches with infinite pains is rather hard for the Western mind to accept. It seems more at home in some Eastern cultures, at least as perceived from the West, where the indi-vidual is routinely subjugated to the group and thought of as being reab-sorbed into the One after death. This is not too far from the mark. Individualism is dealt a glancing blow by Hegel. He is, however, very much a Western thinker in many ways and has a role for the individual person within the larger person of the Absolute and in the political expression of that Absolute, the state. The Absolute, moreover, is a dynamic evolving process (330), just as an individual person is.

For Hegel, everything that is known or understood is related to the Ab-solute Idea or Mind. This Absolute is all-encompassing; so we can make sense of individual things or persons only as parts of the Absolute. "The Ab-solute alone is true," says Hegel,[10] denying any use for a knowledge of some relative "truth" which obtains within a limited context. A piece of a puzzle cannot be understood on its own. As we seek understanding, we move dia-lectically synthesizing opposites until we reach the Absolute, which makes the individual things and persons comprehensible. This process is illustrated when a person thinks of herself as opposed to things outside herself. There is her subjective awareness of the thing outside and the objective existence of that thing independently of her mind. The subjectivity and the objectivity, thesis and antithesis, are synthesized in the Absolute. When an individual person is aware of a thing outside herself, this is the Absolute being self-conscious, rather like Spinoza's God. Individual persons are, then, the way in which the largest person, the Absolute, knows itself. The subjective and the objective are unified in this Absolute (792-93). The object is a thought of the Absolute. The person thinking about the object is the Absolute's self-reflection.

Seen from another point of view, objectively or from the outside, a per-son is, according to Hegel, a mechanism, a chemism, and a teleology.[11] Roughly, that means that we not only have mechanical and chemical aspects but also a system of purposes, both our own and those of the Absolute. Unlike mere machines or chemical reactions, human beings are not merely to be understood in the realm of nature which is governed by necessity. We are the self-awareness of the Absolute and; hence,, free to choose. In the context of Hegel's philosophy this freedom is best understood in Shakespeare's apt phrase, "Destiny shapes our ends rough-hew them how we may." As the great, self-reflecting Absolute evolves through the ages, we are free to go, in various ways, with the flow of this evolution or to fight helplessly against it. We have room for a little swimming across the current, but there is no going against it successfully.

None of what has been said so far implies that the individual person is utterly subjugated to or absorbed into something beyond that individual. Even though all persons are one in that they are all expressions of the Absolute reflecting on itself, there might be many different sorts of self-reflection; hence, room for individuality. The worth of the individual which Kant emphasized, however, takes second place to the worth of the group as the outcomes of Hegel's metaphysics for his moral and political philosophy unfold. Individual political freedom is minimized. Hegel's philosophy of history also leaves scant room for that metaphysical freedom which is opposed to determinism.

To begin with metaphysical freedom and individuality, these are absorbed into the freedom of the Absolute itself. On Hegel's view, history is a record of the growth and development of this large person, the Absolute. What we see in history is the continual revelation of the Spirit or Mind which is the Absolute. The Absolute is evolving towards freedom, but the individual is merely expressing the Spirit of her age, a stage in the character development of a much larger person. She is caught up in and swept along by that Spirit will she, nil she.

> As it is not the brute, but only the man that thinks, he only—and only because he is a thinking being—has Freedom. *His* consciousness imports this, that the individual comprehends itself as a *person*, that is, recognizes itself in its single existence as possessing universality—as capable of abstraction from, and of surrendering all specialty; and, therefore, as inherently infinite.[12]

Here we see not only the familiar theme of rationality as essential to a person but also the unfamiliar idea that both the properties of having freedom and being a person require absorption of the individual, surrendering of specialty, being a part of the infinite, the Absolute.

As for political freedom in Hegel's view, the person who is most free is one who accepts completely the bonds of moral and political duty. This conclusion is also the end product of a line of dialectical reasoning. The thesis is that the individual person has a right to express her freedom by, for instance, accumulating property. Opposed to this are the requirements of morality, the duties which restrict individual freedom. This antithesis is resolved with the thesis into a synthesis in which a higher freedom is found in the harmonizing of the individual will with the universal will. The individual no longer acts for herself but for all through the state. The state too is a person and is "the embodiment of rational freedom."[13] The only acts which one can rationally choose to do are those which are in accord with the public good. Therefore, if one is both free and rational in what one freely chooses, one accepts completely the bonds of social duty.

A theory like Hegel's can easily be perverted to the purposes of a selfish, totalitarian ruler. Hegel's understanding of it was, however, quite the opposite. Kaufmann tells us, "That history is the story of the development of human freedom, is the central idea of Hegel's philosophy of history."[14] Hegel thinks of the Absolute evolving through the history of mankind from the days of the single ruler, to the free society supported by slaves, to the society where all are free. "Universal History exhibits the *gradation* in the development of that principle whose substantial *purport* is the consciousness of Freedom."[15] In spite of Hegel's intentions, his excessive faith in the ability and willingness of people to act rationally leads him to put far too little caution in his remarks about the state. Theoretically, Hegel exalts the individual person as the Absolute being made self-aware. From a theological viewpoint, the Absolute is God. A version of the ancient idea of the divine in persons is thus preserved. One thinks as well of Spinoza's concept of a person. Hegel's views on morality, freedom, and the state are, nonetheless, effortlessly turned in their practical application to the suppression of the individual.[16]

Although Hegel is a mystic of sorts and furthers the Oriental ideal of absorption of the individual person in a cosmic whole, he retains from Kant the requirement of rationality for persons.

Schopenhauer

God begins to disappear

Schopenhauer, whom Stumpf has with apt alliteration called "The Prophet of Pessimism,"[17] moves us further in the direction of contemporary concepts of persons by leaving behind in his account of what is essential to persons both the divine and the rational, intellectual features. In his depiction of persons as totally driven by forces beyond their control one sees a foreshadowing of some of the dim views of persons which became popular in the post-Freudian world.

Schopenhauer takes as axiomatic the principle of sufficient reason "that nothing is without a reason" (345). "Reason" is here used rather like "cause." Once one accepts such a principle, pessimism is justified. Every human action along with every other event must happen of necessity. Free will is dead. We may be aware of our condition, but we can do nothing to alter it. At best one can view the spectacle of the misery of human kind with the compassion and resignation which come from generalizing love for an individual person to love for all persons.

In the course of delineating this cheery doctrine, Schopenhauer generates some interesting claims about persons. Self-awareness is often taken to be an essential feature of persons, but few give an account of what it is. How can the self be, simultaneously, the knowing subject and the object of knowledge? Schopenhauer explains that the self that wills is the object of knowledge for the self as knowing subject. He seems to be telling me that my intellect can step back and take cognizance of that part of me which is moved to action by my will. This use of the term "will" sounds peculiar to contemporary ears since we are used to thinking of will as itself under the guidance of reason. Schopenhauer, however, uses the term "will" as we might use "drives" to indicate deep-seated forces moving the person to act in ways that person cannot control. We can see the strings which move our puppet limbs, but we cannot be our own puppeteers. In self-awareness we come, sadly, to understand and see ourselves as puppets. The intellect is powerless against this "blind incessant impulse" (349). This is most clear in the will to live which normally overpowers reason.

This odd notion of the will as a cause which drives us to do the things we do quite independently of reason is fundamental in Schopenhauer's worldview. This kind of will drives all events in the world. He goes so far as to say the world is will. Clearly then, it would be an error to say that will is merely what later psychiatrists might call a subconscious drive. Will is broad enough to include types of energy and causation which occur in totally non-personal entities. Schopenhauer thus associates what drives persons with what drives any event in the universe. We are not different. We are absorbed into the general, heaving, life-seeking but otherwise purposeless realm of nature. For reasons in some respects different from Schopenhauer's, our contemporaries often view persons as merely more complex processes in the realm of natural processes. Although the scientific backdrop of this contemporary view is more detailed, there is the shared faith in the principle of sufficient reason which motivates both Schopenhauer and these contemporaries to reduce persons to causal processes.

Application to Daphne's case

Hegel and Schopenhauer both, in their different ways, see people as in the grip of large forces beyond their control. It is the Absolute, not the individual person here in the muck of the mundane, who is free. It is difficult to differentiate Daphne from the rest of us on such views. The Absolute is in an odd mood of self-contemplation in her case. She has the advantage over the rest of us of being unaware of her own condition, or so a pessimist like Schopenhauer might think.

Bentham and Mill

The movement of the concepts of person from the religious to the secular realm was accelerated towards the end of the modern period. The positivism of August Comte and John Stuart Mill did something to move metaphysics more into the thought patterns of science and away from those of religion. Religions tend to expect faith on non-rational grounds. They treat the universe as either a person or something governed by an immensely powerful person or persons in whose terms all things have a purpose. What positivism substitutes for this universe with a purpose is a universe in which natural phenomena occur in regular ways governed by discoverable natural laws, but a universe which, in itself, has no purpose. The anthropomorphic and animistic views of the world are replaced with one in which the world is to be understood in terms of its regularity. This view puts persons in a special category, since they have purposes and values while the rest of the world does not. Such an understanding has made the immense power of science possible in the contemporary period and has contributed to its destructive tendencies. If nature is no longer our mother, she can be used like a whore—so one would judge by our present practice in which the planet, like one of the enslaved women on this planet, is being used up. By treating our surroundings impersonally, we have threatened their continuance and, of course, our own. Not only are persons not absorbed into a greater whole, they are encouraged to be so individualistic as to egoistically ravage the world for their personal benefit. Depending on what one thinks the results of less individualistic policies will be, one may find a partial antidote to this rabid individualism in the influence of the utilitarians, including Mill, who advanced positivism against the mother-nature view of the world.

In the interface between the modern and the contemporary periods, Jeremy Bentham and John Stuart Mill solidified and popularized utilitarianism, a view about morality which had been growing in strength since Hobbes' time. Hobbes, Hume, and even Locke foreshadowed what Bentham and Mill were to champion, the utilitarian view that what is good is happiness and that, hence, the right thing to do is what will create the greatest happiness of the greatest number of people. This is a far cry from the more traditional views about goodness and right action. In particular the idea that what is good is what God wills was replaced not only in the writings of these philosophers but in much of the realm of public affairs. Bentham and Mill were passionate, energetic, and effective social reformers.

The new ethics which the utilitarians furthered still competes with ethical views which do not make the rightness of an action depend on the consequences of the action. Utilitarianism is, however, easier to defend than many other views in the contemporary context. Once one takes away a share in divinity as the source of the worth of persons and once one adopts a scientific, investigative attitude to persons, it is easier to support an ethics apparently based on observation. Looking at people's behaviour, we seem to see that they seek pleasure and avoid pain. Thus there is nothing mysterious about the utilitarian analysis of the good as pleasure. No appeal to the intrinsic worth of persons is required.

On the other hand, utilitarians tend to ignore persons as individuals in favour of the mass of persons. If one wants to maximize the aggregate of happiness, attention to the individual is not always necessary. In spite of the best efforts of Mill, this lessening of the importance of individual persons is a concomitant of the rise of utilitarianism and the secularization of the concept of persons which goes hand in hand with utilitarianism. If I have no individual rights, as utilitarians claim, and I cannot say that my soul is special in the eyes of God, then there is nothing to prevent society using me as a means to the end of society's greater happiness, even if that results in my own lifelong abject misery. Utilitarians do a cost-benefit analysis. They find the unhappiness of one person justified by the happiness of the many. Mill thought that the happiness of the many could best be achieved by providing individuals with the liberty to make themselves happy, but that is a social-psychological claim which is open to empirical study. It may turn out to be false. If so, the utilitarian principles justify the absorption of the individual by the state.

One of the things we would like a concept of a person to provide is a theoretical underpinning for a society which is tolerant of individual difference without deifying it. Unfortunately, one can always find social-scientific support for greatly limiting freedom of the individual person, given that one's goal is to maximize happiness. Consider, for example, the uses to which Lawrence Kohlberg's theory of the stages of moral development might be put. According to this theory, very few people ever reach the stage of moral development in which they could properly apply their freedom as Mill would hope they would. They would not pursue their own happiness with respect for other people.[18] This seems to license denying individual liberty to most people and allowing it only to the highly developed few. This looks like a return to Plato's view of a just society in which that few ran the lives of the others. The absorption of individuals by the state is assured.

By another criterion for judging concepts of a person the utilitarians fare somewhat better. In cases of mental incompetence, we would like a concept which does not pin so much on rationality that it excludes a person from consideration because of a loss of rationality. The happiness of a mental incompetent is worth as much as the happiness of the most rational member of society to utilitarians like Bentham and Mill. There are others who distinguish the kinds of pleasures one may have and thus would value simple pleasures less than those of which the incompetent is capable. Most utilitarians would accept pleasure of any kind as on a par with pleasure of any other kind.

This brings us to another feature of utilitarianism which may inhibit the effects of rabid individualism. The idea that the person is the crown of creation and may ravage the rest of the world for personal betterment is blocked by this fact: animals feel pain and pleasure. Since pleasure is the good for utilitarians, the distinction between animals and people is minimized. The line to draw in moral matters is not between the rational and the non-rational but between sentient and non-sentient beings. Singer approvingly quotes Bentham on this score: "The day may come when the rest of the animal creation may acquire those rights which never could have been withholden from them but by the hand of tyranny....The question is not, Can they reason? nor Can they talk? but, Can they suffer?"[19] The heirs of Hume minimize the importance of the person as a metaphysical unit, a chunk of reality, while the utilitarians undermine the importance of the person as a moral unit, one whose interests must be considered above those of other sentient beings. The influence of Hume's metaphysics and utilitarian ethics has the effect of widening our range of concern. As we shall see below, Parfit views this as an improvement. Certainly we have been woefully unconcerned about non-persons in this world, but treating fish and people as on a par is more than most of us wish to do to rectify this wrong. As a culture, we refuse to abandon the concept of a person, but we modify that concept to find a new role for persons in a world which may no longer be dismissed as mere material for our use.

Application to Daphne's case

The utilitarians tend to diminish the importance of the distinction of people from other sentient beings. Whether or not we wish to say Daphne is a person or is the same person will rely on our choice of categories within an empirical framework, but it will have little effect on the moral determination of the treatment Daphne should receive. Though her pleasures may be rather limited from an intellectual point of view, they weigh as heavily in the balance as those of the most refined minds.

What I like about Bentham and Mill

The positivist substitution of the natural world for the supernatural is a good trend in philosophy as is Bentham and Mill's recognition of the importance of pleasure; that is, they are good ideas if one does not make a god of either science or pleasure. It seems to me important to consider the pleasures which are peculiar to people, not just because of their intensity relative to those of other animals, but because of their difference in kind. People are animals who laugh.

Karl Marx and self-realization

We turn now to a system which paradoxically combines great respect for individual persons with the advice that dictatorship will be needed. Trigg claims[20] that romantic individualism seemed to be Marx's aim for those who would enjoy that utopia which Marx predicted would arise once the state had withered away. Could he be talking about *the* Karl Marx? In fact, Marx is known to many of us only through the caricature of his ideas which is seen in the media controlled by those he threatened most. It will take a bit of explaining to uncover the romantic individualist beneath the appearance of the inhumane totalitarian.

Marx might not have too much sympathy with the attempt to understand the concept of person except insofar as that is equivalent to the task of saying what human nature is. On the one hand, Marx seems to have believed that there was no invariant human nature, and on the other that it was the very thing which makes us essentially human, or persons, which is alienated along with the products of our labour in a capitalist society. Consider first the anti-essentialist doctrine that we vary as chameleons against the background of our society: "it is not the consciousness of men that determines their being, but, on the contrary, their social being determines their consciousness."[21]

Some contend that not only invariant consciousness but an invariant human nature is non-existent according to Marx. They attribute to him the doctrine that so-called "human nature" is merely a result of social forces.[22] There is, however, the notion in Marx that capitalist society alienates workers from the products of their labour, and thereby "each man is estranged from the other, as each of them is from man's essential nature."[23] What distinguishes people from animals is that they produce the means of their own subsistence. The need to work and to be fulfilled in work is natural to us.[24] Here again we see the person being defined in terms of ability, but not the mere ability to reason but the ability to labour. Our need to identify ourselves with what we produce by our labour is essential to our being what we are. We are therefore depersonalized when the individual loses the means of production to the bourgeoisie, who distance us from our the products of our labour. Marx is here describing needs and tendencies that, in some sense, are our nature.

Our nature does not, however, go so far as to include patterns of behaviour which many have put under the umbrella of human nature. That people are avaricious traders and fail to cooperate, for example, is something that could be changed, given a sufficiently thorough dictatorship of the proletariat which would enforce cooperation until it became "natural." In the resulting cooperative utopia, the state, that is the dictatorship, withers away once enforcing cooperation is unnecessary. In the cooperative, classless society which Marx envisioned, people would work creatively and be at one with both the products of their labour and the others with whom they created and shared these products. Cooperation would replace competition in our "nature."

Marx thought this development would inevitably come. This conclusion came from his adaptation of Hegel's view of history. Hegel thought that the Absolute moved in its dialectic process through history to become ever more free. Marxist dialectic preserves this as the freedom of the individual in the utopia that must eventually come. In this anarchic, cooperative community we would be as free as Rousseau's noble savages, untrammeled by law. It is here that we see Marx's romantic individualism. Each person ought to be a free, creative being in harmony with other people and enjoying the full use of her abilities to satisfy the needs of all. Marx, however, thought of himself not as a romantic moralist like Rousseau but as a scientific historian and futurist making an accurate prediction of the way that history must evolve.

This raises the question of determinism. If we are unable to resist the currents of history, are we not simply playing roles in a drama written before we were born? Do the concepts of a person which require personal freedom to choose assume what is necessarily false? Marx seems to allow personal freedom in resistance to or acquiescence in the inevitable. We can struggle to bring about or to prevent the coming of a classless society, but it will come in any case. Shakespeare's phrase is apt, "Destiny shapes our ends, rough-hew them how we may." The fine points of the metaphysical debates concerning what freedom is and how people can have it do not seem to concern Marx. His is a philosophy in which the details are not allowed to inhibit the call to action.

The dramatic failure of the Soviet Union to survive and to convert Eastern Europe or its own republics to genuine communist states makes Marx's view of history and of people seem dubious. Admittedly his program required a worldwide revolution so that there would be nowhere for capitalism to breed. That revolution looks like an ever-more distant prospect as people in the industrialized nations, where the workers were expected to rise against the bourgeoisie, take the money and run. Communist revolutions, as opposed to revolutions against communism, were, when they were still occurring, much more likely in agrarian countries of the third world where people had nearly nothing to lose. The abolition of private property appeals mainly to those without any. Marxism is, however, flexible enough to allow for back-sliding. The Marxist faith is that the revolution will come when history is good and ready. While recent events have given capitalists confidence, the long term looks bad for the capitalist system, which is devouring the ground on which it stands. The degradation of the environment may lead to cataclysms which, if they do not promote Marxism, will at least undo its main opponent.

In any case, unless one sees in it the Romantic, beautiful ideals of fraternity and equality and the faith in people as naturally creative, free, and cooperative, the Marxist picture of persons will be unintelligible, and the Marxist fervour for revolution will be seen as pure malevolence. The effect of this betrayed faith has often been a horrific form of totalitarianism in which selfish party bosses enslave a country and degrade the environment even more than capitalist industry. This, of course, is not Marxism. It is what the failed attempts to establish Marxist states have led to, and perhaps this is predictable, given what people are really like. One cannot force cooperation.

In any case, to see Marxists through the caricatures in our newspapers is to underestimate its power as a movement with romantic, humanist ideals. In particular, one must see it as promising freedom and self-realization of the individual person. That is why people fight and die for it. Even within the most capitalist societies, we accept the need for the self-realization of people which Marx preached, and we have accepted many social reforms to this end. Marx would think we will eventually come around once we stop confusing real freedom with the free market. It is not clear to me from reading Marx what this real freedom comes to, but politically, it involves the power to create things in which we take pride and to share them with others in an environment where none are exploited, all contributions are valued, and all needs are honoured. Once one understands the ideal it becomes clear that the main sources of disagreement which most people in capitalist democratic countries have with Marx is over the questions of what people are like by nature and, hence, how to achieve the ideal.

Application to Daphne's case

If the capacity to labour and the need to do so are what is distinctive of persons, then few could have made better claim to the title of "person" than Daphne prior to her illness. She was never still but in sleep. Now it does seem as though the quiet woman who remains has lost what was essential to be Daphne.

What I like about Marx

While Marx's political theories seem ever more difficult to believe, it is hard to disagree with the ideal of a society in which people are each valued for their contribution, whatever it may be, each allowed self-realization and freedom, not merely under the protection of law, but through the voluntary cooperation of all. More pertinent to the topic of persons is the Marxist faith that there is no human nature which we cannot change. Rather than being like all animals driven by will, as Schopenhauer would have it, we can change ourselves fundamentally by changing the society around us. Whether we can effect such changes or not, the relativity of the nature of persons to their environment is an interesting idea.

Kierkegaard's attempt to depose reason

God reappears

In Mill and Marx one sees philosophers who are utterly opposed to the kind of philosophy done by Hegel, though not necessarily the structure of his theories. They might consider such systems as Hegel's to be castles in the air. They wanted philosophy which led to social reform. Yet in their attempt to achieve hard-headed philosophical views and to maintain what Russell would call "a robust sense of reality," each gives some attention to the Humanist and Romantic strains in our concepts of a person. Kierkegaard was a Danish philosopher of the time who gave far more attention to these strains in his own rejection of Hegel's Absolute Idealism. He wanted to preserve, in the face of the scientific investigation of human beings and various kinds of materialism, something essential to persons. Like Schopenhauer, he found this in the will rather than in reason, but, dour as he might have been, Kierkegaard was far from the pessimist Schopenhauer was. Freedom is also central to the concept of a person left to us by Kierkegaard. The themes Kierkegaard pursued became the core of the mighty Existentialist movement in Continental Philosophy in our times.

Most importantly, against those like Bentham who emphasize the good of the whole, Kierkegaard focuses mainly on the individual. Large systems, whether metaphysical or political, are to be understood in terms of the individual rather than the other way around. This is because it is the individual person's act of will, making a commitment, choosing between alternatives which determines what is true. His subjectivist doctrine of truth is summed up in his claim that, "the highest truth attainable for an Existing individual [is] an objective uncertainty held fast in the most passionate personal experience."[25] Ultimately, the individual person must choose what to believe. There is no objective certainty. There is no Absolute.

Free choices are what make us what we are, and choices present themselves to us everywhere. The criteria for choosing are themselves things we must choose on the basis of no higher criteria at all; that is, they are absurdly chosen. Kierkegaard only sometimes restricts this sort of absurd starting-point to the realm of morals or religious faith,[26] separating the kind of truth we can attain to in this area from that of science. Whatever the limits of his subjectivist doctrine of truth, he does believe that people's actions cannot be explained by causes (148). He assumes that freedom of the will is not compatible with causal determinism.

Like Marx, Kierkegaard is fundamentally concerned with self-realization, but he sees it as coming through the exercise of free choice in the development of personality. The Hegelian and Marxist idea that the unfolding of history determines the individual is anathema to Kierkegaard. There is, however, something like Hegelian dialectic in the development of the individual person who, if she develops fully, evolves through three stages of personality through which she is led by guilt and anxiety. The initial stage of the aesthetic person is that of a Sybarite in which the person aims at maximizing her personal sensual pleasure. From this one may move to the ethical stage where she accepts the dictates of a reasoned morality, as Socrates did. This, however, is where Western philosophy has become stuck. Kierkegaard would have us go on to the religious stage in which one overcomes reason, making a leap of faith to believe what is rationally absurd. In this stage one works out her personal, subjective, and unique relationship to God. The ancient Greek ideal of rational ethics is deposed in favour of faith.

Unlike the faith of Augustine or Aquinas, however, Kierkegaard's is a faith in spite of what reason tells us, not one that can be bolstered by argument. Complete self-realization is hindered, on Kierkegaard's view, by the addiction to rationality. His is, however, not merely a non-rational philosophy. Reason must be given full sway during the ethical stage of development; it is just not the be-all and end-all in philosophical method. In this Kierkegaard is out of step with the majority of philosophers throughout history, but his ideas on the limits of reason, often separated from religious views, have been taken up by contemporary philosophers, mainly those in the Existentialist school. One notable philosopher outside that school, Thomas Nagel, currently takes the ability to sense the absurdity of one's life as a defining characteristic of persons.[27]

Reason, the Absolute, and objective truth have been on a less secure footing since Kierkegaard. In particular, the truth about what we are is challenged. The essentially rational nature of persons is disputed. The belief in our participation in some grand Absolute is undermined since the dour Dane wrote.

Application to Daphne's case

It should be noted that the concept of a person which emerges through Kierkegaard and through existentialist writing in general is of a highly developed human being, one who is supra-rational rather than sub-rational. The capacity for choice is fundamental. Thus those who seem incapable of choosing are left out of account. Daphne is incapable of doing what is crucial for persons.

The turn of the century and the screw

Nietzsche and the death of God

Schopenhauer and Kierkegaard wanted to make reason play second fiddle to the will in their descriptions of what we are. Nietzsche was forcefully persuasive for a revision of standard views about what we ought to do and what we ought to become based on the will to power. He exclaims, "the strongest and highest Will to Life does not find expression in a miserable struggle for existence, but in a Will to War. A Will to Power, a Will to Over-power!"[28] A person, no less than a wolf, is driven to dominate. The person, however, seeks to dominate not only her fellow creatures but the entire environment. If this is right, what a choking irony! We have succeeded in over-powering the environment. The struggling biomass on which we live is dying by our hand. Our will to life is killing that on which we depend to live.

Nietzsche saw the wild urge to overpower restrained in the Europe of his time only by the myth of the Judeo-Christian God. This myth was losing its efficacy as a restraint; so, with horrifying accuracy, he prophesied wars of previously unknown violence. People, according to Nietzsche, are different from wild beasts of prey only in the manner of the restraint of their will to power. This will or life force is the Dionysian element in a person, and Nietzsche sees it ideally working in concert with the Apollonian side of the person which provides order, restraint and form (387). The will to power is merely destructive if it is not formed into an act of creation by the Apollonian element of the person.

This synthesis of the Dionysian and Apollonian sides of ourselves is Nietzsche's response to the antithetical concepts of a person which we have seen in the prior history of philosophy. The more Oriental view has the person as part of a mass while the Occidental influence moves the concept further towards that of the individual cut off from the mass. The worshippers of Dionysus became absorbed into the whole of nature in a trance. From this they derived great power and shed responsibility. Apollo, by contrast, was the symbol of the principle of individuation (387). Nietzsche abhorred absorption as much as Kierkegaard, but he also abhorred the Christian doctrine in which Kierkegaard found solace. He derided it as "slave morality." He insisted that it turned love of the earth into hatred (391). He accused it of elevating the mediocre values of the herd above the strength of the great (390).

This is curious, in the large historical picture. Christianity was, in fact, part of the Occidental trend away from absorption of the person in the mass by valuing individual souls and demanding that they be identifiable for judg-ment. Nietzsche, however, thought that the virtues of humility, patience, and diligence which were promoted by Christianity were the virtues that the weak promoted to defeat the strong (389). His hope was that our species might produce Supermen who would rise above the common herd by exercising the will to power. Goethe was his model, not some precursor of Hitler. Such persons as now exist should be superseded by those who would not be afraid to drop the life-negating Christian virtues in favour of the virtue of cruelty—the will to power—which is the source of creativity, on Nietzsche's view. The ideal person would savagely exploit the weak, when necessary, to produce something of greatness.

The most successful executives seem to accept something like Nietzsche's superman doctrine, but they put corporate commercial achievement in place of the cultural achievements which Nietzsche admired. The heads of multinational corporations must accept a large share of the responsibility for the destruction of the environment which they have sought to overpower. It is hard to see how a will to power could generate much concern about future generations, but if Nietzsche is right about persons being fuelled by a mixture of Dionysian and Apollonian urges, the only hope for our survival as a species is in the harnessing of the will to power for the regeneration of our environment.

Nietzsche himself was in such agonizing need of physical regeneration that his writing was, perforce, aphoristic. Ironically, for medical reasons, he depended at the end of his life on the virtuous help which he had despised. Often, he literally could not bear to sit at a desk and write for long periods of time. He produced his ideas in short but immensely powerful bursts of prose, leaving us to fill in the details. What persons are and what they might become has been presented to us only in an adumbrated form. Nonetheless a provocative view as an antithesis to much of what philosophy has told us about ourselves has been flung down as a gauntlet before contemporary philosophers.

Peirce, James, and Dewey: Pragmatism and persons

God's resurrection

Like Marx, Kierkegaard, and Nietzsche, three American philosophers, Peirce, James, and Dewey, wanted to bring philosophy back to earth. Their attitude to systems like that of Hegel was tersely summed up in one of James' letters, "Damn the Absolute!"[29] They, especially William James, wanted to ensure the connection of philosophy with the personal, immediate concerns of our daily lives. While the pragmatists are somewhat more at home with the British empiricists than with the continental rationalists, they thought that both groups were insufficiently respectful of the connections between thought and action.[30] Peirce coined the word "pragmatism" from the Greek *pragma* meaning act or deed (412). To understand what people are saying when they use terms like "person," the pragmatists would ask us to cash it out in terms of what those people using the term "person" would do under various conditions. Action is the underpinning of meaning.

To understand this theory of meaning a little, let us look first at a much simpler concept than that of a person, the concept of hardness. To say that x is harder than y, according to Peirce's theory of meaning, is to assert a series of conditionals. One of these conditionals is this: *if* a sharp point of x is drawn firmly across a smooth surface of y, *then* x will leave a scratch in y. What these conditional statements do is to relate the concept of hardness to things we can do to test for the applicability of the concept. Now to return to the more complex concept of a person, to explain to Peirce what I mean by saying that Zeke is a person, I would have to explain what effects this would have on my actions. I might, for example, say that in choosing between the extreme physical suffering of my dog, which I dearly love, and the suffering of Zeke whom I loathe, I would have to opt for the suffering of my dog. If I could only rescue one of them from a burning building, for instance, it would have to be Zeke. For Peirce, this sort of answer begins to explain my concept of a person. On the other hand, if I were to say that a person is a particular spatio-temporal expression of the ongoing dialectical development of Spirit, Peirce would say, "Whoa! How does that affect what you would do?" or words to that effect. If I told him that there were no practical effects of my use of "person," he would consider that usage empty of meaning. Eventually Peirce gave up this theory of meaning since it led him to subjectivism.[31] The theory of meaning and subjectivism were taken up and popularized by William James.

Peirce's method of looking for outcomes for action was carried on by William James, who wove into it the theme of the importance of the will. Like Schopenhauer, Kierkegaard, and Nietzsche, the pragmatists were willing to dethrone reason, but they did not make the will supreme. James tried to find a careful balance between the two. Unlike Schopenhauer and Nietzsche, who focus on the will to overpower others, James, like Kierkegaard, attends to the will to believe. When it comes to the truth of our beliefs, however, James, like all the pragmatists, takes the truth to be what works. Peirce thought of statements which worked in the sense of standing up to scientific testing. Dewey looked for the social usefulness of beliefs. James is the most relevant to our present purposes since he focused on what works personally. He speaks of passional grounds for belief which go well beyond what we might believe on the basis of scientific evidence.

There are cases in which reason cannot decide an issue even in the way of saying which of two hypotheses would work best for us as a belief. James tells us that in such cases, it is reasonable to follow one's heart—rather than to adopt an agnostic attitude—if certain special conditions obtain. The conditions are that we have at least two clear, live, momentous hypotheses between which we are forced to decide.[32] A poignant instance is the decision between these: "She loves me. She loves me not." These hypotheses are certainly clear, in pragmatist terms, since I know just what I would expect her to do if she loves me. They are live hypotheses in the sense that they have a strong connection with my life since I love her. They are momentous since, whichever I adopt, it will have a profound effect on what I do. They are forced since no answer is also an answer in this case. If I remain agnostic in the circumstances in which I find myself, that is as good as saying she does not love me and acting accordingly. This would be terrible if indeed she does love me. So how would William James advise me?

The option to believe she loves me or believe she does not is living, momentous, and forced, a genuine option in James' terms. In this very special kind of case of a genuine option, and only in such cases, James would tell me to exercise my will to believe.[33] Reason cannot help me. I should believe what I want to be true. I do this. I believe that she loves me. This has profound consequences for action in the way I trust her, confide in her, and commit myself to her. She responds in kind; so now my belief is confirmed. Yet I had to believe it first and have it confirmed later, unlike my scientific hypotheses. The truth, in such special cases, is only revealed if we first believe it. In some cases the truth is created by the will to believe it as it would be if my belief and consequent actions helped her to come to love me after the fact of my believing that she loved me.

One might object that it is possible to proceed experimentally in such a case without adopting the firm belief that she loves me. This seems to me to be impossible if I really love her, but let us give the objection a run. First of all, one must be a very good actor to pursue such an experiment. People are incredibly good at detecting inauthentic behaviour in others. James might also reply that in such a case the decision is not truly momentous for me. It would be momentous if, for instance, I had to take an enormous risk by trusting her—say the risk of my entire psychological, financial, social, or political well-being. One may still call it an "experiment," but that is an odd name for betting one's life. Not mere curiosity or scientific interest but an enormously strong will to believe is required to make even the decision to act as if she loves me. And, in fact, if I really do love her, the devastating effects of dithering with experimentation in any way that might alienate her love make experimentation a fool's game.

Because James has this method of adopting beliefs on the ground of will, he personalizes pragmatism. Peirce and Dewey stick more to the experimental method. Dewey looks at people more as biological problem-solvers trying to survive with intelligence as a primary means of adapting to the environment.

One does not need, on this view, some Kantian notion of persons as ends nor essentialist doctrines about what we are in order to decide what to do. Each decision is taken on the merits of the particular case. The norms left to us by earlier philosophers and religious thinkers have to be taken as some among many that might be useful in solving a particular problem. In general, Dewey looked to the natural sciences for information which would be helpful in such problem-solving. He thought we should pool our wisdom gained from experience to make moral and political decisions. The way to do this was through democracy, on his view. Moral decisions look more like political ones in Dewey's version of pragmatism.[34] The emphasis on the individual comes out in James.

Application to Daphne's case

In general, a pragmatic approach to the problem of understanding the nature of persons and the criteria for their survival over time forces us to look at these concepts in terms of action. We need to know the difference it would make to what we do should we adopt one or other of the many concepts of a person that parade by in the history of the topic. If, for example, it makes no difference to the treatment we accord to a demented person whether or not we say she is the same person she was before the dementia, then the question of her survival becomes uninteresting. Yet surely this would be a peculiar result. We should look then for the difference it would make. One example of a difference is in the gratitude we owe to some people but not commonly to non-persons. A person's good works in the past make us the more willing to make sacrifices on her behalf now. Were she a totally new person, such sacrifices would be completely supererogatory. One should feel no more motivation to make them than one should in the case of beneficence to a total stranger. It seems, then, that from the pragmatist point of view, the capacity to bring about debts of gratitude and their consequent actions is part of the concept of a person.

Another thing that at least James' version of pragmatism brings to the debate about persons is a response to the welter of confusion about facts pertinent to the discussion. In cases of dementia, we have no way of knowing what is happening in the mind of the affected person. Even if we could decide on some firm criteria of adequacy for survival, we might be always unable to decide, on the basis of the available evidence, whether the person we are dealing with satisfies these criteria. For example, if memory of certain crucial events in her former life is required for someone to be the same person, we might never know if she is the same person, since she cannot communicate. Under such conditions, James' passional grounds for belief come into play.

What I like about the pragmatists

The forthright insistence that we say what difference our theories make is refreshing. The idea that our beliefs about persons are relative to social or even personal decisions is interesting. The metaphysical and the moral are knit together in a new way by the linkage of our concepts to our actions through the theory of meaning.

It is interesting that as pragmatism was ushering in the contemporary secular era, James was defending faith, including religious faith, under the conditions discussed above. In our own era faith of any sort is often considered suspect; so we hide it, even our own faith from ourselves. James wryly reports:

> I have long defended to my own students the lawfulness of voluntarily adopted faith; but as soon as they have got well imbued with the logical spirit, they have as a rule refused to admit my contention to be lawful philosophically, even though in point of fact they were personally all the time chock-full of some faith or other themselves.[35]

It is interesting to contemplate the decision to believe or not believe in God as a genuine option, living, momentous, and forced.

We now turn to a group of contemporary philosophers who, unlike most contemporary philosophers, tend to take a great deal on faith.

EIGHT
Our Contemporaries (or Almost)

System builders are still around

Bergson: Seeing ourselves from inside

It is popular today to think that our worship of science and technology has led us astray, that we have ignored Socrates' advice to know ourselves, that our attempt to conquer nature is leading to our own demise, and that we have left something important out in our way of gaining knowledge about the world. Early in this century, Bergson was arguing in concert with such thoughts that the scientific way of knowing is incomplete. Bergson develops a system of philosophy in which the distinction between analysis and intuition is fundamental. Analysis is our typical way of knowing an object. We compare it to other things. We look at its structure and its parts. We represent it in descriptions. In science we do this with mathematical precision. Knowing an object by analysis "implies that we move around the object," in contrast to knowing it by intuition in which case "we enter into it."[1] Knowing a thing by intuition is knowing what it is like to be that thing, to have that thing's perspective in the universe, not to see it from the outside. It is very difficult to get a grip on the concept of intuition, especially as applied to inanimate objects, but, given the topic at hand, we will look only at the more comprehensible case of knowledge of other persons.

Bergson considers the way in which we know the hero in a novel through the detailed story about the character the author has given us. Bergson contrasts this Analytical knowledge of the character with the empathetic knowledge by intuition. Speaking of the story, he says, "all this can never be equivalent to the simple and indivisible feeling which I should experience if I were able for an instant to identify myself with the person of the hero himself" (398). You have to really stand in the hero's shoes to know the hero. You cannot just rely on comparison of the hero to others and such Analytic ways of knowing the hero because these ways all look at the hero from the outside. The inside view which we get by intuition, on the other hand, reveals not what the hero has in common with others, but what is unique to that person. This is the crux of the matter. Analysis gives us the common denominator, the ways in which a person can be compared to others. Intuition reveals the person's essence—which is the central core of

---

Notes to Chapter Eight are on pp. 320-21.

that person and of that person alone—whereby a person can be distinguished from others.

The essence of a person or of anything whatever is inexpressible in symbols. It can only be directly experienced. Analysis, which relies on symbols, of necessity, leaves the essence out. We each of us know ourselves in the direct, intuitive way; so we know how inadequate mere Analytic knowledge of a person can be. Bergson's system is aimed at getting us to take knowledge of ourselves as a model when we try to know other persons and, indeed, all other things.

When we use the method of analysis we are forced to describe persons and other things as if they existed at certain locations in space and time. This, however, is just a useful fiction, an intellectual supposition, which allows our analysis to proceed. It may be useful for prediction and control of events to proceed this way. Science and technology make use of that. We should not, however, confuse this description of ourselves with reality. In reality, as we know from seeing ourselves endure, things are always in the process of change and becoming, not a series of static states at points of space and time. Analysis, in effect, takes a series of snapshots of events and misses the flow and duration of things. Everything is always changing and moving. Reality "is tendency, if we agree to mean by tendency an incipient change of direction" (401).

The whole of reality turns out to be, in Bergson's system, one large creative process called the Elan Vital, of which we are expressions, not parts (402). Intellect, which can only grasp the symbolic output of analysis, cannot make sense of Elan Vital. Only by intuition can we see reality this way. By making us all expressions of a single indivisible process, Bergson has revived to some extent the Oriental absorption of the individual into the whole. On the other hand, persons each have a unique essence on his view. Although we all express the Elan Vital, we all do so in our own ways. Seen from the inside, by intuition, each person is completely unique. Individuality is preserved after all.

Another familiar theme, that of personal freedom, is also taken up by Bergson. Intuitively we know we chose freely, but analysis falsely supports the idea that our actions are causally determined. Bergson appeals more to the strain of romantic individualism which we saw in the very different philosophy of Rousseau than he appeals to the empiricist tradition which he claims for his own.[2]

Whitehead: Persons as processes

The Romantic poets would have agreed with Bergson that science leaves something crucial out of its account of the universe. Expressing his agreement with this tendency in Romanticism, represented in the person of Wordsworth, Alfred North Whitehead says, "neither physical nature nor life can be understood unless we fuse them together as essential factors in the composition of really real things whose interconnections and individual characters constitute the universe."[3] Scientific method involves separating objects and processes from the whole, breaking them down and isolating them for study. This has led to rapid improvement of our ability to manipulate our environment through the prediction and control of events. While it was not so clear in Wordsworth's time that we were destroying the whole of our environment in our attempt to dominate nature, it was already evident that we were destroying ourselves in another way by becoming divorced from nature. Later Whitehead was to take up in the realm of systematic philosophy Wordsworth's theme of holism—the inclusion of the spiritual and the moral as well as the Analytical knowledge of our world. Whitehead developed a philosophical system in which he emphasized process as opposed to isolated objects, and he sought to understand the interconnection of all things.

As with Bergson's system, perhaps one cannot understand Whitehead piecemeal, but for our present purposes what is of interest is that, like Bergson, rather than trying to force persons into the procrustean bed of science, Whitehead takes our experience of ourselves as fundamental and understands other things in terms of that experience. Whitehead tells us that he is closely concerned with what Bergson calls "intuition."[4] What we experience is constant change. We are processes. Rather than a universe populated with static objects, Whitehead presents to us a universe which is like a person on a grander scale. This is a theme we have seen interwoven in other systems. Rather than objects Whitehead speaks of actual occasions which are, roughly, like our experiences, dynamic processes. Thus, instead of reducing persons to aggregates of static, analysable physical objects of the sort that we postulate in order to pursue our scientific aims, Whitehead sees all of nature as an aggregate of actual occasions.[5]

Seeing persons, and indeed anything, as if what science says about them is literally true is, for Whitehead, to commit the fallacy of misplaced concreteness. That is to say, we take the intellectual abstractions of science and treat them as if they were concrete things. The idea that there are bits of matter, for instance, at particular spatio-temporal locations is an example of this fallacy. These bits of matter are merely abstractions, not concrete parts of reality. Where persons are concerned, this fallacy leads to problems like the problem of the interaction of mind and body.

For Whitehead, there is no problem, since mind and body are merely abstractions, not real, static entities which must somehow be shown to interact. They are really just abstractions from the flow of experience, from the actual occasions which make up the whole of the universe. Whitehead speaks of "societies" of actual occasions which we can think of as, roughly, sets of processes. Mind and body are such societies. Just as the body politic is an abstraction, the body of a particular person is an abstraction, a way of looking at a particular set of processes.[6] Mind and body are interconnected, then, just as all things are, for they are composed of interpenetrating processes within the large process which is the universe. More prosaically, mind and body are just different ways we have of looking at our experience. "It is a matter of pure convention as to which of our experiential activities we term mental and which physical."[7] The experiences are real. Mind and body are things we make up to organize our thinking about the experiences. Persons, too, are societies of actual occasions, like eddies in the stream of the universe.

Application to Daphne's case

Bergson and Whitehead probably would find the puzzles about whether Daphne is a person and whether she is the same person she was prior to her illness both puzzles resulting from a failure to see the limits of the conceptual scheme which works well only for scientific investigation. If we populate our universe not with individual entities but with actual occasions known by intuition, then it is merely a conventional matter how we solve our puzzles about Daphne. What is important is not what we call Daphne, but how we understand her changes and her current needs. Standing in her shoes is the task.

What I like about Bergson and Whitehead

The idea that we take our self-knowledge not as a goal but as a starting point interests me. It does seem that I have a certain intimate knowledge of myself that I can only in imagination have of other people or of other things. The notion of people and things as processes seems right from this perspective.

Contemporary Continental Philosophy

The two main schools in contemporary philosophy are often labelled the "Analytic" and "Continental" schools. The Analytic School is the main contender in Britain and North America— although there are many philosophers on the continent who would consider themselves part of this school as there are many continental philosophers who do not reside in continental Europe. Some British and North American philosophers, like Whitehead, defy classification. In any case, the Analytic School is the school I was brought up in. Consequently I am about to give relatively short shrift to the contemporary continental philosophers on the other side of a methodological chasm. As far as I can, however, I will try to draw out some of the influences of this important group of philosophers on our current thinking, on the Analytic side of the chasm, concerning persons. At the very least, like the foregoing historical introduction, this can serve my readers as a menu of ideas. If you find something which strikes you, you will at least know who to read to follow it up in more detail than I can present in this brief survey.

As to the methodological chasm between the schools, it is wide indeed. It is, moreover, only fair to warn those of you who have not yet encountered the chasm of which I speak that many in the Analytic School applaud the sentiments of David Berlinski, "Although great soupy volumes pour off the European presses with the inevitability of death, much of what results calls to mind only the perfect vacuum."[8] How you take this warning about soup, as an indictment of the Analytic School's attempts at clarity or of the Continental School's attempts at profundity will depend on your own predilections. The soup results, according to Leslie Stevenson, from length, repetitiousness, and "a word-spinning delight in the abstract noun, the elusive metaphor, and the unresolved paradox,"[9] but Stevenson thinks that Sartre's *Being And Nothingness*, for example, contains important and deep analyses. I think that Stevenson is right about the continental philosophers having insights worth our attention, but it is not merely a difference in style which separates the two schools. Continental philosophers, at the very least, adopt a different methodology to investigate philosophical questions, and sometimes they are engaged in a wholly different project to that of Analytic philosophers.

Analytic philosophers seek, through objective, logical, rational inquiry, to understand our fundamental concepts. Some philosophers who were at least geographically continental, like Husserl, Brentano, and Meinong, for example, would accept this as their project as well. Others, like Sartre and Heidegger, I suspect, adopt a much more literary approach, even a poetic one. The very word-play, metaphors, and repetition that annoy Stevenson and outrage Berlinski are their means to lead their readers to truths which they may take to be ineffable in the precise language of the Analytic School. The objectivity which Analytic philosophers seek is thought by the continentals to be fool's gold. That is why, like mystics and poets, continental philosophers allow themselves the statement of an unresolved paradox or two in their immense tomes. They seek to achieve with the weight of words what the weight of argument can never achieve. While the Analytic School accuses the Continental School of betraying reason, the Continental School retorts that profundity will not be found within the limits of rational analysis. Since it takes a fair chunk of one's life spent in study to read either school well, it is best to find out early on which kind of method attracts you most.

The roots, at least, of the Continental School are partly shared with those of the Analytic School. Both recognize the importance of the philosophers mentioned in the historical survey of previous chapters. Kierkegaard, however, is of seminal importance for the continental philosophers since he introduces most of the themes of the existentialists. Along with existentialism, phenomenology—the creation of Edmund Husserl—is a key element in the thinking of many of the philosophers on the continent. I consequently begin my too brief exposition of the contributions of the Continental School to our topic with a look at Husserl's phenomenology.

Husserl: Phenomenology

Husserl, who began his career as a mathematician, has a painstaking and highly technical style of philosophizing which has not gained him many readers outside academic circles. This is in marked contrast to Jean-Paul Sartre, who has made his ideas accessible through his literary work as well as in stylistically more entertaining philosophical writings. Nonetheless, Husserl's influence is much felt among us even in lay circles, since it has been transmitted through Sartre and other widely read existentialists, though this is not to say that existentialists generally agree with Husserl in detail. Husserl's influence spread well beyond philosophy, especially in psychology and theology, but in the human sciences generally. What we think of as persons now cannot but be affected by so pervasive an influence.

Although Husserl is moved, like the pragmatists, and like the existentialists, by a reaction to the excessive claims of science to understand us, he is very unlike the pragmatists and existentialists in one key respect. They recommend renouncing the role of spectator and passionately engaging the world through decision and commitment. Husserl seeks, by contrast, to give a rigorous foundation to philosophy by utterly detaching himself from the world. His motive, however, is to save human reason from being misled by a naive scientific naturalism which erroneously seeks to reduce even the spiritual aspects of persons to physical nature.[10] From Husserl's point of view, if we are to understand ourselves, we must adopt a method quite different from that of the natural sciences, and we must give up many of the presuppositions of these sciences.

Science presupposes, for instance, observable objects existing independently of the persons observing them. Husserl wants to restrict attention to the evidence we actually have without such presuppositions; that evidence is our pre-scientific experience. The phenomena of experience—without any assumptions about their causal or other relations to things outside the experiencing Ego—are the data of the phenomenologist. Phenomenology is, according to its inventor, the science of phenomena. It will not replace the other sciences but will provide an adequate basis for their conduct. Husserl explains, in great detail, a method of looking at the phenomena without the influence of all of our assumptions about where they come from and what they represent. This method of *epoche* or bracketing allows us to bracket out all distracting influences and observe the pure phenomena. Husserl tells us in the introduction to *Ideas* that it will take a lot of work to follow the method he outlines, that it is not everyone's cup of tea, but that we should not knock it until we have tried it.[11]

Husserl tells us that we will find, employing *epoche*, that consciousness is always directed to something and that there is always present the experiencing subject or Ego. We will attend to the full richness of our experience, not merely to the limited abstractions of science. We will see that this experience is quite independent of the existence of a world external to the experiencing Ego.[12] Our own consciousness and intentionality, the direction of consciousness to things of which we are conscious, are the fundamental facts to which we have access, not the supposed objective facts of science. These latter are really abstractions, extrapolations from our fundamental experience. Western man is in a crisis, according to Husserl, by virtue of taking science to be the sole source of truth.[13] This direction away from the human and personal to things outside ourselves cuts us off from the basis of knowledge, our own experience. We have to look inward again. This emphasis on the subjective elements of experience and their aspects ignored by natural science is part of what endears Husserl to the existentialist tradition. Nonetheless, there is a strain against that tradition which becomes evident when we see just how restricted is the realm explored by means of *epoche*.

Most of the things that philosophers have taken an interest in are excluded from our attention through *epoche*. This method is only for the study of particular pure experiences, "immanental essences," and is of no use for the study of things we do not meet in pure experience devoid of assumptions. The terms "man," "soul," and "person," are explicitly mentioned as referring to essences which are beyond the pale of phenomenology.[14] These are the kinds of things we can investigate only after we have established the firm foundation needed through the study of our basic experience.

Persons are, for Husserl, transcendental essences; that is, they are not met in our fundamental experience. Neither is the Ego, but it is always there having the experience. We have earlier seen Hume's denial that he can find an Ego in himself. What Husserl has to say in answer to Hume is expressed in a way congenial to both the poet and the mathematician:

> The Ego appears to be permanently, even necessarily, there, and this permanence is obviously not that of a stolid unshifting experience, of a "fixed idea." On the contrary, it belongs to every experience that comes and streams past, its "glance" goes "through" every actual *cogito* [act of thinking], and towards the object. This visual ray changes with every *cogito*, shooting forth afresh with each new one as it comes, and disappearing with it. But the Ego remains self-identical. (156)

There is still a debate in current philosophy about the existence of this Ego. The importance of intentionality, however, is almost universally accepted when the topic of persons arises. Husserl teaches that acts of consciousness are intentional, meaning that they are directed to something.

Persons, for some philosophers, simply are the sort of Ego of which Husserl spoke. Husserl himself, however, thought they were a more complicated kind of thing to be understood only after an ontology (a theory of objects) and an epistemology (a theory of knowledge) had been established phenomenologically as the underpinning of the philosophical and scientific work to be done on persons. He had the effect of turning our attention from the exclusively empirical scientific outlook on persons to the things we can know only subjectively.

Heidegger: Being towards death

Jaspers, Marcel, and Heidegger write in such difficult styles that they seem intent on confirming the saying that the philosopher and the poet are neighbours on separate mountains. Kierkegaard, Jaspers, and Marcel retain a religious motivation for their philosophy, while Heidegger departs from this. Throughout these existentialist writings one finds an emphasis on the importance and uniqueness of the individual person and the theme taken up by Husserl of the distinction of philosophy from science. Personal self-realization is the main focus in Jaspers and Marcel. Heidegger set for himself the question of the nature of Being and produced, in *Being and Time*, one of the most revered works among existentialists.

Heidegger's question is rather more general than our present topic, but his way to an answer it is through the elucidation of persons' awareness of themselves. As did others in his tradition, Heidegger inveighed against the objectification of persons who cannot be understood in the way that the objects of scientific study can be known. The attempt to define "person" by listing the essential properties that a thing must have to be a person is, for Heidegger, thoroughly wrongheaded. To avoid this error of treating persons as definable objects, Heidegger coins his own word to avoid the use of "person," "man," or "human being," which all carry with them the taint of previous philosophy's mistakes. Instead, Heidegger uses "Dasein" which literally translated means "being there." I will stick to using "person" with apologies to Heideggerians. For Heidegger, to understand what Being is, one must understand how a person has being. Like most philosophers on this side of the Analytic/Continental chasm, I do not have too much patience for Being with a capital B. While I cannot be counted on to give a totally sympathetic account of Heidegger's project and achievements, I do wish to draw out some of the themes which he attached to our contemporary concepts of a person.

Three things that Heidegger associates with a person (Dasein) are understanding, mood, and discourse.[15] It is tempting to read Heidegger as treating the capacity for these as essential to the existence of persons, but this would be contrary to his claim that no essence can be given. Under the general head of "understanding" Heidegger speaks of the way in which particular things are meaningful to us in terms of purposes. We encounter things in the world as tools. What they are depends on our network of purposes. Thus the world is a characteristic of the person rather than the person being a *thing* in the world. Each of us has a world which depends on our purposes. Moreover, the mood, say of despair or joy, with which we encounter things will affect as well the way they exist for us. Before we can understand or feel about an object in some way, however, we must be able to talk about it. Thus the world depends on persons, on their understanding, mood, and discourse.

Heidegger teaches that we prepare ourselves to understand Being when we recognize our own temporality, when we recognize that we are living towards our deaths, in the dread of annihilation. The capacity of persons under the heading of mood seems to be most important as a capacity for dread and care. Without these to reveal to us the "nothingness" within us and our temporal finitude, we cannot know what we really are. Only if we recognize our limitations can we live authentically. To live so is to affirm what we really are and live accordingly, not to deceive ourselves with thoughts of immortality or actions appropriate to some other kinds of being than what we are.[16] Understanding our own way of being in this world is a key, for Heidegger, to understanding Being in general.[17]

If indeed the world depends on persons, then there are many worlds. In each one what constitutes a person may be different from what does so in the other worlds. Questions about how we should view or treat others must all have completely subjective answers. The appeal of Heidegger's advice on authenticity, living in the recognition of our own finitude notwithstanding, there are no bounds on what may be justified by such a philosophy. Heidegger's own answer to the question of how to treat others included, as an important part, Nazism. Often this is excused as a naive mistake from which he retreated. Farias argues, however, that Nazism was fully integrated in Heidegger's thought and that he carried it with him to the grave—a good place for it.[18] Be that as it may, it is not clear to me how a subjectivist theory of persons could oppose Nazism or any other doctrine on the grounds of proper treatment of persons. One of the points of discussing persons is to put up the barricades when Nazism and similar doctrines surface.

During the Nazi era destructive experimentation, involuntary "euthanasia," torture, and genocide were carried out on people who had been pushed by loose Nazi theory beyond the pale within which persons were protected. The mentally incompetent were put to death because they were a burden to the state. People were put to death for being critical of Nazism. Individual people were not highly valued. More than the absorption of the individual into the state, however, brought about the Holocaust. The Nazis believed that they could do whatever they wished to the Jews, since they did not consider them full persons. Similarly, the Romans once thought they could treat slaves just as they wished. Slaves were not persons under the law. Settlers in North America, and even some contemporaries in my locale, thought and think of natives of the North American continent as less than persons. Clear thinking about persons is needed as a small but vital part of the rampart that we must erect against such horrific errors.

Sartre: What you do is what you are

Jean-Paul Sartre makes more accessible some of the existentialist doctrines through his literary works, though he also adds considerably to the corpus of inaccessible philosophical writing on existentialist themes. He, like Heidegger, develops an atheistic form of existentialism[19] and, like Heidegger, is influenced by Husserl's phenomenology. A major difference between them is in the focus of their interests. For Heidegger, understanding the person in the world is merely a means to the central question of what Being is. Sartre, however, makes the individual person his main concern.

Action is foremost in Sartre's analysis of persons. It is what we do that is important. Think of the characters in *Huis Clos* if you have read that play. Their hell is to look back on their actions and to be constantly reminded by one another that they failed to come up to their own personal standards. Through these reminders of their own inauthenticity they are denied the temporary solace of self-deception. They must contemplate what they did. To point out Sartre's emphasis on action is not to say that Sartre any more than Heidegger accepts the possibility of defining the concept of a person through consideration of capacities for action or any other characteristics. His motto is, "Existence precedes essence." [20]

To understand this it is interesting to consider the idea of an unnatural act. There are none, as far as Sartre is concerned. There is no pre-existing nature or essence of a person which determines what the individual ought to do. We are completely free to choose, within the limits of physical possibility, what we do, and we are even free to choose the criteria in general according to which we make particular choices. Sartre is an atheist; so he denies that there is any God to foist on us an antecedent nature or essence which would make our action unnatural. First we come into existence, then, after we are able to choose, we make our individual characters or natures. If there were a God, then essence could precede existence, for we could be supplied with a pre-existing pattern of action or purpose to which we ought to conform.

It is tempting to say, paradoxically, that Sartre would say that it is of the essence of a person to be a free agent. The paradox is removed by noticing that "essence" in this claim does not refer to the kind of essence which is preceded by existence in Sartre's motto. The person first exists and then chooses her own pattern of action, values, or purposes—in that sense she chooses her essence. "Essence" in that sense is not a set of defining characteristics like being free, being conscious, or being able to act. Sartre is willing to assert the necessity of various characteristics of persons aside from their being free agents. In this other sense of "essence," in which essences are sets of necessary characteristics, Sartre could admit that there is an essence of persons prior to the existence of individual persons. There are, in other words, characteristics which all persons must have, according to Sartre, to be persons. What he wants to deny is that such characteristics determine what we as individuals do or ought to do. Our actions are free.

These necessary characteristics of persons distinguish people (beings-for-themselves) from objects (beings-in-themselves). A terribly important distinguishing characteristic, dare I say "essential" characteristic, of people, for Sartre, is consciousness. As conscious beings, people, unlike their objects of consciousness, can distinguish themselves from their objects, and choose for themselves the importance and purpose those objects will have. Problems arise, however, when conscious beings contemplate one another. Interpersonal relationships fascinate Sartre and reveal some of the essential or defining characteristics of the concept of a person in his philosophy. An existentialist would prefer to say that they reveal the general framework within which individual persons define themselves, the human condition.

Consciousness, in Sartre's view, is, as with Brentano and Husserl, necessarily directed to something. Sartre also thinks that consciousness makes what is other than itself a mere object. Consequently, two conscious beings who are aware of each other will be trying to make of each other an object rather than a person; "he analyses human life as a perpetual attempt to achieve the logically impossible," says Stevenson in great irritation, and he goes on to say that this contradicts Sartre's claims about our freedom since it seems we must try to make other people into mere objects whether we want to or not.[21] Perhaps Sartre could reply that we are not free to exert some superhuman form of consciousness which does not objectify others any more than we are free to fly by flapping our arms. If so, then he thinks he has discovered some of our mental limits. This is one of several tantalizing suggestions about the concept of a persons which Sartre makes, but I find that closer examination of such works as *Being And Nothingness*[22] does not help to clarify it. Sartre's writing often seems like an enormous impressionist canvas. It does not usually help to understand the work to look at it under a magnifying glass. We are left then with the suggestion that one limit on all persons is that they cannot see other persons as persons. You may have some dark moods if you come to believe this. In any case, it is in the realm of intuitive psychology more than philosophy.

Most philosophical theories about persons either begin from or end in moral pronouncements about what persons ought to do. Sartre has denied that there is anything in the nature of persons that can determine what we ought to do. We each of us must choose our own moral values. Sartre does, however, follow earlier existentialists in condemning inauthenticity, bad faith, or self-deception. These occur, for instance, when a person wants to be a hero but acts in a cowardly way and then pretends that the action was beyond her control. Excuses like, "I was overcome by subconscious forces," or "I didn't know what I was doing," are despised by Sartre. She who gives such excuses is deceiving herself; she is in bad faith.

It seems, then, that while Sartre is willing to promulgate no particular moral view, he does offer a criterion for the acceptability of any moral view. One must adopt it in good faith. The particular standards of action are totally relative to the individual. Sartre cannot condemn Hitler as acting against absolute standards but only as acting against Sartre's personal standards, though in choosing standards for himself, Sartre chooses them for all. As long as Hitler did the same and lived by his chosen standards, Sartre would not despise him for being in bad faith. If, however, Mother Teresa undertook her charitable work in bad faith pretending, say, that she was forced to do it by God, then Sartre would find her life contemptible. This is another feature of Sartre's view to which Stevenson objects,[23] but I believe Sartre would just bite the bullet and accept these consequences. Mother Teresa would be more contemptible than Hitler if the former but not the latter were inauthentic.

Stevenson, like many of us who tear our hair out reading Sartre's philosophical writings, still believes "there is something important to learn from Sartre's deep analysis of how the very notion of consciousness involves that of freedom....The vast verbiage of his philosophy issues ultimately in a directly practical and intimate challenge to us all, to become more truly self-aware and to exercise our power of changing ourselves."[24]

Application to Daphne's case

The themes that the continental philosophers emphasize seem inapplicable to someone who cannot make choices or express them. Like Bergson and Whitehead the continentals would encourage us to drop the conceptual schemes in which our puzzles occur. They tend, nonetheless, to emphasize the relativity or even subjectivity of conceptual frameworks. There is no such thing as "the nature of persons" to which we may appeal to understand Daphne or our role with regard to her. It turns out to be our choice as to Daphne's status that we must examine. She may not be, in Sartre's terms, a being for herself, free, conscious, and able to act. In deciding how to think of Daphne as a being in herself we must choose authentically, not pretending that there is some essence which keeps her in continuation despite our own choices. In some ways, this seems just like saying that Daphne is not a person, since we others must choose for her.

What I like about the Continental School

Husserl makes sense when he speaks of the Ego as that which belongs to every experience without itself being experienced, like the eye which sees but does not see itself except through reflection. What sort of mirror, if any, would allow the Ego to experience itself? Here the analogy breaks down. The reiteration of the importance by Husserl and his school of the role of our subjective knowledge and experience is, in any case, salutary.

The Heiddegerian ideal of living authentically, in recognition of our own finitude, is useful. It leads into Sartre's denial of any human nature to which we must conform, a radical kind of freedom to choose what we are. Sartre's analysis may be deep, but it is muddy. The philosophical problem he leaves us is to see whether his challenge makes sense. Are we free in a way which allows us to change our characters and our moods? Can we overcome the influence of our cultures? I believe that Sartre has, in fact, insightfully described a kind of person, at least in broad brush strokes. I hope, however, that we who fit the description can, in special circumstances, overcome the tendency to objectify other persons and ourselves, for example, when we genuinely love. Sartre might say that I misunderstand entirely the limits on consciousness. My initial reply is that I see the limits of freedom differently, but that leads to a story to be told after this brief survey of contemporary philosophy.

Foucault and Derrida omitted

More recent philosophy in Europe has departed even further from the school in which I find myself. There is a tendency to move entirely from the philosophical method to that of literary criticism and beyond. This is the natural outcome of complete subjectivism. Truth becomes a matter of taste. Rorty describes the new method as creatively ignoring one's opponents. Rather than offering arguments, one develops a new vocabulary and attempts to make one's opponents' vocabulary look bad.[25] Foucault and Derrida may be adopting such a method. I leave them out of discussion here. Some may find that an unforgivable omission, but I can only refer my readers to these authors in the original. They, like poets, defy summary.

NINE
Analytic Founding Fathers

Searching for Precision and Clarity

The group of philosophers which has come to be called "the Analytic School" is very diverse as regards doctrine and even divided with respect to method. Stumpf [1] prefers to call it a "movement" to warn of this diversity. One can think of Analytic philosophy as, in part, a reaction to the previous trends in philosophy, many of which were thought to be extremely unclear in their language, ignorant of or opposed to science, mystical, religious, driven by emotion, and divorced from common sense. While they are very suspicious of the heavily metaphorical language of philosophers outside their group, Analytic philosophers do have a metaphor which tips one off to their philosophical ideals; they like to call themselves "hard-headed." It may be read off from what they oppose that Analytic philosophers emphasize the role of language in determining thought and theory, and they demand clear and precise formulations of philosophical theory. Analytic philosophers often feel bound to take science and common sense seriously, explaining carefully any departures therefrom. On the other hand, they rarely think that common sense is sensible. Common sense is, however, a starting point, not something to be ignored. They often find their theoretical starting points in the science of their day rather than in religion or mysticism. Thoroughly argued iconoclasm is much admired in this school. Many within the Analytic fold are the intellectual heirs of David Hume. Usually they eschew grand metaphysical systems in favour of logical and linguistic analyses of concepts in a context much more narrowly circumscribed than a worldview. The task they set themselves is mainly clarification of the logic and language of science and the everyday conceptual framework.

In this, the last decade of the twentieth century, the edges of the Continental and Analytic Schools tend to blur into one another. In the early part of this century, however, the distinction between schools was much more crisp. The Analytic philosophers universally conceived of themselves as revolutionaries casting out the old order of philosophers, whom they thought of as attempting to go beyond the scope of human knowledge in their metaphysical speculations. These early Analytic philosophers divided into two main streams. One included Bertrand Russell, the early Wittgenstein, and Rudolph Carnap, who thought of formal logic as providing a major key to philosophic understanding. Another stream flowed from Moore, the later Wittgenstein,

---

Notes to Chapter Nine are on pp. 321-22.

and Austin, who thought that in ordinary language the collective wisdom of the culture was to be discovered and improved upon. Philosophers in both streams thought that most of the puzzles of past philosophers and their continental contemporaries could be dissolved in the cleansing acid of logical or linguistic analysis. The single most influential source of this way of thinking is the philosopher I shall deal with first in this school, Bertrand Russell.

Russell: Aiming for scientific objectivity about persons

Some of you may have, on the basis of the foregoing remarks on Analytic philosophy, come to expect that Analytic philosophers would be opposed to everything you hold dear. That is why I begin with Bertrand Russell, a great humanitarian, political activist, and passionate social reformer. It is true that he wished to destroy the sort of philosophy that had led to systems of thought in terms of which some people had found their purpose in life, but he did so because he thought these folk were being led down the garden path. As he puts it,

> Philosophy cannot itself determine the ends of life, but it can free us from the tyranny of prejudice and from distortions due to a narrow view. Love, beauty, knowledge, and joy of life: these things retain their lustre however wide our purview. And if philosophy can help us to feel the value of these things, it will have played its part in man's collective work of bringing light into a world of darkness.[2]

Russell believed that prior philosophers had been led to an unfortunately narrow view of the universe and our place in it by the insufficiency of their tools. He believed that science and mathematics, including the new kind of formal logic, a system of which he and Whitehead had pioneered in *Principia Mathematica*, would open up a great many alternative conceptions where earlier thinkers had seen but one possibility.

There is an apocryphal story about Hegel speaking to an historian who told Hegel that Hegel's system did not agree with the facts of history. Hegel is reputed to have replied, "So much the worse for the facts." This story is used to undermine faith in systems which purport to tell us what life and the universe are all about—systems which admit only one possible way that we and our world might be. The story is designed to move us towards Russell's means of proceeding: when the facts and theory collide, abandon the theory. For this reason, we do not find one theory but a great series of them associated with Russell over his long and incredibly prolific career. Russell makes no apologies for being a moving target. He did not think, as many of his predecessors apparently did, that he had hit upon the absolute truth about us and our universe or that he merely had to explicate his findings in a grand system which could never be fundamentally altered. He adopted instead the attitude of the scientist who tries for some approximation to the truth in his hypotheses, puts them to the test, and abandons them when they cease to come up to scratch.

Russell did not focus on the concept of person in the detailed way that some of his contemporaries like Strawson and Ayer did. The positions, however, which Russell fearlessly took, at a time when they were not at all popular, have had a great influence on the way those philosophers and philosophers since have approached concepts of a person. In particular Russell cast suspicion on the method of grand system-building of the kind exemplified in Kant and Hegel. We have earlier noted that Kant exerted a great influence on thinking about persons. "Kant has the reputation of being the greatest of modern philosophers," says Russell, "but to my mind he was a mere misfortune."[3] Understand that Russell is speaking of one of the few philosophers who is revered on both sides of the Analytic/continental chasm. One certainly sees the iconconclasm here, but this is not mere opinion, Russell's reasons are given for your assessment. In the passage just quoted, Russell is defending Hume's views on induction against those of Kant, but I will leave you to read those in the original if you wish. What I turn to now is another attack of Russell on Kant which affects the central position given to persons with respect to the nature of time and space. It is typical of Russell's wish to preserve a kind of objectivity of the universe outside of people's minds.

Kant argued that space, conceived as something existing objectively outside the observer, must be infinite and that space cannot be infinite. He concluded that, because our concept of space leads us to contradictory results, space was not objective after all, but subjective. Space is in the eye of the beholder. In such a metaphysical view, the person is elevated to being, in effect, the creator of space. Russell informs us concerning space that "the non-Euclideans refuted the argument that it must be infinite, and Georg Cantor refuted the argument that it cannot be."[4] Russell here brings mathematics to bear on a former philosophical stronghold. This is characteristic of Russell and it is his way of bearing out the point made in the opening quotation. Earlier philosophy narrowed our view to one possibility only, in this instance, that space is subjective, a feature of persons. Russell wants to use mathematics and science to undo the restrictive arguments of systematizers like Kant in order to show that there are many possibilities for the way things are and consequently for the way people are. We have to keep our views about reality constantly open to revision in the face of new experience and new scientific and mathematical results. This makes philosophy quite a different discipline to what is being done under the name in the Continental School and what had been done in much of philosophy prior to the twentieth century.

What emerges in the background of the various views Russell adopts as he confronts new arguments and scientific results is a commitment to a generally Humean empiricism. One might expect then that persons would be analyzed away, and to some extent this expectation is realized. Russell certainly is attracted to a bundle theory of individuals on which individuals of any kind, persons, cats, pumpkins, electrons, are to be considered bundles of properties. By denying any Aristotelian substance in which the properties inhere, Russell, in his later works, seems to be leaving little room for a soul or a Cartesian Ego.[5] Nor is the later Russell sympathetic to the mind/matter distinction championed by Descartes. For a while, he calls himself a "neutral monist," that is, one who accepts only one kind of stuff out of which what we normally call "mind" and what we call "matter" is made. There is, however, a distinction in the way we know the two, for "mental events and their qualities can be known without inference, physical events are known only as regards their space-time structure."[6] To clarify Russell's metaphysical view that persons are special organizations of some of the basic things of which everything is made, we need to have a better conception of these basic things.

The philosophical question of what the basic things are is handled in a part of philosophy called "Ontology." Russell's ontology changed considerably over his long career. In the famous, overconfidently titled volume, *The Problems of Philosophy*, he accepted a dualist ontology in which mind and matter were composed of different fundamental objects. Among the physical objects were sense data, "things that were immediately known in sensation," and among mental entities were sensations or experiences.[7] Examples of sense data are patches of colour in one's visual field and the sounds one hears. Russell seemed to think of persons as bodies with associated Egos which sensed the sense data emanating from objects and inductively inferred the existence of those objects.[8] Soon Russell moved to using sense data as the fundamental objects out of which objects external to the mind were constructed, an idea followed up by Carnap.[9] Because he had problems with the nature of the Ego and of sense data, Russell eventually abandoned both ideas, trying to solve his difficulties by the move, in his middle period, to neutral monism. This was an attempt to construct both mental and physical objects out of components which were neither mental nor physical but neutral.[10]

Quine tells us that "Neutrality here has a bias, as it often has in politics; Russell's neutral particulars are on the side of sense data."[11] The status of sense data, mental or physical, was always somewhat unclear, though more physical than not in Russell's treatment. It seems then that Russell, and Analytic philosophy with him, took a step towards materialism. By 1927 he had taken another step inasmuch as he began to analyze sensations as physical occurrences in the nervous system of observers.[12] The view of persons which emerges gets farther and farther from that which had reigned since Descartes of a non-physical being with a physical body at its disposal.

After Russell abandoned the Ego, as Hume had done, and abandoned sense data which were sensed by the Ego, Russell needed a new word for his neutral particulars (fundamental objects that were neither mental nor physical) and he called them "sensa" (690). Pears calls them "appearances" which gives us some handle on what they are, but we must not assume that they are appearances to a person but only things which, if a person were to be able to sense them, would cause something to appear to that person. They are the causes of sensation but not necessarily sensed. Using the word "appearances" for "sensa," Pears sums up neutral monism neatly:

> according to neutral monism appearances are grouped in one way to form physical objects and in another way to form minds. In order to get a physical object, you take all the appearances that radiate outwards from its position in physical space. In order to get a mind, you take all the appearances that start from surrounding objects and converge on its position in physical space. The difference is based on the distinction between input and output. (690)

This is very strange from the point of view of common sense. If I see a red rubber ball, I might think that the appearances of redness, roundness, flexibility and others which it has are somehow given off by something underlying the appearances. Aristotle called the underlying thing "substance." Russell thinks of the ball, however, as just this radiating group of appearances. A person's mind, moreover, at least as far as perception is concerned, becomes a special group of appearances which are not radiating outwards but which are interrelated with one another, causing what we think of as images and memories. Persons are then a combination of the body, which is a group of appearances radiating outwards, and a mind, which is a group of appearances converging on the place where the person's body is. Belief, desire, and action are explained neurologically and behaviouristically by the latter-day Russell (690-91).

Here we see the complete opposite number to continental philosophy which thinks of science as hopelessly inadequate to understanding persons and which points philosophy inward to the knowledge of self gained by introspection. Russell does not ignore introspection, but he tries to balance what that shows him with the results of physics, psychology and other sciences. He wields Occam's razor with zest; this razor is a minimalist principle common in philosophy: entities are not to be multiplied beyond necessity. Russell tries to eliminate any concept he does not need to explain the facts he gets from introspection and from the examination of the world around him. Ideas like that of substance or Being are quickly lopped off as unnecessary appendages.

There is much that is problematic in these views. In particular, it is difficult to see how one can preserve the things Russell promised us in the opening quotation to this section. One is reminded of the sharp-toothed old saw, "The grass never grows green again on ground touched by Analytic philosophy." How can bundles of appearances which are in no ontological way distinct from physical bundles find joy in life, love, knowledge, and values? The only thing which distinguishes persons from trees seems to be our being receivers of appearances rather than just senders. Actually, even trees might receive appearances in a limited way. We are just different kinds of bundles or different sorts of causal networks from trees. Trees might react to incident light by photosynthesis while we might react to a similar appearance by producing images, memories, and behaviour—maybe getting out the suntan lotion. We are more complex, perhaps, but still causal, material systems like the trees.

Of the lofty things mentioned in the opening quotation of this section (joy, love, knowledge, and values) knowledge is the one Russell spends the most time analyzing. The theories of knowledge which he adopts are empiricist theories which vary according to what is doing the knowing. When there are still Egos around in Russell's developing philosophy, they are acquainted with the external objects through sense data. We develop certain beliefs about the objects external to the mind and try to confirm them by seeing what other data we can get experimentally.

At the other extreme of a continuum of views, when Egos have been lopped off by Occam's razor, knowledge is still understood in terms of confirmation of beliefs, but belief or assent to propositions is understood in terms of feelings the person has (691). Love and joy, are of course in this affective realm, and values as it turns out are, on Russell's view, also dependent on feelings, for he is an emotivist in ethics. "Since no way can be even imagined for deciding a difference as to values, the conclusion is forced upon us that the difference is one of tastes, not one as to any objective truth."[13] To call an action good or bad is not to make a claim to knowledge but to say how we feel about it.

Perhaps emotive feelings, like sensations, would be understood by Russell in terms of neurology in his later materialist period. In any case he thought of persons as causally determined physical subsystems of a physically determined universe. "I am persuaded that the behaviour of the human body is governed completely by the laws of physics, and could be worked out by a Laplacean calculator. I say this in spite of the talk of Eddington and others about atomic free will, which I regard as mere anti-Bolshevik propaganda."[14] It seems there is no room for personal freedom. Not only do we get subjectivism in ethics from Russell, but we are treated to determinism as well. By an enormously different route he brings us to the same conclusions about people as, for instance, Schopenhauer.

As for metaphysical views, what emerges in Russell's later writings is a view of persons which is anathema to many because of its materialist foundation but which supports, from Russell's standpoint, many of those sorts of things which the anti-materialist values. Witness the opening quotation to this section. Those who feel this is a cheat will thunder away about the reduction of such precious things as love and values to neurological features of material things. One can see Russell with his characteristic twinkle and mischievous smile saying, "I am quite prepared to listen. What more do you think these things are?" Anything which is unclear or contradictory in response to this question would be summarily dismissed.

On both sides of the philosophical chasm, in the twentieth century, persons have been changed into things which are hardly recognizable to earlier philosophers. Sartre's beings-for-themselves and Russell's irradiations and convergences of appearances are not the sorts of things we once thought ourselves to be. Absolutism has taken a beating as a consequence; both Sartre and Russell makes ethics subjectivist. On the other hand while contemporary philosophers sometimes agree on ending or starting points in their investigations—both Husserl and Russell take our simplest experiences to be fundamentally important for starters—the routes they take us between points are not just different in direction but in the means of transport. Even within schools we see vast differences. This is evident as we move from Russell to his close associate, the formidable Wittgenstein.

Application to Daphne's case

Daphne is, from Russell's point of view, no different in kind to other persons. She is the centre of a vortex of appearances, as far as her "mental' life is concerned, and a radiation of appearances physically. Her neurological disease has, of course, limited her behaviour to a very small repertoire compared to what it was formerly. Like any of us, she is an ongoing series of causes and effects in a material universe. If we wish to use the word "person" to speak of Daphne in some moral sense, then we are merely expressing emotions, not stating facts. These emotions are themselves determined by neurological causes.

What I like about Russell

Russell shows us what we can get if we leave most of the poetry out of our philosophy of persons. Perhaps he has thrown the baby out with the bathwater, but the water was extremely muddy. The trick is to get the baby back, but not the mud. The attempt to work with an ontology of appearances is interesting. Egos and substances, such mysterious things, are not needed if we can make sense of appearances as independently existing entities without the need of anyone to whom they are appearances.

Wittgenstein: A different disappearance of persons

With regard to the relation of words to non-verbal facts, Russell tells us, there is a type of philosopher who maintains that there is knowledge not expressible in words, and who uses words to tell us what this knowledge is. "These include the mystics, Bergson, and Wittgenstein; also certain aspects of Hegel and Bradley."[15] Wittgenstein speaks of using expressions as a ladder to climb to an understanding from which height we can see the expressions as nonsense, and throw the ladder away.[16] This ladder-heaving view Russell dismisses as contradictory.[17] Nonetheless, Russell avers that "Mr. Wittgenstein's *Tractatus Logico- Philosophicus*, whether or not it prove to give the ultimate truth on the matters with which it deals, certainly deserves, by its breadth and scope and profundity, to be considered an important event in the philosophical world."[18] Apparently, even for those who value his work highly, Wittgenstein is a terribly controversial figure in philosophy.

Like Russell, Wittgenstein dallied for a time with an ontology of facts; that is to say, he thought facts were the basic things of which the world was composed. Like Russell, Wittgenstein thought that the world was mirrored by a certain system of logic. Logical atomism was what Russell called this theory. Language consists of propositions which can be broken down, ultimately, into atomic propositions. These correspond to simple facts about the world. All the complexity of the world can be expressed in terms of the atomic propositions combined according to logical operations. In such a view of the world, the self tends to get reduced to a group of facts concerning behaviour and neurology. We have seen this sort of materialist reduction in Russell's view of the mind. Russell is an heir to Hume, and so his student, Wittgenstein seems at first glance. Wittgenstein puts the disappearance of the self this way:

> There is no such thing as the subject that thinks or entertains ideas.
>
> If I wrote a book called *The World as I found it*, I should have to include a report on my body, and should have to say which parts were subordinate to my will, and which were not, etc., this being a method of isolating the subject, or rather of showing that in an important sense there is no subject; for it alone could *not* be mentioned in that book.
>
> The subject does not belong to the world: rather, it is a limit of the world.[19]

As with the original Humean dissolution of the self, the immediate question arises, does this not reduce to absurdity the method which does the dissolving? It does seem to be the solvent, logical atomism, not the concept of the self which is endangered by such conclusions. If one insists on viewing the world through a form of empiricism that only a logician could love, then one will not find oneself. Nonetheless, the idea that the self is a limit of the world rather than a thing in the world may have important uses. It is reminiscent of Heidegger's seeing but unseen Ego. Perhaps the appearance of disappearance is misleading. From an objective point of view the self is not in the world, but subjectively it is the perceiver of the world.

The person left after Wittgenstein's *Tractatus* has done its work is a combination of a body and any other things which can be described as facts in the world plus an encircling limit or self. One has to remember, however, that Wittgenstein is speaking of the world as *he* found it, not simply the world. The self then is the limit of a person's own version of the world, not necessarily of *the* world. For solipsists this comes to the same thing, but for the rest of us, what Wittgenstein has really said is that a self is the limit of a person's world. To know yourself, you must know what, from your point of view, exists. The self is like a vanishing point, a point of perspective from which the world is drawn but not something in the picture.

Wittgenstein is often treated as two philosophers, the early and the later Wittgenstein roughly corresponding with the *Tractatus* and *The Philosophical Investigations*.[20] There are in fact some other developments in between these—"later" sometimes means "from the Blue Book onwards"[21]—but there is a remarkable unity through all his work on the topic of the self and the person. What we have is a philosopher who did not mind changing his views, but who developed a skepticism about any objective self through all the changes. The later Wittgenstein abandoned the logical empiricism of the *Tractatus*, which limited attention to atomic propositions as the fundamentally important kind of language. He later thought of language on the model of a tool box with many different types of tools. His earlier view had been restricted to one tool in the box. Wittgenstein did not, however, give up the idea that linguistic analysis is essential to philosophy, nor does the later Wittgenstein bring much cheer to those who found his earlier views of the person somewhat desiccated. In fact, by applying all the tools in the box, Wittgenstein still constructs a view in which there is no place for a self as the referent of "I" (62).

What seems constant through Wittgenstein's thinking on the subject of persons is that thinking of the self as a particular, as the referent of "I" is being misled by grammar. "I" takes the same subject position in a sentence as the sort of expressions which refer to particular physical objects like London Bridge. To think, however, that "I" in the sentence "I am thinking," refers to something is to be mistaken about the use of "I." To illustrate the mistake, consider a foreign guest who is told, "It is cold outside." The guest then asks, "What is this thing that is cold outside, the cat?" The host explains with patience and amusement that she merely meant to say the temperature was low and that "It" does not refer to a particular thing outside. Wittgenstein claims that we are making the same mistake as the foreign guest when we take "I" to refer to something.[22]

Wittgenstein also makes some brief remarks on personal identity in accord with his general concern to dissolve philosophical problems through careful attention to language.[23] We use personal names in the way we do only because of certain contingent facts about ourselves. Our bodies do not usually change quickly; so we can recognize people on the basis of their appearance. Wittgenstein asks us to imagine that we all look alike but that there are different sets of characteristics associated with different bodies, for example a low voice, jerky movements, and grumpy demeanour or a high voice, slow movements, and a mild manner. If the sets of characteristics stayed in sets but migrated from body to body, then we would be likely to use personal names not on the basis of sameness of bodies but to name sets of characteristics. Wittgenstein then discusses Jekyll/Hyde cases and an example aimed at the memory criterion of personal identity. He supposes a man has two separate streams of memory, one active on even days and one active on odd days of his life. These possibilities are used by Wittgenstein to try to persuade his readers that "the *ordinary* use of the word "person" is what one might call a composite use suitable under the ordinary circumstances. "If I assume, as I do, that these circumstances are changed, the application of the term 'person' or 'personality' has thereby changed" (62). We are free to choose, Wittgenstein thinks, how we are to use the terms in these odd circumstances. Thus, concerning the many similar examples that philosophers have used to try to clarify the concept of person, Wittgenstein would say that the examples show nothing more than that we are free to choose, in unusual circumstances, how we are to use "persons." Once the background assumptions are changed from those with which we are familiar, the meaning of "person" is no longer fixed. One can only speculate on what the new usage might be.

This warning of Wittgenstein's about the chameleon quality of the meaning of "person" is seldom taken seriously. Even philosophers frequently treat "person" as meaningful and clear in extraordinary examples. Wittgenstein believes that "there is a great variety of criteria of personal '*identity*'" to be noticed even in ordinary cases.[24] Some contemporary philosophers like Wilkes do seem to appreciate Wittgenstein's point here. Wilkes, who recognizes the difficulty at least insofar as she avoids fictional examples, still treats the word "person" as meaningful in a constant way when dealing with odd cases like that of multiple personality or fugue sates, but perhaps she thinks it is her Aristotelian reconstruction of the meaning of "person" which allows her to do this, stretching as it does to fit these cases as well as the ordinary ones.[25] Against Wilkes and others who try to establish one usage for "person" to fit a wide variety of circumstances, Wittgenstein seems to be claiming that there are many "legitimate heirs" to the ordinary usage of "person." It seems, however, that most philosophers disagree with Wittgenstein or forget his warning.

Application to Daphne's case

The later Wittgenstein would tell us that the answer to our questions about Daphne depend on linguistic usages. If none of the common usages is developed for the purposes of discussing such cases, then we may simply choose a way of using the terms "person" and "identity" in such a case. There is merely a decision about definition to be made, no profound question about who is who or what is a person. Indeed if we wonder whether Daphne's self remains after her decline, we are merely misled by grammar. The self is not an objective entity but a limit on subjective perceptions of the world. Whatever limit Daphne has now is Daphne's self, but this is a very changeable thing, not at all like a Cartesian Ego.

What I like about Wittgenstein

Wittgenstein is clear about the limits of the strange examples which philosophers frequently use to understand such concepts as personal identity. They may reveal to us the ways in which we use language, but they do not reveal what is real or what is possible. His is an interesting idea, the self as a point of perspective outside the picture. If one stares at the picture, like Hume, one of course finds no self.

Logical Positivism

When I was teaching in Europe in the mid-seventies, I noticed that the defenders of the continental style of philosophizing often took it upon themselves to attack the Analytic School by attacking logical positivism. This was exceedingly strange given that, from the point of view of most Analytic philosophers, these continental philosophers were flogging a dead horse. This sect of empiricism had already died the death of a thousand qualifications. It has, however, considerable historical importance and its influences remain.

Logical positivism was the output of a group of philosophers called "The Vienna Circle" on which Wittgenstein was a major influence. To Wittgenstein they attributed their central doctrine, the verification principle, "that the meaning of a proposition is identical with the method of verifying it—that is that a proposition means the set of experiences which are together equivalent to the proposition's being true."[26] In effect, the Vienna Circle interpreted this in such a way as to accept scientific and mathematical statements as meaningful while rejecting any claims which could not be verified by appeal to the five senses or to logic. Logical positivism contains, then, a theory of linguistic meaning according to which much philosophy consists of meaningless verbiage.

The logical positivists were particularly interested in destroying the German idealist tradition. Such proclamations as "The Absolute is beyond time," were thought to be absolute rubbish by the Vienna Circle. More recent philosophy in the Continental School, while often opposed to idealism, tends to make claims in a way that the positivists loved to dismiss, for example, Sartre's claim that existence precedes essence. It is not hard to see why hatred for logical positivism has outlived logical positivism on the continent.

Much of our ordinary talk about persons would also qualify as meaningless by the verification principle. Unfortunately for the logical positivists, the verification principle also is meaningless when judged by its own lights. It is a self-destructive principle. To see this, consider the statement of the principle: *the meaning of a proposition is identical with the method of verifying it.* There is no method of verifying this statement. The two methods the positivists accepted were the empirical method of science and the Analytic method of mathematics. The statement cannot be verified empirically, nor is it an Analytic statement (a statement known to be true or false by logic alone or one reducible to such a statement by the substitution of synonyms for synonyms). Disagreements about how logical positivism was to handle this problem and how it was to evolve eventually dissolved it as a sect into the wider movement of logical empiricism in which such philosophers as Russell operated, philosophers who did not make such rigid demands on meaningful language. While this positivist view is well and truly dead, the legacy of logical positivism is evident in some contemporary Analytic philosophers' work. This influence is neatly summed up by Passmore:

> insofar as it is widely agreed that transcendental metaphysics, if not meaningless, is at least otiose, that philosophers ought to set an example of precision and clarity, that philosophy should make use of technical devices, deriving from logic, in order to solve problems relating to the philosophy of science, that philosophy is not about "the world" but about the language through which men speak about the world, we can detect in contemporary philosophy, at least, the persistence of the spirit which inspired the Vienna Circle. (56)

While Carnap and others in the Vienna Circle might not like talk about being inspired by a spirit, what Passmore says here is meaningful and true. I speak from experience as one who was brought up in a philosophical tradition which fits Passmore's description. One could not speak to many of my teachers about, for example, Sartre's view that persons, of necessity, try to turn each other into objects. At least one could not express the idea without the kind of linguistic explication which Sartre would find otiose.

Logical positivism is sometimes so approximately construed as to include not only those who accepted the verification principle of meaning but quite different philosophers like Moore, Ryle, and Austin who are properly classified not as positivists but as ordinary language philosophers. Unlike their colleagues in the logical empiricist tradition, they laid much less emphasis on the help to be gained from formal logic and much more emphasis on the analysis of ordinary language. The most important member of this group, where the topic of persons is concerned, was Ryle.

Ryle: Exorcism of a persistent ghost

Ryle shared with Wittgenstein and Russell the Humean view that the self as a separate substance is a myth. Like the later Wittgenstein, Ryle thinks the difficulties we have understanding persons, the self, and the mind all fall away when one attends carefully to language and logic. His classic diatribe against "the Ghost in the Machine" which one finds in *The Concept of Mind*[27] extends the arguments of Russell and Wittgenstein and makes them more accessible.

One of the main battles concerning persons in contemporary philosophy is that between the heirs of Hume and the heirs of Descartes. Ryle lays the blame for our confusion about ourselves squarely on Descartes' doorstep, but he thinks that the arguments of many of those opposed to Descartes are also faulty because they commit an error to be discussed in a moment, an error Ryle dubs "a category mistake" (17). First let us look at the doctrine Ryle opposes.

The roughly Cartesian doctrine Ryle sets out to destroy is what he calls "the Official Doctrine" or "the Myth of the Ghost in the Machine." This is the doctrine that every person is a combination of a material body in a mechanical causal network and an immaterial mind insulated from that causal network. According to this doctrine, "A person therefore lives through two collateral histories, one consisting of what happens in and to his body, the other consisting of what happens in and to his mind. The first is public, the second private. The events in the first history are events in the physical world, those in the second are events in the mental world" (13). This doctrine, Ryle assures us, is absurd. He points to various problems like the difficulty of saying how mind and body interact and the tendency to solipsism if one adopts this doctrine. His diagnosis is that the dogma of the Ghost in the Machine treats the facts of mental life as if they belonged to one logical type or category when they actually belong to another (17).

Ryle illustrates the meaning of "category mistake" only very roughly in a series of illustrations, for instance, this: "A foreigner visiting Oxford or Cambridge for the first time is shown a number of colleges, libraries, playing fields, museums, scientific departments and administrative offices. He then asks 'But where is the University?'" "It then has to be explained to him that the University is not another collateral institution, some ulterior counterpart to the colleges, laboratories and offices....The University is just the way in which all that he has already seen is organized" (17-18). According to Ryle, those who speak of the mind as if it were an entity collateral to the body are misunderstanding what type of thing a mind is. It is not that Ryle wishes to reduce mind to matter or matter to mind, but that he thinks both reductions are ridiculous, since matter and mind are not two contrasting things in the same category. He compares the attempted contrast to that between the sentences "she came home in a sedan chair" and "she came home in a flood of tears" (23). I take Ryle to mean that it would be silly to say that all mental events are really material just in the same way as it would be silly to say that she came home in a sedan chair rather than a flood of tears. Rather than engaging in the old debate among materialists, idealists, and dualists, Ryle tries to make their vocabulary look foolish, as Rorty might say, and Ryle does a fairly good job of this.

This is not to say that Ryle wants to stop altogether the use of terms like "I," "self," or "mind." We do, however, have to administer some astringent correctives to their usage. Ryle points out that "'I' is not an extra name for an extra being; it indicates when I say or write it, the same individual who can also be addressed by the proper name 'Gilbert Ryle'" (180). Ryle is inveighing against supposing that "I" is the name for the self which is to be considered as an immaterial substance associated with the body. He also is unhappy with the idea that "an ordinary person is really some sort of committee or team of persons, all laced together inside one skin." The Iliadic Greeks thought that way; we have seen, moreover, that Plato held that Reason, Spirit, and Appetite were three selves within the person, and many people today still might talk, in Ryle's words, "as if the thinking and vetoing 'I' were one person, and the greedy or lazy 'I' were another" (181). In sentences like, "I caught myself beginning to dream," Ryle does not want to treat the two occurrences of the pronoun as referring to two persons or selves within the person.

To avoid this duplication of persons, Ryle analyzes "I" as an index word, which is today also called an "indexical." Such words "indicate to the hearer or reader the particular thing, episode, person, place, or moment referred to" (179). "Now," for example refers to the moment at which it is uttered. Ryle goes through a number of different uses of "I," "me," and "myself" to illustrate that they may mean "my body" or may just refer to the person uttering one of them. "I am warming myself at the fire," is equivalent to "I am warming my body at the fire," but it is nonsense to say "My body is warming my body at the fire" (180). After going through some more peculiar usages, Ryle returns to the point that these pronouns are indexicals; so in a statement like "I caught myself beginning to dream," there is no reference to duplicate persons or selves within persons. To explicate Ryle, I would paraphrase this sentence just quoted as "Gilbert Ryle at time t' noticed that Gilbert Ryle at time t was beginning to dream, and t' is later than t." Such analyses are intended to show that there is only one person to whom the pronouns refer. One may still, however, be dissatisfied. On introspection one seems to almost grasp an elusive referent of "I." Ryle attempts to take the mystery out of this as well.

Ryle speaks of the "Systematic Elusiveness of 'I'" (186). The general reason for this elusiveness of ourselves when we try to know ourselves is given in Ryle's principle: "any performance can be the concern of a higher order performance, but cannot be the concern of itself" (188). To understand this, consider Ryle's example (187) of a book review. A review of a book is a first-order review. A review of all prior reviews of a book is a second-order review. A review of second-order reviews is third-order and so on. Now the principle tells us that a second-order review cannot be the subject of another second-order review. Consider now my reviewing my own performances with a view to knowing myself. One of the things I must leave out is my current reviewing, which is a performance that would have to be the subject of a higher-order performance later. When I look at myself I always leave something out. This, Ryle thinks, is the source of the elusiveness of self. One cannot describe oneself fully. "Even if the person is for special speculative purposes, momentarily concentrating on the Problem of the Self, he has failed and knows that he has failed to catch more than the flying coat-tails of that which he was pursuing. His quarry was the hunter" (188-89).

Ryle also thinks this principle explains our feeling that we have free will and are unpredictable. Whenever we try to predict our own future actions we will leave something out, namely the current performance, the prediction we are now making. Looking at our past actions, we can see how they could have been predicted by someone in possession of all the facts, but our present self-knowledge is always missing one of the facts (187-88).

It seems, then, that although Ryle claims to dissipate the contrast between mind and matter, what he says is less abrasive in the ears of the materialist than in those of the idealist or the dualist. The materialist who typically accepts causal determinism will like what Ryle has to say about the prediction of human behaviour. It is also clear that Ryle accepts the existence of our bodies. What he says about minds, however, tends to rule out entirely dualism and idealism; for minds are largely known by observable behaviour (59). While Ryle admits that there are things about ourselves which cannot be known by others, things to which we have privileged access, they are, to Ryle, in the main, unimportant. The hallowed souls, selves, and minds within are reduced to a technical trick of inner speech (35). He derides those who make something occult out of this: "They postulate an internal shadow-performance to be the real carrier of the intelligence ordinarily as-cribed to the overt act." Against this shadowy inner mind Ryle claims that de-scribing mind or intelligence is describing conduct (49). This is true of other capacities as well, according to Ryle. "I find out most of what I want to know about your capacities, interests, likes, dislikes, methods and convictions by observing how you conduct your overt doings, of which by far the most important are your sayings and writings. It is a subsidiary question how you conduct your imaginings, including your imagined monologues" (60).

Curiously, Ryle and Sartre agree entirely on the great importance of what we do as opposed to what we imagine we are. Ryle's method, however, is largely opposed to the poetic method of the continental philosophers. The emphasis is on preserving as much as possible of common sense and usage while excising any absurdities and maximizing clarity. His critics might maintain that he has excised anything that was profoundly important in the concept of a person, while his admirers would say that he has banished occultists' mutterings in favour of plain truth. Certainly he has to be reckoned with when we come to give our own analyses of the concept of a person.

Application to Daphne's case

Ryle would tell us that it is silly to ask whether Daphne remains after the ravages of her illness. After all there she is. If we are asking about something other than what we see, then we are seeking a ghost in the machine, like the member of a non-industrialized culture who, on first seeing a locomotive, says "It must have a very powerful spirit!" If we want to know what Daphne is or who, we simply look at what she can do. To ask after the real Daphne within is to make a category mistake. There is nothing over and above that of which we take stock, no more than there is some entity, the University, over and above the buildings and the people in them.

What I like about Ryle

Ryle puts views about persons to be found in the ordinary-language school of thought into relatively sharp focus. He teaches us to be careful about the way we commit ourselves to the existence of things on the basis of the words we use. His picturesque metaphors and the hazy but evocative notion of a category mistake make us careful when we come to say what there is, over and above observable behaviour, in a person.

Taking stock after the iconoclasts

What remains of us after these founders of the Analytic School are through? We seem to be back where Hume left us, no place at all. Perhaps I should say, rather, we have been put in our place. There is no non-spatial Cartesian Ego left. What remains of us is a spatio-temporally locatable set of behaviours and a behaving body which itself is a mere bundle of sensa, to use Russell's term, like any object. Thinking substances, essences, spirit, soul, mind, and self are banished along with the unicorn or, what amounts to a fate worse than banishment, reduced to neurophysiological events. The self is a grammatical illusion. Freedom is impossible. Morals claims are mere expressions of emotion. Some, like Russell seem to be able to think and act as humanists in spite of believing in these iconoclastic pronouncements. This is not logically inconsistent if one describes what one is doing in the appropriate reductionist way. It is, however, difficult to motivate humanism under the stern aegis of reductionism.

In some ways such views simplify things. To ask whether, for example, someone who has permanently lost her mind has survived is to ask either whether a particular body has survived or to ask whether a certain repertoire of behaviours has survived. That explains our tendency to answer "yes and no." Only the body has survived. This simplification of the issue of survival of persons is bought at the cost of trimming the rich fabric of our experience to fit the narrow frame of behaviourist or materialist reduction. Is it really plausible that a behavioural repertoire or a set of sensa can be made to explain what Bergson rhapsodically but unclearly referred to as our intuition of ourselves?

Knowing what it is like to stand in my shoes is to be acquainted with an extremely complex phenomenon, I assure you. To dismiss this as a limit of the world experienced or to reduce it to atoms like sensa is not plausible without a much longer story being told than the cheerful British founders of the Analytic School have begun to tell. One should only throw out bath water after carefully checking for babies. On the other hand, this group of philosophers has shown us just how muddy the bath water is. Their demands for clarity can be met in a salutary way if we avoid oversimplification.

TEN
More Contemporary Classics

Strawson: The concept of person as basic

Not all contemporary philosophers in the Analytic School are suspicious of traditional philosophy, in particular of metaphysics. A major contribution with respect to the metaphysical status of persons was made by P.F Strawson in *Individuals: An Essay In Descriptive Metaphysics*.[1] "Descriptive metaphysics," Strawson tells us, "is content to describe the actual structure of our thought about the world, revisionary metaphysics is concerned to produce a better structure" (9). More particularly, what Strawson wishes to describe comes from the great unsung commonplaces of thought: "For there is a massive central core of human thinking which has no history— or none recorded in histories of thought; there are categories and concepts which, in their most fundamental character, change not at all" (10). Strawson's work on the concept of a person is remarkable in the scope and generality of his undertaking and in his going beyond "the reliance upon a close examination of the actual use of words" (9). His main aim, as regards our topic, is to show that material bodies and persons are "the basic or fundamental particulars, that the concepts of other types of particular must be seen as secondary in relation to the concepts of these (11).

Strawson's route into the forbidding territory of the philosophy of persons is via the traditional mountain passes, the problems of self-knowledge and solipsism:

> Each of us distinguishes between himself and states of himself on the one hand, and what is not himself or a state of himself on the other. What are the conditions of our making this distinction, and how are they fulfilled? In what way do we make it, and why do we make it in the way we do?(87)

Think about how you distinguish two material particulars in the world such as the book you are reading and the telephone. Now think about how you distinguish yourself from other things. It does not seem at all like distinguishing the book from the telephone. You do not hold up some particular, the self, in imagination and compare it to the telephone. So how do you do it?

Strawson sees a person's having an idea of herself or himself as a very strange phenomenon, which he describes in rather Humean terms:

Notes to Chapter Ten are on p. 322.

it might begin to look impossible that he should have the idea of himself—or at any rate the right idea...if it is just an item *within* his experience of which he has this idea, how can it be the idea of that which *has* all of his experiences?(89)

To investigate our idea of self, Strawson turns to the language we use to talk about ourselves, to ascribe things to ourselves. We ascribe some of the same things we ascribe to physical particulars, for instance weight, colour, and position; yet we also ascribe things which we normally do not ascribe to physical particulars like anger, diligence, or, more generally, consciousness. To understand this, Strawson decides to look into our reasons for ascribing consciousness to anything at all and our reasons for ascribing both physical and mental properties to people.

If, however, we look at people who are very young or outside of our culture, in non-industrial cultures, then Strawson's point about what we ascribe does not hold. A child, or a native of North America may feel quite comfortable with expressions like, "The forest is angry." Poets and environmentalists in our culture will also use such expressions, though usually they are meant as tropes to underline our perfidy in sullying our own nest. Sometimes, however, as with the aboriginal peoples, the use is literal and goes with a system of values which is quite unlike the one Kant clarified by distinguishing persons from mere things. Things only have value in their service to persons in the Kantian value system. It is partly because we accept this Kantian doctrine that we are so willing to use up our natural surroundings rather than to preserve them for their own sakes; so Strawson's acceptance of the Kantian doctrine may be backward looking. The point of distinguishing people from mere things was to prevent people being used improperly, but we will have to widen the scope of our protection. This may put a strain on the distinction of persons from mere things. It is to be hoped that we will refine the distinction so as to value some non-persons more highly rather than to value people less.

Having asked why conscious states are ascribed to anything at all and why to the same thing as physical characteristics, Strawson goes on to look at the way we have experiences. He argues that it is a contingent matter that our experiences are tied to our own bodies. The unique role, however, that our bodies have in our perceptual experience explains our attachment to them. This observation about our bodies does not, however, answer Strawson's questions (87-88).

This unique role of the body might go further towards answering Strawson's questions if there were a necessary connection between the body and the experience of the person. The argument that there is no such connection consists mainly of a description of a fanciful case in which a person's visual experience is determined by the bodies of others. Like Kathleen Wilkes[2] I am suspicious of such examples. In the unclear background assumptions which make them seem to work there may be hidden some contradiction. The philosophy, psychology, and biology of perception are insufficiently developed for us to comb this background for such flaws; so it is reasonable to remain, for the time being, agnostic with respect to the contingency of the connection of experience to the body.

What would persuade me that Strawson is wrong about this claim of contingency is sufficient experience of the sort described by the novelist Hesse in *Siddhartha*. Siddhartha, an East Indian mystic, is said to inhabit, while in a trance, the bodies of various animals and said to share their experiences. If I could see the world as if from the body of the Bald Eagle which I sometimes see from my window, and if I could later verify—say using aerial photographs—that my experience culled in this strange way was veridical, then I might accept the contingency of the role of my body in my experience. On the face of it, however, I lean, despite my agnosticism, to accepting a necessary connection of my body to my experience.

Strawson continues his description of the structure of our thought with respect to persons by discussing the Cartesian and no-ownership views.[3] Both of these views he attacks as making the profound error of thinking that there are two senses of "I," one referring to the body and one referring to something else. The Cartesian view is one we have seen in the discussion of Descartes above. According to Descartes, the body is one substance, the mind or Cartesian Ego is another. When we speak of the person we may refer to either or both. Mental predicates are properly ascribable only to the mind and physical predicates only to the body. While Strawson disagrees with this view, he thinks it is at least coherent, but he does not accord the no-ownership view so much respect.

The no-ownership view is one he thinks might be fathered on Wittgenstein and on Schlick, a central member of the Vienna Circle which promoted logical positivism. The no-ownership view is the view that there are no owners of certain experiences which we ascribe to the Cartesian Ego. To use Wittgenstein's example, "I've got a bad tooth," means "This body has a bad tooth," but "I've got a toothache" does not mean "This Ego has a toothache." In fact, where "I" appears to denote the Ego, it denotes no such thing. "I've got a toothache" should be read as "A toothache is occurring now" (91, n.1).

The reason for adopting this strange no-ownership view, according to Strawson, is acceptance of what I shall call the *transferability principle* which is this: "Only those things whose ownership is logically transferable can be owned at all" (98). Of course I could not transfer the ownership of my toothache to you if it is my Ego which has that experience. You might have a toothache but not the experience I had (although it is logically possible that your body not mine had this particular bad tooth). All talk of ownership of a toothache is dismissed, since I could not own that experience in the first place, by this transferability principle.

This no-ownership view is incoherent, according to Strawson. He accuses its proponents of assuming the ownership they are trying to deny when they state their no-ownership view. They must use "my" or some other possessive word to locate the experience. If they eliminate such possessives, they cannot, according to Strawson, talk about the contingent facts of possession of certain experiences by the body in the sense of being causally dependent on that body (the argument for this I will discuss later in connection with Ayer's view.) If these facts are not contingent, then we do not have logical transferability of ownership as required. The no-ownership theorist has to make use of the idea of a person possessing an experience in order to deny that experiences are possessed by persons (96-97).

Whether or not this no-ownership view is Wittgenstein's view, there is a Wittgensteinian ladder-heaving response to Strawson. The no-ownership theorist could say, "Yes, I must use these possessives which reduce my propositions to nonsense, but these propositions are only used to bring you to a realization of the ineffable thing I want to say. Once you see that, you can discard these nonsensical propositions." Of course, if one has no special realizations on hearing these propositions, one can reply with Wittgenstein's authority as well, "What we cannot speak about we must pass over in silence."4

The point of descriptive metaphysics which Strawson seeks to bring out by considering the no-ownership view is that the principle of transferability must be abandoned. There is a non-transferable kind of ownership which is central to our thought about persons. In fact, without attributing them to persons, we have no way of identifying various particulars like thoughts and pains. We need the basic particulars, persons, and this non-transferable ownership to be able to identify and reidentify these items in our scheme of thought about the world.

As to the questions with which Strawson began, on the Cartesian view one need not ask why both conscious and physical states are attributed to one thing, the person, since the person is really the Ego with two other things, body and mind, which it owns. This view, Strawson complains, does not answer why we should ascribe states of consciousness to anything. This seems a rather odd complaint to a Cartesian, for whom the mind is the set of conscious states owned by the Ego. It is the same felt need for ownership of consciousness that drives both Descartes and Strawson. Strawson does not, however, like the sort of owner that Descartes came up with. The alternative no-ownership account is, however, anathema to Strawson.

In opposition to the no-ownership account, Strawson asserts the *ascription principle:* "it is a necessary condition of one's ascribing states of consciousness, experiences, to oneself, in the way one does, that one should also ascribe them, or be prepared to ascribe them, to others who are not oneself."[5] If I say to myself, "No one could love her as I do," then, by this principle, I must be mistaken. It implies that, although no one could have *my* love for her, others could love her in a completely similar way. Others could have experiences like mine. Strawson insists on this ascription principle in opposition not only to the no-ownership theory but to the verification principle of the logical positivists (99-100).

If we accept the positivist's verification principle, then the meaning of "I am in pain" must be very different from "He is in pain" for the methods of verification in the two cases are so different. Indeed, for the first sentence one might doubt the need for verification or the use of the sentence to ascribe a property to a person. Strawson responds (100) that we use language to speak primarily to others; so both sentences would be used to let others know who is in pain. This communication would be impossible if we were ascribing properties to Cartesian Egos which are inaccessible to us. Strawson suggests that (to preserve our ability to ascribe predicates) we must take the concept of a person as primitive. Cartesian Egos, if we wish to speak of them at all, will be defined in terms of persons, not the reverse. "The concept of a person is logically prior to that of an individual consciousness" (101-103).

This taking of the concept of a person to be primitive seems to solve, at one stroke, some thorny problems which have been sticking in the sides of philosophers at least since Descartes, problems like how the mind interacts with the body and how we know of the existence of other minds. Strawson would also make people, not mysterious Egos, owners of conscious states. On the face of it, the solution looks too easy. It seems to amount to saying that we do readily communicate concerning our experiences; so any view that implies there are difficulties with this is suspect. We should first adopt a concept which preserves the possibility of straightforward communication and only then concern ourselves with Egos, other minds, and interaction. From the Cartesian point of view this seems question-begging. Strawson tries to shore it up with a linguistic investigation of the kinds of predicates we use to speak about ourselves.

To clarify the taking of the concept of a person as a primitive, Strawson roughly divides the predicates we ascribe to persons into two groups, M-predicates ("M" for "material," I suppose) and P-predicates ("P" for "person") of which two kinds the P-predicates imply the possession of consciousness of that to which they are ascribed (104). To say that the concept of a person is primitive means that there are not simpler concepts like that of a Cartesian Ego to which P-predicates apply and that of a body to which M-predicates apply which can be combined to make a person. Persons are those basic kinds of things to which both kinds of predicates can be ascribed.

The general argument for claiming that both P-predicates and M-predicates must be applicable to persons (104) I would put as follows:

1. I correctly apply P-predicates and M-predicates to myself.
2. If I correctly apply P-predicates and M-predicates to myself, then I must be able to correctly apply P-predicates and M-predicates to others.
3. If I correctly apply P-predicates and M-predicates to myself and others, then these others and myself must be distinguishable members of a type of thing to which both P-predicates and M-predicates are correctly applicable.
4. Therefore, I and these others must be distinguishable members of a type of thing to which both P-predicates and M-predicates are applicable.

If I have not oversimplified, then we can see from this expression of Strawson's argument where it is most likely to meet challenges: (1) is true enough. For example, I say "I am thinking," or "I weigh one hundred and sixty pounds." (2) is a more general version of the ascription principle which is question-begging from the point of view of the skeptic concerning other minds. (3) just unpacks what is in (2). The part of (2) which is controversial is the part concerning P-predicates.

To be able to use P-predicates of persons, we must have a way to tell when they apply. Strawson tells us,

> What I have said is that one ascribes P-predicates to others on the strength of observations of their behaviour and that the behaviour-criteria one goes on are not just signs of the presence of what is meant by the P-predicate, but are criteria of a logically adequate kind for the ascription of the P-predicate. (106)

This conclusion would solve the problem of skepticism about other minds in what seems too easy a stroke.

Strawson claims, however, that we have to have this conclusion if we are to adopt the conceptual scheme in terms of which skepticism is stated. Thus, when we describe the structure of our thought we see that skepticism is in a way contradictory: "So with many skeptical problems: their statement involves the pretended acceptance of a conceptual scheme and at the same time the silent repudiation of one of the conditions of its existence" (106). This is a bold move against skepticism with regard to other minds. It preserves common sense in the face of philosophical conundrums. On the other hand, it is not at all clear that the condition just stated for the ascription of P-predicates really is a condition of the existence of a conceptual scheme which skepticism must accept. The skeptic may balk at the ascription principle on which this condition depends or may cast doubt on the whole notion of logical adequacy presupposed here. Strawson has merely adumbrated his position.

Strawson reminds us that P-predicates, as with words in general, acquire their meaning in a larger structure of interrelated uses. Those who speak behaviouristically or skeptically about the application of P-predicates are both failing to see the larger picture and supposing, wrongly, that these predicates can be meaningfully used in the narrower context without setting it within the larger one (110). This is an argument for the ascription principle, but it would become convincing only if more were said about the language structure which requires us to have a primitive concept of person before we can have a concept of a Cartesian Ego. In mathematical systems it is often arbitrary which of several concepts one takes as primitive. Why should it be different in speaking of persons?

Perhaps the answer is, from a descriptive metaphysical point of view, partly that we just happen to have this conceptual structure in which the concept of person is primitive. We might have had others, but we do not, and it is far too complicated a structure for us to simply substitute another in a revisionist way. Of course the "we" I use here is "we of the European culture," and it may well be that descriptive metaphysics is culturally relative. I will pursue questions of the influence of culture on our concept of person in my final remarks, but let us stick to Strawson's own program for now.

As to the initial question of why to attribute consciousness to anything, Strawson seems to be saying that one cannot have concepts like that of consciousness without a primitive concept of a person. The other initial question concerning, in effect, why we apply both P-predicates and M-predicates to one kind of thing is also answered by the primitiveness of the concept of a person. We can do none other and still make sense within the larger linguistic structure in which we use such predicates.

In Wittgensteinian terms, the language game in which words referring to persons, P-predicates, and M-predicates are used requires that the words for persons go in the subject place for both types of predicates. The question whether we play this game as a contingent matter of fact or of necessity is not fully dealt with by Strawson, but the answer in his intentionally fragmentary account seems to be that it is contingent and contingent upon what we do. "What I am suggesting is that it is easier to understand how we can see each other, and ourselves, as persons, if we think first of the fact that we act, and act on each other, and act in accordance with a common human nature" (112). It seems that any change of the linguistic structure to allow us to speak differently and see ourselves differently would depend on the way we act and interact.

One interesting example of this comes from Strawson's consideration of a theme that has often cropped up in our investigation of the history of the concepts of a person, namely the absorption of the individual by the group, an absorption which is favoured more in the Orient than in Western philosophy.

Speaking of speculation on the group mind, Strawson says: "The fact that we find it natural to individuate as persons the members of a certain class of moving natural objects does not mean that such a conceptual scheme is inevitable for any class of being not utterly unlike ourselves" (113). If, for example, human beings were arranged into groups which acted as perfectly disciplined military units, with one executive member controlling all their actions, we might think of them as one "scattered body." We would stop seeing individual human beings as persons. This example of Strawson's is fictional, but the Oriental ideal of absorption of the individual allows, in reality, the family sometimes to be treated as if it were a person. The state may also be so treated, and not just in the Orient. Witness Hobbes' *Leviathan*.[6]

The way we speak of persons now and of individuals having separate conscious minds would no longer make sense once we moved to a new linguistic structure in which groups were the basic unit. It would be, within that structure, as strange to talk of the individual mind as it would be to talk of my liver, my kidneys, my heart, and so on, all as individually conscious.[7] Even this latter scenario is not impossible. The Iliadic Greeks may well have thought this way.[8] If so, then Strawson might say that their language would have a different structure from our own, which makes their thought not about persons at all. They were playing a language game in which that concept had no part.

Another way of looking at it is that the various things within a human being that had executive agency were really what were persons for the Greeks. There were many persons within one human body. Strawson's scattered bodies could also be seen as the bodies of scattered persons. The person is the group. When we focus on action and decision-making, as Strawson does, whatever is the agent is the person. It seems, then, that one thing we might glean from consideration of Strawson's example is the idea that a concept of a person is something we cannot do without. When we move to group persons or multiple persons within a human body we merely change the physical realization of our concept of a person, we do not eliminate persons. Strawson, however, must strenuously deny that our actual conceptual scheme permits some of the alternative realizations. Without changing our conceptual scheme, by Strawson's lights, we could not treat Cartesian Egos as persons.

Having struggled might and main against Cartesian Egos, Strawson, in a curious concluding section, considers the idea of a disembodied person.[9] This is not, however, the idea of an Ego with no body. We can, he thinks, conceive of a disembodied person within our actual conceptual scheme only because we already have the concept of a person on which this concept of a disembodied person is dependent. Such a person would see and hear as if she had a body. Strawson's conception of a person, it appears, even retains the common idea of the possibility of survival of bodily death. I say "even" since what is remarkable about Strawson's view of persons is that it accords in many ways with Western common sense on the topic of persons. This is highly unusual for a philosophical analysis of persons. Of course no philo- sophical account can capture all of the richness of the common notion while remaining consistent. The main thing Strawson decides to give up is that ele- ment of our daily chatter about each other which we have inherited from Descartes. Philosophers, however, are bound to remain unconvinced by Strawson. One of the notables of this century who takes on the task of refut- ing Strawson is a part-time member of the Vienna Circle, the great disen- chanted (thus former) logical positivist A.J. Ayer.

Ayer: An unusual view of ordinary people

Ayer begins in a not too propitious way by telling us that he will be discussing persons "in the broad sense that every individual human being can be counted as a person. It is characteristic of persons in this sense that besides having various physical properties...they are also credited with various forms of consciousness."[10] Of course one of the questions in the current debate about survival of persons is whether to confer the status of person upon those human beings who either never achieve consciousness during their lives or who lose it permanently without dying. There are ques- tions as well about the forms of consciousness necessary to being a person. Someone whose consciousness is no more developed than a cat's may or may not be a person according to various conceptions of persons.

Ayer also takes consciousness, at least initially, in a rough and ready way.

> All I can say is that I am speaking of it in the ordinary sense in which, to be thinking about a problem, or remembering some event, or seeing or hearing something, or deciding to do something, or feeling some emotion, such as jeal- ousy or fear, entails being conscious. (82)

Someone who is dreaming but sound asleep or, perhaps, even someone in a permanent coma can be conscious in this sense. Probably a cat can feel fear and see or hear things in a way sufficient to satisfy these examples of con- scious behaviour. We may, however, wish to distinguish between being con- scious in terms of our behaviour, being conscious in the sense of being aware of ourselves and what we are doing, and being conscious in the sense of hav- ing a continuing consciousness of the kind appropriate to persons.

Ayer, however, cannot be expected to solve the myriad problems swarming around our concepts of a person all in one essay, but it is worth noting his very liberal definition of the topic. Some of the problems which Ayer raises, like that of personal identity, require more precise notions of person and consciousness for their solution. The demand for precision, clarity, and attention to language which has become fashionable through the agency of Ayer and philosophers like him almost makes any attempt to deal with the topic of persons stillborn. No sooner does one speak than presuppositions to be clarified prevent one from continuing. Naturally, this leads to a certain amount of glossing over and passing off just to get on with the job. Ayer at least draws attention to the difficulties which appear in his own account by speaking of his approximate usage of "person" and "consciousness" while many others have simply assumed that the meaning of these terms is sufficiently clear.

Ayer attempts to show that Strawson is unsuccessful in his attempt to go between the horns of dualism and materialism. Ayer locates his own view by contrasting it with Strawson's:

> I am...inclined to think that personal identity depends upon the identity of the body, and that a person's ownership of states of consciousness consists in their standing in a special causal relation to the body by which he is identified....This amounts in effect to adopting what Mr. Strawson calls "the no-ownership doctrine of the self." (116)

It is confusing that Ayer's view is not, on the face of it, the same no-ownership view that Strawson was talking about. Ayer speaks of conscious persons owning their states of consciousness. The no-ownership view, on the other hand, is one according to which there is no owner or subject of experiences; experiences just happen, and, Strawson says, "it is a linguistic illusion that one ascribes one's states of consciousness at all, that there is any proper subject of these apparent ascriptions, that states of consciousness belong to, or are states of, anything."[11] Ayer's account looks more like a straightforward materialism rather than the exotic no-ownership view.

Strawson also says, however, that the no-ownership theorist is willing to admit "an admissible, though infelicitous" sense of ownership in which the body "owns" experiences or states of consciousness. As we saw above, Strawson thinks this view is incoherent because the no-ownership theorist helps herself to possessives like "my" to single out experiences thus presupposing the ownership she is denying. For part of Strawson's argument I left a promissory note on which I must now make good. Strawson makes use of the subordinate conclusion that the no-ownership theorist cannot do without these possessives and still maintain the transferability principle. For example, it would be illegitimate to say "my thought" and still require that everything one is thinking could be thought by someone else. It is Strawson's argument for this conclusion which Ayer wishes to undermine.

The no-ownership theorist, in accord with the transferability principle, requires that bodies have experiences as a contingent matter of fact, not of necessity. Strawson's argument puts the no-ownership theorist in the dilemma of either asserting something false or asserting something necessary when trying to assert such a supposedly contingent matter of fact (96-97). To see the dilemma (in somewhat less detail than Strawson presents it) consider a no-ownership theorist, Ludwig, who wants to dispel the illusion of the Ego through talk about the contingent fact that his body, B, has experiences. How can he talk about that fact without possessives like "my" or "Ludwig's"? He can no longer say, "All my experiences are had by body B." When he eliminates possessives he says something false like "All experiences are had by body B." Suppose Ludwig tries another tack by claiming that "All Ludwig's experiences" just means "All experiences had by body B." Then his statement of fact becomes "All experiences had by body B are had by body B." This is a necessary proposition, not the contingent one Ludwig needs. It seems, then, that Ludwig will either say something false or something necessary when he tries to state the contingent fact about the relationship of his experiences to himself.

Against this dilemma Ayer defends the consistency of his own position.

> The position is that a person can be identified by his body; this body can be identified by its physical properties and spatio-temporal location; as a contingent fact there are certain experiences which are causally connected with it; and these particular experiences can then be identified as the experiences of the person whose body it is. There is nothing inconsistent in this.[12]

Ludwig can now say, with Ayer's help, (116-17) that what he means by the original sentence "All my experiences are had by my body B," is merely that if B is in certain kinds of states, then certain experiences are caused to occur. Suppose Strawson then says, "Ah! but these are not just any experiences but Ludwig's experiences, and you have left that out." Ludwig must then reply, by Ayer's lights, that to say experiences are Ludwig's is only to say they occur in body B. The new translation of the original sentence is, "If body B is in certain kinds of states, then certain kinds of events called 'experiences' are caused to occur in body B." Is this contingent?

Whether this last translation of the original claim is really contingent or not is impossible to tell, since it is so vague. It apparently depends on a rough materialist faith that we will be able to spell out scientifically the material causes within bodies of experiences and that we will be able to give a thorough description of experiences as events in material bodies. Depending on unspecified background conditions, on *a general method of individuating events*, and perhaps even on causal determinism being false, this new claim may be contingent. Ayer recognizes the vagueness of such claims and tries to address it, but at most succeeds in pushing the problem back to the problem of what counts as one event (118-21). Ayer has, however, raised some doubts as to the dilemma posed by Strawson. Strawson, moreover, is threatened in his attempt to avoid the seemingly endless debates about the possibility of experiences being merely events in material bodies by speaking not of mind and matter but of persons. Ayer can say that if Ludwig's last translation makes sense and is contingent, then the dilemma is finished as far as materialists are concerned. We are back in the old debate between dualists and materialists which Strawson would like to short-circuit.

Quine: Convention is king

Quine is another major contemporary figure in the Analytic School who puts language front and centre in his consideration of philosophical problems. Quine's remarks on the topic of persons are, nonetheless, critical of the ordinary-language approach. The logical positivists, indeed, the whole empiricist tradition is also subjected to a vigorous critique by Quine, who undermines the distinctions between the Analytic and the synthetic and between science and metaphysics. He is also opposed to that empiricist linguistic reductionism which tries to translate all statements into statements about immediate experience.[13] None of this, however, makes Quine a friend to those who wish to promote grand metaphysical systems to explain persons and their role in the universe. Quine is a special kind of minimalist who values the desert landscape much above the lush jungle where his commitment to the existence of things is concerned.

For Ryle and philosophers like him, to say that John is a person is just to say something, in a very condensed way, about the many things John tends to do. Quine expresses some ire with this and with ordinary language analyses in general:

> There are those who uncritically accept the dispositional idiom as a clear matter of ordinary language. Say what a thing is disposed to do in what circumstances, and the disposition holds no further mystery for them. Solubility in water is the disposition to dissolve when in water, and there is no plainer English than that. Such is Ryle's position in *The Concept of Mind*, where he undertakes to clarify other more obscure and troublesome notions in dispositional terms and is content to leave them thus.[14]

Quine apparently thinks that dispositional talk is not explanatory. This is at least controversial. To say with Aristotle that a stone falls because it tends to seek the earth may explain nothing, but the law of gravity is also dispositional and is explanatory. In any case, Quine attacks both the logical empiricist, like Ayer, and the ordinary language philosopher, like Ryle. Since he attempts to sever both main strands of prior contemporary Analytic philosophy it is hard, at first, to see what he leaves himself as a tether.

Quine is in the tradition of those like the mediaeval philosopher William of Occam who try to eliminate commitment to the existence of anything which is not necessary to explain what we experience.[15] For instance, we have a word "red" in our language so the word exists, but there is no need to postulate a Platonic form of redness as well. This view is called nominalism since the names of some things are accepted as existing rather than the things themselves. Quine's nominalism is in opposition to talk of ideas and concepts yet he wishes to speak of the conjectures and abstractions of scientific theory. This seems impossible, yet Quine assures us,

> There is a way: we can talk of language. We can talk of concrete men and their concrete noises. Ideas are as may be, but the words are out where we can see and hear them. And scientific theories, however speculative and however abstract, are in words.[16]

Thus Quine shares Russell's dismissive attitude to the ineffable and to talking about it or around it. In fact, from such a severe philosophy as Quine's, one can expect a dismissive attitude to many things philosophers have spoken of over the ages. It is interesting to see what can be said about persons in this minimalist framework.

Quine raises, for example, the ancient puzzle of the endurance of the self through change, with a contemporary twist. Undergoing change as I do, how can I be said to continue to be myself? Considering that a complete replacement of my material substance takes place every few years, how can I be said to continue to be myself for more than such a short period at best?[17] Actually there are some brain cells that persist through the change of all other cells in our bodies, but that is small comfort, even to a materialist.

On the other hand, as Quine points out, appealing to some immaterial unifying thing within us is the thin edge of a very large wedge.

> It would be agreeable to be driven, by these or other considerations, to belief in a changeless and therefore immortal soul as the vehicle of my persisting self-identity. But we should be less eager to embrace a parallel solution of Heracleitus's parallel problem regarding a river: "You cannot bathe in the same river twice, for new waters are ever flowing in upon you." (65)

There are indeed few left who would adopt the old animist worldview in which every persisting object, like a river, has a soul. In a way, that is a pity. We might treat the environment with more respect if we saw it this way. We must, however, solve our conceptual problems within the bounds of the resources which we ourselves can accept. Quine's solution is instructive even for those of us who are less committed to minimalism with respect to existential commitments.

While it would be unacceptable for most of us to solve Heraclitus' puzzle by giving the river a soul such as we tend to see in ourselves, it is, on the other hand, suggested that we solve the puzzle of our own continuation by the familiar means we adopt for the river puzzle. Quine sees the river, indeed any persisting object, as a series of momentary stages. One cannot bathe in the same river stage twice but one can bathe in the same river twice. Different stages will consist of different waters, but they are all stages of one river (65). Similarly, Quine would see persons as a series of stages. You are not the same person-stage you were ten years ago, but you are the same person.

Quine, since he sees all individual objects as processes, develops an ontology, a theory of objects in general, which makes it easy to speak of one object through great changes. I will adumbrate that ontology here and apply it to persons, but you may retain the distinction of person-stages from persons without accepting the ontology.

Quine proposes a rather radical conception of what counts as a particular thing. To understand it, we need to get at least a loose grip on the concept of a four-dimensional space-time worm. Imagine, unappealing though it may be, a bookworm has gnawed its way through this book from cover to cover. As you turn the pages you see holes in various places. Since the worm bored through at various angles the hole may be in the top, middle or bottom of the page—different positions in space. Each page was bored through at a time. Each page represents a stage of the worm's progress. The pathway through space-time which every object takes is somewhat like the record of the worm's progress through the book. Objects are, therefore, called space-time worms. They are four dimensional since they occupy three dimensions in space and one in time. At any given moment in its existence, an object exists as a stage of its whole progress through space and time. But suppose that there are some pages of the book with no holes and some pages with several holes (our worm cannot bore backwards any more than we can reverse time.) Quine is willing to countenance objects which are many places at one time, scattered objects. Water is such an object. At any given time its parts are to be found in many locations. Objects also need not be continuous. They can skip a page or more in the great book of the universe.[18]

This view is radical because it allows us to take any assemblage of particles of matter at any times and call them a particular object. For the most part, of course, the objects we are interested in, rivers, people, and such, are not discontinuous in time or not noticeably so. A river might dry up for a while. Can a person have gaps as well? One hears tell of various cases of apparent death and revival. There are science fiction cases of prolonged hibernation or being dissolved and reconstituted, as in *Star Trek* teletransportation. Certainly Quine would have no objection to calling Captain Kirk a single object even though there are times during teletransportation when Kirk does not seem to be anywhere. What would Quine say about these various stages of Kirk before and after teletransportation being the same person? He thinks that such examples merely demonstrate deficiency of the word "person."

Any coherent general term has its own principle of individuation, its own criterion of identity among its denotata. Often the principle is vague, as the principle of individuation of persons is shown to be by the science-fiction examples; and a term is as vague as its principle of individuation.[19]

In the world according to Quine, as medicine progresses we may be confronted with things which we are at a loss to classify. Our current means of individuating persons will not help us. New conventions will have to be fashioned.

One final point on Quine's contribution to the current debate on persons is in order. Much of the contemporary literature has to do with the topic of personal identity which concerns the question, "When is person x the same as person y?" Quine reduces questions of identity, whether diachronic (across time) or synchronic (in the timeless present) to questions of kind membership. The real question we are asking is not about identity but about how best to construe the term "person."[20] Once we have made a decision about the nature of persons, we will be able to decide whether Kirk is the same person after being beamed up or whether the old Kirk has been killed and a new one very much like him created. This is reminiscent of the warnings of Wittgenstein on this topic.

Philosophers like Strawson, Ayer, and Quine laid the groundwork for much recent Analytic philosophy. Now we move into the discussion of the current debate, which always looks to this groundwork as something which it must include, replace, or adapt. Before that, however, let us look at what we can do with what we have taken just now from contemporary Analytic philosophy.

Applications to Daphne's case

According to the metaphysical views adopted by Strawson, Daphne may or may not be a person or the same person we once knew, depending on what P-predicates we can truly ascribe to her. But what is it to be the same person over time as these predicates change? For Ayer, Daphne is the same person, since her body remains. For Quine, it is simply a matter of how we wish to talk. Our conventions for the use of "person" are, perhaps, not suited to such cases as Daphne's. We must decide how to extend those conventions if we wish to use the term.

While he leaves us up in the air, Strawson makes some interesting remarks about personal identity and reidentification.[21] By taking persons as primary, he believes he has avoided concerns about the unity of consciousness within these topics. Hume's problem, for instance, of finding an enduring self vanishes when the self or consciousness is conceptually derivative from the primitive concept of a person. What we reidentify are persons, and we need to make use of their bodies to do so. However, "the criteria of personal identity are certainly multiple. In saying that a personal body gives us a necessary point of application for these criteria, I am not saying that the criteria for reidentifying persons are the same as the criteria for reidentifying material bodies" (133). We identify people by focussing on the body and applying M-predicates and P-predicates. That done, we can now identify and reidentify the consciousness of a person even if it should migrate from one body to another. Strawson leaves it an open question how we should deal with extreme cases in the real world, like that in which a person becomes demented, or with other science-fiction puzzle cases, but he thinks that, if we take the concept of a person to be primitive, then we will have no trouble with identification and reidentification in the normal cases (133-34).

In a case of dementia in which the set of P-predicates is greatly reduced while the set of M-predicates is reduced far less, it seems we are met with a person, by Strawson's lights, but whether we are met with the same person is another matter. While that will depend on the relative weights we assign to various criteria for reidentification, it will not depend, according to Strawson, on the unity and continuity of a primitive item called "the demented person's consciousness." Once we stop looking for this non-existent item, we will look at the whole person and see her consciousness as defined in terms of that person rather than the reverse. We will stop asking questions like, "Is the same person still in there since this fall into dementia?" Instead we will ask, "How should we weigh intellectual ability as a predicate required for continuity?"

There remains the question, which Strawson leaves open, of how we are to assign such weights. Reidentifying persons becomes a matter of assigning weights to various criteria; that is, it is a matter of deciding what is important about persons. Quine would say that we can choose any convention we wish. Strawson lets himself be guided by respect for the structure of the conceptual scheme we actually employ (138). The difficult task remains of describing that conceptual scheme with respect to the reidentification of persons.

It also seems unclear whether Daphne is a person at all, never mind the same one we knew, on Strawson's account, since some P-predicates seem to apply to her, but most do not. She may smile. We might say she is happy. It is difficult to suppose, however, given the extent of her brain damage, that she is thinking of things in the way that we do. Perhaps if we decided how to assign weights to certain P-predicates we could not only answer the question whether she is a person but also answer the question whether she is the same person we knew prior to the brain damage. Quine would say that choosing our conventions about what counts as a person will also settle issues concerning identity. It becomes clearer why Ayer would want to short-circuit this whole discussion and say we merely have to determine whether the body is the same body.

What I like about these contemporary philosophers

Strawson's attachment to our pre-existing conceptual scheme is refreshing, since so many contemporary philosophers encourage us to abandon it. Taking the concept of a person as primitive may be a very useful device as long as the conceptual scheme is recognized as culturally relative. The primacy of actions of persons in our understanding of them is a good idea, especially with regard to actions of persons on persons.

We should retain from Ayer the idea of the importance of the body to our concept of a person, but we need not make it all-important. Ayer and Quine make us reflect on the conventions which Strawson tends to view as part of an ongoing conceptual scheme which weathers changes of time, nation, and place. The challenge is to keep some of Strawson's insights in spite of the corrosive effect of Quine and Ayer's arguments. This requires that these insights be supported by different sorts of arguments. In the search for such arguments in later chapters, we will hear the echo of Quine's warning about the inapplicability of some of our conventions to new cases.

ELEVEN
Wiggins And Williams

Wiggins' Individuative Naturalism

Wiggins, in the course of writing detailed essays on the concept of identity, has much to say about personal identity and the concept of a person.[1] He calls his view "individuative naturalism."[2] It is naturalist in that *person* is treated as a natural kind by reference to which we individuate its members. *Person* is a substance concept which applies or does not apply to a living being its whole life through. By contrast, *infant* is not a substance concept. It applies during part of a life (24-25). Persons are coextensive with members of *homo sapiens*, so spatio-temporally continuous living human bodies serve to identify persons,[3] but persons also have irreducibly psychological properties supervenient on their neurophysiology.[4]

While Wiggins believes that we must individuate people under a natural kind, he does not accept the relative identity thesis. This is the view that identity of thing under one kind does not imply identity under other kinds. For example, in cases of dementia, it might be tempting to say that the demented individual is the same human being but not the same person as existed prior to the dementia, since many human attributes are still present after dementia sets in, while properties like rationality and self-awareness are gone. Wiggins says, however, that identity cannot be relativized in this way and retain its formal properties of transitivity, reflexivity, and symmetry.[5] It is sufficient for our purposes to note that Wiggins holds that if we identify some being as the same human being whom we once knew, and that human being is also a person, then we have identified the same person as well. If indeed philosophers ought to speak of persons in Wiggins' way, this blocks many attempts to say, in a philosophically significant sense, that one is no longer the same person after losing one's mind. Denial of sameness of persons is often a preface to ethical considerations; so Wiggins' claim is of great importance in areas of philosophy other than metaphysics.

In terms of the history of the concept of a person, Wiggins is lining himself up squarely with the Aristotelians against the supporters of Locke, who take continuity of consciousness to be the criterion of identity and who suppose that it is logically possible that we change bodies. Aristotelians think that the person or self is the form of the living body, hence inseparable from it.

Notes to Chapter Eleven are on pp. 322-23.

177

Aristotle's view about the inseparability of souls from bodies, which Wiggins thinks is nearly correct, is this: "So there is no call to ask whether the soul and the body are one, just as there is no call to ask this question with the wax and the impression in the wax, nor any call to ask this question for any substance and the matter of which this substance is composed."[6] Unfortunately for this view, Wiggins notes, a body is a substance, yet a dead body is not a person.[7] It seems, then, that the soul, or self, or person is separable from the body. The very brief form of Wiggins' answer is that the person is inseparable from the living body. The person is not, however, merely the living body since the person has irreducibly psychological properties (58).

Since Wiggins is not willing to identify the person with the living body as materialists do, one may wonder why he is not willing to accept the dualism of Locke. He defends Locke against Butler's objection of circularity of the memory criterion for identifying persons and thinks that Locke is right to emphasize self-awareness, a profoundly important feature of persons.[8] Wiggins proceeds by revising Locke's account to overcome the problem of the imperfections of our memory (155). In the end, however, Wiggins argues that a biological underpinning is needed for the consciousness of persons and that Lockeans overemphasize the intellect. The continuity of a ballerina needs explaining as much as that of a philosopher (160).

Part of Wiggins' argument for his doctrine that persons are substances, organisms more specifically, is the inadequacy of the denial of this doctrine. If we take persons to be defined by their functions, then the resulting concept is inadequate to bear the weight which is put on it from a moral point of view (185). Although Wiggins denies ethical naturalism, he asserts a neighbouring doctrine that the nature of persons is the basis of value in the sense of causally enabling objective agreement between persons (186-87). Concerning this difficult doctrine Wiggins asserts:

> If freedom and dignity and creativity are what we crave, we shall find more promise of these things in the Heraclitean prediction "You would not find out the bounds of the soul, though you traversed every path: so deep is its *logos*" than in the idea that it is for men to determine the limits of their own nature, or mould and remake themselves to the point where they can count as their very own creation. (187)

This can be understood partly through seeing that Wiggins holds that the functional account of persons allows what counts as a person to be a matter for interpretation while his own account makes it a matter for discovery. Person is not only a natural kind but a kind of such depth and complexity that Heraclitus' prediction is born out.

Another dangerous path that Wiggins claims to avoid by means of his own theory is that taken by those who see persons as mere social constructs. Such is the concept used by the social manager who would engineer society to the manager's own political and moral specifications. This limits human potential, and such constructs, once in place, are resistant to reform (180-82). Those who try to be something more or something other than the manager's concept of a person allows are blocked by the social norms hallowed in terms of persons. If, on the other hand, we think, as Wiggins does, that what persons are is generally specifiable in biological terms but infinitely variable in the irreducibly psychological attributes which we may discover to be supervenient on that biological basis, then we do not limit human potential through the narrow vision of the social manager.

A person then is a substance. If we have the same animal, we have the same person; for however one identifies a thing it is the same thing. The spatio-temporal continuity of the living body will, therefore, be sufficient to individuate the person. The sense in which Wiggins accepts that the person transcends the body is that the person is realized in the living body. One can abstract the person from the body, but not in practice separate the two. The criticism which quickly comes to mind in the light of current philosophical debate on persons is based on the possibility of brain transplants in which a person seems to leave her body, except for the brain, behind.

Wiggins is highly and rightly suspicious of science fiction examples. Of Shoemaker's brain transplant case in which the character of the person goes to a new body with the brain Wiggins says: "We are deceived by the high-quality of the actors and mimics we see on the stage if with the help of greasepaint and props they have made us think this is as (relatively) simple as the transposition of music from one instrument to another" (189). Certainly it may well be in this and in other cases of radical change, including fission cases, we can appear to describe them without contradiction only because they are so badly underdescribed.

There may be another reason for thinking the various science fictions impossible. Wiggins uses a view based on Leibniz and Putnam which makes natural kinds determined by lawlike principles discovered by attention to an arbitrary good specimen of the kind (169). We take, for example, arbitrary good specimens of gold, which we have known for centuries, and discover the properties of gold as a natural kind. Now "person" may be a sortal term, such as "gold," based on lawlike principles. We thought we could imagine making gold from base metals in certain ways which turned out to be impossible. Similarly, we think that persons can change in ways which threaten the use of spatio-temporal continuity of the living body as a criterion of identity. These may turn out to be impossible as well once we understand the lawlike regularities underlying the concept of a person. This remains an open question.

We may possibly be able by some process, not involving the philosopher's stone, to synthesize gold. It would be real gold for all that. If, by some much more miraculous process,[9] we can synthesize people, then they would be real people, made of flesh and blood. They would not be just good-looking automata. If, by contrast, we accept mere automata because they function as people, then we open ourselves to the objectionable views mentioned earlier. What persons are becomes open to interpretation. We would still, therefore, by Wiggins' lights have to distinguish between real persons and artifacts which function like some persons if we want the concept of a person to bear the moral weight we put on it.

One response to this claim about moral weight is that given by Williams, whom we are about to discuss. Williams says that the concept of a person simply will not bear this weight, and we should reject this concept as a foundation for ethical thought.[10] Before we consider Williams' alternative conception of a person, let us look at an example of the use of Wiggins' concept of a person in moral discourse.

A person's dementia, a radical change of psychological properties, does not, by Wiggins' lights, destroy her as a person. It would be foolish to say that she has a different body although it has changed in some respects, including important neurophysiological respects. Since Wiggins argues against the use of relative identity to say that the sufferer of dementia is the same living body but not the same person, and since he denies that the person is separable from the body, he must count her as the same person through the radical changes.

A possible objection to this analysis using Wiggins' concept of a person can be worked out using the idea of our irreducibly psychological characteristics supervenient on our neurophysiology. Can Wiggins not say that while the person cannot exist without the living body, the living body can exist without the person? Yes, he can. Probably he would do so in the case of a neomort. All of the psychological properties formerly associated with such a living body are gone. The dementia patient has certainly lost her intellect, but Wiggins thinks we place too much emphasis on intellect. Her remaining psychological properties, for instance perceptual and emotional ones, may well qualify her as a person on Wiggins' view; hence she is, on that view, the same person who once had a great intellect.

There is no doubt that a dementia patient no longer has the capacities she once had. By the functionalist account of persons which Wiggins criticizes, such a patient would be gone, though her body remains, like a computer which has been disabled and can no longer run the program we knew as a person. Wiggins rejected this account as unable to bear the moral weight we put on the concept of a person. In this case, one would be released from obligations to the patient which were undertaken so long as she lived. By Wiggins' account of persons, such a release would be premature.

Williams takes a dim view of the concept of person just adumbrated since he thinks that concept is not a true sortal or natural kind concept. That is why he does not trust it to bear the moral weight that Wiggins puts on it. Williams takes persons to be merely bodies, as we shall see.

Williams' bodily criterion

Short of saying with Ayer that persons are merely bodies—sometimes this is restricted to bodies of the human kind—Williams argues, like Wiggins, that bodily identity is a necessary condition of personal identity.[11] That is, if person A is the same as person B, then A has the same body as B. Williams denies, however, that A's having the same body as B is enough to guarantee that A is the same person as B. Williams' thesis that bodily identity is a necessary but not a sufficient condition of personal identity, if true, would rule out the very popular view, for which Strawson argued, that one could survive apart from one's body.

The essential point in Williams' argument to show that bodily identity is always necessary to personal identity is that any criterion of personal identity has to have a user (14). The attempts by Locke and others to explain personal identity without the body rely, in Williams' opinion, on presupposing an impossible viewpoint from which to observe the non-bodily features of persons. This viewpoint is neither that from within the person (subjective) nor that from without (objective). The use of criteria like self-consciousness and memory is illegitimate since these are not observable from the objective point of view (14-15). From the subjective point of view, the question of identity cannot arise (13). What we use to identify a person are actions and events, but we cannot associate these with a person without first identifying that person by means of her body. There are two points I wish to examine in this sort of argument: the viewpoint problem in general and the question of personal identity from a subjective viewpoint. We will see in a later chapter on Thomas Nagel that Nagel takes seriously the idea of a view from nowhere.

Even if one agrees with Williams concerning the viewpoint argument, the idea that a criterion of identity must have a user needs qualification. To require that a criterion of identity in fact be used by someone to make an identification is probably requiring more than Williams does here. Philosophers are not prone to restrict attention to what may be put to practical purposes. Let us suppose that he is saying, rather, that the criterion could possibly be used. Williams seems to be saying that I cannot use criteria like memory to identify others since I can have no access to their memories. What is required, then, is an argument to show that it is not possible to know another's memories. Such an argument is not given. Only an assertion about lack of access to the mental events of another bolsters this claim about memory (14). Is mind-reading logically impossible? Even supposing that Williams is right about this impossibility, there remains the question whether a criterion of identity might not be correct even if it were inapplicable to the identification of others. That is to say, the criterion might contain a metaphysical truth but our knowledge of identities of persons might be limited by our not being able to apply the criterion.

Williams considers Locke's use of memory as "what makes a man be himself to himself " (13). Williams tries to show that this is absurd. His argument is puzzling, but it is his reply to objections that reveals what has gone wrong. He imagines this objection:

> "You have argued," it might be said, "that no man can use memory as a criterion of his own identity. But this is just what shows that memory is the essence of personal identity; figuratively speaking, memory is so much what makes him a certain person that when provided with certain memories, he cannot doubt who he is."

To this objection, Williams replies, "A man who has lost his memory cannot say who anyone else is, either, nor whether any object is the same as one previously presented" (14). It appears that Williams is treating the memories used to identify a person as coming in an all-or-nothing package. That is, however, not the way memories are packaged. Apparently one can be in states in which large parts of memory are lost, like transient global amnesia or epileptic automatism,[12] not knowing who one is, but knowing much about other things and people. One can retain complex abilities and characteristics without remembering one's own history. Once memory of one's own history returns, one cannot doubt who one is.

My reply to Williams is a two-edged sword. If memory, during a state of epileptic automatism, for instance, is nearly intact except for memory of personal history, then memory of personal history does not seem essential to personal identity. This is hardly what the objection intended to support. I agree, however, neither with Williams nor an opponent diametrically opposed, a Lockean for instance. Memory of personal history is one of many marks of personal identity, including the body, personality, abilities, and other memories of the person. What I take from Williams, then, is the point that Locke and others have overemphasized the role of memory of personal history. On the other hand, Williams goes too far in his rejection of memory altogether but more of this towards the end of this work.

Personality also comes under withering fire from Williams' position. William's resurrects the famous Beauchamp case of dissociation of the personality reported by Prince[13] to consider whether one may individuate personalities independently of the body. Beauchamp was reported to have various personalities in complicated relationships. Some of her personalities knew the doings of the others and some were supposedly in ignorance of others. Williams seems, at some points in the argument, to take it at face value that some of her personalities could not remember what others had done (17). This is a matter in some doubt. The symptoms described by Prince are sometimes thought to have been produced by Beauchamp out of Victorian modesty and a desire to please Prince.[14] Whether the Beauchamp case is reliable evidence or not, let us assume for the sake of argument that Beauchamp's reported symptoms are possible. Note that the memories which make a person herself to herself may be lost and regained if such symptoms are possible. While this occurs, other memories remain intact, in the Beauchamp story. Self-identification through memory seems to make perfectly good sense for Ms. Beauchamp in spite of Williams' claim that such self-identification is absurd. It seems then that the shaky evidence which Williams accepts, if it really is acceptable, provides a counter-example to his anti-Lockean claim. But let us see how Williams is using this Beauchamp case. His purpose is not to deal with the memory criterion, but to attack personality as a criterion of identity.

With respect to individuation of personalities, Williams claims that they are particulars only in the sense that character is a particular, "a sense which is grounded in the particular body."[15] Here, of course, he is only speaking of the publicly observable personality and character. This is a point well taken. We could not begin to speak of Ms. Beauchamp's various personalities without first identifying her by means of her body. Her personality or personalities and her body are both part of what makes her Ms. Beauchamp; that is they are parts of her identity, but we can know of that identity primarily through observation, which gives the body its central position in identification. This should not in itself impugn personality as essential to the identity of the person. It makes, rather, a point about how we may come to know that person.

Williams wishes, however, to claim more than this. Character and personality are not genuine particulars, he claims. They are parasitic on the body for their status as apparent particulars (17-18). If this is so, then not only are they not the primary way in which we identify people, they are not metaphysically primary in the identities of people. The person is the body, and the personality is merely a set of properties of the body which may change without changing who the person is. Whether or not personalities are essential to persons, all Williams' argument shows is the epistemological point that the way we come to know them is through the body. This depends on our particular viewpoint from which we come to know persons. Williams' argument depends on saying that it is the only way we could gain such knowledge. This is the point of his saying that a criterion must have a user, and there must be some viewpoint from which we make the identification.

This brings us back to the viewpoint from which we apply a criterion of identity. Williams argues that it must be either subjective or objective, and then rules out the subjective viewpoint. We have just seen that it is not ruled out. It turns out then that publicity is not essential to identification. Ms. Beauchamp could identify herself when in possession of the appropriate memories. All those views of persons, like Locke's and Descartes', which result in criteria which are heavily dependent on subjective evidence, have not been laid to rest by Williams' argument thus far. Williams has, however, given us reason for caution in adopting Lockean or Cartesian positions by pointing out the epistemological importance of the body from the objective viewpoint. The subjective viewpoint, while not vanquished, is limited. It is logically possible that there may be incorrect self-identification of a kind as reported in the case of Ms. Beauchamp. Should I wake up convinced that I am Bernard Williams, I could perhaps be persuaded of the falsity of that self-identification. One identifies oneself through one's body, personal history, abilities, and personality as others identify one. In cases of amnesia or dissociation of personality, the objective check of others may be needed to aid self-identification. If we could accept Williams' metaphysical position that persons are thinking bodies, we could simplify our conception of such difficult cases. Ms. Beauchamp would remain Ms. Beauchamp throughout her radical changes, according to Williams, while she must go into and out of existence frequently on Locke's view.

Williams puts up three main contenders for the understanding of what persons are. Two of these we have discussed earlier. The three are Strawson's view that persons are unanalysable subjects, Descartes' position that persons are Egos in bodies, and the position Williams himself supports, that persons are thinking bodies. We have seen how Williams treats positions like those of Descartes and Locke, which have the Ego or the consciousness housed in a body and able to change residences.

Williams puts forth a variety of objections[16] to Strawson's position that the concept of a person must be taken as primitive, making persons unanalysable subjects in terms of which such things as person's minds and person's bodies must be defined. One of the simplest of Williams' objections is that treating persons as bearers of both M- and P-predicates is too inclusive, since animals may also bear both (66). This is indicative of the general thrust behind Williams' objections. It shows that Williams does not take seriously the idea that the concept of a person is primitive, for his objection depends on taking that concept as defined in terms of M- and P-predicates. If there is to be any defining in this neighbourhood, it will have to be of the predicates in terms of persons, not the other way around. While I do not dispute that Strawson has insufficiently defined these predicate types, that does not, in itself, defeat the view that the concept of a person must be taken as primitive. One may object that Strawson has not satisfactorily shown us that so doing will lead to advantages in metaphysics. Williams may contend that taking persons as bodies which think, material things to which psychological predicates are applicable, is a preferable basis for theory.

One of the objections to his own position considered by Williams is that persons who once had bodies can survive in a disembodied state, that is, without bodies. Williams warns that this way Cartesianism lies. Apparently, while he takes Strawson's view of persons seriously, Williams thinks that a reduction to Cartesianism is a reduction to absurdity. Nonetheless, the possibility of disembodied persons is widely accepted, often for religious reasons, and our language reflects that. It is natural enough to speak of shaking off these mortal coils and departing from the body. Nor is this just figurative. Even the non-religious tend to take seriously the often reported out-of-body experiences had by people near death. Williams must argue that this common way of talking rests on a metaphysical error.

Williams first points out that supposedly disembodied persons would be indeterminate in many respects, just like fictional characters. There is no answer to "How much does Sherlock Holmes weigh?" nor to "How much does Julius Caesar weigh?" given that Caesar is now disembodied. Williams adopts a principle that, he claims, excludes such entities as disembodied persons from existence: "If we are given a specification of a thing of a certain sort, and are told that it exemplifies no determinates under determinables associated with things of that sort, we can standardly conclude that it is not the specification of any real thing of that sort." (70). The application of this principle in the present case is simply question-begging. Why should we assume that disembodied persons should be determinate with respect to weight as embodied persons are? Is it that weight is essential to persons? Then one has assumed that persons are material or have an essential material component. Whether it is possible that persons can, like Cartesian egos, have psychological without material features cannot be determined by the principle Williams adopts until we have decided what things of that sort, persons, have as determinables. Only if material properties must be included among these determinables will disembodied persons be ruled out. Since the reasonable alternative (of saying that disembodied persons do not have such things as weight among their determinables) has not been dealt with, Williams further arguments against the unreasonable alternative of saying that disembodied persons have a determinate weight of zero must be put aside as amusements.

Williams might retort that the onus is on those who imagine that there could be such things as disembodied persons to say what their class of determinables is. We know, roughly, for real people in what respects they are determinate. The answer that disembodied persons would be determinate only in those respects which do not require a body might elicit the response that there are none; all psychological properties are dependent on material bodies. This claim brings us to what Williams calls "the micro level" (64) of neurology and questions as to the causes of the psychological characteristics of people. The question then becomes one for empirical science.

The philosophical questions which interest Williams arise not primarily from science but from consideration of the way we speak. For example, "Jones" and "Jones' body" are not interchangeable *salva veritate*; in other words, we can say true sentences using one of these two phrases which will become false sentences if we substitute the other. It seems, then, that these two refer to different things; hence, the person-as-body thesis seems wrong. In a way this is tricky for Williams since so many of his arguments rest heavily on our use of language, on what we may plausibly say. As he points out, however, there are phrases which are synonymous in some contexts and not in others; so we cannot rest much on the contrast between these two phrases in some contexts (74). Williams is, moreover, revisionist in his metaphysics. He wants to change the way we standardly speak about persons.

Williams examines the difficulties of separating material from psychological properties of persons. This is just the problem with Strawson's M-predicates and P-predicates revisited. Descartes takes extension to be the fundamental property of material things—their being in space and time. Williams thinks that defining material properties in terms of extension would exclude such properties as being observable by physicists as a property of material bodies (75). That depends, however, on our analysis of observability. Williams looks at perception and memory as effects with causes in the body (75-76); so he should see observability in the same terms. One can, it seems, accept extension as essential to material objects and say, consistently with Williams' other views, that observability is the potential of objects to cause our perceptions. This would not help Descartes as it reduces psychological events, perceptions, to material events.

The difficulty here is to say something on either side of the issue without begging the question as to the truth of materialism, dualism, or idealism. Williams tries to be neutral prior to his apparently materialist conclusions but remarks that it is "far from clear that the idea of causal relations obtaining in an immaterial substance could be anything but utterly mysterious" (75-76). Idealists would say the same about causes in matter. Dualists, however, suffer from the interaction problem here, and it is mainly against Cartesian dualism that Williams seems to defend his person-as-body thesis. It seems, not too surprisingly, that Williams' rejection of Cartesian dualism leads him to materialism.

Williams glosses his objection to dualism in terms of class membership. If whales are mammals, then being the same whale is being the same mammal. Similarly, being the same person would imply having the same body, if the necessity-of-the-body thesis is correct. There is an infelicitous lack of parallel here. In any case, against this putative parallel Williams considers Shoemaker's science fiction brain-exchange case. Two people have their brains exchanged and their personalities go to the new bodies along with the brain. Williams seems to accept this as possible. In response to Shoemaker, Williams refers to a problem—which Williams also attributes to Strawson—namely, that Shoemaker must say how it is that the ascription of bodily properties to persons is not the ascription of anything to bodies (79). One would have to be able to say following a brain trade, for example, that a person who used to be six feet tall with grey hair is now five feet tall and has not yet turned grey.

Putting aside the question as to the logical possibility of Shoemaker's example, it is odd that Williams requires of Shoemaker that he overcome linguistic conventions when Williams was not willing to take them that seriously in his own response to the objection concerning interchangeability of "Jones" and "Jones' body." Shoemaker could simply say, emulating Williams, that we ascribe properties sometimes to bodies and sometimes to persons; which it is depends on the context of the utterance.

Williams also considers a science fiction case in which the information in one person's brain is recorded and transferred to another. Again, the logical possibility of this is not questioned. Since the contents of our minds seem to be heavily dependent on the actual structure of our brains, it seems that minds cannot be thought of as software to be recorded and transferred, leaving the old hardware behind. Let us grant, for the sake of argument, that the background assumptions could be spelled out so that such transfers are logically possible for beings like ourselves.

Williams is concerned that such transfers could be made in more than one case, creating a number of people who are exact copies of the original person. They cannot all be identical to the original. This sort of copying is called "reduplication" and seems to lead to puzzles if we depart from the bodily criterion of identity. Williams considers a way out for those who think in terms of character as a criterion of identity. Two tokens of persons cannot be identified with a third token. The problem of reduplication might be overcome, Williams speculates, if we think of persons as types, as classes of bodies (80). This is, however, no advance. Williams considers what it would be like to fall in love with a person type and to want to be near any of several tokens of that type. "Much of what we call loving a person would begin to crack under this, and reflection on it may encourage us not to undervalue the deeply body-based situation we actually have" (81). As you will see in a later discussion, Parfit is not so concerned with tokens as with types. In his revisionist way, Parfit embraces the very conclusion which Williams finds repugnant. Williams, however, is also revisionist and admits that his own view may seem odd, entailing as it does that one who loves a person loves a body, but "the alternatives that so briskly flow out of suspending the present situation do not sound too spiritual either" (81). But must we really accept his view that the main remaining alternative to considering ourselves as bodies is to consider ourselves as types? I have tried to cast some doubt on his arguments leading to this conclusion.

Williams' arguments, however, make it difficult to keep to the Aristotelian position defended by Wiggins and even more difficult to occupy the large opposing fort where defenders of Cartesian egos or Lockean consciousnesses reside. In particular, Williams has, through his consideration of reduplication, made it very important for any concept of a person to find an anchor lest it float into the region where persons become types of things and particular individuals may be just tokens of that type, more like particular copies of an frequently printed book rather than like precious crystals each of which is unique. Williams chooses the body as the anchor.

Regarding the moral import of the concept of a person, Williams writes:

> The category of person, though a lot has been made of it in some moral philosophy, is a poor foundation for ethical thought, in particular because it looks like a sortal or classificatory notion while in fact it signals characteristics that almost all come in degrees—responsibility, self-consciousness, capacity for reflection, and so on. It thus makes it seem as if we were dealing with a certain class or type of creature, when in fact we are vaguely considering those human beings who pass some mark on a scale. To make matters worse, the pass mark for some purposes is unsuitable for others. If *person* implies something called "full moral responsibility," the lowest age for entry to the class that has traditionally been entertained is seven, but anyone who has lived with a six-year-old, or a two-year-old, has vivid reasons for thinking of them as persons.[17]

If, on the other hand, we accept the claim that the capacity for reflection and self-consciousness are the effects of causes "running through the body." as Williams puts it,[18] then, whether or not we accept fully that persons are bodies, ancient concerns about responsibility arise. The problem of causal determinism, that there seems to be no room for people to have responsibility if all their thoughts, feelings and actions are caused by material phenomena, surely must be faced by any view that answers "Yes" to "Are persons bodies plus their psychological effects?" At this level at least, Williams' views on persons have a very direct impact on moral theory.

That is not to say that moving away from Wiggins' notion that person is a sortal concept does not radically alter the ways in which that concept can be used in moral theory. If we must, moreover, disabuse ourselves of the opposing concepts of a person as a personality, Cartesian Ego or Lockean consciousness, then these other ways of making the concept bear moral weight evaporate. Even if we can get over materialist determinist difficulties with motivating moral discourse at all, we will still have to forego Locke's forensic concept of a person and Wiggins' sortal or natural kind. We will not be able to talk of the rights of persons. If Williams is right, ethics has become a very different subject.

Application to Daphne's case

In terms of my constant example, one who becomes demented, if Williams is right, is certainly the same person, dementia notwithstanding. It would be foolish to argue that her body is not the same body. What we see is, moreover, still a thinking body, though the level of thought is diminished nearly to the vanishing point. Depending on the height at which one puts the pass mark on certain scales, one might wish to say that the dementia patient is not a person, but this would be perhaps more revisionist than Williams would wish to be. In this identification of the patient, Williams would, then, probably agree with Wiggins. But what follows from this identification regarding the patient's right to treatment or our duties to keep her comfortable? Nothing at all for Williams. What we ought to do has to be determined, according to Williams, without appeal to, say, the dignity of persons. Saying the patient is a person does not necessarily put her into the same class as you just because we say that you are a person. Person, for Williams, is not a sortal concept as Wiggins would have it.

Daphne is the same person she was prior to her misfortune, according to Wiggins' theory. This is morally significant since, for Wiggins, a person is a particular kind of creature, not merely a conscious body which can perform certain functions. A difference in kind is the moral basis for a difference in treatment.

What I like about Wiggins and Williams

Both Wiggins and Williams make the body important without actually identifying persons with bodies. Williams, however, comes closer to this position than Wiggins. Wiggins reminds us of the moral import of the concept of a person. Williams, through his iconoclasm against the spiritual or moral importance of persons as persons, drives us to clarify the way in which the concept of a person can be central to our moral thinking. Williams provides us, I believe, with a good example of the sort of revisionism which banishes concepts of a person to the museum of philosophical curiosities. Some such concepts,. I will eventually argue, hold on to the door-posts and will not be forced into this unseemly retirement. For now, I will explicate more of this revisionist work in current philosophy of persons.

TWELVE
Nozick's Self-Makers

Crazy solutions

The concept of a person is slippery. The problems which we encounter over the ages trying to explicate it are legion. Nozick admits that the solutions on which he speculates are crazy but thinks that, since all the sane solutions have been tried without success over the centuries, it may be that only the crazy solutions will work.[1] Some of the things he proposes do seem daft, but I will try to show how he is driven to them. What they reveal for those of us who hold out for sanity is important.

Crucial to Nozick's understanding of persons are two ideas, that of a closest continuer and that of reflexivity. Roughly, closest continuers of past people are the present people who resemble those past people most. Reflexivity has to do with a peculiar way some things, like references of words, have of looping back on themselves. The keystone in Nozick's arch of ideas between the concepts of a closest continuer and reflexivity is that of an action which creates the person who does it. As long as you can buy the notion that an act can take place independently of the person who seems to perform that action, you will feel at home with Nozick. Before you turn the page crying "This way madness lies!" understand that the theory is able to account for some of our common sense views and to explain how they are sensible in spite of the powerful reasons to the contrary which are the heritage of philosophical thought about persons. While Nozick seems to put at least some of his speculations forth without full conviction, he does think they have some merit in providing us with fresh ways of wrestling with old problems (114). He is right about that. Just in case you lose patience as we follow Nozick through some difficult concepts and some strange examples, I hereby issue a promissory note: before the end of this book I will put some of what you read in this chapter to good use in talking about real people.

CC (Closest-continuer) theory
What a CC is

The question about persons which Nozick faces first is a familiar one by now, unless you just opened this book to this page and began here.

Notes to Chapter Twelve are on p. 323.

What makes a person at one time the same person at a later time? To construct examples I will use the names "Tom," "Dick," and "Harry," but these need not be different people and they need not be male. Names are like that nowadays. Well, then, consider any person Tom on New Year's Eve, 1990 and any person Dick on New Year's Day 1991. What are the criteria, once Tom has developed into Dick, for Dick being the same person as Tom? What criterion should we use to identify people over time? Nozick's answer is roughly that the identity of a person depends on who, among all the available alternatives, is the best candidate for being that person. If Dick is the best candidate for being Tom, Dick is called "the closest continuer of Tom" (33). Now let us see what makes a candidate the best one or what makes a continuer the CC (the closest continuer).

The CC of a person is caused by that person

Nozick describes the closest continuer of a person as not merely someone closely resembling the original but someone whose properties are like those of the original because the original's properties *caused* the continuer's properties. As an example of such a causal connection of properties, suppose Dick has strength of character because Tom did, for instance, because Dick is just a later stage of a person who was previously called "Tom." This causal connection does not, according to Nozick, imply temporal continuity. People might have temporal gaps, as do the messages sent on telephone wires (35). Thus all views, like that of Wiggins for example, which require spatio-temporal continuity for persons to continue are dismissed. "Continuer" really means "resembler" here.

The similarity metric: Weighted dimensions of closeness

So much for the concept of a continuer. To understand the other half of the phrase "closest continuer," namely "closest," is a difficult task indeed. Nozick speaks of a set of weighted dimensions and features in a similarity metric by means of which closeness is to be measured (37). By "weighted dimensions" he seems to mean the properties of people, like having strength of character or having curly hair, plus the weight we give these properties in judgments about identity. Think of Nozick as developing a suggestion we saw from Strawson in chapter ten concerning the weight we might give to the M and P properties which tell us who is who.

Whether Dick is really Tom will, of course, depend a lot more on their shared strength of character than on their sharing the same kind of hair. Character is, therefore, a dimension of much greater weight than hair-style. What Nozick calls the "metric" is a complex of causal and qualitative dimensions of the person, to each of which we assign weights. This metric has to be taken into consideration in making judgments of closeness of continuation, but Nozick does not say in detail what is within the metric. He is offering a general schema to be filled in by whoever is making the judgment of identity. There are limits, however, on the ways we can select and weigh dimensions and thus fill in the schema. Nonetheless, there is not one correct answer to the question whether Tom is Dick. According to the metric Dick selects, the answer might be "yes," while you or I might correctly deny this if Dick is too much changed from the Tom we knew, according to our metric. Harry might be closer to Tom as we see it. Closeness of persons, hence identity as well, is relative to the metric used in judging it.

In spite of this relativity, not anyone can be identical to Tom. There are four kinds of limits: CC limits, that is, limits intrinsic to the concept of closest continuers; mono-relatedness which has to do with predecessors as well as continuers and is not as bad as it sounds; metaphysical limits on classification; and, finally, social limits. Dick has a long way to go before he gets to be Tom, but I will have to consider each of these limits before a picture of Nozick's theory begins to emerge.

CC limits

Nozick points out that although we make different judgments of the identity of persons, we are still using the same general schema for making such judgments, and he thinks that his schema fits the judgments we do, in fact, make. Even though we can always pick a metric to suit a particular judgment about, for instance, whether Tom is Dick, "it does not follow that every group of judgments can be made to fit." While individual judgments may vary, certain combinations of judgments are ruled out. You might, for instance, be able to adopt a metric under which Tom is Dick, but then you could no longer deny that Sally is Mary once you have chosen your metric. Picking a metric is deciding what you mean by "closeness of continuation" for persons, and that ties you to a whole set of identity judgments (38). One cannot make such judgments lightly, I suppose, since they affect one's own case.

Mono-relatedness

Just as there are continuers of persons, as Dick might be of Tom, there are predecessors of persons, as Tom might be of Dick. Roughly, the person most closely resembling Dick who came before Dick is Dick's closest predecessor.[2] Now Nozick requires that for Tom to be Dick, not only must Dick be Tom's closest continuer, but Tom must be Dick's closest predecessor. This he calls "mono-relatedness" (42). To see why Nozick does this, consider Harry, who is more like Dick than Tom is and who exists along with Tom on New Year's Eve. Even though Dick is Tom's closest continuer,

Harry might be Dick's closest predecessor. In that case, I think, Nozick would not think either Tom or Harry was identical to Dick. Now you might remember the causal condition on closeness and ask how on earth Dick could arise causally from both Tom and Dick. Well it could not happen in the real world, so far as I know. Nozick, however, takes all examples to be relevant as long as they are of logically possible events. Now a fictional case in which Tom and Harry are in a terrible accident and clever surgeons cobble together Dick from the pieces is, although disgusting, *apparently* logically possible. It is an example which is underdescribed, so we cannot be sure that it is logically possible. Nozick's condition of mono-relatedness is intended, in any case, to rule out the identification of Tom and Dick in such cases of merging of persons. If thinking of persons merging is too strange, consider a case of two rivers flowing into one another at a fork. Nozick would not count the resulting river as identical to either of the rivers upstream.

While we are on the topic of identity, note that Nozick does not think that mono-relatedness is sufficient to make Tom identical to Dick, but it is necessary. In other words, if they are merely mono-related, it does not follow that they are identical, but if they are identical, then they are mono-related.

Metaphysical limits

The job of such classifying concepts as the concept of a person, according to Nozick, is to maximize the unity of a class of entities. This is to be done by maximizing the differences between classes and the similarities within classes in our classificatory scheme (86). Persons, therefore, should be a lot like each other and as little as possible like non-persons. It is then not arbitrary, not merely conventional, what we call a person, nor is it arbitrary who we say is who. We need to follow a reasonable set of principles of classification. It follows that if I try to look upon my grandfather's departed pet cat as my closest predecessor, I can be making a mistake through adopting a classification scheme which fuzzes the border between persons and non-persons. I cannot, however, be wrong about who it is for whom I am seeking a predecessor. I am trying to figure out who I am in such a case, however badly I may be doing it.

One of the results of maximizing similarities among persons and maximizing their differences from other beings is the narrowing of the class of persons in some respects and widening of it in others. There are many human beings who, if included in the class of persons, would prevent maximization. One might include, for example, only those with the linguistic ability to say "I" meaningfully and those who will develop this capacity. (Nozick's reasons for this will be revealed later.) This might exclude some severely retarded human beings but include Washoe, the chimpanzee who uses sign language, among persons. Nozick, an old hand at bullet-biting, should be willing to accept such a consequence, but he seems not to bite. At least he does not explicitly include non-humans in the class of persons. In any case, his general principles for classification limit what kinds of identity judgments he is willing to countenance.

Social limits

What happens if Dick tries, when deciding on his own metric, to include Harry's body or part of it as Dick's own? Assuming that Harry and Dick have distinct bodies, this will be frowned on in most societies, at least where slavery is unacceptable. Society limits our acts of self-creation. To this point Nozick says:

> Rewards and punishments will lead to a boundary in a particular location along innate salient features or dimensions. Recalcitrant individuals who act on their deviant classifications wherein part of their own body includes someone else's arms, will be punished, institutionalized, or killed. Usually, the mutual compatibility of self-definitions occurs with less hardship. (108)

The class of innate, salient features might include a great deal. Nozick does not help us with examples other than the inappropriate claiming of another's arms. The term "innate" leads me to suspect that he is thinking of features common to human beings rather than socially determined features. Not enough is said here as Nozick is just skimming over this point, but I will develop it when I come to pontificate on the ways I think we should develop a concept of a person.

Self-creation and reflexivity

We ourselves are each, in part, responsible for determining who, by our own lights, preceded us and who continues us (105). This gives particular tang to the question, "Who do you think you are?" We create ourselves—at least we share in our own creation—by deciding how we measure closeness of continuation. The self conceives of itself as a listing and weighting of the dimensions in the metric used to measure closeness. Nozick sums this up, "Which continuer is closest to a person depends (partially) on that person's own notion of closeness" (106). Nozick does not attempt to say how much weight should be given to self-conception in the metric for closeness, but it must be considerable. He thinks that what distinguishes selves from other things and gives them special dignity is their self-synthesis, their determining their own identity (107).

The idea that we somehow create our own characters or personalities is not an uncommon one, but usually half-baked. Nozick, however, is a rather thorough and systematic baker. Although he takes on the whole person, not just the person's character as a self-made item, he still makes the notion of self-creation somewhat plausible. One must, however, be able to imagine actions as events which may exist independently of the person whose action it later turns out to be (88-89). The act of self-creation exists prior to the self which it creates. Suppose, for example, that in the year 2000 Dick chooses a metric for determining his closest predecessor and continuer. According to this metric, Tom in the year 1990 was Dick's closest predecessor, and Harry in the year 2010 will be Dick's closest continuer. This newly unified person, Tom-Dick-and-Harry, only comes into existence when Dick's action creates this person. Once this person exists, Dick's action is this person's action. Dick, of course, cannot choose any old Tom and Harry. There are limits on the choice of metric, which were described above. But Dick can choose prior to the coming into being of the person Tom-Dick-and-Harry.

Accepting actions which create people appears, initially, like giving up on people. Actions may be among the events which make up persons but which may be described without mentioning persons. This seems to lead to what I call "impersonalism," the view that people are not necessarily part of our description of reality. We could just describe the actions and leave people out of our account of what exists. If, however, as Nozick apparently sees it, one of a series of actions may be an act of self-creation, then, it seems to me, it is not possible to describe the action without mentioning the person created, the self which is synthesized. This is a good feature of Nozick's view, that people are real, not merely convenient fictions. By contrast, Hume, whom we wrestled with in chapter six, made people disappear from his account of reality by his use of the device of actions existing independently from people. Parfit, who comes later in my account of contemporary philosophers, also favours impersonalism.

Reflexivity

Reflexive self-reference

Part of Nozick's explanation of self-creation involves an examination of the ability of people to say "I" in a special way. "I" is an indexical, and we have seen in the discussion of Ryle's exorcism of ghosts how words like "I," "this," "here," or "now" index an item in our scheme of reality. For example, when I say, "This tomato here on the window sill is green all over now," I pick out an object at a particular location in its journey through time and space. There is no contradiction in my pointing to the same tomato days later and saying, "This tomato here on the window sill is red all over now." The indexicals keep straight which stage of the tomato's ongoing development I am indicating.

If, however, I use the word "I" to refer to myself, then "I" is an indexical of a very special kind. The difference between this use of "I" and the use of "this" is in the *reflexivity* of the use of "I." Nozick explains:

> Some indexical terms have a reference that not only varies with the context of their utterance, but also depends essentially on the very utterance in which they appear; for example, "this very phrase" refers to that phrase itself, and "I..." refers to the producer of that token itself. Let us call such linguistic devices *reflexively self referring*. (74)

To put this a little less carefully (but perhaps more understandably) what "I" means, according to Nozick, is "the thing that is referring to itself by using this particular instance of the special indexical word 'I.'" "I" is special in that it points back at itself when we use it. The essence of the self is the capacity to meaningfully say "I" (79). Another way to understand reflexively self-referring terms is to say they are those which depend for their reference on the very utterance in which they appear. To know who or what "I" refers to on a given utterance of "I" we must know more than what is making the sound. A tape recorder may be making the sound, but it is the person who meaningfully said "I" into the microphone to whom this token (or instance) of the word "I" refers. Nozick has, thus, defined "self" in terms of the ability to use language in this special way.

It is not, then, the ability to speak or reason which distinguishes persons from beasts and machines which may possibly acquire these abilities to some degree, it is the ability to say "I" and mean it. If Washoe the chimpanzee or multiple-parallel-processing computers can do this too, then they are selves with us, by Nozick's rules.

Nozick has clarified two things about his view of persons with this linguistic approach to the self. First, it is clear that *person* is not a species-specific concept like *human being*. Second, the act of self-creation can be carried out through an act of reflexive self-reference. One need not speak the words aloud, I suppose, but when one says or thinks "I" and simultaneously has in mind some metric for closeness of continuation, then one creates oneself anew.

Think about a famous saying from Descartes, "I think therefore I am." Could this be false? Applying Nozick's view, it could be. For example, in saying "I" a person may be trying to create something which goes beyond the limits that were specified above on making choices regarding the metric for measuring closeness. If Dick is saying "I" in such a way as to include Harry's arms in the reference of "I," then Dick's act of self-creation fails and Dick is not who he is saying he is when he utters "I am." Perhaps it would be preferable to say that Dick has not said anything rather than that he has said something false, since his use of "I" is non-referring. I prefer to say that Dick has made a fictional claim as if it were a statement about reality. As Nozick puts it, "'I exist' might, strictly speaking, be false, in that the preconditions for the perfectly accurate use of the 'I' are not satisfied." (667).

Nozick also says that no thing in any possible world which always lacked the capacity for reflexive self-reference could be me or you (78). This, however, is not clear without looking at an example. "Always" is ambiguous. We might say, for example, that the stage or stages of Daphne following her last decline into dementia always lack the capacity for reflexive self-reference; hence, by Nozick's criteria, Daphne ceased to exist upon becoming permanently demented. On the other hand, we might say that Daphne no longer has, but once did have, the capacity for reflexive self-reference. In that case, the demented Daphne would be a later stage of the same person as Daphne the philosopher. Nozick takes the former stance and would say that Daphne, once she has finally lost the capacity for reflexive self-reference, is no more (78). Nozick of course makes the allowance for some periods of loss of the ability of self-reference without loss of self to provide for the brief interruption of the capacity for reflexive self-reference when, for instance, we are asleep. But he also makes an exception for those who have not yet developed the capacity of self-reference (78). This creates an interesting asymmetry in his view. A fetus is a self as long as it will develop the capacity for self-reference, while a senile adult who has permanently lost the capacity is no longer a self. I wonder why he does not say the self is born with the capacity for reflexive self-reference just as it dies when that capacity dies. Perhaps the answer lies in the apparent fact that the fetus has the potential to develop the capacity while the senile adult does not.

Another interesting feature of Nozick's account is that there seems to be no theoretical limit on how often one could recreate oneself through reflexive self-reference nor any limit on changing one's mind about who one is. It might, however, be difficult to be sincere about frequent changes if one is mentally stable. Perhaps this could be worked into the social limits on one's metric discussed earlier. There are also the limits imposed by the metaphysical principles of classification. If people become too volatile, going into and out of existence all the time, it might be difficult to unify them in a class.

Reflexive caring

The theme of reflexivity, of things feeding back into themselves, is crucial to Nozick's understanding of a person, as we have already seen through his analysis of the meaning of "I." Nozick also imports this feature into his understanding of our concern for our selves. Oddly enough, care for the self as the self, not as a bearer of some property or properties, is required by Nozick. The care is reflexive, looping back on itself the way the reference of the word "I" does. More precisely, it is care in virtue of a feature of the act of caring. Creation is an act of caring for the thing created; so self-synthesis is an act of caring for oneself (109-10).

Four possible theories of identity of persons over time

Without saying which he favours, Nozick throws out four possible views about identity for us to kick around. To avoid any further technical terminology and to simplify these theories, I will use the metaphor of a cartographer mapping a previously unmapped river. The cartographer must decide at various points in his journey down the river whether a body of water is the same river, a tributary, or an effluent. Nozick, because he takes seriously the logical possibility of odd things happening to people, must face similar decisions. He thinks, for instance, that people can possibly split into two people as a river splits into two rivers at a fork.

The first theory

The first theory is that identity over time follows the path of closest continuity. A person would be a series of things each of which was the closest continuer of the one before. Death is the end of continuity. Our intrepid cartographer travelling downstream would compare bodies of water to what he had just travelled over. Like Nozick, he would use a metric, a set of scales of similarity, to make a judgment about which body of water was the closest continuer of the river. At a fork in the river the cartographer would proclaim one fork an effluent and the other the river. On this first theory, if the river forked so neatly that there were two equally close continuers of the river, neither of them would be the continuation of that river being mapped.

In Daphne 's case, most of us would agree on continuity in spite of massive changes up until Daphne became demented. At this point, the different weights people give to the body, the personality, dispositions, abilities, and the mind would give different answers concerning her survival. If we use Nozick's first theory of personal identity and do in fact give different weights within the metric of closeness, our infrequent disagreements about survival could be explained as differences in choice of a closeness metric. Whether one is the same person after a major change would seem to depend on who is making the judgment. Nozick, however, takes the closeness metric each person chooses for herself as the important one for identifying that person. Within the limits mentioned, you are the best judge of who you are. This leads to puzzles in Daphne's case, since she changed her metric as she lost her intellectual abilities. At the end of her ability to consider such matters it was by no means clear on what Daphne put great weight where closeness was concerned. Perhaps Nozick would be willing to say that Daphne, at the point of ceasing to be able to keep a metric in mind, becomes a person only to others. Her incapacity to evaluate herself makes her like a child. She becomes, in some sense, less of a person since she loses that self-determination which is the source of a person's dignity. From this point of view there is some truth in the adage that one must value oneself to be valued by others, though the adage is interpreted in rather a new way. Valuing oneself comes through self-creation, as an act of reflexive caring.

If we think of the river once again, we can see how Nozick's first theory allows for having many rivers made out of one stretch of water. We might call a river from its origin to the ocean one hundred miles distant the "Blue River." But a shorter stretch within the Blue from mile ten to mile ninety of the Blue River might be the Shiny River. Within the Shiny River we might have the Moon River which goes from mile twenty to mile eighty of the Blue River. Various acts of self-creation in a person's life could have the effect of creating people within people in the same way.

It seems that, on Nozick's first theory, "Who's who?" becomes a question with more possible answers than seems plausible. The answers depend not only on who you ask but also on *when* you ask her. Daphne, before she lost the ability to do philosophy, put enormous weight on that ability. She would, perhaps, have had difficulty in conceiving of a continuer of herself who could not participate in that activity. Later, when participation was no longer possible for her, she saw herself as a continuation of the former Daphne, although it pained her greatly to be unable to do philosophy. She began to see other things as central to her being the person she was. In Nozick's terms, the later Daphne considered herself mono-related to the earlier Daphne, while the earlier Daphne would perhaps have denied this. Daphne the philosopher had a life which was part of the life of Daphne who came later like the Shiny River is part of the Blue River. The later Daphne created a new self including the earlier Daphne while the earlier Daphne created a self which ended prior to the later Daphne. Since Nozick's view allows for many acts of self-synthesis associated with one body, Nozick is committed to the view that there may be many people associated with one body over a lifetime. Closeness of continuation may not be completely arbitrary, but it is certainly flexible

The strangeness of Nozick's first proffered concept of personal identity, illustrated by the example of Daphne before and after she lost her most cherished ability, does not go away when we switch to any of the other proposals for identity that Nozick gives us. Nonetheless, Daphne thought of the woman whom she knew would result from her illness as someone other than herself, and there is some sense in this. The other theories, while strange, all capture something sensible as does the first theory.

The second theory

The first proposal was that identity follows the path of closest continuation. Nozick then modifies this to overcome what he calls the overlap problem. The problem, which I will explain through the river metaphor, is that two continuers might exist simultaneously, and we might have reasons to think of both of them as the closest. His solution is this: "Entity X follows the path of closest continuation, unless it is a short path."[3] To clarify both the problem and the solution, imagine that the Blue River forks, and the part that is most like the Blue before the fork ends after a short distance (which corresponds to a short-lived continuer on the short path of continuation). The less similar fork which continues on for a long way would be the Blue River on this second theory of Nozick's, but it would only be the Blue after we had come to the end of the short fork of the river. This is rather odd. Say that the short fork is one mile long. Then one mile after the fork, the long fork becomes the Blue river. From the fork for one mile along the long fork, there exists a very short river which is not the Blue.

This short-path condition only comes into play when there are two or more candidates for being a continuer of an earlier stage of a person. It is quite ad hoc. If the closest continuer dies off, we switch conveniently to the next closest and much longer lived continuer. This has the same subjectivity as the plain vanilla variety of closest continuation, and it does nothing to overcome the difficulty that there may be many people associated with one body. Nozick would, perhaps, not consider these objections to be real problems for his view. He bites the bullets on which other philosophers only nibble. There is no doubt that Nozick accepts a best-candidate theory of personal identity with all of its odd consequences.

The third theory

The Blue River, on this view, would not include the short fork but simply go along the long fork which is a less close continuer of the Blue before the fork. This third proposal for defining personal identity is that, instead of switching at the end of a short path of life—a short-lived closest continuer—one simply ignores the short path and becomes the second closest continuer at the fork in one's life. If we are not looking at this from some timeless viewpoint, we will have to wait to see how long a continuer lives before declaring it closest. Later stages of a person will determine whether earlier stages are part of the person or not. This is not quite as odd as switching to the second-closest continuer after a short-lived continuer as in theory one. Nonetheless, it is strange to think that I might not be the same person who began writing this book if I should die before I wake tomorrow and some reasonable facsimile comes along to finish this book. and my life. Perhaps that is ruled out by the social limits on continuation.

The fourth and, mercifully, last theory

Finally Nozick proposes what I will call an "ur-person," an original which every later stage must closely continue. Using the Blue River metaphor, the Blue might, at its delta, divide into many rivers. Part of this river and part of that could be cobbled together as the Blue. The stretches of water which most resembled the pre-delta Blue would be the Blue. Similarly, if the person divides in a kind of tree structure, then there may be segments of many different branches which would be assembled into one person because of their closeness to the ur-person. While I like the idea that there must be something central to all stages of me as I flow through life, I do not think that this quite captures that idea.

All of these theories of identity which Nozick puts forth have a drawback from within the closest-continuer theory. That theory subjectivizes identity and these are attempts, albeit unsuccessful, to objectify identity. For example, a person-stage on a short path of life would consider herself to be the closest continuer of a predecessor which some other second-closest continuer would also take to be her predecessor. To say that one of them is right is to defy the principle of self-creation, the principle that who a person is depends heavily on that person's own metric for closeness of continuation. The weight given to a person's own metric, does not, therefore, remove the puzzle about who is who in every case. There could still be competing continuers, each of which had excellent grounds to think the other an impostor.

Some applications of CC theory to puzzle cases

The science fiction puzzle cases dear to the hearts of philosophers talking about persons are solved by Nozick's theory in a way which he thinks preserves some important intuitions about persons. The main intuition he ignores is that someone who was very much like me but an impostor would not be me even if he sincerely thought he was me and even if I were so insane as to agree with him. Nozick's theory also allows one to say that the impostor is me from the impostor's point of view but not me from mine if I am not deluded into agreeing with the impostor. This flexibility of Nozick's view does not help us much when we are trying to understand what persons are with a view to answering moral questions. If, on the other hand, we assert one of the four proposals for identity considered above as an objective answer to the question of personal identity, then we must delete the self-creation of individuals from the closest-continuer theory. Yet this self-creation is the source of the dignity of persons.[4] If we can agree on some general conception of a person, then this objection does not arise. We each will allow others, within the limits of the general conception, to determine their own identities (106). But how are we to agree on the general conception? Perhaps we are to choose among the four possible theories of identity adumbrated earlier. Nozick must have made such a choice, for he offers the following solutions to the standard philosophical puzzles about personal identity.

Duplication

If I were duplicated, and both I and my double survived the process, then I would be me and my double would not be me, according to Nozick's application of his theory (38). I suppose this is because I am causally better connected with my earlier stages than my double is. If others, not me and my double, were making the judgment as to closeness of continuity, then this conclusion that the double is not me might follow, but given the vagaries of the act of self-synthesis and the importance of self-conception in that mysterious act, Nozick should not be so quick to judge. What if I develop a self-conception and my double develops a self-conception such that both of us agree that my double is the closest continuer of my earlier self? It looks like I would no longer be me, my old self, that is. Even without this subjective element, it is not clear that Nozick is entitled to claim that the double is not me. Recall that the closest continuer of a person does not merely resemble that person but is someone whose properties are like those of the original because the original's properties caused the continuer's properties (35). But that is true of both me and my double with respect to my old self prior to duplication. My old self is the cause of us both. Here Nozick might have to retreat to the concept of a normal cause, or the right kind of cause, but that is notoriously relative to the norms we choose. Perhaps Nozick would say that the norms are given by the social limits on continuation. If I and my double emerge from Williams' duplicating machine, our society would count the person who resulted from ordinary human reproduction as the real person.

Various thought experiments resulting in a CC

Nozick considers the following cases to be cases in which the result is the closest continuer of the original: the brain is transplanted to a clone; the information in the body is transferred to a clone; there is a half-brain transplant with full psychological continuity, and the original dies; or half of the brain is destroyed. Even if we ignore the vast under-description of such cases, and accept them as logically possible, Nozick's conclusions about closest continuation ignore the potential interference of self-conception. He is at most entitled to conclude that these people could be the closest continuers of the earlier people who gave rise to them if they choose their closeness metrics in certain ways. The weight given to self-conception makes this claim trivially true. Because of this weight, anyone can be the closest continuer of anyone who went before (38-48). Nozick might protest that the limits described earlier apply and would limit who is who. However, the social limits in such science fiction cases are simply not known. Our society has not had to face such oddities yet. It is hard to see how the other limits could be used to make decisions in such science fiction cases either.

Nozick admits to having some trouble with certain kinds of duplication via transplantation of split brains. What really bothers him, however, is the overlap, or short-path case (47-48). I suggest, however, that closest continuation has been so weakened by the weighting of self-conception that no case is problematic, but this success is bought in a problematic way. We can be who we want to be. Again, to repair this Nozick would have to give far less importance to self-conception, which would undermine his view of the dignity of persons (107). Having dignity depend on self-determination has something right about it, but perhaps the idea needs much modification before it is workable.

What a CC theorist cares about

Fission is death but not disturbing

Since closest continuation determines what we should care about, according to Nozick, it is crucial for Nozick to repair his theory to avoid the consequence that closest continuation is a purely subjective matter. Otherwise the theory produces the view that we should care about whatever we do care about as regards survival. For example, perfect fission of a person in which there are two equally good candidates for closest continuer is a case, according to Nozick, in which there is no closest continuer. The original no longer exists. Nonetheless, the original should not care. What is important is the survival of what would be a closest continuer if it were unique (63). Fission where is thy sting!

When reflexive caring was discussed above, the point was made that in the act of self-creation we care for ourselves as ourselves, not as a mere collection of characteristics which could be had by someone else. Nozick seems to forget this when he discusses fission. What seems evident to me is that we do and ought to care about survival of more than merely a closest continuer. It is not just important to me that someone very much like me will wake up tomorrow; I want to wake up myself. The puzzle of how to understand this is a Gordian knot, but Nozick tries to slice through it at a stroke, and perhaps misses the import of it. A mere closest continuer is not enough for survival of the subject of experience which is at the core of the person. For instance, Tom might choose a metric which makes Tom the closest continuer of Tom's twin brother, Dick, and there is a causal connection between Tom and Dick; so CC theory does not clearly prevent Tom from being Dick's closest continuer except by social limits. Let us suppose those limits have changed. This is at least as possible as Nozick's examples. Now, clearly Tom and Dick do not share one subject of experience. What Dick wanted to survive was not just someone who could continue his genotype, personality, plans, and projects, but the very subject of his experiences. I think that it is perfectly reasonable for Dick to care about this continuing subjectivity and not just the continuing similarity which Tom can provide by taking over where Dick left off.

I can only be content with my replica as a closest continuer if I care not for myself as myself but as the bearer of certain properties which will be continued in the replica after I am destroyed. This is contrary to what Nozick says about such replication in a case of perfect fission (63). I am not supposed to care that there are, if I perfectly divide, two replicas and no me. I am supposed to care merely about somebody very much like me—the instantiation of properties which I now instantiate. Something has gone wrong with Nozick's view of caring. Perhaps no reasonable view can deal with a case of perfect fission, but then such fission may not be possible. The idea that we should care for ourselves as ourselves ought to win out for Nozick's supporters if a choice is to be made between this and his solution of the fission puzzle, namely saying that neither product of fission is the original person. One should also be suspicious of the facile solution to more mundane cases like that of the twin brother taking over. Similarity is not enough.

In fact, the datum that Nozick wishes to explain, that our care about our closest continuer is disproportionate to its degree of closeness of continuity, is explained only by denying the closest-continuer theory. If, for example, I find that there exists a nearly perfect double of me who is causally unrelated to me, hence not my continuer, I will care much more about my closest continuer. This double is not my closest continuer, since he is a person causally unrelated to me. My care for my closest continuer in this case is not because of its closeness via causation but because it is more likely to be me than my double. What I want to survive is me, not merely someone remarkably like me. Nozick tries to address this concern in his talk of reflexivity, but he ends, as I have been trying to show, by neglecting his own insights regarding reflexive caring.

Self as property

The view that the self is but a property of a body is one that Nozick flirts with. He puts it forth as a curiosity which may put old problems in a fresh light but which is insufficiently illuminating to adopt as a position (114). If Nozick were to adopt this position fully, caring for oneself as an object, the self, and caring for the instantiation of a property would no longer be opposed. There would be no self as object to care for. In a case of perfect fission, the property of being myself would be doubly instantiated. When my replicas say "I" they will not be referring to me, nor to any individual: They will be asserting that they have a certain property which I used to instantiate. This points once again to the absurdity of fission, since the property of being myself must be uniquely instantiated, but Nozick actually takes the self-as-property view to provide a solution to the fission problem (112). Unless the self-as-property is tied to a particular body as it is in Aristotle's enmattered-form conception of persons, then problems are likely to arise. We will have Williams' oddities, as in his example, discussed in the previous chapter, of falling in love with a person type as opposed to a person token. Those who wish to follow Nozick's lead should read "dead end" on the person-as-property view or go back to Aristotle.

Application to Daphne's case

An earlier and a later stage of what appears to be one person need not agree on who is who. Daphne, in fact, once held that her ability to do extremely abstract work in philosophy was a necessary condition of her continuation but, after losing that ability, she no longer thought so. In Nozick's terms the earlier Daphne would not count the later Daphne as a continuer, while the later Daphne would count the earlier Daphne as a predecessor. Now that Daphne apparently has no self-conception, she is still the closest continuer of the earlier Daphne according to those who give bodily continuity great weight in the metric for determining closeness. Since Daphne herself can now neither affirm nor deny this weighting of the body in the metric for closeness, she is deprived of one of the essentials of dignity on Nozick's view—self determination. This is one of those intuitively correct consequences which flows from Nozick's apparently wild view. Daphne herself held that she would be deprived of her dignity if allowed to live without her intellect, and intellect is essential for making decisions about the metric, hence essential for self-creation or self-renewal. This is, of course, a matter of degree. Someone with Down's Syndrome might have sufficient intellect for such purposes, but someone as severely limited as Daphne has nothing of what one normally calls intellect.

What I like about Nozick

Nozick's craziness is a good thing. Although I wish to stick closer to common sense, Nozick's abandonment of old sane solutions which have not worked drives us to dig in our heels. It forces those of us who think there is something right in the old views to ferret it out. It forces those of us who find something right in Nozick's relativism to say how it might be limited to prevent every Tom and Dick from being any Harry. We need to add to the limits, particularly the social limits, which Nozick acknowledges.

The importance of similarity in our idea of continuity of people cannot be underestimated. Nozick takes it apart and puts it back together in a useful analysis. While closest continuation is not all there is to continuity, it is a major feature. A metric of dimensions is a good figure for understanding what Williams has called a series of sliding scales.

Being a person is also something of a boot-strapping operation. Nozick has given us one of the clearest discussions of the apparently insane topic of self-creation and has managed to inject some sanity into it. He has linked this usefully to the analysis of our use of "I.," a vexed subject indeed. We will have to keep this contribution in mind as we come to consider what makes a person herself to herself.

I hope I have managed to convey some of the dizzying effect one may experience in a brisk climb up the steep slopes of Nozick's book *Philosophical Explanations*. What is harder, if at all possible, to convey, is the view which one surveys after this steep ascent. It is worth a look, but I would like to stick closer to common sense about persons, and that is feasible, Nozick's doubts notwithstanding.

THIRTEEN
Parfit: The Oxford Buddhist

The creed of selflessness

Parfit, like Williams but unlike Strawson, whom we discussed above (in chapters ten and eleven) is a revisionist in metaphysics. He is not content to describe the way we do think about persons but wishes to change it. Parfit is, in fact, an iconoclast where traditional concepts of a person are concerned. His motives for trying to discourage us from taking ourselves seriously include a moral one; he wants to make people realize that selfishness is irrational, even more so than you might have thought. Of his strange views about people he says, with typical understatement:

> Most of us would accept some of the claims that I shall be denying. I shall thus be arguing that most of us have a false view about ourselves, and about our actual lives. If we come to see that this view is false, this may make a difference to our lives.[1]

In fact, any converts to Parfit's view would have such a radically different self-conception that their lives would be changed beyond their imagining.

In popular Western representations of Buddhism, the self is something to be abandoned, excess baggage on the way to enlightenment. In effect, this is Parfit's view as well. Parfit tries to convince us that our selves are not what we should care about. Parfit's argument is general, opposed not only to Cartesian Egos but to anything like them, Christian souls, for instance, which would be an indestructible, unchanging part of a person. As I did with Nozick, I will try to convince you that Parfit's arguments challenge us in interesting ways though, as always, I will hold out for a stronger representation of Western common sense in our favoured concept of a person.

Parfit says that he will answer these questions:

1. What is the nature of a person?
2. What is it that makes a person at two different times one and the same person?
3. What is necessarily involved in the continued existence of each person over time?

After posing these questions, Parfit says "In answering (2) and (3) we shall also partly answer (1)" (202). Does that mean that he will answer (2)

Notes to Chapter Thirteen are on pp. 323-24.

and (3)? In charitable moods, I take him to be just pointing out the relation between the questions rather than issuing a negotiable promissory note, but I will argue that he certainly does not pay off any such note. The theory of personal identity in Parfit's main work on persons, *Reasons and Persons*, is circular (216). He abandons the concept of the nature of persons rather than explicating it. Nonetheless, his views are provocative.

In terms of philosophers whose views were adumbrated earlier in this book, Parfit, by his own lights, is updating Locke in opposition to the followers of Descartes. I see him as owing as much to Hume as to Locke. Recall that Hume looked for himself, found nothing, and concluded that selves are fictions. Descartes thought that our selves were indivisible, hence indestructible. I will call the view that there are such indivisible Cartesian Egos the *indivisibility thesis*. This indivisibility thesis of Descartes' is Parfit's main *bête noire*. In these pages I will often speak of Parfit's opponents as the Cartesians, meaning Descartes' followers, but anybody who believes we are indivisible is welcome to be offended by Parfit, and, slightly less so, by me.

Parfit defends four main conclusions about people which I put forward here in brief along with some names by which I will refer to them:

1. (the *divisibility* thesis): We are not indivisible Cartesian Egos; rather, we are complexes of psychological and or physical things which may be divided;
2. (the *indeterminacy* thesis): We are indeterminate in the sense that the question "Am I about to die?" does not always have a definite answer;
3. (the reducibility thesis, or *reductionism*): It is theoretically possible to describe all of reality, including the unity of consciousness and the unity of a whole life, without mentioning people, since people can be reduced to the various things which make them up as complexes;
4. (the *fundamental value* thesis): Personal identity is not what fundamentally matters, but psychological continuity and connectedness do matter fundamentally. Roughly, whether you survive should not concern you as much as whether your mind survives.

The last three conclusions are supposed to follow from his first conclusion (217), that we are complexes; so I will first consider that view and its immediate consequences.

Four ways of seeing people

Divisibility: People as complexes

Since Parfit denies the existence of any continuing and indivisible self, soul, or Ego, people are, instead, made up of psychological and/or physical events. As an empiricist, Parfit thinks the matter of our divisibility should be judged in the court of experience. He notes that there is no experience which is generally acknowledged and is evidence for indivisible selves. If, for instance, people had memories of earlier lives which could be demonstrated to be genuine memories, then Parfit would be prepared to reconsider (227).

One might think that the obvious rejoinder here is, "I do experience myself!" Parfit's response here is to point out that an indivisible self or Ego cannot be detectable in the way that changeable objects are. If an ordinary object is replaced by another object, we may notice the switch because of the difference in the features of the two objects. Egos, however, are things without features of that sort. The features of people, like being happy or being six-feet tall, can change, while the Ego remains. Parfit wonders how we could tell if the Ego was switched with a different Ego since both could support the same psychological features and both could be associated with a single body. Parfit attacks all followers of Descartes by using the relay-race argument. Parfit says that they "accept the possibility described by Locke and Kant. On their view, the Cartesian Ego that I am might suddenly cease to exist and be replaced by another Ego. This new Ego might inherit all of my psychological characteristics, as in a relay race." The Ego according to this version of the indivisibility thesis Parfit calls "the featureless Ego." "And it is not clear that Cartesians can avoid this version of their view" (228). On this version of the indivisibility thesis, it seems possible that one Ego could be replaced by another Ego and no one could notice. Neither the evidence of introspection nor publicly observable events would tell us of the change. Being something of an empiricist, Parfit thinks this makes the unintelligibility of the featureless Ego (perhaps of any sort of indivisibility thesis) probable, but he is content to rest his case on the facts (228). The gauntlet has been flung down. The Cartesian must show how it is possible to detect a change of the Ego, soul, or whatever is the indivisible entity associated with the mind or body.

What is a Cartesian to do in the face of Parfit's attack? One could say that the Ego is not featureless. It does, after all, have features like indivisibility and determinacy. These, however, are not the sort of thing which we can detect empirically. I can see changes in my body. Introspectively, I can notice changes in my psychological makeup. How could I know if the current Ego has left some other body and mind and entered ? This seems to make a change without a difference. On the other hand, if one gives the Ego features, like consciousness for example, then it becomes changeable and no longer the indivisible and indestructible thing which Cartesians want. These remarks apply equally well to Christian souls or any of the purportedly indivisible things which guarantee the identity of a person through change.

Cartesians can take some *small* hope in this, however: Parfit's two arguments strain against one another. The reincarnation argument complains that there is no evidence of Egos and the relay-race argument seems to rest on the idea that there could be no evidence of Egos since they are featureless, thereby undetectable. Now suppose that through hypnotism people were able to get accurate memories of former lives. If I could, for example, remember where I had hidden treasure in a former life, and such experiences became common, then Parfit would, by his own lights, accept Egos. In that case, it appears that they are detectable after all, although the detection is indirect. Egos, the Cartesian might say, could, at least in theory, become associated with new bodies, but they would carry memories and other psychological events with them. The Ego is not the mind, for the mind is changeable, but where the Ego goes, there goes the mind.

This sort of response would only serve to clarify but not to defeat Parfit's' objections to the Ego. Parfit could say that there is no way to tell one Ego from another, hence no way to tell which Ego is dragging a particular mind around. Even if there were excellent evidence of reincarnation, there would only be inclining reasons to believe in Egos or souls or some such indivisible component of persons with no guarantee that such indivisibles were not switched from time to time in an undetectable way. Such a response would show that undetectability is the truly objectionable feature of "featureless" Egos according to empiricists like Parfit. One need not be a very thoroughgoing empiricist to find the possibility of a relay race of Egos rather disturbing. Parfit has at least put the defenders of indivisibility on the defensive.

Aside from these two arguments against the indivisibility thesis, Parfit argues that that thesis is too hard to believe since it conflicts with what we believe about our own continuation through time. This brings us to indeterminacy.

Indeterminacy: Dead, alive, or maybe

To parody Parfit's indeterminacy thesis, old people never die, they just fade away. As the pieces of the complex person are lost, the person gradually goes out of existence. Parfit argues mainly by presenting examples to convince us that we believe in our indeterminacy, hence in our divisibility. In other words, by trying to persuade us that there are situations in which the question "Am I about to die?" has no definite answer, Parfit is trying to convince us as well that we are not Cartesian Egos. If we were, people would be alive or dead with no gradual fading away. Cartesian Egos have no parts; so they cannot go out of existence bit by bit. Parfit, moreover, varies his examples to deal with purely physical change as well as purely mental change within persons; so Parfit's arguments do not depend on a real distinction between psychological and physical events. In other words, he is, in his theory of persons, not presupposing any of the three views, materialism, dualism, and idealism discussed above in chapter one.

Parfit uses prominently some science fiction examples, as philosophers are wont to do. This has the disadvantage of making philosophy look silly to intelligent lay readers. Even worse, it allows philosophers to speak of events as if they were logically possible without troubling to describe these events in detail. The minimal description may conceal logical inconsistency. Parfit tries to avoid this charge by claiming that he uses the examples only to reveal what we *believe* about ourselves as persons, not to argue for any conclusion about what we actually or possibly are. His argument against Cartesian Egos is that it is too hard to believe Descartes' view since it requires us to believe in our determinacy. We are supposed to see this by contemplating some science fiction.

The spectra example

His main fiction involves the spectra. The spectra ought not to be taken to show anything about what is possible. They may show that the indivisibility thesis is hard to believe. This is, in principle, *all* they could show, given Parfit's admission of the limits of the method of science fiction examples (200). The psychological, physical, and combined spectra examples are cases of the gradual change of a human being (231-43). Parfit might be (in lurid imagination if not possibility) changed from the kind of human being he is into one much like Greta Garbo, mentally, physically, or both. In a smooth and very gradual spectrum of change there is no clear point at which one can say that Parfit is no more, and some other person has come into existence. In other words, there is no place to draw the line, in the psychological or the physical spectrum of change, at which Parfit dies. This is taken as showing that we believe in indeterminacy; we believe, according to Parfit, that there is not always a definite answer to the question, "Am I about to die?" The belief in indeterminacy is inconsistent with the belief in our indivisibility. A Cartesian Ego cannot be gradually changed into something else since it cannot be changed at all. Change involves division into parts so that some parts may be hived off and different ones added.

The Cartesian could just bite the bullet here and say to Parfit that this Greta-Garbo-like person just *is* Parfit so long as the Ego remains. Parfit could reply that this only goes to show that the indivisibility thesis is too hard to believe. But Parfit's own alternative, embracing indeterminacy and losing oneself via Oriental absorption is, however, no joy either. Parfit tells me that if I die and am survived by a replica which is psychologically continuous and connected with me that I should view that as about as good as (or as bad as) ordinary survival. I am supposed to be happy that this impostor, a mere replica of me, will sleep with my lover and write my book. More of this story, which is Parfit's teletransportation example, later. The point here is that Parfit's main reason for rejecting the indivisibility thesis is that it is implausible. He then gives us a view which he admits (200) is very hard to believe. This does not seem like progress. Nonetheless we can learn from Parfit's explorations.

One thing we learn from such science fiction puzzles whether of the purely imaginary or the possible variety is that our common conceptions of persons are capable of dealing with persons as we commonly find them, not with special cases. Elements of our common conceptions can, however, provide us with more durable concepts of a person which will not break down as we approach new scientific facts. Medical technology is presenting us with puzzles about what we believe ourselves to be. These puzzles may not be as strange as Parfit's cases, but they do stretch our conceptions of ourselves. At this point I will merely issue another promissory note to deal with real people and to try to preserve much of what Parfit abandons. Parfit at least illustrates some traps we will have to avoid to continue thinking of ourselves as in some sense indivisible and determinate.

Reductionism: An impersonal universe

Another of the consequences of abandoning the Cartesian way of thinking of people is that the old glue that held a person together, the Ego or the soul, is gone. In particular, Parfit faces the problems of how one's consciousness remains a unified whole rather than a series of disparate events and how one's life is unified in spite of the vast differences between different stages of that life.

I will be so bold as to claim that common sense tells us that there is a unity of the consciousness of each healthy person. Memories, feelings, desires, and beliefs of which we are conscious may be united by the ownership of an person who has them. For example, the experiences I have had are united by their being *my* experiences. They can be widely separated in time and extremely different, but they are bundled together by being one person's experience. The unification of a person's whole life is done in similar fashion. What makes my life one unified life is my ownership of it, and I am an entity existing apart from all that changes in my body and my mind during that life, *if* I am an indivisible thing like a Cartesian Ego. My persistence as a consciousness through change and the unity of my whole life are explicable for those who believe in the indivisibility of persons. The unity is preserved through the ownership by the Ego, soul, or whatever else in us continues indivisible and indestructible through change.

Parfit, thinking as he does that these two unities, of consciousness and of a whole life, are to be explained without the benefit of our indivisibility, thinks that the explanation must lie in the interrelations of the mental events and their relations to the brain. All this can be described, he supposes, without reference to the person. There is no owner of the experiences over and above the set of experiences and the body. Like Ayer, Parfit embraces what we saw Strawson deride, in chapter ten, as the no-ownership view. The world, according to Parfit, can be fully described without referring to persons (217). Persons are ways of conceiving of some groupings of the furniture of the universe but not themselves pieces of that furniture. Similarly, we could refer to Granny's living-room furniture as some kind of unified whole. At auction, however, the same pieces would just be the red-plush sofa (Oh! where are its doilies now?) the ottoman, and the overstuffed chair. They could be described well enough without mentioning either Granny or her living-room, bitter though the thought may be. "Person," as used by Parfit, seems to refer, conventionally, to a series of mental and physical events which we group together for convenience but need not have grouped together at all.

On the other hand, Parfit, in the same breath as denying that we are entities existing separately from our bodies, actions, and mental events, asserts that "a person is an entity that is distinct from his brain or body, and his various experiences. A person is an entity that *has* a brain and body" (471). It seems that "distinct" does not mean "separate" here. While a person may be inseparable from her experiences, it is wrong to say a person is *identical to* her experiences. Parfit elaborates:

> A reductionist can admit that...a person is what has experiences or the subject of experiences. This is true because of the way in which we talk. What a Reductionist denies is that the subject of experiences is a separately existing entity distinct from a brain and body, and a series of physical and mental events. (223)

The crucial thing here is that people are a function of the way we talk. Conventions—not souls, Egos, or other separately existing entities—make people. Parfit's people are just handy shopping bags into which we put a series of events, but the events are distinct from the bags. We could have packaged these events differently.[2] Note, we could not package one series of events as two different people, but we could package it either as a person or in some impersonal way.

This reductionism which I have earlier referred to as "impersonalism," the assertion that the universe is describable without reference to people, is the opposite of Strawson's view, in chapter ten above, and to common sense. It is explicitly (x) revisionist metaphysics, an attempt to change what we believe ourselves to be. The opposition to common sense is not, however, total. Parfit is trying to get rid of ghostly items like souls or Egos while retaining the common sense idea of the person as distinct from the person's experiences. This is a good idea which I will try to preserve and elaborate in a way different from Parfit's when I come to my own theory of persons. For now, I want to explore some other interesting claims of Parfit's concerning what we should care about.

Fundamental value: People do not count

The value we attach to ourselves should, by Parfit's lights, be attached rather to a series of psychological events. We care too much about the shopping bag and should concern ourselves about certain of the contents. To illustrate his departure from common sense, Parfit tells a science fiction story. Parfit uses the story of teletransportation to look into what we believe about ourselves and what we care about. It is also his vehicle for answering the sorts of questions which we have seen Nozick fretting over in the previous chapter with thought experiments concerning the overlap of people upon duplication of a person. Recall the metaphor of a river which divides into two streams; the most similar to the original river is very short. Nozick would consider the less similar but longer of the two streams the continuation of the river. So, hang onto your hat, here is a synopsis of Parfit's story (199) of a person dividing as a river might divide.

The teletransportation example

Imagine yourself to be living in a future century when people routinely travel from one planet to another by teletransportation. Typically you step into a scanner, on Earth perhaps, press a button and lose consciousness. After what seems like a moment, you awake in a Replicator on, say, Mars. The scanner on Earth destroys your body, including your brain, while recording the exact states of all your cells. This recorded information is transmitted to the replicator on Mars by radio. The replicator on Mars then produces from new matter a body exactly like yours in every detail. This is teletransportation, which some consider a form of travel.

One day you step into a brand new scanner on Earth and push the button, but you do not lose consciousness. You are then told that the new scanners do not destroy the body on earth but merely replicate it on Mars. Unfortunately, the new scanner is defective, and has damaged your heart. You will die in a few days. Your replica on Mars is healthy.

In Nozick's terms from the previous chapter, the earthly you is the closest continuer of the person who stepped into the scanner on Earth, but the next closest continuer is to be much longer lived. This is a case of overlap in which personal identity follows not the path of closest continuation, since this is such a short path, but jumps to the replica on Mars. But Parfit does not accept Nozick's theory. The earthly you might have some difficulty thinking that the person on Mars is the real you. As Parfit points out (201), when you have your heart attack on Earth, thanks to the damage done by the scanner, your exact replica on Mars will feel no physical pain. The replica, however similar to the person who stepped into the scanner, is not you.

Parfit's reasons for thinking the replica is not you are unclear, as we shall see in the coming discussion of personal identity. Now, however, I am interested not so much in his acceptance of the common sense opinion that the replica is a different person, but in his claims about how one ought to think about dying and being survived by a replica. He claims that this is about *as good as ordinary survival* (201). What is fundamentally valuable about you will survive. While Parfit's views on who is who seem ordinary enough as contrasted with Nozick's, his views on what is fundamentally valuable seem skewed. Surely, even if you are very unselfish, it should be little consolation to you that you are to be replaced by someone who will take over your life. Given that this replica is someone who will take over your love life, it would be understandable if you felt a jealous rage against the impostor.

This is one of those instances in which we see the force of Parfit's general comments on his theory: "I believe that most of us have false beliefs about our own nature, and our identity over time, and that, when we see the truth, we ought to change some of our beliefs about what we have reason to do" (ix). To persuade you that you should feel not rage but relief at the existence of the replica, Parfit argues (346) that acceptance of divisibility and reducibility of people makes the question of who is who much less important. Since there is no soul or Ego, saying that you are the same person whom your mother cradled in her arms at age one, is merely saying something about relations between experiences in a human life. Rather than fretting about the way in which one experience led to another, Parfit would have us concern ourselves with the quality of the experiences. Whose experiences they are is merely a question of the way in which experiences are connected but not as important as what kind of experiences they are.

I think that the idea behind this argument is that our relations to our future selves are no stronger than our relations to other people existing with us now insofar as the production of value is concerned. If you love somebody right now, that relationship is much more important than the relationship you have to your future self—perhaps some senile old crock in years to come with which you, now, have very little in common. Should you care more about that old crock than others around you now? If you can use your resources to make others happy now, this would be, on my interpretation of Parfit, far more rational than hoarding them up to provide for that future crock. Indeed, if Parfit is right about people, the truth will set us free by breaking down the walls of our irrational selfishness.

Saints are unconcerned about themselves and concerned about others. That is not, however, what Parfit thinks is rational. To be concerned about others is to be concerned about people. A person, whether oneself or another, is not a proper object for moral concern. Persons are, after all, merely conventional groupings of events. What is fundamentally valuable is the experience of persons. As a utilitarian in moral theory, Parfit is concerned with maximizing happiness; whose happinesses increases is not of great moment. Utilitarians are routinely criticized for insufficiently valuing individual people in their attempt to get the greatest happiness for the group. Parfit thinks that the utilitarian moral position becomes less implausible when we understand that people are not what counts (346).

Personal identity: Who's who

To see better why himself and other people are of little concern to Parfit, we must consider Parfit's views on personal identity, that is on the question of what makes a person at two different times one and the same person. Since a person is a complex of things rather than a Cartesian Ego, personal identity must depend, for Parfit, on relationships among the things in the complex.

The circular criterion of identity

Parfit sums up his view on personal identity as follows:

> Our existence just involves the existence of our brains and bodies, and the doing of our deeds, and the thinking of our thoughts, and the occurrence of certain other physical and mental events. Our identity over time just involves (a) Relation R—psychological connectedness and/or psychological continuity, with the right kind of cause, provided (b) that there is no different person who is R-related to us as we once were. (216)

More simply put, each person is just a river of events. Some of these events are mental events linked together by an unclearly specified kind of linkage which Parfit is calling "relation R." Examples of the events in the river could include instances of thinking, remembering, dreaming, emoting and so on. Parfit says that this river must have *the right kind of cause,* meaning it cannot be artificially produced, I suppose. So much for part (a), now let us see what happens in Parfit's part (b) in the foregoing quotation.

In part (b) of his identity criterion Parfit wants to rule out a fork in the river so that two different people in the present will not turn out to be identical to one past person.[3] This seems reasonable enough, but part (b) makes Parfit's criterion of personal identity a circular criterion. We must use (a) plus (b) to tell when we have a different person. Part (b), however, relies on difference of persons. Parfit's criterion seems to depend on itself.

All in all, this is not too propitious a beginning. In much earlier work Parfit gave a version of the identity criterion which was not circular since it did not include the word "different," but that version will not work unless we understand it to implicitly include the word "different."[4]

What Parfit may be trying unsuccessfully to do here with his rough criterion of identity is to define identity in terms of R without running into Williams' reduplication problem, which was discussed in chapter eleven. If people can be copied, then criterion (a) is not enough to guarantee personal identity. Parfit thinks duplication of R (roughly duplication of consciousness of a person) is possible. (His reasons for believing in this possibility will emerge later.) He adds criterion (b) to rule out problems which might arise if people were copied or their conscious states were copied. Roughly he does not want someone's consciousness splitting into two streams to make two people identical to the one whose consciousness split. Part (b) says that if the river forks, identity is lost.

Another feature of Parfit's identity criterion, (a) plus (b), which needs clarification is the relation R itself. Parfit does not try to give any precise definition of its components, psychological continuity, and connectedness. He does say this: "*Psychological connectedness* is the holding of particular direct psychological connections." "*Psychological continuity* is the holding of overlapping chains of *strong* connectedness."[5] The psychological connections which Parfit uses as examples are memories, beliefs and desires, but he allows "any other psychological feature" to qualify (205). This gives us only the weakest grasp on what R is. That is less of a problem if Parfit is not really concerned to give a precise definition of identity, but it is a bit odd insofar as Parfit holds that R itself is what we should care about instead of caring about our personal identity. As we saw in the last section, people are not what count; their experience is what is fundamentally valuable. R is what holds experiences together in a sequence. Parfit, moreover, sometimes speaks not of experience but says that R, however it is caused, is what is fundamentally valuable. I can understand a utilitarian caring about the quality of experiences, but I am not sure why it should be so important that experiences be connected or why the relationship connecting them should be glorified. Indeed, if I am willing to give up on my continuation as a person in favour of the continuation of my mind in some other person, why should I not take a further step and say that any continuity is unimportant. I should only desire that experiences similar to my best experiences be had by me or others. Admittedly, for certain experiences, like writing the book Parfit was writing when he made these claims, continuity is needed.

Parfit's attempt to revise Locke is probably what drives him to use R as the all-important part of persons. Locke, whose views were discussed in chapter five, told us that memory held a person together over time. Parfit wants to broaden this to include any psychological features which connect persons from moment to moment. He also wants to allow for loss of memories, beliefs, and desires by a person. As long as there are overlaps of my memories I can be said to have continuous memory even though I do not remember what I did when I was ten years old. I do remember what I did when I was twenty, and when I was twenty I remembered what I did when I was ten. This is enough for continuity of memory and continuity of the person, according to Parfit.

Parfit seems to be trying to avoid Reid's brave officer counterexample to Locke[6] in which the officer has memories of his boyhood which he loses by the time he becomes a general. The problem for a memory criterion of identity is that the boy and the general are both identical to the officer while the general is not identical to the boy. On Parfit's view, they are one person because overlapping connections are enough to do the job of maintaining a person's identity as long as there is only one stream of such connected events with no forks.

To fully reveal Parfit's picture of R it remains to be said what makes connectedness strong. To say I am R-related to some person yesterday is to say I have enough psychological connections with that person, for example, enough shared beliefs, desires, and memories. Parfit elaborates,

> Since connectedness is a matter of degree, we cannot plausibly define precisely what counts as enough. But we can claim that there is enough connectedness if the number of connections, over any day, is *at least half* the number of direct connections that hold over every day, in the lives of nearly every actual person. When there are enough direct connections, there is what I call *strong connectedness*.[7]

This is confusing and seems confused. The term "direct" is left vague. Worse, being a matter of degree is not related to imprecision as Parfit supposes. Support for a bill in the House of Commons is a matter of degree, but we can still precisely define enough support for a bill to pass. Parfit does, in spite of his disavowal, define "enough connectedness" by drawing a line at a certain degree of connectedness. I suppose he means to say that there is no non-arbitrary line to draw. To add to the unclarity, we are left unsure about what the connections are. Memories are the most obvious candidates. We are left unsure about what it is that Parfit thinks we should care about and what personal identity is, on his view. Both depend on R.

Let me try, a little more sympathetically, to see what Parfit probably thinks of as the same person. Perhaps Parfit should be saying first that if the body and the psychological states of a person, Tom, are strongly connected to the body and the psychological states of a person, Dick, then Tom is Dick. It does not work the other way around, though. That Tom is Dick does not guarantee that Tom is strongly connected to Dick. Second, he could mean that if you are one in a series of people, each of whom is strongly connected to the preceding member of the series, then you are identical to all the people in the series, as long as the series does not fork into two series. For example, if Tom is strongly connected only to Dick, and Dick is strongly connected only to Harry, then Tom, Dick, and Harry are all stages of one person even if Harry is not strongly connected to Tom. Thus I am the same person whom my mother held in her arms when I was two. I am not strongly connected to that person, but I am part of an appropriate stream of people, better, an appropriate river of psychological and bodily events, running from that gurgling two-year old to me. As a reductionist, Parfit could just talk about the events in the river without mentioning people. The concept of a person is just a useful way of talking about a continuous, non-forking river of events of a certain kind.

Recall the questions Parfit seemed to promise to answer:

1. What is the nature of a person?
2. What is it that makes a person at two different times one and the same person?
3. What is necessarily involved in the continued existence of each person over time?

Parfit claims that an answer to questions (2) and (3) will partly clarify the nature of persons, since "to be a person, a being must be self-conscious, aware of its identity and its continued existence over time" (202). Question (1) is answered by saying we are complexes. Questions (2) and (3) were answered roughly in terms of continuity of a river of experiences and bodily events. This tells us something about what kind of complexes we are, and what it would be to be aware of ourselves, not as Egos, but as a series of related events passing through time. To really get a grip on Parfit's answer to (2) and (3), we would have to have a definition of "direct connection," and we would have to have some understanding of a non-forking series of events which did not depend on the identity of persons for its explication.

Cartesians and other believers in souls or Egos would, in any case, think Parfit has thrown out the baby with the bath water. In a sense he would agree, for the baby was a fiction on his view. The answer to (2) shows that personal identity is a rather trivial matter. In fact, I think he is just trying to say enough about personal identity and the nature of persons to show us that in such concepts we will not find what really matters to us. I will think of Parfit as saying that R is what matters in our futures, and if it turns out that one can only be R-related to one person, then identity matters, since it is always accompanies R. Perry, who agrees with Parfit in large measure, puts the point by saying that the importance of identity is derivative.[8] We only should care about identity because R normally goes with it.

Although Parfit promises to give a criterion of personal identity, and does give a bad one, he also denies that he is offering a criterion of identity at all. He says he is a reductionist and that reductionists should not bother with offering such criteria, for personal identity is not what matters to them. In the particular context of this denial Parfit may just mean that it is not important for reductionists to decide among materialism, dualism, and idealism as they interpret relation R; thus they need not say what kind of thing, a body, a mind, or both, must survive for identity to be maintained.[9] In any case, Parfit appears to agree with Strawson's comment that personal identity is a problem of relatively minor significance.[10] Whatever Parfit intends, it seems to me that we need to know more fully what personal identity is before we dismiss its importance. We also need to know an awful lot more about R before we take it seriously as the fundamentally valuable thing about us. A little more about R can be gleaned from Parfit's real-world examples.

Parfit in the real world

Parfit, sensitive to the charge that too much rests on dubious thought experiments, seeks confirmation of his views in the findings of psychological research on commissurotomy patients and then extends this to more science fiction examples of brain bisection and brain transplanting. Parfit's argument is predicated on the idea that commissurotomy results, or may result, in a divided consciousness. "What is a fact must be possible," he asserts, "And it is a fact that people with disconnected hemispheres have two separate streams of consciousness—two series of thoughts and experiences, in having each of which they are unaware of having the other."[11]

Commissurotomy is an operation on the brain which does not split the brain in half as is done in science fiction examples of brain bisection. Links between parts of the cortex, the upper brain, are cut, but the lower brain is not disturbed. This lower brain is completely indispensable to psychological functions. Philosophers should be more cautious than Parfit in making pronouncements about what actually happens to the consciousness of a person after commisurotomy. The empirical evidence is difficult to interpret.

This empirical evidence has led Trevarthen, a psychologist and psychobiologist, to comment:

> The tests of Zaidel and Sperry have shown that both hemispheres of commissurotomy patients have awareness of themselves as persons and a strong sense of the social and political values, or meaning, of pictures or objects.[12]

It is a testimony, however, to the difficulties in the interpretation of this evidence that the same psychologist says, a few paragraphs later,

> It does not appear necessary to imagine the "self," which has to maintain a unity, is destroyed when the forebrain commissures are cut, although some of its activities and memories are depleted after the operation. (746)

While it may seem very odd to speak of each hemisphere as being aware of itself as a person while there is but one self, one can remove the apparent paradox. Happily for Parfit, the means of removal is incompatible with the Cartesian view of persons. It seems that in such patients consciousness is not unified. That should not, however, be so surprising. It is not unified in people without commisurotomies either. The unity of consciousness, which the Cartesian explains by the mysterious Ego and Parfit explains by means of the mysterious relation R, needs no explanation. It is a myth.

Before I go on to myth-bashing, you may have noticed that I have attributed to Parfit views which are at odds with each other, namely that the unity of consciousness is to be explained by the relations among experiences[13] and that consciousness is not necessarily unified (247). Perhaps he thinks that unity of consciousness is the norm, and that needs explaining, while exotic cases like commisurotomy examples show that there are exceptions to the norm. In fact, there are mundane cases of disunity of consciousness in totally normal people. Indeed, commisurotomy patients usually behave normally. I do not wish to defend the Cartesians against Parfit, but to point out that he brings out many dubious cases of unnecessary ammunition to fire at Descartes.

Parfit, you see, thinks that showing that the division of consciousness is logically possible shows that the Cartesians are wrong about our indivisibility. As Parfit puts it, "This is one of the points at which it matters whether my imagined case is possible. If we could briefly divide our minds, this casts doubt on the view that psychological unity is explained by ownership" (251). Parfit imagines a commissurotomy patient who is capable of dividing his consciousness at will and working on two different problems in these two streams of consciousness. If this is possible, then Parfit believes he has some evidence against the view that we are each indivisible subjects of experience uniting our experience as ours. This view would entail, implausibly, that Parfit's commissurotomy patient is two people in one body, by a psychological criterion of personal identity. Parfit himself avoids this only by means of the circularity of his criterion which was discussed earlier.

Wilkes' extended discussion[14] of disunity of consciousness shows that the real-life cases are less dramatic and less clear-cut than Parfit supposes. Wilkes points out that for commissurotomy patients, "The disunity holds against a background of 99 per cent unity. It is not far-reaching, does not consistently disrupt ordinary purposive action, tends to affect *only* the level of consciousness, and is avoided whenever possible" (156). Wilkes also is convincing (148) on the point that exotic cases, like that of commissurotomy patients, are not needed to illustrate disunity of consciousness. Imagine yourself driving a good friend to work on a route you take routinely. You have an animated conversation with the friend with one part of your consciousness while another part takes care of the driving. At the end of the drive you might remember only the conversation although you exercised appropriate caution and reacted to various traffic events along the way. This would not make you a special case for philosophical explanation, nor should we think this of the commissurotomy patient. Even if the disunity is more dramatic in some cases of commissurotomy, not much philosophical hay can be made from this. A similar lack of hay is evident in the other real-world examples Parfit uses, but I shall content myself with his commissurotomy case as illustrative of the problems besetting such examples.

What hay can be made, Plato bailed long ago. As we saw in chapter three, we have a complex sort of consciousness, not an indivisible, unified whole. This is grist for Parfit's mill, but it does not ensure the logical possibility of all sorts of weird and wonderful science fiction.[15] Indeed, there is no need for it. Consciousness is clearly complex. This does not entirely defeat Cartesians, of course. The Cartesian can say that the consciousness is the changing part of the person while the immutable Ego owns this consciousness or even these consciousnesses if there are several in one person. In other words, the Ego is not the consciousness, but what has the consciousness, divided though consciousness may be into various streams.

If Cartesians say this, however, then Egos seem not really conscious of themselves. Consciousness is of thoughts, feelings, and other things with detectable features. Egos cannot even detect themselves, since they do not have any properties which are detectable by consciousness. This would just bring us back to the argument discussed earlier in this chapter that there is nothing to prevent an undetectable relay race of Egos through a human being. Each Ego in turn would support the same stream of consciousness in the same body.

Application to Daphne's case

If Daphne is a person at all, on Parfit's account, she is a different person from one hour to the next. Her short-term memory has long been dysfunctional. Her cognitive ability seems to be like that of an infant. Psychological continuity and connectedness, which Parfit thinks are crucial, are just what she has lost. Even if Parfit were willing to entertain concepts of a person on which Daphne survived the ravages of her illness, he would say that she lost what matters. Daphne was certainly of the same opinion prior to her descent into dementia. She did not wish to have her body live in that state.

Parfit's consideration of the spectra is particularly apt for Daphne. There are spectra of change, physical and psychological, beginning with Daphne the brilliant philosopher, a healthy vibrant woman, and ending with Daphne, ten months later, infantile in mind and nearly so in body. Parfit would say that this is a perfect example of a person's indeterminacy. It is not clear when Daphne, the philosopher, ceased to be. Different elements of the complex that was Daphne faded away at different rates. In any case, by Parfit's lights, what happened to Daphne in the first few months of this terrible period was the equivalent of ordinary death, although the exact point of death could not be determined.

What I like about Parfit

It is good that Parfit reminds us of our complexity. Parfit has at least undermined Cartesians and others who support the indivisibility, determinacy, and irreducibility of persons. We may wish to retain some version of these properties for ourselves, but probably not the ones Descartes had in mind. While I share some of Wilkes' concerns about Parfit's examples, they may, nonetheless, serve to prod us into re-examining our beliefs about ourselves. Parfit, in throwing out the baby with the bath water, has shown us what sort of baby we are seeking, and it is not a Cartesian Ego.

Parfit has also given us some serious challenges concerning the clarification of our ways of valuing ourselves. I cannot, however, accept all of Parfit's views about what should matter most to us. Psychological continuity may be important to an intellectual, but much less so to an athlete. Parfit, like Aquinas, has elevated intellect to too high a pedestal. Body-based views of the person have something to offer which Parfit neglects. Like Locke he is overvaluing psychological continuity, as philosophers like Wiggins, Williams, and Wilkes would remind him. Nonetheless, there is some merit in considering later stages of ourselves less important to us now than other people at present might be. I should not, for instance, value my own comfort in retirement as highly as the present comfort of those I love. It is hard to argue with the need for some sort of war on selfishness. Nonetheless, the casualties are too high as Parfit conducts it.

Parfit also encourages us in other ways to be here now. My later self might concern me less than my present self, especially if I think I will become very different from the person I am now. In anticipation of a diminution of my faculties, should I not spend my resources on the stage of my life when I am most capable of appreciating the results of such expenditures? Again Parfit pushes us to the limit, and we may not all wish to join him there. In any case, we are challenged to say why we should value later stages of ourselves as much as we appear to do.

Parfit has tried to convince us, in effect, that persons are not nearly as long-lived as the associated human beings. Since psychological continuity and connectedness are more fragile than their physical cousins, a human being may house a series of persons. There is something right about this, but it goes too far, as with most of Parfit's theses. Again we are challenged to come up with a concept of a person which allows personal identity to be a little more robust than on Parfit's view without making it implausible at the other extreme. It may be implausible to say that a zygote is the same person as the adult who later develops from it, but must we join Parfit in making people so volatile that they do not last from one six-year stage of an adult to the next?

We should, perhaps, be somewhat revisionist, replacing the implausible views we have. We should not, however, replace them with outrageous views which only a philosopher could love. I accept Parfit's objection to the Cartesian view that it is hard to believe. Let us apply the same objection to Parfit and move on. What is plausible in Parfit's view will surface again in the round-up of ideas later as a new theory of persons is offered.

FOURTEEN
The Nagelian Perspective

Thomas Nagel thinks that Parfit and others, in trying to be objective, leave out something crucial about people, namely, their subjective viewpoint. We have been trained by many generations of philosophers and scientists to distinguish between mere appearance and reality. The way things appear, from a subjective point of view, is not necessarily the way things are, objectively. In *The View From Nowhere*, Nagel sets himself the task of combining the subjective perspective of a particular person inside the world with an objective view of that same world.[1]

The objective view is emphasized by most writers on the contemporary philosophical scene to the exclusion of the subjective viewpoint. The pundits Nagel opposes would suppose that, even if one is subjectively aware of what is real, the same reality could be viewed objectively—indeed, the objective view would be superior. The underlying assumption is this: that there is in a subjective view of reality nothing different in kind from that which is observable objectively.[2] Against this claim, Nagel maintains the irreducibly subjective character of people's minds.[3] He thinks that objectivity is a valuable method of understanding the world but is overrated by those who think it is complete in the absence of the subjective viewpoint (5). People cannot be understood in a purely objective way.

The objective perspective

The incompleteness of the objective perspective

Parfit, as we saw in the last chapter, believes in reductionism, the view that one could describe the universe completely from an objective point of view without mentioning people at all. The opposition, however, between Nagel and Parfit is not so clear-cut as this would suggest, since Nagel holds as well that the difference between subjectivity and objectivity is a matter of degree:

> A standpoint that is objective by comparison with the personal view of one individual may be subjective by comparison with a theoretical standpoint still farther out.... We may think of reality as a set of concentric spheres, progressively revealed as we detach gradually from the contingencies of the self. (5)

Notes to Chapter Fourteen are on p. 324.

In spite of this fading of subjectivity into objectivity, people and their points of view are ineliminable elements of Nagel's world, while people are just series of objectively describable events on Parfit's view.

Objectivity as method

To get a preliminary grasp on Nagel's distinction of objective from subjective viewpoints, it is useful to reflect on some simple experiences of reality which people have. Suppose Tom and Dick are measuring the size of an object, say a cube of metal. We expect them to come up with the same answers to our questions about the height, width, and length of the cube. If, however, one of them describes it as grey and the other disagrees, calling it "blue-grey," then we are not so surprised. Colour is unlike size.

An example which Nagel develops (75-77) to explicate the objective/subjective distinction concerns such differences as the one we just noticed regarding size and colour. The distinction of primary qualities of objects from secondary qualities has been used to explain the difference of colour from size. The primary or objective qualities of objects are supposed to be the properties they actually have independent of the perceiving subject, while secondary qualities are the powers of objects to evoke a certain experience in a subject of experiences like you or me. Size is supposedly a primary quality while colour is a secondary quality. We can, however, take this old objective conception in which size is a property not relative to the observing subject and create new explanations in which size is no longer a primary quality. In Einstein's relativity theory, objects are not absolutely equal or unequal in size but only so with respect to a frame of reference. Einstein moves us out to a larger sphere of objectivity.

From the new perspective which Einstein fashioned we can explain why, from the old perspective, we took size to be a primary quality. Size appears objective locally, but at extreme speeds and distances depends on the observing subject. As we move from the way Galileo might have viewed size and colour to the way Einstein viewed them, we move from one of Nagel's concentric spheres of objectivity to another. We detach ourselves further from the contingencies of the self; for we now see things from a perspective which is not limited by the speed at which and distances over which our poor little bodies can travel.

If we now go back towards the centre of the concentric spheres, and temporarily accept again the old primary/secondary distinction, we can see how, from Galileo's perspective, colour is not an objective or primary quality, though it seemed to be so in the smaller sphere of objectivity from which Galileo made his expansion. Colour seems like a primary quality of things until we notice that some people have different colour perceptions from the majority. These examples show us that in thinking both colour and size are objective we are in a smaller sphere than when we move to thinking colour is secondary in Galileo's sphere. This expands farther to Einstein's sphere in which both size and colour are seen to be secondary.

Objectivity is, according to Nagel, merely a method of gradual detachment from the subjective point of view, and that is why the difference between the objective and the subjective is merely a matter of degree. Galileo is more objective than his predecessors and less objective than later scientists. One might wonder if it is possible to find some all-inclusive, absolute sphere of objectivity which would get us past any subjective elements in our thought.

Subjectivity is, however, incompletely reconcilable with objectivity, and objectivity is always limited, as Nagel sees it (3-12). Our concepts become more objective by taking old objective conceptions together with an understanding of *ourselves* and putting the two together. The new conception explains how we had the old, given our subjective outlook (5-6). The two perspectives are thus inextricably intertwined. Even the objective method has people's subjectivity at its core on Nagel's account of the matter.

False reductions of the subjective

Consider, now, in light of Nagel's opinion on the nature of subjectivity and objectivity, the reductionist thesis Parfit has presented. This is probably a case of what Nagel would call a false objectification or false reduction which merely reduces the explained rather than improving the explaining. The examples, however, which Nagel gives of such false reduction applied to people are not examples of Parfit's sort of reduction. Below I will show how Nagel attacks materialism, the view that everything, including each person, is made merely of matter, and a special case of materialism called "functionalism" (10). Functionalism—the idea that the computer is the right model for the mind[4]—is a view on which there is only a material brain and a program on which it runs, nothing mental beyond that. Parfit, on the other hand, only wishes to reduce people to mental and physical events without prejudice as to the nature of such events. Parfit can accept the falsity of materialism and functionalism while retaining his sort of reductionism.

Getting people out of the picture, however, even if one does not reject irreducibly mental states, must be wrong given that people and their perspectives are ineliminable parts of the world. Such ineliminability is what I take Nagel to be pointing to with his claim that subjectivity is the core of all objectivity, the centre of all the concentric spheres of reality. Thus, although Parfit's view is not the direct object of Nagel's attack on reductionism, Nagel should consider it as false as any other sort of reductionism which leaves out the subjective viewpoint.

Objectivity is relative to the discipline

To add to the restriction of the objective viewpoint, Nagel thinks that objectivity varies from discipline to discipline.[5] This relativizes objectivity rather than having it serve as some universal, absolute standard by which to judge what we believe. Although Nagel does not make use of the relativity of the objective in this way, it could be argued that an objective description of the world which excluded people would have its objectivity only relative to the discipline in which the description is given, say physics. This would not provide objective reasons for another discipline, say psychology, to consider people eliminable. The reductionist thesis is probably understood by its defenders as being quite independent of disciplines; yet Nagel's relativizing of objectivity seems on the face of it quite plausible. At the very least, Parfit's reductionism is in need of clarification. In what discipline does Parfit envisage his unpeopled description of the universe?

The subjective perspective

Irreducibility

The irreducibility of the subjective to the objective comes up, so Nagel argues (8), in ethical values and truth. Neither subjective nor objective values can supersede the other, yet they do not coexist without strife, and the same can be said of truths, as Nagel sees them. The concept of a person is, in my opinion, at the centre of the vortex created by these opposing currents of objectivity and subjectivity. Nagel's insistence (9) on opposing the scientism which requires us to neglect the subjective is, therefore, especially welcome. Parfit is not alone among the influential writers[6] who have led many to believe that we can say what we need to say about ourselves while totally neglecting our subjective viewpoints in the world. It is this that leads them to suggest that personal survival is not what fundamentally matters. Nagel argues for the value of the subjective. I believe that this entails the importance of the very person who is the subject of the experiences. Replicas will not do.

Mind

Given Nagel's attitude to subjectivity and its importance, Nagel can be expected to attack vigorously the attempts of his contemporaries to understand people in terms of our objective understanding of machines. He does not disappoint this expectation:

> The reductionist program that dominates current work in the philosophy of mind is completely misguided, because it is based on the groundless assumption that a particular conception of objective reality is exhaustive of what there is. Eventually, I believe, current attempts to understand the mind by analogy

with man-made computers that can perform superbly some of the same external tasks as conscious beings will be recognized as a gigantic waste of time. The true principles underlying the mind will be discovered, if at all, only by a more direct approach.[7]

To understand ourselves, we must look at ourselves, not at machines which can mimic some of our linguistic behaviour.

While Nagel does not yet know how to understand mind, he rejects materialism, idealism, dualism, and no-ownership theories as implausible or unintelligible and asserts a *dual aspect* theory. In other words he rejects the view that people are just physical bodies, the view that they are purely minds, the view that they are a combination of both, and the view that experiences can exist independently of the people who own those experiences. Instead of these he accepts the view that a person is one being made out of one kind of stuff with two sorts of features: a material aspect and a mental aspect. He forthrightly admits that talk about this dual-aspect theory is largely handwaving (29-30). Waving hands is, in any case, better than clenching them or wringing them in face of the inadequacies of the other kinds of theories.

Given the blanketing snowfall of Parfit's influence, I will just single out one part of Nagel's argument driving us in the direction of a dual-aspect theory, the part which counters Parfit's reductionism. Reductionism is closely related to the no-ownership view accepted by Wittgenstein and Ayer and attacked by Strawson, as we saw in chapters nine and ten. Of this no-ownership view Nagel says:

> I suppose I should also consider the "no-ownership" view according to which mental events are not properties or modifications of anything, but simply occur, neither in a soul nor in the body—though they are causally related to what happens in the body. But I don't really find this view intelligible. *Something* must be there in advance, with the potential of being affected with mental manifestations. (60)

The reductionist description of the world suffers from the same lack of intelligibility. If we try to describe, say, our own perceptions as events rather than as things which happen to us—all in aid of deleting people from the description—we fail to describe what really happens. From a subjective point of view, I have a perception. That is part of the world which gets left out when the physical concomitants of my having the perception are objectively described.

The question then arises for Nagel, who is the owner of mental events? Since they must be events in some soul or self, what constitutes that self? His answer is that the brain is that self.

The self as brain

According to Nagel, I can truly say, "I am my brain" (40). The self just is the intact brain. Nagel admits this is an empirical hypothesis. What he supposes is that the brain is the seat of the person's experience, a conscious organ (41). It follows that without survival of the intact brain, there is no survival of the person. Nagel rejects many thought experiments that seem to show otherwise. Such experiments confuse metaphysical with epistemological possibility (42). What we *can be* should not be confused with what we *can conceive of ourselves as being.*

It might seem that Nagel is a materialist since he identifies self with brain. In fact, however, he believes that the brain has irreducibly immaterial properties (30). He believes that physical parts of persons can have mental units (51). He knows that this raises many difficulties for which he has no solution. His general tendency, however, is to preserve the richness of what is to be explained rather than to reduce it to something that can be handled given our limited conceptual framework and tools.

Nagel's method avoids the common philosophical failing which Abraham Kaplan called the principle of the drunkard's search.[8] As the story goes, a drunk is on his knees under a lamp-post. In response to a query from a policeman he says he is looking for his keys. "So you think you lost your keys here?" asks the policeman. "No," replies the drunk, "I think I lost them down the street, but it's lighter here." Nagel looks in the dark where answers to our puzzles about persons are more likely to be found. This leads him to unsupported speculation like that about mental properties of physical parts of us. Better that we have such speculation than a reduction of mysteries to things we can understand when it seems clear that the mysteries are not adequately captured in these reductions. Reductionism, it seems to me, is guided by the principle of the drunkard's search that we should look where it is lightest, beneath the lamp of empirical, objective science.

Panpsychism

One problem that arises from Nagel's conception of the brain having irreducibly mental properties is that other things may have such properties too, even if they are not the sorts of things with which we would normally associate mind.[9] The view that things other than people have minds or at least mental properties is panpsychism. Nagel takes this to be a serious problem with his dual-aspect theory. A conceptual revolution is needed to overcome such problems, on Nagel's view (51-53). Leibniz, Schopenhauer, and Whitehead, among the dignitaries whom we have briefly interviewed in these pages, would reassure Nagel on this point. They accept forms of panpsychism. The revolution anticipated by Nagel may lead us ultimately to see people as distinct from other things only in the degree to which they have mental properties. On this view, mind is particularly well-developed in people, less so in other animals, and very dim in vegetables. Certainly it is revolutionary to say that carrots, in even an extremely limited way, have mental as well as physical properties. One could, however, limit mental properties to those things with brains rather than buying the whole panpsychism theory.

Against Parfit: Not *R* but the brain

Recall Parfit's spectra examples—science fiction cases of gradual physical and mental change of one person into another person. Parfit's physical spectrum case was designed to show that the continuity of the brain is a matter of degree and that, in any case, not the brain but relation *R*, which includes psychological continuity and connectedness of the person, is what really matters. Nagel asserts that the actual cause of such continuity is what matters, namely the intact brain. Otherwise, he claims, personal identity would be illusory. Nagel has, however, no clear answer to the question "Why does the brain matter?" (45) Perhaps for both Parfit and Nagel, the answers given to "What matters?" are close to bedrock assumptions on which the rest of the position is built.

One motive which Nagel does not mention for clinging to the brain, but which may be active behind the scenes in Nagel's presentation, is the only Tom and Dick principle.[10] That principle, which underlies the argument of Williams in chapter eleven, says that if there is a question whether person Tom is identical to person Dick, then that question can be answered by appeal only to what Tom and Dick are like. Properties of other parties are irrelevant to the identity of Tom to Dick. This seems like a reasonable principle, but best-candidate theories of personal identity deny this principle. Such theories determine who is Tom by looking for who, of various people, is the best candidate. If Dick would be best but for the existence of Harry, then not only Tom and Dick are relevant to the question of whether Dick is identical to Tom (who existed earlier than Dick and Harry).

For example, we have seen Nozick's best-candidate theory in chapter twelve, or, in chapter thirteen, the theory based on *R* which Parfit flirts with but probably does not need to defend. Best-candidate theories tell us that if there is some third person, Harry, who might, along with Dick be a candidate for identity with Tom, then we choose between Dick and Harry by checking to see which satisfies the identity criterion best. Parfit might think that if Dick is more *R*-related to Tom than Harry is, then Dick is identical to Tom while Harry is not. If Dick and Harry are equally *R*-related to Tom, then neither is identical to Tom, going by the way Parfit speaks of his cases of personal fission. If Tom divides, becoming Dick and Harry, then properties of Harry are relevant to the identity of Tom to Dick contrary to the only Tom and Dick principle. The sameness of the intact brain provides a criterion of personal identity which is immune to such science fiction fission cases. Even if the brain is divisible without the death of either half, the resulting halves are not to be identified with the original whole brain.[11] Nagel thus has a way of preserving our intuition that there is something under our consciousness that would preserve us even through radical changes in our mental life. Parfit seems to bite the bullet here, in effect denying this intuition about survival and denying the only Tom and Dick principle.

With Parfit: Denial of the indivisibility thesis

Parfit and Nagel, in spite of their differences, do agree on some controversial theses. They both deny the indivisibility thesis of Descartes. This means that Nagel should accept indeterminacy of people. In fact, he does not think that there must be a definite answer to the question whether a particular experience is my experience. Nor does Nagel balk at believing that there could be two experiences both of which are mine but which occur in different subjects (45). A single brain can continue in existence but with a radically different mental life after some extreme experience. This preserves the intuition that one can lose one's intellect and/or memories but still be the same person. In a case where large and important areas of the brain are altered, brain identity may be a problem for Nagel's view even if personal identity given the sameness of the brain is no longer a problem. The self as brain may not do all that the simple, indivisible self was supposed to accomplish, but it is better than the alternatives, if Nagel is right (44).

Nagel, it appears, adopts a divisibility thesis which leads to *some* forms of indeterminacy of persons. But Nagel does not want to go to the extent that Parfit does in claiming that a person is a complex of things more like a nation than like a Cartesian Ego. Nagel admits that his reasons for resisting are question-begging:

> One of the conditions that the self should meet if possible is that it be something in which the flow of consciousness and the beliefs, desires, intentions, and character traits that I have all take place—something beneath the contents of consciousness, which might even survive a radical break in the continuity of consciousness. If there were no such thing then the idea of personal identity would be an illusion, but we are not in that situation. (45)

Since Nagel insists on the intactness of the brain to fulfill this condition of the self, he would have to accept the odd consequence that one who survives the destruction of half of the cortex and who seems to be the same person by macroscopic observation is not the same person as the original victim of the brain damage.

Worse than this, the molecules that compose the brain change. Does this mean that the brain does not continue? If it does continue through this change, then the brain's structure, not the particular material of which it is composed, seems to be what is important. Nagel's view might, therefore, run afoul of Williams' reduplication argument. If we could produce a second brain identical to the first in structure, we would have two candidates for being a single person.

Since Nagel insists on actual causes of R (psychological continuity and connectedness), he might count only the first brain as determining the original person and the copy as having the wrong kind of cause to be the original person. A duplicate person might be, except for causal history and spatio-temporal location, indiscernible from the original. She would believe she was the original. Nonetheless, that causal history explains how she came to be, hence who she is. In this, Nagel agrees with Kripke,[12] yet another famous philosopher who barely gets mentioned in these pages. Nagel notes that Kripke comes close to a dual-aspect theory operating through his claim that biological origin is the source of identity. Nagel disagrees with Kripke, however, as to the possibility of mental events without the brain. Nagel suspects that the conceivability of such detached mental events is dependent on our mental concepts grasping only one aspect of the mind.[13] When we think of our visual experience, for example, we may think of only one aspect of it and thereby delude ourselves into supposing that it can be consistently conceived of as existing independently of the brain.

In summary, then, Nagel rests identity of persons on identity of brains. He recognizes that identity of brains is problematic. He chose brains, in any case, because he thought that what mattered in survival was the actual cause of R. When confronted with a case of two brains similar in structure or function, Nagel would look to see if one of them had the right kind of cause. If so, it would be the same brain we started with. It appears then that, for Nagel, what causes us to be as we are is crucial for our being who we are and, at the same time, is what matters about us. I should care about whether I survive, not just about whether my mind survives in someone or other. Personal identity and mattering are together again. This reunion, at least, is intuitively correct.

What is unintuitive is that the cause matters so much. Just how crucial is it that I am the result of a particular sperm and egg? Could not one of that sperm's squirmy brethren have contributed equally well to my birth? There seem to be a number of possible causes of my being which would not crucially have altered me as a person. Once we admit this, however, we stray from the causal theory which Nagel seems to be adopting from Kripke.

A good reason for Nagel to cling to a causal theory is his opposition to functionalism, the view of the person as biological computer. Once one gives up particular causes, like a sperm and ovum, one is thrown back on the structure of the brain as the crucial thing about it for purposes of identity. Since every molecule of the brain will change every six years or so, there is no way to use a same-matter-same-brain criterion of identity. Structure is all that is left. Structures, however, can be duplicated, opening a Pandora's Box of problems with which we have seen Williams, Nozick, and Parfit struggle. So Nagel is left with a brain caused in the appropriate way which has mental and physical aspects.

Problems

The difficulty of defending a dual-aspect theory

Nagel is defending very difficult ground here. Bravely, he tries to take a position between the dualist and the materialist in the full recognition that, like a pacifist protesting at the battlefront, he will be caught in the crossfire. The materialist will say that his talk of irreducibly mental properties of the brain is unfounded while the dualist will say that his identification of the self with the brain is unintelligible. Although Nagel admits to hand-waving and question-begging, he thinks the alternatives are even less able than his view to preserve both our subjective impressions of ourselves and our objective knowledge of our biological components.

Terminological problems

The terminology of Nagel's difficult position is somewhat puzzling. Nagel speaks interchangeably of personal identity and self-identity, seemingly making no distinction between selves and persons (37). On the other hand, the self is defined as the same subjective consciousness (33). While subjective consciousness is usually essential to our view of what we are, it is also usually a somewhat narrower concept than that of a person. Perhaps self-identity and personal identity always go together, but they must not be exactly the same thing.

Nagel also gives us his empirical hypothesis that the self is just the person's brain. Here the self is clearly distinct from the person: "What I am is whatever is in fact the seat of the person TN's experiences" (41). Here TN (Thomas Nagel) is a person who includes the brain which is the self. It looks like the self is the subject of experiences if a seat is a subject; hence, the brain is the subject of experiences. We have already seen that the brain may survive a radical change in consciousness; so the subject of experiences is clearly not the consciousness.

Collecting all the bits, we seem to have the *person*; the *self* (which is also called the *subject* and is perhaps the *brain*); and the *consciousness* as, perhaps, three distinct entities. To this list we must add the strangest of them all, the *objective self*. The picture we have prior to adding the objective self is of persons as normally conscious beings who may, however, lose their consciousness and remain the same so long as they retain the same brain.

The postulation of the objective self

In his quest to accommodate the objective and subjective perspectives to one another, Nagel postulates the existence of the objective self, a self each of us has but which has *no point of view*. This "true self" (61) is abstracted from the person by treating that person's experiences as data for the construction of an objective picture (62). This objective self functions independently of the person (65) but is inseparable from the person (61). By taking the view from nowhere this autonomous objective self helps in the reconciliation of the subjective and objective perspectives (66). This will take some unravelling in terms of the meanings of what we say about ourselves.

From a semantic point of view this objective self idea allows us to distinguish three different meanings of the sentence uttered by Thomas Nagel, "I am TN." It could be the content-free "TN is TN," or the practical communication, "My name is 'TN.'" As a communication of the objective self, however, it says that the objective self is getting its sensory information about the world through the person TN. Nagel is replying to those who think we are misled by linguistic considerations into manufacturing a self from a misunderstanding of the use of "I" (57-60). That is, he is replying to the no-ownership view. The apparent strength of the reply depends, however, on one's intuitions about the existence of something in oneself fitting the description of the objective self.

Intuitively it is possible to stand back from ourselves and take an objective look at ourselves and the way others see us. Even in the midst of great anger, one can see the anger as absurd from the outside. Nagel takes this kind of data seriously and drives the conception of persons from the contemporary unified picture back to a pluralistic conception. There are various decision-makers within one person. This is somewhat reminiscent, in its pluralism, of the ancient Greek idea of a person as containing various autonomous decision-makers—an idea used by Wilkes to hammer Parfit, as we saw in the last chapter.

Nagel's pluralism with respect to persons is certainly every bit as strange as its Iliadic cousin to contemporary understanding of the person. We could perhaps become accustomed to thinking of the self as the brain, but the objective self which takes the view from nowhere is an odd item indeed. Williams, in discussing identity criteria for persons, and insisting that they must be used by someone, has objected to the intelligibility of the view from nowhere long before Nagel makes use of it. Commenting on Hume's speculation on what we would see if we could see clearly into the breast of another, Williams says,

> Others, in criticizing or expanding Hume's account, have written in terms that similarly require an externalized view of the contents of a man's mind, a view obtainable from no conceivable vantage-point. Theorizing which is in this sense abstract must be vacuous, because this privileged but positionless point of view can mean nothing to us.[14]

It certainly seems to mean a lot to Nagel, but he warns against giving it a metaphysical interpretation, although it is real.[15] How can something be real and not countenanced as a real object by our metaphysics?

This difficult doctrine is illuminated by another passage:

> The fact that I seem able in imagination to detach this perspectiveless or objective self from TN [i.e., Thomas Nagel] does not show that it is a distinct thing, or that nothing else about TN belongs to me essentially. It does not show, as may at first appear, that the connection between me and TN is accidental. It does show, however, that something essential about me has nothing to do with my perspective and position in the world. (62)

It turns out, then, that the objective self is real, but not really a distinct object from the person. It is a device for seeing an objective but non-physical part of a person. Is it intelligible Williams notwithstanding? It is indeed difficult to moderate this debate concerning the possibility of a privileged but positionless point of view.

Williams is objecting to this viewpoint because no person could take it. Nagel might agree that no *person* could take it, but insists that *a part of a person* could. Stand back from your passions and notice, from no point of view, what you are experiencing. This essential part of you which does the standing back, rather standing nowhere, is your way of being objective about your subjective experience.

One may answer these instructions in a Humean way, saying that there is nothing corresponding to the objective self which one sees when one introspects. Nagel might reply that it is the objective self which is doing the introspecting. We should not look for a distinct thing or a little person within doing this, but "a distinct part of the mind" viewing the mind's experience (66). Here again is the pluralism which is contrary to many of our current ways of thinking and speaking. It is not contrary to all. You may find that you are *of two minds* about it.

While the objective self is still somewhat nebulous, it does tug at one's intuitions. There is an odd phenomenon of standing back from oneself even in moments of great heat. It is especially noticeable when one feels the absurdity of life.[16] The phenomenon may, however, be something more evident to those who have meditated on it than to others. My willingness to entertain, tentatively, Nagel's concept of an objective self as an essential part of a person is utterly dependent on my awareness in myself of this phenomenon of my standing back from myself even though there is nowhere to stand. It is quite possible that some do not experience this, whence their Humean replies to Nagel.

Application to Daphne's case

Daphne was the victim of massive scarring of her brain which altered nearly everything else about her. In spite of the changes to the brain, it is the same brain, by the causal criterion of sameness; so Daphne still exists as the same self. The self, however, is not identical to the person. Nagel does not tell us enough about the relationship, although he speaks as if self-identity and personal identity always go together. Daphne's former kind of consciousness is gone, although the seat of consciousness remains. The current consciousness appears to be very limited. The personality is reduced to mere remnants. The capacity to interact with others is nearly absent. Would Nagel be willing to say, therefore, that a different person is now related to that continuing self, that brain? If so, then why is it the brain that matters? If not, then what is a person over and above the brain which that person has? Nagel's account, while insightful, is very incomplete.

What I like about Nagel's account

Nagel sees that there is something essential about the physical aspect of a person, although he does not take this insight far enough. Most importantly, he also articulates some of the uneasiness we reasonably have with reductionism. What reductionists leave out is our subjective viewpoint, and that is essential to persons. Nagel rightly resists the contemporary fashion of scientistic adulation of the apparently objective output of the empirical sciences. Nagel's analysis of the distinction between the subjective and the objective seems right. The proliferation of terms Nagel adopts to apply this analysis to persons is forced partly by the variety of questions about persons which is masked by a minimalist approach.

After too short a visit, we must bid a fond adieu to Nagel's territory in order to begin to draw together some of the ideas of the contemporary notables I have selected for comment.

FIFTEEN
Collecting Ideas

Ideas from ancient Greece and Rome

The belief in a perfect world of Forms apart from the muck of the mundane in which we are mired is very pretty, but I put it with the belief in Santa Claus as a device for changing behaviour. It is good to temporarily suspend disbelief and act as if these things were so. There is, however, more in the Forms than in Santa. The Forms, with apologies to Plato, may be thought of not as real but as ideals to help us to organize our thought and action. It is useful to ask what the Form of a person might be. If we can construct a model and hold it before our minds, then we will be better able to say when a particular human being has enough resemblance to the ideal or model to be included in the class of persons.

There is another kind of form which is inspired by what was discussed in connection with Aristotle and which is even more useful. Aristotle's forms are not other-worldly ephemera. The form of persons in general is a set of abilities. The foremost of these abilities is rationality, broadly construed to include much more than merely logical thinking. Logic can lead us from foolish starting points to foolish conclusions. Rationality includes the choice of good beginnings. Among the other important abilities which distinguish persons from other kinds of being are social and political abilities. Fundamental among these is the ability to communicate with others of our kind. There are also very basic abilities which are part of the form which are nonetheless not themselves distinctive of persons, like the ability to move oneself. If we consider all of these various abilities as necessary to any person, counterexamples spring readily to mind. There are, obviously, people who cannot move themselves. There are irrational people as well. These counterexamples require that we say how one can be a person, albeit a deformed person, with only some of the abilities. Since nobody is perfectly formed, we are all in some sense "deformed." If we use this as a technical term rather than an insult, it can help to draw together ideas about what we are.

As will become clear, my perspective is fairly heavily influenced by Aristotle. This is partly because I hitch my wagon to Western common sense, and Aristotle is one of the originators of what has come to be common sense. It would be anachronistic to say I will develop an Aristotelian concept of a

---

Notes to Chapter Fifteen are on pp. 324-25.

person, but the inspiration for some of my theory blows from this doughty ancient.

As we try to make sense of the forms of people, both people as a class and people as individuals, we must keep in mind the lessons of the ancients which point to a complex, not a simple, indivisible self. Whether we call the parts of the self, "Reason, Spirit, and Appetite" or use contemporary psychiatric jargon, we must admit that a person is at times at war with herself or doing several things at once. This is inexplicable with a simple, indivisible self like a Cartesian Ego.

The Roman adaptation of the Greek ideas includes, importantly, the invention of the concept of a person (*persona*) as a concept distinct from that of a human being. Although there are those who wish to eradicate this ancient distinction, the anti-abortion activists for example, it is a distinction worth preserving. However we arrange our concepts, we must be able to tell when a person so loses the form of person as to be a mere human being or when a human being has not yet acquired that form.

Freedom starts to come into the picture in ancient times as well. The idea that slaves were not persons under late Roman law is a particularly nasty recognition of the importance of freedom in concepts of a person. As well as political freedom and its moral basis, there is linked to notions of person the idea of metaphysical freedom. Persons, unlike automata, can be confronted with genuine choices. Most of us believe this, however difficult it may be to say what the freedom to choose is. We think we are responsible for our own actions. Of course, as we saw in chapter three, the Stoics and Plotinus thought this while thinking that all of our actions are determined. I find this paradoxical. Give me freedom.

Individuality as a part of what we are begins to grow in ancient times as well. The importance of the person as an individual over and against groups of persons, for example the state, is weaned in ancient times. It has become common sense in the West that the individual's interests, not merely the interests of the group, must be considered.

Mediaeval and Renaissance influences

Augustine keeps a version of Plato's value hierarchy alive, as Plotinus did before him. The world is arranged via a system of values, with God at the top. For Plato the Form of the Good was at the top. For Augustine, people are valuable to the extent that they resemble God. This is a little easier to comprehend than resemblance to a form. God can be thought of as the ultimate person. In this system angels are better than us, but we are better than animals. Whether or not you think of God and angels as real or merely ideals, you probably think of people as more valuable than animals.

This is a part of our common sense which is much under challenge nowadays. Nonetheless, with restrictions, there is something right about this. For example, it seems reasonable to allow animals to suffer in medical research so that people will have their suffering relieved. Much animal suffering, however, is inflicted for minor pleasures of people. This would not be justified simply by valuing people more highly than animals. Nevertheless, there is something right in the notion that people have a greater moral value than chimpanzees because of their greater resemblance to some ideal, some form, as the source of value.

Another contribution of Augustine's is the addition to the list of capacities of persons the capacity for mutual love. There is a strain, however, in Augustine's emphasis on love over abilities like the capacity for rational thought. This might put some dogs above some people on a scale of resemblance to the ideal being, if that ideal is framed more in terms of love than rationality. While being a person is partly an affair of the heart, it is not only this. There are, of course, varieties of mutual love which require more intellect than a dog or even a chimp is likely to muster. In any case, we need to keep open a large place for the capacity for mutual love when we come to speculate on the form of a person.

Aquinas goes back to the intellect as a primary feature of us, and takes up the Aristotelian banner. There is, however, a new element. On the one hand, following Aristotle's general way of thinking we would say that the potential person, the human infant, becomes a person in realizing some preset end or purpose. On the other hand, the role of the person in making herself is greater on Aquinas' way of thinking. Because we are responsible for forming our own characters, becoming a person is a boot-strap operation. There is something right about this paradoxical position on which we must try to get a handle. Perhaps Nozick's views on self-creation will help.

A theme that takes root in the mediaeval period flowers in the Renaissance. We have seen, for example, Erasmus weaving into the humanist strand of thought on persons the idea that we achieve merit through our exercise of our freedom. Our dignity and moral worth come to depend on our own achievements. Of course a great achievement, in this context, may be merely in using well the poor hand that we are dealt by the accidents of birth. Through Augustine, Aquinas, and Erasmus, the importance of the individual and of what the individual does become further entrenched in our ideas of the worth of the individual as a person. For the religious, the value of a person resides officially in the approval of God. It is up to us, however, to choose to be either sinners or saints. This makes a person's worth depend ever more on that person. That is a development that I wish to further with a gentle sort of individualism as a part of the concept of a person I put forward.

Help from the earlier moderns

Locke is the first to make the concept of a person a central issue. Ever after concepts of a person tend to be tied to moral concerns, especially Locke's worry about responsibility. Unlike Locke, I think people are responsible even for things they do not remember doing, but there is much in Locke that is useful. Like him, we should rule out appealing to religious solutions to philosophical problems. If our concept of a person, for example, is inadequate for telling who is who, it is not acceptable to say that God sorts that out. We should also follow Locke in trying to keep the debate among materialists, dualists, and idealists from clouding the issue. We want a concept of a person which will work with any of these metaphysical foundations.

Like both Descartes and Locke, we should attend to the subject of the experiences which a person has, but with Hobbes, we ought to remember the importance of the body. This does not rule out idealism. The idealist can reinterpret body-talk as talk of ideas in minds. Whatever bodies are, they are crucial to people. Leibniz reminds us to remember also the non-conscious aspects of people which harks back to Plato's spirit and appetite as parts of the self.

Hume's view that there are no people is an excellent prod. We must keep in mind his arguments against the self if we are to say anything sensible about it. His iconoclasm with respect to personal identity must also be faced squarely. There is, moreover, a theme in Hume that I will develop—conventionalism. The nature of persons is not something which can be discovered independently of a culture and its conventions.

Kant makes persons ends rather than means to achieving ends. The dignity of persons and respect for them as individuals with rights as opposed to mere parts of a larger society are things we should preserve. The strong linkage of the metaphysical, epistemological, and ethical concerns about people is another valuable part of our Kantian heritage.

Contributions of the later moderns

Bentham and Mill, through making pleasure the foundation of morality, would undo Kant and allow people to be mere means. Although I think this is devoutly to be avoided, we should take from them the reminder that pleasure and pain are central to the concerns of people. We can admit that unnecessary suffering is evil. We can wish to protect animals from it. To value, as most of us do, people over animals, we must fashion a concept of persons which explains the difference. Otherwise we would be guilty of demanding a difference in treatment when there is no difference in kind. This is just what racists do.

Kierkegaard and the existentialists generally take the capacity to make free choices as central to what we are. This theme of freedom we have noticed in earlier philosophers. Marx, on the other hand, reinforces the idea of the relativity of people to their social and political environment. These need not be incompatible ideas, however. What we are, in general, may be socially determined, while the choices we make as individuals will create what we are as later individuals.

Contemporary pieces of the puzzle

The cultural relativity of the nature of persons is also furthered by pragmatist thinking. Any claims we make about people would have been assessed by James, Dewey, and Peirce by checking to see what difference it would make to accept such claims. It would be wise to ask ourselves what social and personal difference is made by accepting any concept we cobble together from these pieces of past philosophy.

Some continental philosophers we have considered, Heiddeger and Sartre, reinforce the theme of the importance of personal choice and our subjective point of view. Such mottoes as "we are what we do" can be useful points of departure in our search for ourselves. Existence does precede essence insofar as one first exists as a human being, then gradually develops capacities which admit one to the class of persons, and, by choice, fashions an individual essence. The difficulty will be in making this boot-strapping operation understandable through a clarification of the two kinds of essence. Husserl, also in this continental tradition, influences me, somewhat in the way that Wittgenstein and Nagel do later, to see as crucial the unseen seeing part of myself but not to treat it as simply one of the items in the world which I see. It is a challenge to make something other than tongue-twisters out of the things to be said about the viewpoint of the subject of experiences.

In the Analytic School of philosophy, Ayer revives the body-based view of people while Strawson picks up one of the continental themes in emphasizing the primacy, for our understanding of people, of personal interaction. Strawson, however, unlike many philosophers in both schools, does not wish to shock us with the novelty of his views. Like him, I will take our pre-existing conceptual scheme as a guide. The difference is that I explicitly take this scheme to be culturally relative. To some extent, this is also a way of following Quine. He takes persons to be matters of convention. Like Quine, I think that once we can say what people are by specifying clearly the conventions regarding our use of the word "person," we can then understand what it is to be the same person over time.

In Wiggins and Williams we have seen further exponents of the body-based view of persons. Unlike Ayer they recognize the importance of the body without insisting that it just *is* the person. I will emulate them in this. We have seen Wiggins' warnings about the dangers of functionalism. While I will take them to heart, I will try to come up with a theory that takes the abilities of a person to, in part, define that person. Mine is not, however, a purely functionalist account. Williams is also concerned about the socially relative concepts of a person as an adequate basis for morality. He gives us instead a theory of person as a natural kind. I would like this to work, but it does not. We have to grasp the thistles of relativism.

Williams, on the other hand, thinks that the concept of a person is of little use in moral theory. I will side with Wiggins here, but I will try to overcome his conclusion that accounts which do not treat the concept of a person as a natural kind cannot provide for the moral weight that this concept must bear. I think that "person," like "infant," need not apply to a being from conception to death. I like Wiggins' revival of Aristotle and will use some of this groundwork, emphasizing the Aristotelian notion of the *psuche* discussed in chapter three.

As we come to the very, very contemporary philosophers whom I have selected for comment, my debts grow larger. Nozick, for all that I reject closest continuers as not close enough, sets up some general structures which are a good support for my view. The weighted dimensions of Strawson or the series of sliding scales spoken of by Williams become Nozick's metric. This is a good device, though I have a somewhat different application. Nozick's views on self-creation and the use of "I" will also be incorporated.

Parfit, like Williams and Hume, often serves as the opposition to my view against which background I illuminate what I wish to say. Nonetheless, I accept the anti-Cartesian arguments which Parfit offers. Instead of Parfit's determined revision of our conceptual scheme, I support Strawson's descriptive metaphysics. The importance of psychological continuity and connectedness cannot be denied, but there are other kinds of continuity and connectedness to which we must give equal weight.

Although I found Nagel's account incomplete, his discussion of the distinction of subjective from objective is very valuable, extending and clarifying as it does some suggestive remarks from earlier philosophers like Wittgenstein and Husserl. Like Nagel, I think the bodily basis of persons is to be found mainly in the brain. Nagel's most valuable contribution, however, is the opposition to Parfit's reductionism and to pure functionalism by means of the subjective viewpoint of persons.

What a concept of persons should preserve

The overview of the history of Western concepts of a person makes the construction of yet another such concept a little daunting. Metaphysically, it should tell us what persons are, in general, and what makes a person at one time the same person at another time. Epistemologically, it should help us make judgments about knowing who is a person and who is who. Ethically, it should help us make moral judgments about the treatment appropriate to persons. We have seen some philosophers despairing at finding any concept filling such a tall order. But the view that any concept of a person is inadequate to such tasks or to much of anything else is a mistake. This concept is central to Western European culture. This anthropological claim requires some support before we launch into the assembly of further desiderata for a concept of a person.

The centrality of a concept of a person

One might well argue that the concept of a person is merely a recent Western European invention, a cultural peculiarity rather than something central to our understanding of human beings. Marcel Mauss, while arguing for the importance of some concept of a person, gives a great deal of evidence opposed to associating persons with human beings in our one-to-one Western fashion. He details the ways in which other cultures see something like a series of persons through a single human life or a single person through various human lives. He tells us, "Those who have made of the human person a complete entity, independent of all others save God, are rare."[1] Are our memories just the ghosts of persons past? Or could it be that our bodily lives are just channels for persons who precede and survive those bodily lives?

Clifford Geertz, after investigating the Javanese, Balinese, and Moroccan ways of defining persons, concludes that

> The Western conception of the person as a bounded, unique, more or less integrated motivational and cognitive universe, a dynamic center of awareness, emotion, judgment, and action organized into a distinctive whole and set contrastively against other such wholes and against its social and natural background, is, however incorrigible it may seem to us, a rather peculiar idea within the context of the world's cultures.[2]

One might say, if Geertz is right, that our concept of a person is a defining characteristic of Western European (including British North American) culture.

The anthropological data should at least give us pause. Perhaps current skeptics are right that the concept of a person should not be given the pride of place that it has had in Western philosophy since Locke's time. A look at cultural differences and at the sweep of the history of the concept does, at the very least, motivate our taking stock of the sort of concepts of a person which we are willing to take seriously and at the functions we expect them to perform.

For many British and North American philosophers, the main concepts of a person which are considered in the ballpark tend to be versions of Locke's concept of a person as a continuing consciousness. Wilkes notes, however, that the word "conscious" in the sense of "inwardly sensible or aware" only came into our language around 1620, and that neither the ancient Greeks nor the contemporary Chinese have such a word.[3] Even in contemporary Western European culture, we rarely limit the concept of a person, as it tends to be limited in philosophical discussion, to some sort of continuing consciousness or potentially conscious being where consciousness may be narrowly construed in terms of intellect.

Wiggins, whose individuative naturalism was discussed above,[4] points out that boxers and ballerinas as well as philosophers are persons.[5] Our putting intellectual ability foremost in our discussions of survival has a parochial flavour. Philosophers dealing with the subject of persons tend to ignore most of the aspects of persons and to concentrate on those abilities that persons need to do philosophy. That is how Descartes got the idea that we are essentially thinking things. The emphasis on ratiocination and, in Locke, the emphasis on memory is, I think, due to this philosophocentricity. Recent philosophy has not changed the fashion much except to try to reduce these abilities dear to the minds of philosophers to abilities of the bodies of philosophers. I would like, instead, to keep an open mind about what kind of concept of a person will be useful.

There is of course the danger of keeping my mind *so* open that everything falls out. To prevent fall-out, I will Moore[6] myself to Western common sense in my search for live hypotheses concerning the concept of a person, and I will try to get clear about what those who are not among the skeptics expect a concept of a person to do for us.

General features of a person to be preserved

Looking at the history of what philosophers have thought about people we see certain especially general features which their concepts of a person strive to maintain. These give us, in effect, a list of desiderata for any concept of a person being proposed. Any concept acceptable in Western eyes will have to allow for people to be complex individuals who are nonetheless irreducible and indivisible. They must be continuous and determinate. Persons have a certain mysterious cachet as well; they should be indefinable. All of these features need further explanation.

Complexity

People are many-splendoured things. In this I agree with Parfit. We have various parts, bodies, conscious and non-conscious faculties, for example. Views like that of Descartes which try to make us simple atoms which are indivisible by virtue of having no parts are on the right track for the wrong reason. We have some kind of indivisibility, and Parfit's reductionism is wrong. We are, nonetheless, complex.

Irreducibility

This is one of the features that Parfit tried to persuade us to abandon. Not just Descartes, but most of the philosophers we have discussed would wish to preserve this feature of persons in their concept of a person. Positively put, irreducibility requires that what we call persons must be more than merely the sum of their objectively describable parts. One cannot adequately describe a person by merely describing objects, events, or processes none of which is a person. To abide with Strawson in the realm of descriptive rather than revisionist metaphysics, we should preserve irreducib-ility in our metaphysical views about people, recognizing that what we are describing is relative to Western culture. At the same time we must recognize what philosophers from Plato onward have emphasized, that we have an inner complexity. Irreducibility cannot be purchased at the cost of oversimplifying ourselves, pretending we are indivisible atoms of some sort like Cartesian Egos or souls.

From the moral standpoint, metaphysical irreducibility may be very significant. If, from a moral point of view, people deserve special treatment, then people must be special. What makes people special, what makes them ends rather than means in Kant's sense, may well be, in part, that people cannot be reduced to the things which are mere ends. Our dignity requires a contrast of ourselves with our social and natural background, else we are mere cogs in the social wheel or elaborate natural processes. Reduction is all very well if we wish to abandon entirely individual rights and to embrace instead the ideals of benefiting the social commonwealth or furthering ecosystems. Consequentialist ethical theories can benefit from the reducibility of persons, as we saw in looking at Parfit's views. Most non-consequentialist ethical theories, however, can tolerate no such abandonment. My presupposi-tion is that our Western ethical mainstream is non-consequentialist (in the sense that it requires that we look at more than just the consequences of an action to determine whether the action is right). The ethical mainstream of our culture requires the dignity of persons to underlie such things as rights and virtues which underlie non-consequentialist moral reasoning.

Epistemologically speaking, it would be easier if our concept of a person made a person a possible object of knowledge by acquaintance. Irreducibility seems to muddy the waters somewhat. A person's objective features do not in sum make the person, but they are the features with which we can be acquainted; so there is something mysterious about knowing a person. Consequently it is difficult to identify and reidentify another person with complete confidence. It would be easy if there were some unchanging mark of the person on which the irreducibility depended. If this mark could be objectively known then one could reidentify people with relative ease. There is nothing, however, which serves to identify people as fingerprints serve to identify their bodies. Judging from my experience of myself, however, I expect bodies and people to be correlated one to one. Admittedly, generalizing from a single case is not ideal, but that is the limit of the empirical evidence we can have.

Self-knowledge, however, is another matter. Descartes was right to say that what we know about ourselves is not little. The subjective knowledge of a person by that person is of great importance and is closely tied to irreducibility. The ancient exhortation "know thyself" cannot be followed by merely investigating one's own characteristics as one would those of another. In fact, our knowledge of other people and things is based on our subjective self-knowledge. Bergson is right to take the self as the starting point in our search for knowledge of other things.

The viewline

Knowing one's own current subjective viewpoint and its history, that is knowing one's *viewline*, is a large part of self-knowledge. My subjective *viewpoint* is the place from which I seem to be seeing the world at a given moment. My viewline is the locus of my viewpoint through space as it appears to me over time, that is, my series of viewpoints through my life. As I will argue, roughly following Nagel, this viewline is what makes us irreducible. Before coming to the difficult matter of discussing viewlines, however, I will mention some of the other features of people which will depend in part on subjectivity.

Individuality

Many of the same comments apply to this criterion as to irreducibility. That is because we are only individuals if we are not reducible to other smaller individuals which make us up as, for instance, a society is made up of us. If, to pursue an example of Strawson's,[7] there were groups of human beings who acted with one intellectual and emotional accord with such precision and unanimity that activities of members of the group could only be understood as part of an action of the group, then such a group of human beings would, nonetheless, not be an individual person. "One person, one body" seems to be one of our cultural mottoes perhaps because each of the members of the group would have a subjective viewline not shared by the others, however neatly they combined their wills in the objective realm. From an epistemological point of view, our classificatory criteria would be far too weak if we allowed such groups to be persons. We would not know who was who. In moral debate we tend to suspect the claim that the various human beings making up the group could not be held praiseworthy or blameworthy independently of the group. The buck of moral praise and blame stops with the individual. One cannot hide in the group. Individuality is dependent on irreducibility.

At the same time we must recognize the importance of society for our individuality. Some of the philosophers we have considered, particularly Plato and Aristotle, thought of people as importantly social. We need to understand ourselves not as metaphysically dependent on some larger group, but as fulfilled only in such a group. Even the hermit depends on society as a foil to make sense of her life. This does not mean that we should elevate the state, as we have seen Hegel doing, to that in accord with which the rational individual must act to be "free."

The idea of our individuality harks back to the property of persons which we saw the mediaevals calling "self-existence." This is the idea that people are not essentially parts or properties of other things. We are individuals in our own right.

Continuity

One of the preoccupations of the metaphysicians looking at persons is that of diachronic identity—the question of what preserves the individual through change. Its epistemological cousin is the problem of reidentification. The metaphysician looks for the source of the continuity while the epistemologist seeks some mark whereby we may know it. Where continuity is concerned, I would turn Hume on his head and say that the one case where each of us does have direct knowledge of a continuing thing is our own case. The continuity of other things we understand by reference to our own continuity. I am influenced by Bergson in this.[8] Objective knowledge is a pale probabilistic reflection of subjective certainty. Unfortunately, even this subjective certainty is no unshakable certainty about others or even ourselves on the view I will propose.

Continuity is also necessary as a precondition of much moral thinking about persons. To say I am responsible for what I have done is to say, among other things, that I am continuous with he who did the action. If one makes continuity too fragile, as does Locke with the memory criterion or Nozick with the self-creating closest-continuer theory discussed above, then we let people off the hook too easily. It is also dangerous, from an Occidental perspective at least, to make continuity jump the bounds of a human life so that I become responsible, for instance, for what the holder of my title did prior to my birth. That is not the least bit counter-intuitive in some cultures, perhaps, but I am standing by Western common sense as much as possible in the delineation of a workable concept of a person.

The metaphysical problems which surround the attempt to describe what keeps people continuous are the problems of personal identity. A satisfactory answer to the question of what makes a person at one time the same person at another time may or may not help with the epistemological problem of continuity. How we know who is who will depend on the knowablity of whatever it is that, metaphysically speaking, makes people themselves. Kant's doctrine of the noumenal self which was discussed above is an example of a metaphysical solution which makes the epistemological problem insoluble. I wish to avoid this as much as possible.

We know ourselves, subjectively, partly because we remember a viewline which our present viewpoint continues. We may, however, know ourselves well or badly. Unfortunately, some segments of one's viewline bear little relation to the objective locus of one's body through space. Suppose Tom in Toronto gets stoned on acid and watches a movie taken as if through the eyes of Dick in Vancouver. His viewline may not correspond to the objective location of his body if the drug causes him to shut out completely his awareness of being in a theatre. Tom may know himself in a way which is good for Dick but bad for Tom during the time of the watching of the film.

Nor does the viewline guarantee continuity. It may, after all, have gaps when we sleep. The subjective part of a person alone is not enough to guarantee continuity, but the continuity of the person can be guaranteed partly as Wiggins and Williams would have it by the continuity of the body. The subjective component is, however, necessary for indivisibility and irreducibility, as will be explained in the next chapter. A person, according to the concept I will explicate, must have a body, a viewline, and a set of abilities to continue through time.

Determinacy

The question "Am I about to die?" is metaphysical, a question about existence, about continuity of an individual. If it is always to be answerable, there must be some definite end-point of every individual. That is another tall order for a concept of a person to fill, but it is too tall and not needed. The assumption that we cannot have irreducibility and continuity without complete determinacy is an unwarranted assumption. A person's life is not an off-on switch. Admitting some vagueness about the beginnings and ends of people's lives without thereby falling into reductionism is one of the tasks I set myself. I shall have to accept the epistemological consequence that it is sometimes impossible for anyone, even the person herself, to know whether that person continues in existence. I think, however, that this can be made more plausible than at first it seems. I saw it happen to Daphne. Morally speaking, there is in the vagueness of beginnings and ends of people much difficulty about matters such as abortion and promise-keeping. We must, however, accept Aristotle's advice and not seek more precision than our subject matter allows.[9]

Indivisibility

Sometimes it seems reasonable to say one cannot speak of parts of persons except in the sense of body parts. We must be wary, however, of the mediaeval motivation for this. Indivisibility would provide us with indestructibility, something we might wish for but cannot necessarily be expected to have. I do not wish to argue for or presuppose any religious doctrines such as that of an immortal soul. The heritage I wish to preserve is secular, although the origin of much in that heritage is religious. Both the religious and secular traditions emphasize the importance of knowing oneself. Self-knowledge, however, requires a kind of indivisibility. But note, it need not be so mysterious as the indivisibility of the soul or of the Ego. I know who I am partly by knowing my viewline (the locus of my experience in space and time as it appeared to me, the history of my subjective viewpoint or perspective). One must have a unique subjective viewpoint from which one sees the world to be a self-knowing subject, and a viewpoint cannot be divided without becoming two. This indivisibility of viewpoint is morally important as well inasmuch as I cannot know what I have done unless I know my own viewline.

There is no infallibility here, since people can be fooled by tricks of memory to taking into their own viewline a sequence of perspectives which came from, for instance, a motion picture. One would have to be in some rather unusual state to suppose that one was living through what one was merely seeing depicted, but this can happen. More commonly we misremember the source of some of our remembered images. Usually, however, we are morally certain about what we have done and have not done because of the viewline from which we witnessed the events in which we took part. The viewline is not an objective part of these events. We should say, following Wittgenstein as explicated above in chapter nine, that a viewline is not in the world but a limit of the way one sees the world. One cannot split such a limit. In that sense we, who contain such limits, are indivisible, but not indivisible in the way Descartes supposed.

Indefinability

Indefinability is the linguistic counterpart of irreducibility. If one of the fanciful machines discussed above—Parfit's teletransporter or William's duplicator—could read the information in a human and produce an exact copy, the result would be a replica rather than the person associated with the original body. Even before making sense of such difficult doctrines as the mediaeval doctrine of the intransmissible essence of the person[10] we have a kind of indefinability. To support the metaphysical difference between a replica and the original coming out of the teletransporter, we note that they are different because they have different current viewlines now, although they seem to remember the same past viewline. As Parfit would express it, however, the replica has only a quasi-memory, not a genuine memory, of the events as seen from the shared viewline. From an epistemological perspective, the replica cannot have the self-knowledge that the original can have even if the replica seems to remember a segment of the original's viewline. The replica is deceived by the quasi-memory of this segment of the original's viewline. This has moral importance, since moral responsibility cannot be replicated. The replica might admit guilt for a crime of the original, but the replica is deceived and should not be punished. Naturally one must put forward with caution the role of the subjective viewline in establishing ethical responsibility, else we end with something like Locke's implausible view that we are not responsible for what we do not remember. Certainly, I will say more about viewlines as I develop a view through which I attempt to preserve our indefinability.

Freedom

I agree with the ancient Romans, with Leibniz, and with contemporary existentialists that our freedom is essential to us as people. If our actions are all determined by things over which we have no control, for instance, determined by things like prior causes, then we are mere automata, not people. We would not be responsible for anything we did in that case. On the other hand, the attempts to make sense of the concept of freedom through the history of philosophy have foundered on conundrums. I believe the jury is still out on what freedom is and whether it is possible. Nonetheless, we have a rough idea of what concept it is we are seeking to clarify. It would, however, take a rather long book to say what can be said on this topic. Instead I will offer you, in the spirit of William James[11] and Blaise Pascal,[12] a wager.

Bourgeois' bet

I speak only to those who agree that freedom of the will is essential to people. You are confronted with what James would call a genuine option: you can choose to believe that you are free or that you are not free. Reality may or may not correspond with your belief. You may really be free or you may really not be free. Consider now the four combinations of belief and reality. First, suppose you believe you are free, and you are free. In this case, you possess two benefits. You believe the truth, and you can live your life according to this true belief as a person. You win. Let us move to the second possibility: if you believe you are free but you are really not free, then you are an automaton programmed with misinformation. You lose. In the third case, you believe you are not free and you are right. Now you are a correctly programmed automaton. You lose. Finally, you might believe you are not free when you are, in reality, free. You would really lose badly in this case, for you would be a person who throws away freedom.

Since you do not know whether you are free or not, you have to adopt a belief under conditions of rational uncertainty. I suspect that after thorough philosophical investigation, no matter how hard you try, you will not be able to convince yourself fully by means of rational argument that you are free nor that you are not free. All you can do is place your bet. The only way to win, for those who think as I do that freedom is crucial, is to bet that you are free. James would not like this way of putting it, but he might say instead that since you are confronted with a genuine option, you are justified in believing whatever you want to believe about your freedom. I believe I am free.

Enough has been said about the ideal functioning of a concept of a person. The time has come to put the pieces together and fashion a concept that will work.

SIXTEEN
A Bourgeois Concept of a Person

Persons in a nutshell

Very roughly speaking, you are what you can do. You do not actually have to do it, just be able to. Abilities mark off not only individual persons but the class of persons as a whole. Thus abruptly and unceremoniously summarized, my view is bound to spark many objections. So it should. There is, of course, more to us than our abilities. The summary statement of what we are gives only the scent of a theory which must be pursued through some rather dense thickets.

My view of persons is essentialist. Essentialists try to explain the nature of things by talking about the elements a thing must have to exist. Water, for example, is essentially H_2O. Being H_2O is *essential* to all samples of water. They may have other features, being muddy, clear, solid, liquid, or vaporous. These are just *accidental* features. It is fairly clear what the essence and accidents of water are. Persons are another kettle of fish.

To explain persons by describing the essence of a person we would have to list the elements essential to being a person. I will talk about the *general essence*, which includes those elements which all persons must have, and the *individual essence*, which is the essence of an individual person. My view, however, I dub "Byzantine essentialism" because it has, compared to the simple essentialism described above, a structure of Byzantine complexity. That is necessary because of the wild variation within the class of persons and within individual lives of persons.

Rather than saying that there are features which all people must have, I am forced to say that there are features most of which they must have most of the time. Some of these are *subjective*, like the conscious and non-conscious mind, the viewline, which is a series of viewpoints, and the experiences had from the viewline. Others are *objective*, like the body or the publicly testable abilities of the person. All this is without prejudice as to whether mind and body are one thing or two. Putting all the bits together, I get a kind of essentialism which is intended to preserve the general features of persons which any common sense, secular, and Western concept of a person ought to have, namely the ones distilled in the last chapter.

Not only is my view Byzantine, it is relativist. Like Strawson I think of myself as doing descriptive, not revisionist, metaphysics. What I take myself to be describing, moreover, is not some absolute which is independent of

---

Notes to Chapter Sixteen are on p. 325.

time, place, or society. Most essentialists with regard to persons think they are describing *the* concept of a person not merely *a* concept. This concept I describe is intended to work for us here and now, we who are heirs to the philosophers dealt with in this book. That is no small ambition, though more modest than the intention of most of those philosophers. I hope to produce an understanding of persons which is also cross-cultural in the sense that people from other cultures who may not yet have any of the Western concepts of a person will find this one attractive or at least not as repulsive as some of the others.

Subjective elements of persons

The viewline

Indivisibility

One of the things which preserve the indivisibility and irre-ducibility of persons is the viewline. I have said that my subjective *viewpoint* is the place from which I seem to be seeing the world at a given moment. My viewline is the locus of my viewpoint through space as it appears to me over time, that is, my series of viewpoints through my life. Think of your viewline as a history of the places from which you *seemed* to be sensing the world. It is really a view, hear, touch, taste, and smell line. Rather than being just one more item in our subjective experience, it is the series of apparent places from which we have such experiences. It is an indivisible feature of persons.

Viewlines are indivisible in the sense that each viewpoint in a viewline is indivisible. If I seem to be seeing things from a certain perspective, that perspective cannot be split in two. It can change. It may even be shared with another person; that is, viewlines may intersect. One viewpoint, however, cannot divide without becoming two different viewpoints. This provides us with indivisibility. Not just persons, however, but any experiencing subject has such indivisibility; a cat does for instance. The viewline on its own is not enough to be the essence of persons.

Viewlines may appear to be divisible in some of the examples we have considered, like the fanciful example in which Tom gets duplicated, resulting in two people, Dick and Harry, both of whom seem to remember Tom's viewline. This duplication may not really be possible, but it helps to ferret out what we believe about our viewlines. What happens here is that Tom's viewline has forked into Dick's viewline and Harry's viewline. Which fork, if either, is a continuation of Tom's viewline? The one that corresponds to Tom's body continues Tom's viewline. Tom's body is the body which is part of the complex, the person, Tom. This body has a different history from that of the duplicate. The correspondence of viewline to body is somewhat com-plicated. Tom's body is *usually* objectively in a location which is Tom's subjective viewpoint. The body also directly causes Tom to have the viewline he does. This provides a close link of Tom's viewline to Tom's body, which helps us understand what is really happening in cases of apparent division of persons and their viewlines.

Let us say that of the two people stepping out of Williams duplicating machine, Dick has the original body of Tom while Harry has one which was produced as an exact replica. Tom is Dick, but not Harry. Tom and Dick have one viewline. Harry only seems to share the part of that viewline prior to the duplicating. Harry, though, is a newborn with false memories of Tom's viewline. Tom, a.k.a. Dick, got his viewline through the use of Tom's body. Harry got only a short segment of his remembered viewline through the use of Harry's body, and this is his real viewline. The viewline he remembers as a result of duplication of Tom's memories is not Harry's. Bodies can be traced through time objectively as what we saw Quine calling "space-time-worms." Harry's body begins in the duplicating process. It is distinguishable from Tom's; hence,, Tom is not divided nor is his viewline. Harry is a mere replica even if his self-knowledge is imperfect and he believes he is Tom.

Suppose now that Harry says he has as much right to the remembered viewline as Tom since viewlines are subjective and he has the same subjective impressions of having sensed the world from places that Tom has. We could reply that memories of viewpoints are not viewpoints. Tom seemed to see, say, Niagara Falls from the Canadian side in June of 1994. Harry did not exist until August of 1994; so Harry only remembers this viewpoint, he did not have it. It is an objective fact that Harry did not have that subjective viewpoint. He has false memories of a viewline up to August of 1994, and a genuine viewline after that. It turns out that Tom has not divided into Dick and Harry.

Tom is indivisible in the sense that he has an indivisible viewline. Of course Tom is a complex including many things like a body, a viewline, and a mind. These are not accidents of some indivisible Ego, as Descartes might have it, but they are all essential to Tom. Tom is, therefore, also indivisible in the sense that we cannot permanently separate the various essential parts of Tom while Tom exists. More of that when we come to look at Byzantine essentialism in detail.

It might be thought[1] that if a person's brain could be divided and the two halves transplanted into bodies so that each half-brain carried the viewline, then a person and a viewline would have been divided. Our brains are not, however, so divisible.[2] The two halves of the cerebellum are different in function and do not carry the same memories. The lower brain is not divisible at all. If the reply is that this is merely a fact about us which does not exclude the logical possibility of such division, then the point has been missed. Creatures with brains so unlike ours would not be individuals as we are but pairs of individuals sharing most of a body, the brain excluded. If there were such pairs, we might be willing to revise some of our conventions about persons, but that is too speculative for all but science fiction fans. A workable concept of a person need not take such under-described cases, even if they are indeed logically possible, as a threat They are not much more odd than the case of Siamese twins, and do not provide a counterexample to anything I have put forward.

Irreducibility

Consider our earlier discussion of Parfit's objections to our irreducibility. I reject Parfit's reductionism or impersonalism not because I believe I am a separately existing entity, a Cartesian Ego for instance, but because impersonalism leaves *me* out of the universe, and I am sure I am in it. I am not merely a useful fiction but a person knowing the world along a particular viewline. This is an adaptation of Nagel's response to Parfit which we also considered above.[3] To preserve Nagel's point and some important characteristics of people we do not need a Cartesian Ego, a Christian soul, nor any other device which makes either being a person or being the same person like having a switch off or on. A person can, like a flame, gradually come into being, grow more intense, then gradually go out of being.

Admitting, as I do, that human beings are to a greater or lesser degree persons and that each person is to a greater or lesser degree herself is not admitting that people may be reduced to the objectively describable events or processes that make them up. This theory is not to be caught in the snares of Parfit's continua examples described above in chapter thirteen. Parfit accepts the obvious, that people seem to change by degree, only by promoting the outrageous, that there are no people. To keep both people and the gradual evolution and devolution of a person, I will use two kinds element in my concept of a person: the subjective kind like the viewline and the publicly inaccessible portions of the mind generally, and the objective kind like the body and publicly testable abilities.

Glover has a nice example to make the point about the irreducibility of the subjective to the objective. Imagine seeing on TV a composite drawing of a dangerous criminal accompanied by a verbal description. You say derisively, "What good is that? That could even be me." At this point the police knock on your door. You have been framed. You discover with a shock something about the picture and the description. What you have discovered can only be visible from your viewpoints or along your viewline. You could say with Glover, "however detailed or accurate it is, I do not get a shock until I realize the description is of me."[4] No objective description would give the same shock without the same realization. Parfit, it seems, would leave something out in his supposedly complete, objective description of the world if he indeed mentions no people in this description.

The conscious and non-conscious mind

If I think, feel emotions, or have sensations, then I have a mind, however you may wish to analyze the concept of mind. I am willing to suppose that dogs have minds, but what makes people different from other beings is partly the degree to which they have minds. Some human beings are limited to the mental capacity of dogs. They may have the potential to become persons, but they lack an essential characteristic of persons. That does not mean they should be treated like dogs. They have human rights, if not the rights of persons. I will adumbrate a distinction of these kinds of rights in the next chapter.

Private and public abilities

We are essentially what we can do. Persons probably can think and perhaps feel emotions to a greater degree than non-persons. There are two great obstacles to specifying such degrees precisely. For one thing, the degree is culturally determined. Person is a concept relative to Western culture which is a rather hard thing to pin down, real though it may be. The concept of a person, in general, then relies on the amount of such things as intelligence and emotional sensitivity which are generally required in the West to join the persons club. The second great obstacle is the inaccessibility of certain subjective features of persons. This affects not only what kind of thing a person is but who is who. Some of what we can do is private. Mozart could supposedly compose an aria in his head and write it down later. Only Mozart knows for sure if this is so.

Examples: love, spirit, and aesthetic sense

Inspired by Augustine, I will try to say something about a subject concerning which almost every philosopher ponders but few wish to speak. Love is left to the poets. Some forms of love, however, seem to be peculiar to persons. Love can also illustrate the distinction of public from private abilities. Recall Ross' brave definition: "Mutual love seems to be a blend of virtuous disposition of two minds towards each other, with the knowledge which each has of the character and disposition of the other, and with the pleasure which arises from such disposition and knowledge."[5] Of all the kinds of love, mutual love between two people seems to me to be the sort which is peculiar to persons. The love of the parent for the child may be fiercer in a mother who is human than in a bear, but the love seems to be of like kind. It can be all *one way*. An infant may be permanently comatose but not less loved. What partly distinguishes people, however, is the way they interact, a point I take from the earlier discussion of Strawson. It is, then, the capacity for *mutual* love which is peculiar to people. This is not to deny either that a mother bear may love her cubs in some other sense of "love" or that some human beings are incapable of love.

Let us suppose that some human being, say Hitler, is incapable of taking part in a genuine mutual love. Does this incapacity rule Hitler out of the class of persons? The essence of a person which defines the class of persons is not so simple as a set of necessary conditions which are jointly sufficient for being a person. It would seem reasonable to say that Hitler is a person, albeit incomplete. Part of his potential is unfulfilled. He would not be such a monster, however, were he not a person. In using the capacity to love, like the other capacities mentioned here, we will have to fashion a concept of a person which is flexible enough to allow for persons of various kinds, even monsters who are in some remarkable way deformed. Being a person admits of degree.

The ability to participate in mutual love of the sort described by Ross requires a mind of a kind which bears probably do not have, judging by the behaviour towards each other of mother and father bears. Some would say that many a human being is ruled out of the class of persons if the capacity for mutual love is necessary. It is very hard to tell if this is so, given that we cannot peer into the hearts of human beings to detect the virtuous dispositions of which Ross speaks. We guess people's dispositions on the basis of behaviour. Even if we do not know for sure exactly how large the class of persons is, we can say roughly what kinds of being we think are in it.

Love illustrates another feature of persons which makes it difficult to be precise about the essences of persons in general or of individuals. Suppose Tom discovers that he loves Mary. He might have come to love her all unaware. Tom's non-conscious mind can do all sorts of things to which Tom is not witness. Our subjective experience is not only inaccessible to others, it may be inaccessible to ourselves. This leaves us not so much knowledge as good guesses about who is a person and who is who. Even our self-knowledge admits of degrees.

Recall also the notion of spirit as the intentional togetherness of beings who are for themselves "I" and for others "You."[6] Primates can have spirit in this sense, but people develop the capacity to a degree of intensity and complexity that is staggering. The ways in which people unite with one another are almost infinitely variable. This distinguishes our behaviour from that of other higher primates whom we think of as acting "instinctually." The scare quotes on this term indicate my inability to say what it really means, but at least our patterns of behaviour are much more complex and unpredictable than those of non-persons.

Another example of distinctive abilities of persons is the capacity to exercise aesthetic sense. Most non-persons seem not to decorate their environment nor themselves unless it is to some practical purpose. People, however, produce and consume art, especially visual and auditory art,. in great quantity and variety. Certainly there are people with no aesthetic sense or at least people who fail to exercise and develop this capacity. It is *one* of those capacities in a group from which human beings must have at least one to some degree to be a person. Hitler might have aesthetic sense or spirit but lack the capacity for engaging in mutual love. This keeps him in the class of persons but not as a very sweet sort of person.

Anything which makes us think of people as special, as different from most animals, is a candidate for being in this grab bag of capacities from which a human being can draw to gain entrance to the persons club. Specifying the set of such capacities precisely is an ongoing and partly scientific labour. We used to think, mistakenly, that only people kill members of their own species. Do only people laugh with true humour? As we sort out the capacities peculiar to persons (not that all persons have them) we find that we may have them only to a greater degree than non-persons. This I will discuss below under the heading of "thresholds." Remember too that some human beings lack even the most rudimentary capacities of persons. People may choose, as well, to develop or not develop these capacities.

Self-creation and its limits

It may seem strange that self-knowledge can be imperfect. Since we choose what we are, it would seem that we know precisely who is who in our own cases. Difficulties with self-knowledge become apparent, however, when we look in more detail at this self-creation. Some of the philosophers discussed above have been helpful in delineating the peculiar bootstrapping operation which makes each of us who we are. This process is one in which there is a confluence of the subjective and objective elements of persons. We are what we can do, but we must give objectively acceptable weights to the various abilities in order to distinguish one individual from another and to distinguish people from non-persons. Something analogous to Nozick's metric of weighted dimensions is what we need here.

When people talk of finding themselves, they are probably engaged in discovering their own abilities and dispositions and deciding the degrees of importance of these. They are making the non-conscious conscious. When Tom discovers he loves Mary, in the way described by Ross, and puts that at the top of the list of important things he knows about Tom, he is finding himself—finding out what he can do. His capacity for love may survive even the tragic break-up with Mary which is all too likely in a graceless age. Our capacities may be longer lived than the exercise of them; hence we may outlive our most important deeds.

Epistemic and metaphysical social contracts

To say what we value most about ourselves is to choose what we are. The choice, however, is a choice within limits. These limits help to delineate the concept of a person. The limits can be thought of along the lines of social contracts. The social contract is a device usually used in ethics. For example, we might define what is fair by saying that it is what is according to the rules of an ideal social contract. This is the contract that equally powerful and intelligent self-interested beings would choose to run a society if they did not know what advantages or disadvantages they would have in that society. The choices we make about what to accept in our essences are choices which have to be in accord with an ideal metaphysical and an ideal epistemic contract as well as the more usual ethical social contract. What norms are ideal is, however, a culturally relative matter.

The question as to how we know who is who, for instance, will depend on the ideal rules for reidentifying people. These will be, in turn, influenced by the ideal metaphysical rules for saying who really is who. Suppose Tom, scion of a wealthy family, is lost for twenty years. Two people, Dick and Harry, show up claiming to be Tom. Dick resembles the former Tom most in character, general appearance, and in knowing the things Tom knew, but Harry has the same fingerprints as Tom. We would choose Harry as the inheritor of the family fortune. This tells us something about the epistemic and metaphysical social contracts for both the general essence of persons and the essences of individuals.

If you were choosing rules for reidentification you would demand that sameness of body be essential for sameness of the person would you not? Otherwise, some impostor could take your place. Against Parfit, and Nozick, most of us would say that having somebody remarkably like us take over our lives is not the sort of continuity we wish. Individuality as summed up in the "one person one body" motto is a part of our contract. This tells us, then, something about persons in general as well. They must have bodies and each must have only one. Must they be human bodies? At this time, yes. Extraterrestrials may land, causing us to change the rules, but that is still science fiction. Chimpanzees or dolphins may in future seem to us to have abilities which gain them entry to the club. What is important here is that we admit that it is what you can do which makes you a person, not your species.

Wiggins' individuative naturalism is much opposed to this, as we saw in chapter eleven. He thinks that persons are a natural kind of creature, and that if we are entrapped in contrary views, we will not be able to maintain the moral importance of the concept of a person. Just the reverse is true. Being a member of a particular natural kind has no special importance morally. This view could be called "kindism" by analogy to racism. Racists take irrelevant naturally occurring characteristics to be morally significant. The morally relevant features of people are among their capacities, such as the capacity for mutual love discussed above. Not what kind of thing you are but what you can do, think, and feel determines how you ought to be treated and what your obligations are. Being of the human kind is just an accidental feature of persons even though it is, to the best of our current knowledge, a universal feature of persons.

It is crucial that one recognize the role of the subjective features of persons as well as such objective ones as sameness of body. Suppose that we have no fingerprints to go on. Does that mean that Dick, who has the winning hand with regard to other objectively determinable features, is Tom? No, it merely means he would be mistaken for Tom. Our metaphysical social contract does not specify that Tom is whoever we would take to be Tom. Rather, Tom is the one we would take to be Tom, using our standards for reidentification *if we could know which viewline was caused through which body.* From the inside, subjectively, Harry can know he is Tom even if he cannot prove it objectively. Normally, you know who you are, even if the rest of us do not. That is because you remember your viewline. If you think your viewline is that of Napoleon, we put you in an institution. We do not always know who we are, but usually we do.

This shows that the viewline plus the body is essential to individual essences. The essence of persons in general would also include these. To be a person one must have a body which causes a viewline. If the body or the mind ceases to function utterly and permanently, then a person ends, though a human being may continue.

It also becomes clear in what sense our essences are intransmissible; that is, we see how individual persons cannot be defined in terms of their objective features. Whatever we include in our objective descriptions of Tom, Dick, and Harry, it will not be enough to capture the viewline. One might suppose that this is merely an epistemological limit. We have no way of assigning coordinates to time and space and saying which of Quine's space-time worms would fully match Tom's viewline. But the viewline may not fully match any worm in real time and space. Tom's dreams or illusory experiences may affect it. He might have some experience of virtual reality. While the viewline is not at Nagel's innermost sphere of subjectivity, it is close. We cannot get there from here, outside Tom's mind.

What this tells us about people in general is that they have an indefinability, and, as we have seen, an indivisibility and irreducibility as well. What you see is not all that you get when it comes to people. To be in the class of persons, one must also be self-creating. This is part of the source of our dignity as persons: we choose what to value in ourselves. We are responsible for what we are. This distinguishes us from other intelligent beings we know about. Chimpanzees may have ninety-eight percent of our chromosomes, some self-awareness, and the ability to learn limited languages, but unless they are self-creating, choosing their own individual essences, they are not people. Until we change our minds about how much chimpanzees can do, we will not count them as persons. Nonetheless, they should get more consideration, because of their similarity to us in capacities, than they do get.

The results of the investigation so far are that persons are, although complexes of many elements, nonetheless indivisible, irreducible, and indefinable. To understand better how individuals create themselves, we should look more closely at the objective elements from which they have to choose.

Objective elements of persons

The body and associated public abilities

To accommodate the point discussed in connection with Wiggins, that ballerinas and boxers are persons as much as philosophers, we can look at the degree of weight attached to bodily features by the individuals possessing them. We need not go to the extent of adopting Wiggins' view that person is a natural kind. We have noticed that having a (probably human) body is essential to persons, but for each individual the importance of the body may vary. The boxer may value his physical strength much more highly than his intellectual ability. He is most himself at peak performance. He defines himself in terms of what he can do physically. If he could, at the height of his powers, see his future body as a punch-drunk wreck sweeping the gym floor, then he might deny that the sweeper is the same person as the current champion. He has chosen, perhaps unwisely, to be very short lived as a person.

This does, after all, seem to be a complete departure from common sense. The one-person-one-body motto is being taken in only one direction. If there is one person, then there is one body. On the other hand, if there is one body, there is not necessarily just one person. I think, however, that we in the West sometimes take the motto only in the first way, even if we are not consistent about that. We often seem to talk as if having the same body were necessary but not sufficient for being the same person.

Consider the return of the long-lost Tom once again. Harry is seen to be Tom because the fingerprints match. Harry also chooses to own what Tom had been able to do. Suppose, instead, that Harry says of Tom, "That was somebody else." He no longer has Tom's abilities or even memories of Tom's viewline and never reacquires these. In this extreme case, we might be willing to say that Harry is a different person, since Tom's body no longer embodies the same form it once did. Some things essential to Tom are missing. There can, in theory, be a series of persons associated with one body. It is just a very rare sort of thing if this happens. Most of us choose an essence so as to survive and do not undergo whatever extreme experiences turned Tom into Harry in the case where Harry no longer has Tom's individual essence. We are, however, reluctant to admit such cases as genuine. We would prefer to say that Harry is Tom but deficient in self-knowledge through his loss of memory. The differences must be truly extraordinary before we say that a body no longer embodies the person it once did.

Our social contract is a little ill-defined in this area. Perhaps the rule once was that such self-defining choices as Harry's were unacceptable, although that may be changing. At least in cases of multiple personality, which have the imprimatur of psychiatrists, we tend to make moral allowances for more than one person per body. But this is not all. Self-creation could make possible persons within persons as well. The boxer as an old man and as a boy may include in himself everything that was or will be taken in along the viewline associated with the body that grows from that of the boy to the body of the old man. The boxer in his prime may repudiate this. The boxer in his prime is a person contained within the larger person determined by the choices of the boy and the old man. This, again, is not common sense. Perhaps we should say, rather, that the most inclusive person associated with a body really is the person, while the included "persons" within are just special stages of that overall person. The act of self-creation which really counts is the one which encompasses most of the viewline. In cases of extreme dissociation, we could admit that a person has been destroyed by mental illness although the human body is alive and is the body of some person or other.

This way of thinking explains why we should value our moral, emotional, and intellectual abilities more than our purely bodily abilities. The boxer should think of his courage as more important than his left-hook. The ballerina should honour her dedication more than her stamina. It is such features which are primary in the saying that we are what we can do. In the case of the philosopher, pure intellectual ability may be chosen as foremost. This too is a trifle dangerous. A beneficent disposition is longer lived than brilliance. If we wish to maximize longevity, wise self-creation values long-lived features. While some may value intensity more than such staid features as longevity and continuity, they are not in accord with common sense.

The body, seen as a space-time worm in Quine's way, is continuous. This makes persons largely continuous. We may have periods of absence from our bodies. Morally, madness is accepted as such. Nonetheless, we each wake up in one body every day and remember a viewline. That the complex which is the person includes such a continuous body is sufficient for continuity of a person through most of the life of a human being, though the person comes into being after the human being and may well go out of existence before bodily death. Elements of the complex gradually come together and may gradually disperse.

A degree of determinacy is also preserved under the present concept of a person. The question "Am I about to die?" has relatively clear answers in most cases. In the face of extreme change one can ask whether the abilities one values most will survive. Even if the body is going to live on, we can know that what is essential to us will not. Daphne knew this. The exact point of death may be unknowable. While I do not know how to make sense of life after death, meaning life of the person after death of the person's body, it is some consolation to preserve life during life. The person lives during most of the life of the body, usually. In cases like Daphne's, the body may live on for a rather long time while it no longer embodies the form or supports the essence of the person who used to inhabit that body.

Objective indivisibility

There is a kind of indivisibility of the person from an objective standpoint. It is fortunate, moreover, that objective indivisibility, like the subjective kind, need not be bought at the cost of accepting the featureless Ego. Must the impossibility of division imply having no properties? Why can it not be that the person is indivisible in the sense of having certain *essential* properties which are bundled together in an individual essence if and only if the person exists. If the essence is divided, the person is no more. One does not have the absolute indivisibility of the Democritean atom but the indivisibility of a democratic house which cannot stand divided against itself. Like a democracy, a person can survive considerable internal conflict but not unending civil war. The essence of the person must be intact for the person's survival.

Byzantine essentialism

Part of the difficulty with the contemporary discussion of the essential characteristics of persons is the frequent assumption that these characteristics are all-or-nothing. But being a person is not like being a light which is turned on. It seems relatively easy to say what is essential for the light to be on, and if any of the conditions in the essence is lacking, say there is no current through the filament, then the light is not on. People, however, have much more flexible essences than that. They can lose some of their essential characteristics to some degree or lose them temporarily while remaining persons.

We do not, for example, fall out of the class of persons just because we go to sleep. If having a viewline is essential to persons, it is essential in a flexible way. We must have a viewline *enough* of the time. We look to our social contract to say what is enough. If Tom has only one lucid minute per day, he is no longer able to do the things which made him Tom. He is not the person he was, but a living human body. We ought to treat that body with respect, but we could be quite paternalistic to the human being called "Tom" without harming Tom as a person. Often, however, the case is not even this clear-cut. We should do the best we can with the limited knowledge available to us to determine whether a given human being is a person. A reasonable social contract would put the onus of proof on those who wish to deny the status of a person to a human being.

Of course, even a light bulb is not really limited to being either off or on. It might be dim or flickering. We might be unsure whether or not to say it is on or off. All of us flicker. We go to sleep at night. All of us are dimmer at some times than at others. We can do less well the things which are essential at some times or we can do fewer of them. Persons remain persons and remain particular persons to a degree of frequency and intensity. Be careful if you constantly hear people saying of you, "She's not quite herself today."

Using general and individual essences

The essentialism I defend is not entirely at odds with Parfit's view of which I have been critical. In fact, I think Parfit is an essentialist of an odd sort. The particular realization of the relation R (psychological continuity and connectedness) is what makes a person who she is, on Parfit's view.[7] Since R is fragile and short-lived—at least more so than are living human bodies—persons are ephemeral entities flitting in and out of bodies. It seems that what is needed to preserve common Western beliefs about persons is an essence that is more robust than R in the face of changes which we all live through as persons.

Complexity

Essentialism is a difficult doctrine since it is easy to put too much or too little into the essence. If there are a great many features which are required for being a person, or features which are short-lived, then it is too easy to disqualify many human beings as persons. The claim from the pro-choice camp, for instance, that persons are essentially self-aware would seem to rule us all out if we are asleep. Something has to be said about how such features can come and go in persons. If on the other hand we put in too few features or features which are too readily retained, the class of persons widens so as to become useless. This is what happens, for example, when pro-lifers say that having human chromosomes is all that is essential to persons. This makes human cancer cells grown in a petri dish persons. The error on both sides of the abortion debate is oversimplifying. We must keep the complexity of persons in mind and make the essence of persons support such flexibility.

We must take account, moreover, not only an essence of persons in general, but an essence of each individual person. Again, the difficulty is in specifying this individual essence in a plausible way. If we have too fleeting features in the essence of an individual person, then people will not last any longer than a new car. That is why the boxer is unwise to try to create himself as the champion. The fleeting essence is, as we saw in chapter thirteen, also what we get from Parfit. Putting in too many features will have the same effect. If, on the other hand, we put in too few or too easily retained features, Parfit can evolve into a Greta Garbo and still survive.

What goes wrong in this latter case may be that the essence of persons in general is mistaken for the individual essence. At each point in the spectrum of gradual change of Parfit into Garbo we consult our concept of a person and say, "Yes, there is still a person present." That is not, however, to say that the *same* person is present. The essentialism I seek has to allow for the belief that a human being can change so radically as to become a different person. I think that those who disagree with the possibility of such change most likely retain a belief in a soul or Cartesian Ego. Retaining just the viewline from this Cartesian view, let us try instead to make sense of people using an essentialism in which a viewline is the indivisible essential feature.

The seed of a believable essentialist view has been sown by Wilkes.[8] Wilkes, however, does not directly concern herself with the questions of individual essences. Perhaps she thinks the survival of persons through change is a matter settled if she answers her main question. Her question is, "What is a person?" She answers (211), relying on Aristotle, that a person is an embodied form and a formed body. Aristotle did not, however, have a separate word to distinguish persons from human beings.[9] Wilkes ignores this, although it may be as significant as something else which Wilkes[10] emphasizes, Aristotle's having no word for consciousness. In any case, I think Wilkes has Aristotle right, and I wish to go beyond Wilkes' Aristotelian views on persons in general to a view of individual essences of persons which will fit with Wilkes' position and assimilate the insights but not the shortcomings of some of the other views I have discussed. Wilkes' position on the general essence of persons will also be revised to take into account the variability of persons as complexes.

Continuity

Let us recall Nozick's social limits on closest continuation and think of how these limits affect genuine continuity of a person on my view. Suppose that the limits of variability seem to have been passed. A woman comes forward claiming to be Jones, but she is physically, and in all other ways we can detect, extremely unlike Jones. She is socially unacceptable as Jones. Could she not still be Jones? She could on my view. It is not what her community members accept but *what they would accept if they could know her viewline* which is necessary to her identity.

It is, however, not merely some private and apparently non-physical aspects of Jones which make her who she is. The separation of the physical from the non-physical aspects of persons which is the tendency of the Cartesian view is impossible on Wilkes' view, which I am adapting and extending here. One consequence of this, it seems to me, is that one who is destroyed and replicated is really destroyed. The replica is a mere replica. The original embodied form is gone, as Wilkes might say following Aristotle.

Taking the embodied form as essential to the person usually prevents long temporal gaps in persons. That provides for one of the features I like, namely continuity, albeit of a rough variety. The viewline alone does not provide continuity; but an objective part of the person, the stream of matter through time which is the person's body, is more stable. This is what motivates some of the body-based accounts of a person such as those of Wiggins and Williams.[11] We need not, however, merely by accepting Wilkes' account, take the body plus the form as a materialist conception of the person. Whether the form is immaterial or not is a question for another inquiry, and I do not wish to get bogged down in the debate here.

What Wilkes says about forms of persons in general is suggestive of a way for the essentialist to proceed in the search for an understanding of individual essences. One hopes for further gains in the direction of common sense. The form of a person is supposed to tell us what the nature of persons is. The individual essence of a particular person would, if we knew it, tell us what the nature of that particular person was, hence, under what conditions that person would survive changes to the body. We should try to understand the individual essence, then, as the form of the individual along the lines of the form of a person generally. Before looking at survival on this kind of essentialist view, however, I must get more of the view out. Consider first the form of a person in general.

The form of a person is a special case of the form of an organism. The form of an organism is its *psuche*. Wilkes represents[12] Aristotle's concept of the *psuche* as a pyramid of abilities. Organisms which are not persons have some of the abilities in the pyramid of abilities associated with a person. The higher the animal, the more of the pyramid it takes in. What distinguishes persons as a class from other organisms is that our *psuchai* include, over and above the abilities of other higher organisms, the capacity for rational thought, both practical and theoretical (210). Crucially, this capacity for rationality includes the potential to be a social animal (234). The ability to reciprocate with rational beings is essential to being a person.

How then do we know when there is life during life? That is, how do we know when the survival of a person goes with the survival of the corresponding human being. It is not enough to know what the class of persons is. We need to know something of diachronic identity (identity over time) as well. Suppose that we follow the essentialist's inclination and say that a thing remains the same over time just in case it retains its individual essence. What will an individual essence for a person contain over and above whatever in the *psuche* is essential to remaining in the class of persons? Well, we could throw in the fleeting characteristics, psychological continuity and connectedness, whatever they are.[13] But then one is certain to get a relay race of various persons through the body. With all that ephemeral stuff being essential, the person has to change as the stuff changes, often.

On Wilkes' view of persons, while one has certain capacities, one retains the status of person. I envisage an essentialism for individuals compatible with this essentialism for the class of persons. Roughly, one is what one can do. An individual essence might be fleshed out in terms of a particular set of capacities peculiar to an individual, over and above those essential for that individual to stay in the class of persons. Also in the essence is the viewline, the series of subjective viewpoints of that individual. To be who I am, I must have my past and present viewpoints. I need not remember all of them, the whole viewline. Nonetheless, having that viewline is part of what I am.

One advantage of thinking in terms of what the individual can do is that some abilities can survive considerable physical and psychological changes. One of Wilkes' many examples[14] is of a doctor who suffered an attack of epileptic automatism while interviewing a patient. Although the doctor remembered nothing of the interview, he discovered from his notes that he managed to conduct a reasonably efficient medical examination. The doctor was, apparently, a person throughout the attack. Was he the same person before, during, and after the attack?

Of course I do not want to say, with Lockean respect for memory, that the doctor lost one of his essential capacities, namely an important part of his memory, and therefore went out of existence, to be replaced during the attack by a replica. That would not be a gain for common sense. To merely take a particular realization of the form which makes one a person and call that particular realization an essence would be too ham-handed. Some of the capacities in that essence might be *temporarily* lost. These capacities may also admit of degree. Even the memory of the viewline is variable. It is significant that, as Wilkes describes the case, the doctor owned proudly the actions which he could not remember doing. We do not have to remember our experiences to have had them. The doctor did have the segment of his viewline during the attack, but lost the usual benefit of it, since the portion of his viewline running through the examination is lost to his memory. Our viewlines, however, always become lost or strange as we sleep, perchance to dream. Since memory is one of these varying capacities, our retention of our past viewline in memory will also vary in degree.

Determinacy

Essentialism seems to preserve our determinacy as well, though only in a metaphysical sense. The question, "Am I about to die?" always has an answer, but it is not always one that can be known. One cannot always know whether certain thresholds have been reached. It might be impossible to check on the survival of a person in a case where introspection is needed to view some part of the essence. For example, I might wonder whether I have sufficient emotional intensity to still be the person whose memories I share. My viewline may be the same, but that is only a necessary not a sufficient condition for my survival. If I am sinking below the threshold, there is not a continuing person there to do the introspection needed. Yet nobody else could investigate by introspection the presence of some capacities in the essence to see if they are at levels above their thresholds. In this way, self-knowledge can be imperfect even for self-creating beings.

We are, in spite of these epistemological difficulties, metaphysically irreducible, determinate, and as continuous as we should be. "Am I about to die?" always has a definite answer in terms of thresholds, although those near death may not be competent to give the answer. Those near death may be poor judges of their own thresholds, given their altered mental states. While most of our abilities are open to objective determination, it is interesting that our objective and subjective components get quite tangled up here. This epistemological problem, fortunately, does not prevent us from consolidating our metaphysical gains with respect to the concept of a person.

Return, too, to the question of life during life for such persons. Is there only one person associated with a living human body throughout its life? Not quite. It seems that a human being gradually develops capacities, hence gradually grows up to be a person. One can also gradually go in the other direction as one approaches senility. During that part of the life of the body in which one is above the threshold, however, one remains one person. In most cases, this is through most of a human life. I may reasonably refuse to take responsibility for something I did as a child because I had not fully become myself then. My children may not blame me for things I do in my dotage since I will have gone by then. There is, then, not life during life but life during most of life, usually. The Cartesian Ego and the Christian soul are attempts to provide continuity from conception to bodily death, but that is rather too much to ask.[15]

Individuality

One does, moreover, retain a variety of individuality on the essentialist view. A group of bodies cannot make one person, since their viewlines would be different. It may however be a bit too much to intone the one-person-one-body principle. There usually are not several persons having a single body at one time. One might think that the body is just a container for capacities and that it is easy to have differing sets of capacities associated with the same body in a Jekyll and Hyde fashion. If we add to a person's capacities, however, we are usually not adding another person but merely adding accidents to the essential capacities already there. Theoretically one could add enough capacities to kill off one person and bring another into being within a single human body, but the likelihood of this is diminished by the subjective viewline. Perhaps multiple-personality cases are genuine cases of multiple persons in one body, but I rather suspect that it is a case of one person with a great mental deformity. One person is having trouble keeping track of which self she created.

People with no illness at all, however, can undergo radical change with no threat to the one-body principle. Suppose, for instance, I recall being a skid-row bum who reforms and becomes a social activist working to eradicate poverty. Probably I will accept the blame for my earlier condition, to some degree, and the praise for pulling myself out of it, to some degree. I will own the earlier limited capacities even though I seem to many to be a new person because of much higher present capacities. The kind of epistemic and social contracts we accept in the West allow for considerable variability in characteristics and abilities of persons over time. It is reasonable for Jekyll to accept Hyde's actions as his own. One who forgets her drunken spree should also own it, even though the viewline is forgotten in that segment. She has reason to suppose that her viewline continued and that her capacities, albeit diminished by the genie in the bottle, were sufficient to maintain her as the same individual during her spree.

Once again I have made use in my argument for Byzantine essentialism of the viewline. This is not strictly speaking an ability, although one could speak of that person's ability to know the world as if from a particular perspective in space-time. In any case, the crucial thing is that one cannot have more than one of these perspectives at a time, hence only one viewline. The thought experiments in which people divide like amoebae, if they show the essentialist anything about what we believe ourselves to be, show only that we may believe a person can be replaced by two remarkably similar people. A point of view cannot divide. A viewline can fork as a river forks, but after the fork there are two people.

We have subjective as well as objective individuality. Recall the theological use of *persona*, the Latin root of person, to mean something which is self-existent, that is, not a property or a part of another thing but a thing in its own right.[16] The individuality provided for persons, on my essentialist view, makes us self-existent. We are not just part of a larger whole; we are individuals. Larger wholes, like societies, do not have one viewline.

Indefinability

The theological use of *persona* which we have seen stemming from developments in the Middle Ages includes intransmissiblity of the person's essence or indefinability (354). There are also two senses in which persons are indefinable, on the view I am adumbrating here. First, a definition conveys objective information and cannot, therefore, capture the viewline. Second, while the objective information in an individual essence can be conveyed in theory, in practice it is too Byzantine in its complexity to be recorded. The person herself is the main record of what she is.

By now it is clear, I hope, that I accept to some extent Wiggins' claim, discussed in chapter eleven, that

> If freedom and dignity and creativity are what we crave, we shall find more promise of these things in the Heraclitean prediction "You would not find out the bounds of the soul, though you traversed every path: so deep is its *logos*" than in the idea that it is for men to determine the limits of their own nature, or mould and remake themselves to the point where they can count as their very own creation.[17]

Viewed objectively, persons do have this deep nature which can only be partially known. This does not prevent us from making some choices subjectively, culturally limited ones, about what we are as individuals within the class of persons; thus far but no farther I am willing to go with Nozick. From Nagel I take another crucial point in this discussion, that we have an irreducibly subjective component.[18]

The union of all these elements creates a new view of persons different from each of the theories which provided these elements, for each of these theories left out something crucial which another recognized. Putting all the foregoing views together, we come up with a fairly common sense picture of persons. Indeed, it was Western common sense which guided the selection of elements from the earlier theories. We retain important features of our Occidental heritage, but they are cleansed of contradiction. We are each *complex, individual, irreducible, determinate, and continuous* (through much of our lives while awake), *indivisible and indefinable* in some reasonable senses of these terms which I have specified.

There is, however, the wrinkle for the essentialist that a series of persons can possibly be associated with one body, as on Parfit's view. This is the relay-race objection. This, however, is not likely on my essentialist view and certainly not required by Byzantine essentialism as it is by Parfit's essentialism. The capacities at the centre of what we are tend to be rather hardy. Very radical change may push us below the threshold of our own individuality, but usually we also lose the form of person as well as our own personal essence. Radical change not leading to death makes mere human beings of us, more likely than not, as, for example, when brain damage leaves the mere shell of a person.

We lose our freedom, in that case, and paternalism towards us becomes appropriate as it was before we grew up enough to pass the threshold. We may still have considerable moral worth as human beings, but not that special dignity which attaches to persons. If we are judged to be permanently below the threshold, we will be viewed differently from children who wear their potential to become fully developed persons as a special badge of worth. It is, however, medically possible to do such things as head transplants now. Who knows how this and other medical marvels will influence our metaphysical, epistemic, and social contracts insofar as they regard who is who. I consider it a strength of my theory that it allows in a limited way for but does not require the association of a series of persons with one body.

Another strength of this essentialist theory is that a we avoid the distraction of worrying about the sameness of the body over time. Supposing that every molecule in the body is replaced every six years, we can still speak of the same stream of matter through the form. The form helps us pick out the beginning, end, and other boundaries of the space-time stream of matter. The form, remember, is a set of abilities. One becomes a person on acquiring the appropriate set and at the same time becomes differentiated from other people by the particular set of individuating capacities which make up the individual essence. Keeping the thresholds in mind, we can say, theoretically at least, when the person begins and ends which will be after the body begins and, in most cases, before it ends.

Freedom

Now, what about all that moral importance, social worth, dignity, and so forth that motivates the search for yet another concept of persons? While I think the individual essentialist view has a chance of preserving certain large chunks of common sense, I admit that it departs from our current legal notions of sameness of persons. That is, however, inevitable, since our current legal notions are occasionally far from common sense. There are, however, some interesting connections of the view with the notions of Roman law which I see as partly fathering our current common sense. What gave persons in ancient Rome their dignity, moral, political, and legal worth was their freedom, and freedom was understood in terms of capacities. Freedom was understood as the "natural power to do what you please unless you are prevented by force or law."[19] On the essentialist view I put forward here, an individual person is defined in terms of her powers to do things plus the body and the viewline.

Thresholds

Both the individual essence and the general essence for persons will, it seems, have to allow for considerable flexibility. Our capacities may not only admit of degree individually, but the degree to which we have a complete set configured appropriately may also vary. This suggests various thresholds.

One threshold below which one could not fall while remaining a person or remaining the same person would be, very roughly, having a minimum number of capacities in the general or the individual essence. Focussing on the individual essence, for example, if one suffered the permanent loss of one's normal conative, locomotive, and affective abilities, as well as of memory but retained intelligence, probably one could no longer be counted the same person. Here we depart from the current usage of "person" in law, but not in common sense. It is reasonable to say that the person who is devoid of her former desires, physical abilities, and emotions, and who does not remember us, is not the person we knew even if she has sufficient rationality to stay in the class of persons.

The first threshold, then, is a threshold of quantity. There must be enough of the essential capacities in a being if that being is to be a person. Not all of the capacities, however, must always be present. Hitler is still a person, though a monstrous one, if his capacity for love is absent. The general essence of persons includes many features, but we do not have to have all of them all of the time. If Hitler now begins to lose his other conative abilities as well as memory and cognitive abilities, he at some point crosses the line from the class of persons into that of human former persons. The line is fuzzy since the essence is culturally determined, and cultures are fuzzy. There are other things which blur the line too. There is another kind of threshold, which I will come to later, applying to features individually. This makes quantity of capacities not the be-all and end all of the general essence.

It is no doubt a gross oversimplification to speak in terms of a minimum *number* of capacities in the essence. Certain configurations of capacities would have to be present. The ways in which capacities might be added or removed could have incredible complexity. During a quorum call for capacities in the essence, there might well be particular capacities in a particular configuration which must be present for an individual to be a person or to remain the same person. I envisage here a general core of capacities which are necessary but not sufficient for being a person and a further core for survival of the particular person. These capacities would not form the whole essence but only a particularly important part of it. If they come and go, one flickers.

A person who is temporarily insane is genuinely temporarily not herself, or, less paradoxically, temporarily not housed in her body. Some part of her essence may be missing. A person may, for instance, be thought to have taken leave of the body on conative grounds. Someone who undergoes a drug therapy, then does without compunction something evil may be acting totally out of character. While that person lacks her essential shame, she is not responsible for the behaviour of her body. Courts have sometimes taken this position to excuse such horrendous crimes as matricide, at least when the killer was not conscious of having done the crime.

There might, in addition, be thresholds of each individual capacity. Once one permanently loses a certain degree of recall, for instance, one could not be counted as having the capacity for memory that was once part of one's essence. It would be quite difficult to tell where exactly the threshold for a particular ability or the threshold for the total essence would lie. This does not mean that there can be no such thresholds. The varying difficulty we have with Parfit's spectra might just reveal our varying degrees of confidence in our knowledge of our thresholds, our knowledge of who we are. It is too easy to say, however, that the metaphysical facts are totally independent of our epistemological difficulties. After all, as there is an element of self-creation in our choices of what experiences to own, indecision can be deadly. Given, however, that one has chosen oneself, one has a determinate threshold whether or not one is completely competent to judge its nearness of approach.

In some cases, as with persons who have Alzheimer's disease, a human being seems to fall below the threshold in various capacities, especially memory, and then to come back. It is as if the person is fading in and out. On this essentialist view, that is just what is happening. A person can be temporarily suspended, reinstated, and suspended again in the same body.

It might be objected, however, that this form of essentialism is just a dressed-up version of the old person-as-programmed-meat view, functionalism. What is primarily different is this: functionalists leave out the subjective elements and the particular body is of no importance to them. The essences of persons, moreover, are enormously complex—Byzantine in their complexity. The comparison with computer programs is entirely unenlightening, since we have no examples of computers, outside of fiction, which can act as human beings do in a human society.[20] Even if we did have such formidable, free robots, their programs might be quite different from our essences. If they had essences like ours, they would be persons, but how can we say whether such machines are possible? We cannot describe them in enough detail. We have enough trouble trying to convince ourselves that *we* are possible.

Admittedly, there are many problems with the view I am proposing for development. The pursuit of an essentialist doctrine using the idea of thresholds is somewhat Byzantine. People, however, are somewhat Byzantine. We can clean up the theory only if we ignore our own complexities. We are not much like nations. We are not much like computers. Nozick's closest continuers are not close enough. In fact, there is nothing I can name that is anything like a person, with the possible exception of the higher apes. It seems worthwhile, then, to put forward a program for investigating a rubbery, gappy, fuzzy, complex essence unlike the essences of non-persons. If this Byzantine theory should work, it would show that we do not have to go all the way with Parfit into the arms of Buddha merely to escape featureless Egos.

SEVENTEEN
Applications of My Concept of a Person

Fairness and the social contract

I will ask for your patience with some fanciful metaphors which follow. These allow me to simplify and condense the thinking behind social contract theories of morality, particularly a notion of *fairness* developed by Rawls[1] which I adapt here to suit my concept of a person (which Rawls does not share). A smattering of such theory will illustrate briefly some applications of the concept of a person developed in the previous chapter. First there is the metaphor of an ideal social contract. This is the contract each person could agree to with assurance of getting a fair deal. The contract would govern all behaviour of persons to persons. Our moral rights are the rights we would have under the terms of such a contract.

Now consider an even more fanciful metaphor to specify roughly the method for determining what those rights would be under such an ideal contract. This metaphor makes limited sense, but is intended not as a genuine possibility but only to reveal what we believe about fairness in terms of two concepts: the *original position* and the subordinate concept of a *veil of ignorance* (12, 17). Of course the beliefs I reveal are my own. I hope they are shared by many, for I think they are in accord with Western, common sense, secular morality. Whether or not you agree with these beliefs about what is fair, you will, I hope, find the way of thinking about what is fair useful for revealing your own beliefs on the issues considered here.

Suppose that a new anesthetic has been developed which makes people temporarily amnesiac. They retain their general cognitive and conative abilities, but they forget who they are and where they are. They are temporarily blind. They cannot feel their bodies except to the extent that they can speak coherently. These people, though rational, are behind a *veil of ignorance* about their own personal advantages and disadvantages in society. They do not know if they are crippled, average, or athletic in their bodily capacities. They do not know their positions in society, what sort of personalities they have, nor any other personal information—not even their genders or ages. They retain general knowledge about the human condition, but no particular religious or moral beliefs. This peculiar drug is put to an interesting political use.

Notes to Chapter Seventeen are on pp. 325-26.

Under the auspices of the United Nations, a committee of volunteers takes this anesthetic drug in order to sit down and write a charter of rights of persons to apply throughout the world. They communicate with each other only indirectly through intermediaries. As much as possible, the veil of ignorance is thickened. Even white lies are used. The anesthetized committee members are told that when they come back to normal they may be mentally impaired or much more brilliant than they seem to be now, and they believe this white lie, although in fact the volunteers who have been chosen are equally intelligent, rational people who will remain so on coming out of the anesthetized state.

These volunteers are also told that they must decide what the rights of persons are by forming the basic rules according to which societies will conduct themselves. They are instructed to think only of their own self-interest, not of any moral principle, and they obey this instruction. They are told to put forward rules that people, given their natural sympathies, could actually follow. The volunteers on this committee are, as nearly as possible, in the *original position*. They are equally powerful, intelligent, self-interested people who will decide what rules should be in the ideal social contract.

The point of the foregoing barely bearable metaphor is to explain how social contract theorists might try to resolve moral disputes by asking what rules we would agree to if we did not already know what advantages or disadvantages we have, that is from the original position, behind a veil of ignorance. These fair rules tell us what our moral rights and duties are as persons. The self-interest condition is not there to produce egoism, nor would it. By acting in their own self-interest the volunteers would act in the best interests of any person simply because they are so ignorant about themselves, about their own advantages and disadvantages. For all any volunteer knows, she could be anyone. To help themselves they would be forced to choose rules that would be best for anyone governed by these rules.

In light of the social contract between persons as chosen in the original position, an important general principle of moral theorists is illustrated. Moral rules must be *universalizable*: what it is right for a person to do is right for any similarly situated person to do. For instance, when a doctor behaves in a certain way towards a patient, the patient should be able to agree that if the patient were the doctor, the patient would have behaved in the same way. The rule being followed by the doctor should be one that would have been chosen behind a veil of ignorance. Behind that veil there is ignorance about the relative positions of the people in the situation in which the rules are applied.

Even though the concept of a person explained in the last chapter is a concept heavily dependent on abilities, using a social contract theory would prevent the distribution of wealth or pleasure in a society on the basis of ability. The Nazis thought the disabled should be killed. Various schemes for developing meritocracies have been proposed by other groups. These schemes are opposed by the universalizability of moral rules which the social contract theory and most moral theories adopt. There might be different rules for those who are outside the class of persons than there are for those who are in that class, but within that class there is no favouritism for those already favoured by naturally occurring advantages in ability. Those behind a veil of ignorance, not knowing what their own abilities would be, would fear such favouritism and prohibit it. A person with common sense would protect herself by ensuring that advantages are not distributed in ways which might deny her access to those advantages.

Now it may be objected that we cannot tell what people would choose in the original position. Perhaps they would be gamblers and choose favouritism in the blind hope of being among those favoured by the rules. But common sense is opposed to such blind gambling. The volunteers would not take silly chances with their lives. The standards of common sense which have guided this investigation throughout are not precise. Nonetheless most of us are, I suspect, fairly confident of our ability to decide what would be a reasonable bet in the circumstances I described to illustrate the original position.

Of course you, personally, might be inclined to take some bet which is not reasonable just because you have a higher than average (hence uncommon) tolerance for risk. Still, I ask you to judge my pronouncements about what people would do in the original position remembering that they are rational by the standards of Western common sense. It is common sense to minimize risks when venturing into the unknown. You may not wish to do so, but if you think of the volunteers as exercising this kind of caution, then you can see what sorts of rules they would recommend, hence what sort of moral theory is proposed here.

It might still be objected that even rational people have irrational moments. People are generally unpredictable. Since the fanciful metaphor to illustrate the original position is contrived at best, I have no objection to making it more so and specifying that those in the original position are so psychologically stable as to be always guided by common sense in their decision-making. After all, this need not be a description of a possible situation or a likely situation but only of a situation which illustrates a kind of social contractarian view. Objections to my claims about what the people in the original position would choose should be not of the form, "I would not do that," or "Real people might not choose that way," but "That is not a bet a person would make in her own self-interest and in accord with Western common sense concerning risk-taking." While there are likely to be disagreements about what the volunteers in my illustration of the original position would do, there is, I believe, a large measure of agreement. I hope to employ that measure as I make a very broad and quick survey of ethical issues revealing, generally, the intended moral application of my concept of a person.

Allocation of scarce medical resources

The rules chosen in the original position would include rules for allocating scarce medical resources to people rather than to human beings who are not people and are not likely to become people. But the committee would not accept a rule that says that those who have advantages shall get more advantages within the class of persons. Fearing having, for instance, a body which limits abilities, a volunteer on this committee would ask for democracy within the class of persons. Fairness of allocation of resources among persons would not treat the accidental advantages of birth as merits. From the original position we would not accept a rule which tells us to save the most able-bodied and brightest people first, since we volunteers would have no good reason to think we are among those people.

The rules for allocation within the class of persons would be closer to a first-come-first-served rule, but that rule would have to be qualified. Clearly a person with a fatal disease and weeks to live should not block a person with a chance for a long life from receiving treatment. Volunteers would consider their best interests over a lifetime, for they do not know their own ages. Unfortunately, decisions are rarely so clear cut. There are many things that we might weigh in the balance, such as gratitude for past actions and abilities and propensities to perform future actions for which we would be grateful. Providing rules which do not conflict with ordinary human sympathy requires attention to these matters.

Suppose, for instance, in a medical centre in the far north where resources and time are limited, we are faced with saving a drunk well known as a drain on the community or saving a surgeon who has come to donate services to the community. Are we really to flip a coin? Would we choose, in the original position, a rule which would deny the surgeon the care because she lost the coin toss? From the original position we might try to choose rules that would favour the surgeon since we would wish, in self-interest, to promote the society which results from such allocations. We might be willing to take our chances of winding up as the drunk in such a situation. Nonetheless we would frame our rules so that there is a heavy onus of justification resting on the shoulders of those who would depart from the first-come-first-served rule. The right to life-saving medical treatment of the individual would have to be weighed against the rights of others. In the case of the surgeon and the drunk, we honour more rights by saving the surgeon because of the dependence of others on the surgeon. Seen from the original position, it is a better bet that we would be helped by this weighing of rights than hurt by it. But some will smell a whiff of sulphur here. If we really were to put such rules into practice, would we not be sliding into the pit of moral consequentialism where the end justifies the means? I think not, and I think the volunteers would not like consequentialism. The social contract theory, however, tries to get some of the advantages of consequentialism without becoming totally governed by consequences.

In the original position, we would surely be reluctant to choose the simple consequentialist rule that whatever is in the interests of the majority is what is to be done. The volunteer knows that when she comes out of the anesthesia and returns to normal life she may sometimes find herself in a happy minority at an advantage over most others, and she would not, therefore, choose a rule which always wipes out that advantage. On the other hand, she might well find herself, on occasion, in a majority which suffers because a few have most of the advantages. She might make a trade. She could limit the depth to which she might be allowed to fall into a disadvantageous situation by limiting at the other end the height of the advantages she could enjoy. Rather than getting rid of all differentiation of people's positions, she might accept rules which would provide a safety net at the bottom and a ceiling at the top. No person could be treated as if she did not count and no person's merits could be trump. It is common sense to hedge one's bets.

The way that consequentialism is limited in rules chosen from the original position may be illustrated if we vary the story of the drunk and the surgeon. Suppose the drunk has arrived earlier than the surgeon and treatment of the drunk is under way. Treatment would not be abandoned in this case to save the surgeon even though this would have a better outcome for the community as a whole. The anesthetized volunteers would want advantages, once gained, not to be totally volatile. From the original position both totally egalitarian societies and meritocracies would look bad because of their tendencies to reverse allocations already made and thereby to undo advantages which have been gained without force or fraud. The volunteers would want a stable society, and hence, would oppose rules that take away advantages which were gained without force or fraud as opposed to luck or pluck. Common sense would tell the volunteers that their rules should allow them to hang on to what they have. On the other hand, they would want to arrange things so that nobody can monopolize advantages.

Not just new and exotic treatments but standard health care becomes more scarce as populations increase and economies founder. Not only concerning life-saving medical care but about health care in general questions are being raised about the allocation of this care on a first-come first-served basis. Ethics committees in hospitals, for instance, may be asked to suggest policy regarding the reserving of some treatments for those who are not so infirm or advanced in age as to make the outcome extremely dubious. A physician remarked to me, in the context of discussing this issue, that 50 percent of health-care dollars in BC, Canada, are spent on people in the last six months of their lives. Long-term care facilities may house many patients who are well below any reasonable threshold for being persons, hence below the threshold for being the persons their families knew before advanced age or illness robbed those persons of their capacities.

Problems arise also at the other end of human life. In neonatal care units we spend millions saving newborns even after a mere twenty-week pregnancy. These newborns will probably have ongoing health problems all of their lives. As our health care systems stagger under the weight of supporting such patients as if they were persons, we need to separate clearly the treatment which is the moral right of all human beings from the treatment which is the moral right only of persons. The rights of human beings are not a matter of genetics, but had by virtue of the close relationship between the class of persons and the class of human beings. As far as we know, given that Byzantine essentialism is correct, all persons are human beings, though not all human beings are persons.

We already make many decisions in accord with that concept of a person which I adumbrated in the previous chapter. The medical profession in my locale has stopped doing many life-saving operations on patients who appear to be clearly below some threshold. For example, one hears that fewer bypass operations are being done on senile ninety-year-olds. If resources are dedicated instead to a forty-year-old person whose abilities are obviously above the thresholds, few would take the reallocation amiss, given that there are not enough resources to give all who wish it the operation. First-come-first-served is a rule which is constantly being qualified. We ought to devote resources first to people and only then to those human beings who are no longer (and likely never again to be) or not yet (and unlikely to become) people. Resources are not so tight that we are unwilling to err on the side of generosity in letting human beings be treated as people, but having human chromosomes is no longer a guarantee of treatment, if it ever was.

On the other hand, those who are not persons may have certain rights as well under the terms agreed to by the volunteers. For those outside the group of persons it would be reasonable to differentiate treatment on the basis of their similarity to persons and on the degree to which they have a chance of becoming persons. Their similarity engages our sympathies. Consideration of sympathies is necessary for making the rules of the sort that people can follow. The potential to be a person is, moreover, all some of the volunteers may have, as far as they know, once the exercise is completed.

As seen from the original position, egalitarian considerations have a qualified use within groups of people. This is a block to attempts to differentiate treatment on the basis of the degree to which a patient is a person unless all other things are equal. That is, if there is no other way to decide how resources are to be allocated in some situation, then those with their feet most firmly planted in the circle of persons would have the advantage.

For those outside the circle, however, to decide on allocation the rules might well look to the degree of similarity to persons or to the degree of potential for becoming persons. I seem to remember an outcry in the press when a well-known chimpanzee who had demonstrated certain cognitive and conative capacities like ours was to be used for vivisection. Well you might ask about the other chimpanzees who are used in this way without any notice being taken. Animals who are more like people than are some human beings should be accorded special respect because of their capacities. The volunteers in the original position would, in self-interest, demand respect for such abilities so that their own would be respected. They would not wish to undermine the sympathies of persons for persons by allowing people to act harshly towards those who resemble persons. It is reasonable for the volunteers to bet that they would have need of such sympathies.

Informed consent and access to information

From the original position we would choose rights to information prior to giving consent to operations or to our use as experimental subjects. Indeed, we would want information about ourselves generally. These rights apply to all research on persons and to government record-keeping. They are urgent questions as well in medical practice. By the nature of medical practice, the patient cannot have as much information as the practitioner. One very difficult policy to state is that regarding the degree to which consent must be informed. This will depend partly on the degree to which the patient is a person. Roughly speaking, the more one is a person the more one has the capacity to assimilate such information and make a judgment on one's own behalf. From the original position we would choose to give the patient's own view of the patient's competence a very heavy weight in these matters. In short, we would oppose paternalism because it is a reasonable bet that we volunteers would turn out to be the best judges and protectors of our own self-interest when we got back to our ordinary lives.

Yet doctors in my neck of the woods have been brought up in a somewhat paternalistic medical culture. Legal difficulties to one side, probably the moral question most physicians would ask themselves is "Would this information do my patient more harm than good?" The culture is changing, however, to admit that the autonomy of patients who are persons must be respected even when some harm will be done by such respect.

To see the knife-edge on which doctors must balance principles, consider an example. While diagnostic test results are generally considered information to which competent adults have a right (as autonomous persons), if a gynecologist has a young patient who presents as a woman but is diagnosed as having testicular feminization and, consequently, a male chromosome profile, full information will not usually be disclosed to the patient. If the patient were told that she had the profile of a man, the patient might suffer from difficulties with gender identification. In some cases full disclosure has led to extreme psychological trauma and even suicide. Clearly health-care professionals may come under conflicting requirements in cases of autonomy and access to information. From the original position we would want our autonomy respected, but not if it would injure us to no good purpose.

This illustrates the mammoth task of the volunteers in the original position. With each of the rules they would put forward in the original position, they would have many paragraphs of general exceptions and examples as guidance for the decision-makers in the societies trying to abide by these rules. It is, nonetheless, not an impossible task. It is more difficult than, but comparable to, the task each of us might face in writing a living will to specify what should be done in a future veiled from us by our ignorance of the future state of our health.

Moral limits on research and experimentation

The primary issue here is informed consent. Informing subjects fully may destroy a research study and inhibit the discovery of important data. Failing to inform them may constitute a breach of their rights as persons. This dilemma is mainly faced by universities and research hospitals, but the debates about informed consent are relevant to ordinary medical practice in many areas. For example, informing a patient about the details of a procedure may lessen the opportunities for success if the patient is sufficiently fearful. Once again, health-care professionals are expected to make a judgment about which takes precedence, the autonomy of persons or doing what is best, medically speaking, for patients. From the original position we might well decide that autonomy can only be overruled if severe harm is likely to be avoided by withholding information from the patient.

We may, however, forgo considerable benefits from research if we insist on informed consent. Consequentialists might think the concept of a person too weak to stand in the way of the general increase in human happiness that might come from less hobbled research. From the original position, however, we would want to be sure that we were not going to be used, without reasonably informed consent, as laboratory rats. While fully informed consent is impossible without giving the subjects an education like that of the experimenters, it is usually easy enough to see what the experimenter would be interested in knowing if the experimenter were in the subject's shoes. From the original position, one does not know which shoes one will wear. The rule is, therefore, that the experimenter should tell the subject what the experimenter would want to know if their roles were reversed and if common sense guided risk-taking. This ensures treating the subject like a person rather than an experimental animal. It would mean foregoing some experiments which would be impossible with such reasonably informed consent.

Once again, we must distinguish between merely human beings and persons here. We tend to protect all human beings from harm in experimentation, but informed consent is only possible for persons. The protection for all, moreover, is justified in the original position by concerns about persons being mistaken for mere human beings. In some cases, it is clear that we are dealing with a human but not a person. We allow experimentation, for example, on neomorts in hospitals with the consent of the next of kin. Because the neomorts' brains are not functioning, they are not persons. On the other hand, those whose brains function sufficiently to maintain them as living human beings without life-support systems but who probably have no significant cognitive function would not be thought to be proper subjects for experimentation. For instance, some human beings in long-term care facilities would be in this category. Perhaps if we were as certain as we are with the neomorts that these human beings would never again be persons, we would not have quite the same qualms, but their similarity to us is greater; so they would not likely be treated like neomorts. The general rule chosen from the original position might well be this: when in doubt, protect a human being as a person should be protected. Since the volunteers are betting on rules with their own self-interest in mind, however, they would have to weigh carefully their chances on the one hand of being a person who is mistaken for a merely human being in a vegetative state and on the other hand being a person who suffers because of the lack of knowledge which might have been gained through more liberal experimentation. The volunteers might, however, let the general rule stand in any case just to support sympathy for human beings on which so many of their interests and the usefulness of their rules would depend.

Non-human experimental animals might also be accorded more respect according to the rules of the social contract than they are currently accorded. In their own self-interest the volunteers would want to have the advantages which come to people from the use of animals in experimentation, but the volunteers would also want to inhibit needless suffering in any sentient being, not just those which resemble us. To allow suffering is to undermine one's own security by undermining the sympathy on which security rests. The ideal of the dispassionate scientist would not be favoured by those in the original position. It is an ideal of scientists, not a view likely to appeal to those who are trying to minimize their risks in accord with common sense. I think the volunteers would want to promote a robust sympathy for sentient beings more than they would want to promote uninhibited scientific experimentation on sentient beings.

Euthanasia

Euthanasia is taking over from abortion as the topic of biomedical ethics most in the public eye and before the courts. Consequently it provides excellent examples of pressures on ethical decision-making which may go on in medical settings. Attention to even the abbreviated discussion here could, perhaps, urge the debate within those settings in new directions.

It is useful to distinguish at least six kinds of euthanasia: *voluntary* (the patient requests death), *non-voluntary* (the patient is incapable of making requests), *involuntary* (the patient requests life-saving aid which is denied),[2] and each of these three may be *active* or *passive*. This last distinction is hazy. Is doctor-assisted suicide active or passive? In accepting a patient's refusal of life support is a doctor causing a death or merely allowing a patient to cause her own? Disagreements here are not merely about the moral value of actions of persons but about what constitutes an action and what constitutes a person. Actions are, roughly, the behaviour of human beings caused by the intentions of the corresponding persons, and corresponding persons are as described in the last chapter. On this view, not giving a patient antibiotics when the patient has pneumonia is as much an action as giving the patient a lethal injection. The question in either case remains, "Is euthanasia morally justified in this instance?" Given this rough characterization of action we can consider what to say about the six kinds of euthanasia.

Acting in their own self-interest but behind a veil of ignorance about their lots in life to come, the volunteers would choose contractual terms that would make life worth living, as much as possible, no matter what lot is drawn. On the other hand, they would also, perhaps, permit the termination of the life of a person were it to be a totally unbearable life. A human body which was not a person could, under very special circumstances, permissibly be killed too. If brain damage, for example, in that body were so severe that no person is really present in it, killing that body would not be killing a person. Different rules would protect human beings who were not persons, though the volunteers would want to severely restrict harm to human beings as well. The self-interest of the anesthetized committee, the choosers of rules in the original position, would lead them to provide for their continuation if they are having lives worth living and, otherwise, their deaths at their considered and reasonable request, if they could make such a request.

Voluntary euthanasia

From the original position, then, one would want the power to end one's life if it were truly unbearable. People make mistakes about their future degree of suffering and about its probable duration. Sometimes they are glad to have lived after all, sometimes not. Voluntary euthanasia, therefore, should be allowed only under strict controls to prevent the patient from accepting euthanasia because of pressure, misinformation, or temporary despondency.

One should also be able to make the choice of death while still a person and have it carried out later when one is no longer able to commit suicide. This would usually be called "active euthanasia." When only the human being remains, but the person has, prior to falling below some threshold, requested euthanasia, it should still be carried out. I suppose it could be called both "active" and "voluntary" in such a case, though some dispute the use of voluntary acceptance of death when much time has elapsed since acceptance was expressed. In the original position, however, we would choose to be in charge of our own bodies even when we can no longer control them, if only to prevent the mere behaviour of those bodies from being mistaken for our actions. The dignity of persons depends on persons' wishes about their own bodies being given great weight in any decision about how to treat those bodies. The volunteers would, in any case, be making a reasonable bet if they put forward rules which protect persons' power over their own bodies.

It seems we should not rest too much on the distinction between "passive" and "active." These terms have no precise meaning, but active euthanasia is, roughly, the mercy-killing of the patient by some other person assisting while passive euthanasia is mercifully letting the patient die, or benign neglect. Neglect, however, is not always as benign as more vigorous steps to bring about a patient's death. In the original position we would choose a rule by which we could get help to end our own suffering in a hopeless case. Avoidance of needless, pointless pain is the way of common sense. Some may choose to suffer to the end, but it should be a choice. If there is a point to suffering to the end, it should be a point of the patient's. As usual, I assume that it would be a reasonable bet, a rule of common sense, from the original position, to keep our options as open as possible and keep as much control as possible over ourselves in the rules we choose. If we had to make rules to govern us in an unknown future, it would make sense to maximize the personal choices we would be permitted in that future.

Non-voluntary euthanasia

In cases of non-voluntary euthanasia the will of the person or the remaining human being to be killed is not knowable with any certainty.

One can consult those who knew the person when communication was possible, and make the best guess. Protecting ourselves in the original position, we would want to distinguish two main kinds of cases. In the first, the patient cannot request euthanasia, because the patient is no longer a person. A patient in a permanent coma, for example, is a living human being but not a person. In cases like this, non-voluntary euthanasia is permissible. In cases, however, where there is some reasonable expectation of revival of a person in the body, non-voluntary euthanasia would not be permissible. The volunteers would choose to err on the side of keeping human beings alive pointlessly as long as the cost of this policy is not prohibitive. It would be in their interest to protect themselves in case of a future loss of abilities which might prove temporary, though temporary against all odds. On the other side they would have to weigh the costs to themselves of keeping others alive pointlessly. Probably the best the volunteers can do here is give guidelines for judgments to be made on a case-by-case basis. A chance of recovery should normally be a reason for keeping a person alive. This is consistent with saying that extreme circumstances make for harsher choices. For example, triage has been used where resources are very scarce.

In the second kind of case, much rarer, a person exists but cannot communicate. One could even be conscious but so severely injured that one cannot give instructions even by a sign. In the original position it would be rational to put stringent restrictions on non-voluntary euthanasia to ensure that it was only used on persons in cases where the patient could be shown, with moral if not epistemological certainty, to be incapable of regaining the capacity to decide for herself. In the original position we might, out of self-interest, wish to have a decision made for us on the basis of what a reasonable person would do if so terribly injured. Medical experts could determine the likelihood of survival and the future condition of the person so far as could be known. If the prospects were only for agony, for instance, then non-voluntary euthanasia would be justifiable. Once again, I think common sense tells us to pick a rule which promotes our survival only if our lives are worth living. If possible, one's own judgments about what life is worth living should be used to decide one's own case.

According to some principle which I have failed to master, stopping life-support systems is often considered morally permissible in cases of non-voluntary euthanasia, while giving a lethal injection is not. The first is considered passive, the second active. The only morally relevant difference I can see is that the lethal injection is liable to be quicker, more effective, and less likely to cause pain to what may be, in some way, a sentient being. The similarity of this being to a person should at least move us to minimize pain. People in the original position would take sympathy into account and rule in favour of euthanasia in such cases. Common sense urges us to end pointless suffering, but we must be at great pains to ensure that there is no reasonable expectation of the suffering human being becoming a person again who is able to decide for herself whether to live or die.

The law is not in accord with morality on this; so further moral questions arise about the legal risks, if any, which health-care professionals are morally obligated to take to do what is right for their patients. In the original position one would not know whether one would wind up in the position of the patient or the doctor. The rule might be framed that a doctor who could relieve extreme suffering through euthanasia with minimal personal legal risk ought to do so. Risk, however, becomes a morally adequate excuse for not acting in such cases at fairly low levels of risk, since those in the original position would exercise common caution. In self-defence, they would excuse readily in such cases a doctor's unwillingness to cause a death or to provide the means for others to do so. It would still be incumbent on all to seek a change in the law if the moral rules put forward by the volunteers were, indeed, at odds with the law.

Involuntary euthanasia

A person who chooses to live should be allowed to do so. Here, however, the distinction of active from passive begins to have some purchase. The ninety-year old who is suffering terribly but afraid to die should generally be relieved as much as possible of pain and kept alive, but not at the cost of a misallocation of medical resources according to our earlier discussion. Such a patient could be allowed to die if the motive of mercy is combined with that of saving another person who can benefit much more from resources. In the original position, though, I suspect that considerations of autonomy would win out, denying the permissibility of any *pure* case of involuntary euthanasia. Even a patient who is suffering the tortures of the damned who chooses to live should not be shown to death's door actively or passively *if* the resources are available without misallocation to honour the patient's wish to live. Nonetheless, I would expect the volunteers to weigh more heavily the importance of having their lives saved when they might have much life left to live than the importance of having their lives saved when they are nearly sure to die soon. This too seems to be common sense. Common sense prevails in moments of calm reflection, though one may lose sight of it when one is on one's deathbed. The volunteers might agree to rules in the original position which they know they might not wish to follow under some circumstances in the real world. We make rules which force our future selves to be sensible.

Daphne's case

Daphne, who requested euthanasia frequently during the three months prior to her final descent into dementia, is now in the condition she feared and wished to avoid via euthanasia. Daphne now is certainly not the person who existed before dementia overtook her. It is very doubtful that Daphne remains in the class of persons. She was reduced to being first like a babbling infant and then like a silent one with no potential to develop as an infant would. Now that her chance for a remission is certainly gone, her request for euthanasia should be honoured, on the face of it. The volunteers would want their wishes concerning their bodies to be followed after their minds had gone. At the very least, we ought not aggressively to try to keep Daphne alive.

Things are, in life, rarely so simple as they are in the abstract. In this case we discover conflicts of rights. First there are the rights of the physicians to refuse euthanasia. They would suffer sever legal sanctions if they practised it. This excuses them from following Daphne's wishes.

Even the less controversial claim that we ought not to preserve Daphne in life is difficult to defend. Daphne's parents cannot believe that she has lost her former capacities except for what she has obviously lost—her abilities of locomotion and speech. They cannot believe what the neurologists say. As they see her, she is simply trapped in a body which is out of her control. They strive heroically to maintain her in life, and have spoken of pursuing alternative treatments to what standard medicine offers. The massive scarring of Daphne's cerebral cortex makes it certain that their view of the facts is incorrect. The intellect cannot survive the death of the brain tissue which supported it, nor can any treatment bring it back. They are willing, however, to hang on and hope for a miracle. Her parents spend most of their time and efforts on this. Saving Daphne is their life.

The conflict of rights is primarily between the right of Daphne to determine what should happen to her body and the right of her parents to keep her alive and pursue various treatments. Not all cases of conflict of rights are this difficult. The parents' rights to protect their daughter with help from Medicare would be extinguished, for instance, if Daphne were completely braindead, but she is not. Daphne still has apparent emotional, though not cognitive, responses, limited though they may be.

Reflecting on the original position, we get some help with resolution of conflicts of rights, but many points remain moot. If we are willing to allocate medical resources to keep human beings in Daphne's condition alive, then it is hard to see how we could deny her parents reasonable access to some resources. If the rules we make in the original position take into account that we can only follow rules which accord with our sympathy for persons, then we would arrange for honouring a parent's right to enlist society's help to battle for the survival of a son or daughter even when the prognosis is opposed to any return of the abilities of persons. When there is no probability of recovery, such a right can be extinguished by competing rights of other patients to medical resources. This is vague at best, and there would have to be limits on the type and quantity of resources used to keep a human being alive for the sake of her parents.

In cases like Daphne's and in less clear cases in our society where medical resources are not yet taxed to the bitter limit, we fall back on the principle that when we are in even the slightest doubt we should treat a human being like a person. Indeed, even when our doubts are insignificant we tend to do so, at least when other persons' rights or sympathies for other persons promote such treatment.

We are not, however, taking the global view that those in the original position would be partly inclined to take. The world as a whole is reaching that bitter limit. If all resources were distributed without regard to nationality, we could not support human non-persons in life at the expense of people elsewhere in the world. Daphne herself was greatly opposed to the systematic wastefulness of the West and had great compassion for all who suffer. She would have, I believe, agreed that euthanasia in cases like hers would be morally right even if it were considered non-voluntary and active.

The volunteers, however, are to make rules which people who feel ordinary human sympathy could follow. We know, moreover, that our sympathies vary with proximity of persons to us both in geography and in personal relations. This undermines the global view. The volunteers would realize that rules which required distribution of medical or other resources without regard to the proximity of people to those doing the distributing would be rules that people could not or would not follow. Rather than distributing resources without regard to nationality or kinship, the rules chosen by the volunteers would require that people throughout the world be helped to attain some minimum standard. A global safety net would be the object of the rules. In case the volunteers found themselves on the outside of the resource-controlling countries looking in, they would want such a safety net. They would realize, however, that sympathy operates in such a way as to prevent any egalitarian distribution. To require such a distribution would make the rules ignored. This is a case where half a loaf is better than none. Putting this together with another bit of common sense, that charity begins at home, we modify the distribution of resources which the volunteers might otherwise like to make. Rules applicable by those with ordinary human sympathy do not include a rule requiring parents to let their own children die to preserve others with a better chance of a life worth living.

Discussing allocation of resources on a hospital ethics committee, a doctor remarked to me that our society has to relearn when it is right to let people die. Part of the problem is that our sympathy for the parents in Daphne's case makes us want to do things which are not necessarily in Daphne's interest nor in the interest of society. In the original position we would be willing to allow for what would otherwise be unreasonable treatment of a patient to alleviate the distress of others, but only to the extent that it put no one at risk. From a global point of view, our medical practices put others at risk, and they are beginning to do so even here at home. The volunteers would be ignorant, of course, of their economic circumstances. It would make only limited sense for them to assure those like Daphne her current treatment at the expense of those who are clearly persons in need of life-saving aid but who cannot afford it. We are not at that point yet, at least not locally. Sympathy still wins over harsh necessity within the wealthy countries.

The volunteers would put persons first, but in Daphne's case it is difficult at best to see how to do so. Daphne's own wish for euthanasia should be taken seriously. Her parents' right to protect her is very strong. Her parents are, moreover, currently persons while Daphne is no longer. This does not extinguish Daphne's right, but it affects her interests and capacity to suffer in ways which the volunteers would have to consider when deciding how conflicts of rights are to be decided. The right of persons elsewhere to medical resources, however, abets to some extent Daphne's right to die. We could, nonetheless, cut many luxuries before cutting medical care to human beings like Daphne if we wished to provide better care elsewhere in the world.

The question seems, therefore, to come down to the competing rights of Daphne to euthanasia and of her parents to protect her. If it is a harm to Daphne to keep her alive and as comfortable as possible, then it is a harm that no person experiences. The harm to her parents, on the other hand, to be deprived utterly of their hope would be almost unbearable. The volunteers would protect the interests of persons much more than those of merely human beings. Daphne cannot now suffer as her parents can. Even though Daphne was a person when she requested euthanasia, it seems that to put persons first and follow rules consistent with sympathy is to support the parents in Daphne's case as long as Daphne is kept comfortable and the use of resources is not extreme. Her parents, on the other hand, cannot require the rest of society to provide aggressive, invasive treatment, nor are they morally licensed to inflict unnecessary suffering on Daphne through such treatment. Our duty to Daphne is to keep her as free from pain as possible. Our duty to her parents is to give them the resources, short of aggressive treatment, to keep Daphne alive. This seems to be the way to put persons first without ignoring the rights of past persons or of present human beings.

Abortion and infanticide

Here the central concept is often seen as the concept of a person. Pro-life groups argue that abortion is always morally wrong since it is the killing of an innocent person. Pro-choice groups deny that the fetus is a person. This opens up much larger questions which affect most medical care: "What is a person?" "What are the rights of persons over and above those of human beings?" and "Does the potential to become a person confer any rights?" A program for answering the first question has been suggested in the last chapter. The answer to the second and third questions are hinted at in this chapter by looking at the rules we might choose in the original position. Each of these rules defines a right and, for persons, a duty. Since those choosing rules in the original position would want to protect their future selves, there would be a general prohibition against us killing innocent people who are not attacking us. This rule gives each person a corresponding right to life and a correlative duty not to kill other innocent people who are not attacking her.

A right to life is a poor thing, however, if it is not accompanied by a right to life-saving aid. A rule would be accepted which requires us to come to the aid of other people whose lives are threatened as long as we can do so without great harm to ourselves or others. How great a harm must be to provide an excuse for not aiding is a vexed question. I will reserve it for brief treatment by examples in the sections on foreign aid and future generations below. Here I will merely say that while we may not be required to be good Samaritans, the opposite extreme is not likely to be acceptable to the volunteers either.

The right to life and the right to life-saving aid, however, are not obviously rights of a fetus. A fetus has not yet developed the capacities which take it across the threshold from being human to being a person. Persons in the original position would want rules to save persons, but not necessarily rules to save all human beings. Since they do not know whether they will be persons or only potentially persons when the anesthetic wears off, the volunteers would be careful not to dismiss the interests of those who are not yet persons. A common presumption is, moreover, that a human being is actually or potentially a person; so any denial of rights to human beings would have to be carefully weighed.

The similarity of merely human beings to persons is also relevant in this regard. The fact that a fetus at an early stage of human development has fingers and the fact that it has gills are both relevant. The one arouses our sympathy while the other distances it. Compatibility with sympathy is a feature to be taken into account by any set of rules which is actually to be followed.[3]

When I am sleeping I have only as potentialities certain capacities which make me a person and other additional capacities which make me the particular person I am. Nonetheless, I expect my rights as a person and as *this* person to be respected. I may not be killed, and promises made to me may not be broken, just because I am not currently able to do the essential things on demand. Of course capacities are always potentialities in the sense that they are the potential to do certain things when they are required. We may, however, not be able to do things on demand when we are in various states from sleep to transient global amnesia. In these cases, though, there is good reason to believe that the abilities will be revitalized. The potential of the fetus is somewhat different.

Believing that people begin at human conception, some wish to treat fetuses as people. Fetuses, however, do not yet embody the essence needed to make a person. The question is begged, "Why treat something which is clearly not yet a person as if it were?" Even if we accept, just for the sake of argument, that fetuses should be treated as if they were persons, we can see that abortion would still not be completely ruled out. In the original position, a volunteer would not know if she would eventually be a woman needing an abortion for physical or psychiatric reasons. A person who is being attacked, even by an innocent, may rightly produce even a deadly defence in some cases. The right to self-defence can overrule the right to life.[4] But this still avoids the main question, since few pregnancies are this threatening.

The difficult question is "What moral limits, if any, are there on the right of women to choose to end a *healthy* pregnancy?" These limits, once we know them, can be modified to the degree that the health of the fetus or the mother are threatened prior to our facing the decision about abortion. To say that there is no moral reason to protect a fetus from abortion is to ignore the matters of similarity to persons and the potential to become a person. Since those in the original position would take sympathy into account, they would recognize that abortion late in the term would have to be justified by much more pressing interests of persons than abortion earlier in the term. And since they would want a rule which protects themselves when they are temporarily unable to function as persons, they would allow the potential to become a person to weigh in the balance when the decision to preserve or take human life is contemplated.

This potentiality too would increase as the pregnancy continued. As the fetus gains a greater probability of survival, it is has more potential to become a person. Thus the common idea that abortion becomes morally less permissible the closer to birth that a fetus gets is buttressed by the conceptions of a person and of the social contract used here. On the other hand, the mother, as the most affected person, would be given strong rights to autonomy and bodily integrity by those in the original position. Within the limits of sympathy, the mother's rights would generally be more powerful than those of the fetus, as the rights of persons usually are over those of the merely human. The volunteers would be more concerned to protect their interests as persons because they would be more capable of suffering and pleasure as persons than human beings. It is common sense to worry more about what may happen to you when you can know about it and care about it than about what may happen when you would not know what hit you.

The foregoing raises the spectre of infanticide. There are few taboos stronger in our culture than that against killing innocent children. Yet newborn infants are not persons. Their potential to become persons, however, is increased by birth since the probability of their surviving to become people is greater than the probability of survival prior to birth. Our sympathy is also greatly increased once the infant is living in the world like ourselves rather than within the mother. Infanticide commonly goes beyond the limits of our sympathy.

It is useful to look at a culture in which infanticide has been deemed permissible, the Inuit culture. At times infants were put to death when there were insufficient resources to keep the community from starving if there were new mouths to feed. In harsh conditions, a choice had to be made between the survival of a community of persons and the survival of a newborn infant. To suppose that a human infant had an absolute right to live in such circumstances would be to condemn the community to slow suicide. When food was plentiful, the Inuit would demonstrate the devotion to their young that one would expect of sympathetic people. The rules put forward by the volunteers would have to be variable with conditions. They would put persons first and protect human beings who are not persons as much as possible while preserving persons.

The right to life of persons generally outweighs the future interest[5] in a personal life of human beings who are not yet persons. To illustrate the concept of a future interest, consider a purchase of a valuable piece of art. The purchaser has, let us suppose, paid half the cost down and is paying the remainder of the price in installments. On full payment, it is agreed, the purchaser will become the owner. Until then the purchaser cannot take the art. Nonetheless, the purchaser has an ever-strengthening future interest which, from a moral point of view, prevents the current owner from doing whatever she pleases. The current owner could not, for example, exhibit the work under risky conditions. Similarly, the closer a human being comes to being a person, the stronger entitlement that human being has, under the rubric of future interest, to such things as life-saving medical treatment. In a culture like that in the West, where resources are currently plentiful, the future interest of an infant is very strong indeed.

If we took a global view, then this future interest is weakened in competition with the rights of the needy persons already in existence throughout the world. Of course the sympathy for those close to us, particularly our own offspring, makes a usable set of rules take the global view only insofar as is necessary to provide some global safety net. No rule which required people to deprive their own newborns to save strangers in the Third World would be compatible with ordinary human sympathy. Restricting the number of children per couple in the wealthy countries would, however, be reasonable, assuming that a child born among the wealthy will use about eight times the resources of a child born in the Third World.

Even looking only within our own society, there are cases where the future interest would be weak, indeed cases in which infanticide as a form of non-voluntary euthanasia would be permissible. Consider cases of birth defects too severe to allow a chance of development of the human infant into a person. If the prognosis is for two weeks of agony before an inevitable death, it would be better to kill a newborn infant than to merely allow it to die through the supposedly benign neglect of passive euthanasia. The very sympathy which prevents killing in most cases requires it in rare cases. Some cases will be very difficult to decide since we will have varying degrees of certainty about the chances a particular infant has to develop into a person. In our decisions, we should keep in mind the rights of the mother and other closely affected persons. These rights may outweigh the future interests of the infant. Fortunately, the cases in which these rights and future interests conflict are *relatively* rare. They are, however, heart-rending where they do occur, and we need strong principles such as those I have been suggesting to deal with them. We should put people first just as the volunteers would require.

It may be thought that the deck is stacked if we ask the volunteers to write rules concerning abortion. Even behind the veil of ignorance they would not believe they might be fetuses. They are, however, unaware of their capacities. It might turn out that they are only potentially persons once the drug wears off, so far as they know. They would have to offer some protection to potential persons. Still, it makes more sense to be concerned about protecting one's life after one has developed to the point of being aware that one is a person. A failure of this protection could cause the volunteers greater suffering than a failure to protect merely potential persons. It is common sense to worry more about losing your life when you could agonize over it than about losing it when you would not be capable of valuing life.

Genetics and human reproduction

Questions frequently raised here concern the moral implications of selective abortion, genetic engineering, surrogate motherhood, and the rights and duties of biological parents. As we confront these issues, there are reasons to treat human beings who are not yet persons differently from persons. A look at some cases may illustrate the employment of the concept of a person introduced in the last chapter.

Selective abortion

Treatments for infertility, for example, may give rise to multiple pregnancies. This requires the abortion of some of the fetuses in such a case to maximize the chances of the others being brought to term. The rights of the parents as people are put foremost here. The future interests of the aborted fetuses as human beings are not dismissed, but they are outweighed by the rights of the parents plus the future interests of the fetuses which do live. The volunteers would be unlikely to change this current policy, given that they would put persons first.

On the other hand, another case of selective abortion illustrates the ways in which cultures may collide because of disagreement about or lack of a concept of a person. Ultrasound clinics have opened that offer parents the knowledge of the gender of their fetuses. It is alleged that in some cases those who are anxious to have a male child abort female fetuses. Here the future interest of the female fetus in becoming a person outweighs the wishes of the parents as we see things in the West. Unlike infertility, the lack of male offspring is not, in Western culture, often considered a significant harm to the parents. Human fetuses may not have a right to life, but they have a strong enough future interest in life to outweigh mere preferences as opposed to rights of persons. Putting persons first does not mean that any interest of a person will outweigh any interest of a non-person.

Population control

It is doubtful that the volunteers would uphold what we may suppose to be a right to have as many children as we wish. The whole discussion of fertility here has been, after all, within the context of affluent Western culture. If we were to take the global view, limits on the resources we use, including those we use by having children, might well be considered the right of those who are cut off from resources. Fertility clinics would perhaps be contrary to the rules the volunteers would write. Childless couples could be helped to adopt orphans from the Third World. Similarly, those with a strong desire for male offspring would be the objects of intensive education aimed at making the world's people care for the children who are already here rather than having many children to assure that one is a male. The desire to reproduce one's own genotype, however strong a drive it may be, can be sublimated in an affluent society, and there are many orphaned children elsewhere in the world needing our care. This moderates the effects of sympathy for the childless. To protect themselves, the volunteers would wish to restrict the creation of new people in cases where people in existence were unable to live good lives because of inadequate resources. Against this, the volunteers would have to weigh the degree to which having their own children would be essential to the development of their own capacities and thus to the enrichment of their lives as persons.

In any case, any restrictions on such personal matters as reproduction would have to be imposed in a way compatible with a counterbalancing interest of the volunteers. They would want to be as free as possible to make choices for themselves. For example, in case they turn out to be on the outside looking in, the volunteers would want to make sure that efforts to control population in the Third World were not coercive but aimed at bettering the economic circumstances of the people there, giving people the incentives and the education needed for them to want smaller families as we do in the wealthier nations. Giving women control of the use of their bodies for reproduction would probably also be favoured by the volunteers whose gender has been concealed from them.

Genetic engineering

Now that it seems imminent that geneticists will be able to stitch in genes for tallness, athletic ability, and other characteristics which parents may wish to have in their offspring, the question arises whether we should limit intervention in the development of the fetus. Are genetic alterations significantly different, from a moral point of view, to other advantages parents give to their fetuses and to their children? Certainly if there is a danger that the alterations will realize part of Mary Wollstonecraft Shelley's nightmare in the novel *Frankenstein*, then the future interest of the fetus and other potential victims would outweigh the parents' wishes. Stringent precautions must be taken to ensure fetal health and human development whether or not genetic alterations are induced. The self-interest of those in the original position would require this; they would not want to live in a world full of failed experiments.

Within reason, the rights of the parents to enhance the lives of their offspring are again foremost, and genetic alteration might be permissible by the volunteers' rules if it is known with reasonable degree of probability to be beneficial to the fetus while unlikely to harm anyone else. After all, the volunteers would take into account their possible future role and desires as parents. It is difficult, however, to predict future harms coming from such radical changes. What if the people in the affluent countries could be made biologically superior to those elsewhere? Genetic engineering could widen the gap already existing between rich and poor both globally and within nations. The volunteers would try to make rules that would not exacerbate existing inequities. Use of genetic alteration would have to be strictly controlled to make sure that it was beneficial to most persons, not just a lucky few.

Surrogate motherhood

The questions here concern primarily the rights of the so-called "surrogate" mother. She, as a person, has a right to bodily integrity under the terms acceptable in the original position. She cannot be treated as a baby factory, nor can the fetus which is dependent on her body be thought of as the property of another. Those in the original position would be more concerned about protecting their interests in case they wound up in the mother's shoes than they would should they turn out to be one of those wishing to have someone else bear a child. The reason is that the mother is generally more vulnerable to harm, and the volunteers have no idea whether they are likely to be in the situation of the mother.

The resulting child in such a case might be in some ways better served by being placed in the care of the couple who hired the woman to bear that fetus. Usually the couple is wealthy and the mother acts out of financial necessity. Nonetheless, the future interests of the fetus cannot outweigh the right of the mother to determine what happens in her body. After the birth, the mother should also, if competent, be allowed to parent the child if she chooses. In the original position, those choosing the rules would frame them in such a way as to give themselves rights acquired by extending themselves physically as the mother has done. Rules which ignore the strong bond between mother and child and the sympathy which people have for the mother in this instance would be defeated by the conditions on the volunteers' choices. The disappointed couple might still have some rights to recompense for support given to the mother during the pregnancy. Perhaps they could even be given the option of co-parenting the child. Again, in the position of the volunteers, it makes sense to hedge one's bets to protect one's future interests, but they would protect the most vulnerable first. Common sense requires this of those who might turn out to be among the most vulnerable.

Foreign aid

Recall now the committee choosing the rules, a committee struck by the United Nations to hammer out a revised charter of the rights of people throughout the world. The participants, behind a veil of ignorance as they are, would not know what countries they come from. They would come up with rather different rules for distributing the world's wealth than do the wealthy and powerful nations of the world. These rules would, if the committee members each assiduously pursued her own self-interest, reflect approximately a twenty percent chance of landing in an economically good situation and an eighty percent chance of landing in a bad one. The volunteers who are instructed to act on self-interest would not want such a punitive redistribution of wealth as to destroy their luck if they were in wealthy nations. They would, however, insist that much more be done to give the poor a reasonable return for their labour and resources, most of the benefits of which flow rapidly into the wealthy nations. To develop to the fullest of one's abilities, to be as much a person as one can be, one needs ample resources. Personal development is, for most human beings, dependent on economic development. Much of what is now considered charity coming from the wealthy to the poor would be duty under rules framed by the volunteers.

Heading into the unknown, the volunteers would want a chance for the best but not for the worst. It would make sense for them to limit the worst-case scenario for their futures even at the cost of limiting the best outcome. It would be wise for them to ensure that the duty of all was to provide a minimum standard of living for everyone in the world. This might involve population control, but probably the rate of increase of the population goes down as economic well-being goes up.[6] Providing themselves with a safety net would be common sense caution for the volunteers even if it meant that they could only have the potential to be millionaires instead of billionaires should they make a lucky landing in the real world. Certainly a right to life-saving aid would be a minimal part of the safety net. The wealthy would be required to overcome famine in other parts of the world.

This raises the question to what degree the wealthy could be obligated to suffer to aid the poor. The volunteers, remember, make their decisions based on self-interest. Since they have a chance of being wealthy they do not wish to allow rules which require extreme sacrifice to aid others who are starving abroad. In any case, our sympathies are directed mainly at those with whom we are in close contact; so no rule requiring saintliness in aid of foreigners would be acceptable to the volunteers who try to fashion rules that people with ordinary human sympathies could follow. The volunteers might accept a rule which says that, far beyond the basic necessities, the wealthy could keep enough wealth, hence enough power, to ensure reasonable security. They could keep the wealth needed to respond confidently to natural disasters and the attacks of other people. Even by such a generous standard, we have a surfeit in the industrialized nations which should be used to fashion a global safety net to prevent any person from falling out of reach of a minimum supply of food, shelter, and medical care.

Future people

The metaphor of the committee of anesthetized volunteers has been stretched to its limits. We can, however, extrapolate beyond them the notion of fairness which emerges from the preceding examples. Imagine, although it takes quite a feat of imagination, that the volunteers do not know when they will live. Ignorant as they are about some facts they might believe a white lie to the effect that some of them will be preserved for life in the future. Would they share our current rules for preserving resources for future generations? In self-interest, they would not want any generation to sacrifice its economic and personal development entirely for the people yet to come. Nonetheless, they would look askance at our current profligacy in using up whatever comes to hand. Sustainable development of resources would be, in the hope that one can make practical sense of it, a requirement laid down in the original position.

Current people would be required to keep options open for future generations as well. If we can use wind, geo-thermal, wave action and solar power sources to supplement or replace the use of non-renewable resources and nuclear power, we ought to do so. In other words the volunteers would choose rules which bias decisions about resources so as to avoid doing anything irreversible. This reversibility rule and several other rules offered by Goodin[7] as an improvement on simple consequentialist reasoning characterize the application of common sense in the original position to management of resources for the future. The volunteers would be potentially at risk if they allowed current generations to leave radioactive waste as a legacy to future generations in the hope that they will find some way to deal with it. In effect, nuclear plants are forever. The decision to use other power sources is reversible. Some of Goodin's other suggestions are that decisions be biased to do the following: make the worst possible outcomes of our decisions as good as we can ensure, give special protection to the vulnerable, create sustainable benefits, and avoid causing harm as distinct from merely foregoing benefits. These are the sorts of policies which would be reasonable from the point of view of the volunteers who want to protect themselves wherever and whenever they land in society.

The interests of future generations cannot be ignored. At the same time future persons cannot be treated in the same way as existing persons. We do not know whether people will exist at all in the future. It would not make sense to sacrifice every luxury now to extend the best possible resource allocation to the future. We can still put currently existing persons first without ignoring future generations. We should not mortgage the future to provide current luxuries and preferences, but we should not sacrifice current persons' needs to those of persons in an uncertain future.

Respect for persons

Feminism

From the original position, the desire of women to be treated as persons is completely reasonable. Ignorant as they are of their gender, the choosers of rules in the original position would wish to maximize their own chances of personal development. This is primarily a matter of exercising and improving upon one's capacities, given the way persons are understood in the previous chapter. Barriers to occupying any position in society which are based not on ability but on gender would be struck down by the committee.

Some feminists, however, have asked for reverse discrimination in order to bring the genders into a balance of power. The idea is that to break some of the invisible barriers, glass ceilings, and the like, we need to give women the advantage men have had for so long. A person on the committee would be concerned about turning out to be of a gender which is at a disadvantage and so might allow the judicious use of some tools like reverse discrimination as a last resort. These tools would have to be carefully guarded to ensure that a balance was created between the genders rather than a new form of imbalance, since only by ensuring balance would those behind a veil of ignorance, which conceals their genders even from themselves, be likely to protect themselves.

Racism

The issues here are similar. Racists fail to treat some people as persons. They do this by not recognizing capacities, and by preventing the exercise of capacities in some visibly different group of people. Behind the veil of ignorance one does not know one's own skin colour. Rules, and tools like reverse discrimination, would all be directed by the volunteers at giving every human being a reasonable chance to develop as a person. The volunteers would support the ideal of equal opportunity since they would have no idea what skin colour or what opportunities they might have.

It is worth noting as an aside that equal opportunity can only make sense for those who have the autonomy of persons. That is why it is a mistake to try to capitalize on the gains made against racial intolerance to institute the same policies where intolerance of the mentally handicapped is at issue. Certainly the mentally handicapped should be better treated, but it is folly, in some cases, to treat them as if they had capacities other people normally have. Under the banner of equal opportunity, some students have be "mainstreamed' in my locale who are ill served by being in a classroom which is hopelessly beyond their level of competence. Others have benefited greatly by mainstreaming, but individual cases must be judged in terms of capacity. Mental ability cannot be treated as an irrelevant characteristic like skin colour when such decisions are made. What is fair in preventing racial discrimination does not necessarily work in every case where a group is singled out for different treatment.

Slavery and prostitution

What is wrong with people being bought and sold like commodities is simply that it is grotesquely unfair, as can be seen by contemplating the rules we would make from the original position. Self-interest would surely motivate the volunteers to rule against any sale of persons. The capacities which give people their dignity are largely ignored in such transactions. Even if a slave is valued for her ability to write poetry or do mathematics, a great wrong is done in reducing her achievements to commodities. One is most oneself when one is exercising one's capacities to the fullest, and it is precisely then that it is most horrible to be treated as the property of another. People in the original position would want to be able to take their places in the class of autonomous beings.

Slavery has not been wiped out in our world. People are still bought and sold as if they were machines made to perform labour. Much more common than the purchased labourer, however, is the prostitute, a form of slave in many cases. Most obviously when a prostitute is under the control of a pimp and forced to work to enrich that pimp, a prostitute is a slave. When there is no pimp, the question still arises whether the alternatives are so bleak that prostitution is a form of self-enslavement to a series of masters. Examples are not so far to seek, but an obvious one is that for children in the slums of third world countries who must sell themselves to live, prostitution with no pimp is still slavery.

It is a moral commonplace that it is not only wrong to enslave others but morally wrong to offer oneself as a slave. From the position taken here, the sin is in both cases the same: one denies the existence of a special class, the class of persons. One reduces persons, in such acts, to the level of a trained dog, a being which cannot choose what it will be. This right to choose for oneself would be fundamental to the volunteers as they tried to ensure their future well-being. A rule against slavery would be part of the safety net they would weave to ensure that no person could fall too far, no matter how unwise her personal decisions. Of course such a rule only makes sense within a network of rules ensuring that no one falls so low economically as to be reduced to slavery for survival. As in the other issues discussed here, the volunteers would exercise common sense caution if they fashioned safety nets to prevent themselves from falling too far. These nets would be worth the price which might be ceilings which prevent them from rising too high.

Civil liberties

Those in the original position would want to retain as much individual freedom as possible while protecting the global community by controlling such personal matters as reproduction. Most of us would prefer to be the judges of what is in our own interest as opposed to having the state decide for us. Freedom of speech, association, religion, and movement are fundamental to putting people in charge of their own further development as persons. Where restrictions are necessary for the general good, as with population control, the volunteers would make rules that bias policies in favour of eliciting voluntary change. Education and economic betterment are, from the volunteers' point of view, far better means to controlling population than law. If more coercive measures like economic disincentives are used to bring about the good of the global community, these should be applied in the same way to all, without favouritism. Many special interest groups have taken of late to calling their privileges "rights." If we look at these from the original position, we can, perhaps, better distinguish the two. At least the traditional civil liberties and other means essential to the maintenance and development of the capacities of persons should be protected as rights. It makes common sense for the volunteers to promote these.

Moral relativism

A favourite question of students in introductory ethics classes is "Who's to say?" A favourite answer of mine is "You are." There seems to be a common view that what is morally right depends somehow on persons, times, or places. At its most extreme, relativism becomes subjectivism, the view that what is morally right depends on each individual person's values. Usually the relativists one encounters are closet absolutists believing as they do that there are some absolute values which everyone must accept. For example, they often say "You shouldn't try to push your values on me! Everyone's got his own." This, if it means anything, is contradictory. The relativist is saying that it is absolutely morally wrong to interfere with others' moral decisions since morality is relative to individual values, not absolute. But this is to say that something (interference) is absolutely wrong although nothing is absolutely wrong. Another way of exposing the problem is to reply to the relativist who demands to be let alone, "But *I* value interference."

Usually the absolutist tries to pin the relativist in a contradiction,[8] then goes on to promulgate some rule or rules of conduct which are said to be independent of when or where or by whom an act is done. Utilitarians ask us to look only at the consequences of the conduct. Maximize happiness and minimize suffering is the one rule of the hedonistic, act utilitarian[9]. The concept of a person becomes relatively unimportant, since any sentient being can be happy or suffer. Hence the distinction between the wider class of human beings and the narrower included class of persons which I have been trying to make is not morally significant on this view. Other moral theorists, non-consequentialists, emphasize the importance of something in addition to the consequences. Often the additional things are moral rights.

For every right there is a rule. The rules chosen in the original position, for example, correspond to a set of rights of persons and duties of persons. Suppose, for instance, the volunteers accept the rule that people ought to give life-saving aid to those people (at least those in their immediate vicinity) who are in danger of dying as long as the saviours can do so without serious injury to their bodies or their life prospects. The rule would have to be further qualified and hedged to avoid counterexamples, but some heavily qualified rule of that sort would be in the self-interest of the volunteers. Now if Tom sees Dick drowning, Tom has a duty to save Dick, and Dick has a right to be saved, under the social contract rule; that is, Tom has such a duty if Tom, for instance, need merely throw in a life preserver. The question then arises, are such rights and duties absolute, or are they relative to persons, times, and places.

I wish to say that there are some senses in which rights are relative, but that they are objective. Using Nagel's view on objectivity which was briefly explicated above, I will say that rights are to a high degree objective. That is to say that rights are mainly independent of the values of individual persons. Rights are, though, fundamentally rights of persons and, as I have argued, person is a concept relative to cultures. Indeed there may well be cultures without any morally important concept of a person.

To illustrate, imagine that I am in a moral dispute with someone from a society which wants to revive an ancient custom that requires that women be burned alive on their husband's funeral pyres. My opponent accuses me of cultural imperialism when I try to persuade people of his locale to prohibit the practice. In his culture, he tells me, it is nonsense to attach great importance to individual human beings. There is no clear concept of a person in his society. The family is the morally central unit. Any individual within the family may be sacrificed for the family's well-being just as we might remove tonsils from a human body as a preventative measure. The idea of persons and their rights as individuals makes no more sense to him than the rights of tonsils would to us. I would reply that I see it as my duty to change his culture. I would rather be politically incorrect than derelict in such a duty. I should work to change any culture, my own included, which treats people in a way so obviously inconsistent with the rules which would be chosen from the original position. While the nature of such rules may be moot in some cases, there can be no doubt in this one. The volunteers would rule against practices like this sacrifice of women since it is clearly in their interest to protect themselves from such practices. Those who argue for such practices usually know they are not going to suffer from them.

My decision has the appearance of being independent of my culture. My opponent, however, responds that the original position which I imagine makes no sense to him. What is a committee of persons? Make it a committee of families, perhaps, and the rules would alter to preserve less fanatically the individual. My opponent and I are clearly embedded each in his own culture as far as our moral thinking goes. Even if we put a high value on tolerance of the customs of others, there are limits to my tolerance if I take people and their rights seriously. There is no *absolute* standard to which we in the West can appeal as we argue with the indigenous peoples of the Americas or the people of the third world about dignity and respect for persons. This is not to say that anything goes, or that when in Rome we should do as the Romans do. There are various kinds of *objectivity* available to us even if no *absolute* standard is available.

First we can be objective in the sense of following non-contradictory sets of moral principles. My opponent cannot say that each culture determines its own morality; so my culture is morally wrong to interfere with his. This puts an absolute value on non-interference which would make him an inconsistent relativist. I could simply and truthfully say that my culture values interference where the fundamental rights of persons are at stake. Secondly, we can have the objectivity that comes from the veil of ignorance. As this element of the social contract is understood, the rules are those which would be in the interest of any person in any culture whether or not she thinks of herself as a person. There is then, a vast difference, to my opponent's objection to having the concept of persons introduced to his culture and his objection to having a foreign religion foisted on his people. Although we are a proselytizing culture, not all that we preach is religious in source nor need it be in the narrow self-interest of our own culture. Indeed, if we acted according to our own rules across cultures, we would treat other peoples of the world much better than we do. It is objectively right that we reform our own conduct and interfere with the conduct of others when it is not in accord with the rules that would be chosen from the original position. The unfortunate spouse on the funeral pyre might well agree.

The moral rectitude of this interference is, nonetheless, relative to Western cultural concepts like that of a person. If I pretend that our morality is absolute, I contradict myself as a moral relativist. Yet I comfort myself with the objectivity of the moral claims which are based on the social contract. Concerning cultural interference I can say that I do not wish to change other cultures except insofar as they undermine persons. It is unfortunate that I must choose between my respect for cultures and my respect for persons, but persons must win. Mine is a Western morality. This is figuratively represented in the metaphor by the volunteers' use of Western standards of rationality and common sense as they choose rules in their self-interest.

The moral view adumbrated here is one which is intended to have a broad appeal since it takes seriously the rights of all persons at all times everywhere. It is a nod in the direction of the unattainable absolute standard of morality. While it fails to achieve such a standard, since person is a relative concept, my view does not devolve in the other direction to subjectivism.

Human rights as opposed to rights of persons

It might be thought, however, that we could escape this cultural relativity by appeal to *human* rights instead of the rights of *persons*. Could we not use a social contract for the purpose of deciding what rights human beings shall have with the result that persons would have only human rights along with human non-persons? If the committee members could be ignorant of their status as persons, then they might decide questions differently concerning such matters as abortion, for example. But if the idea is to suppose that the volunteers are not necessarily persons, this is to suppose a contradiction. If any social contract is to be made, the makers have to have the abilities of persons pertinent to the making of a contract; hence, they must be persons, not mere human beings. It is, after all, impossible to be ignorant of one's capacities exercised in making a contract while one is making the contract which concerns honouring those very capacities. Even the general knowledge of people and the human condition which those in the original position must have would assure them that they are not mere human beings who lack the capacities of persons. Acting in their self-interest they would give themselves special rights over and above any they would give to human non-persons.

Most of the rights human non-persons which would be granted by the volunteers in the original position would be granted because these humans will be persons or have been persons. Some will be granted because of our sympathy for those who resemble persons. To say, however, that human beings deserve different treatment from that accorded to other animals simply because they have human chromosomes,[10] for instance, seems rather arbitrary. Chimpanzees share much of our chromosomal makeup. They, however, seem to be unable to become persons who are self-creating. They apparently cannot choose what they want to desire, but act on desires they have by nature. If, however, they can be shown to have the capacities for free will and self-creation and other capacities above the threshold for persons, then their non-human character would be morally irrelevant. They would have the rights of persons. If they only come close to being persons, but are below the threshold, then they may acquire some rights by virtue of their resemblance to persons. As for human non-persons, while it may be useful to distinguish between human rights and rights of persons, the former are dependent on the latter. Furthermore, although human rights are possible given the rules fashioned by the volunteers, human non-persons could not have duties since they do not have the ability to do them.

On the other hand, we have already built into the fiction of the original position the idea that the volunteers might be fooled into thinking that it is possible that they would be merely potential persons once they were removed from the original position. They might be in some state of suspended animation, they are told, to live as persons in a future generation. To thicken the veil of ignorance, they might also be given to believe that the effects of being volunteers on this committee could result in their becoming merely human non-persons. I still think that common sense would guide them to give rights primarily to persons and only in a subsidiary way to non-persons. After all, there is less point to having advantages of which one could not be aware than to having advantages which one can enjoy as a person. As a mere human one could enjoy pleasure and suffer pain. Persons have, however, much wider scope for their enjoyment and suffering. People can anticipate a future life or an imminent death. Non-persons do not have the capacities needed for such anticipation.

Human rights would reflect the need for rules which can be followed by people with the sympathies we typically have. This is built into the instructions given to the volunteers. Considering our sympathies for human beings whether persons or not, we would make rules against cruelty to sentient beings. Not only would such rules be of the kind which people with typical sympathies can follow, they would be in the self-interest of the volunteers if only since what is done to sentient beings who are not people may very well be extended to people. It is also self-interest to avoid having one's own sympathies offended. People in the original position know they have human feeling. Even dead human bodies have rights since there is some behaviour towards them which would not be tolerated by people in the original position. In general, the volunteers would tend to disallow anything which undermines sympathy for those like the volunteers, whether like them only in outward form or in capacity to suffer. It is common sense to minimize cruelty in the community one must join.

So what should we do?

From the history of what we have believed ourselves to be, I have cobbled together a concept of a person. It is interdependent with social contracts of a moral, metaphysical, and epistemic kind. It is Byzantine in its complexity. It gives us initial answers to the questions "What is a person?" and "What makes a person at one time identical to a person at another time?" Supposing that I am right in my speculations as to which elements of our views about what we are can be consistently and fruitfully maintained, the question now arises, "What good does it do us?" The pragmatists discussed in chapter seven would want to know how such a concept would affect us if we were to take it up into our lives. That has, I hope, been partially answered by this chapter on applications. In general I would say this: as the secret to survival is knowing what to throw away and knowing what to keep,[11] one should develop one's essence, one's special capacities, to the fullest. One should cherish and preserve these individuating capacities. This is what lies behind the advice to be oneself and to live life to the fullest. One should also promote a world in which people can live well. Seen through Western eyes, this is only common sense.

Notes

Notes to Chapter One

1 G.E. Moore, *Principia Ethica* (Cambridge: Cambridge University Press, 1971), p. 13.
2 P.F. Strawson, *Individuals: An Essay in Descriptive Metaphysics* (London: Methuen, University Paperbacks, 1959).
3 Amelie Oksenberg Rorty, "A Literary Postscript: Characters, Persons, Selves and Individuals," in *The Identities of Persons* (Berkeley: University of California Press, 1976), p. 301.
4 Adolf Trendelenberg, "A Contribution to the History of the Word Person: A Posthumous Treatise by Adolf Trendelenberg," trans. Carl H. Haessler, *Monist* 20 (1910): 336-63, 353.
5 Ibid., p. 338.
6 Immanuel Kant, *Grundlegung der Metaphysik der Sitten* [Foundation of Metaphysical Ethics], 1785, quoted in Trendelenberg, "A Contribution," p. 337.
7 Max Black, "The Identity of Indiscernibles," *Mind* NS 61 (1952): 153-64.
8 Warren Bourgeois, "The Identity of Indiscernibles" (doctoral thesis, University of California, Irvine, 1979), chap. 1 and pp. 33-47.
9 Milton C. Nahm, *Selections from Early Greek Philosophy*, 3rd ed. (New York: Appleton-Century-Crofts, 1947), p. 91.
10 Abraham Kaplan, *The Conduct of Inquiry: Methodology for Behavioural Science* (New York: Chandler Publishing, 1964), p. 11.
11 See, for example, the discussion of Bernard Williams and Derek Parfit below.
12 Kathleen Wilkes, *Real People: Personal Identity without Thought Experiments* (Oxford: Clarendon Press, 1988), pp. 6-12.
13 Ayer attributes this *bon mot* and decisive objection to Ogden and Richards. See A.J. Ayer, "The Concept of a Person," in *The Concept of a Person and Other Essays* (London: Macmillan, 1963), pp. 82-128, p. 101. The general idea is that those who have sensations have minds; so materialists in denying their own minds deny they have sensations. Global anaesthesia deprives one of sensations.
14 Ludwig Wittgenstein, *Tractatus Logico-Philosophicus*, trans. D.F. Pears and B.F. MacGuiness (London: Routledge and Keagan Paul, 1961), 6.54, p. 74.
15 Wittgenstein, *Tractatus*, 5.64, 5.641, p. 58.
16 David Berlinski, *Philosophy: The Cutting Edge* (Port Washington, NY: Alfred Publishing, 1976), p. xi.
17 Environics is one such polling company.
18 Herbert Morris, "Persons and Punishment," *The Monist* 52:4 (October 1968), reprinted in Joel Feinberg, *Philosophy of Law*, 2d ed. (Belmont, CA: Wadsworth, 1975), p. 582.

Notes to Chapter Two

1 Solomon Asch, "The Psychology of Relativism," in *Social Psychology* (Englewood Cliffs, NJ: Prentice Hall, 1952), reprinted in Arthur J. Minton, *Philosophy: Paradox and Discovery* (New York: McGraw-Hill, 1976), pp. 215-22.
2 Harry G. Frankfurt, *The Importance of What We Care About* (Cambridge: Cambridge University Press, 1988), p. 81.

315

3   Ibid.

4   Richard Rorty, *Contingency, Irony, and Solidarity* (Cambridge: Cambridge University Press, 1989), p. 74.

5   Ibid., chap. 4.

6   Ibid., p. 44.

7   J.N. Findlay, *Values and Intentions* (New York: George Allen and Unwin, 1961), p. 399.

8   Bernard Williams, *Ethics and the Limits of Philosophy* (Cambridge, MA: Harvard University Press, 1985), p. 114.

9   W.D. Ross, *The Right and the Good* (Oxford: Oxford University Press, 1930), p. 141.

10   Steven G. Smith, *The Concept of the Spiritual: An Essay in First Philosophy* (Philadelphia: Temple University Press, 1988), pp. 63-64.

11   Ross, *The Right and the Good*, p. 141.

12   Rorty, *Contingency*, p. 44.

13   Aristotle, *De Anima*, in *The Basic Works of Aristotle*, ed. Richard McKeon (New York: Random House, 1941), pp. 535-606.

14   Blaise Pascal, quoted in Lyof N. Tolstoï, *Life* (London: Walter Scott, 1889), p. 3.

15   Daniel C. Dennett, *The Intentional Stance* (Cambridge, MA: MIT Press, 1989), p. 32.

16   Thomas Nagel, *The View from Nowhere* (Oxford: Oxford University Press, 1986), p. 16.

17   Rorty, *Contingency*, p. 44.

18   Thomas Nagel, *Mortal Questions* (Cambridge: Cambridge University Press, 1979), p. 13.

Notes to Chapter Three

1   David Ross, *Aristotle* (London: Methuen, 1949), pp. 240-41.

2   Kathleen Wilkes, *Real People: Personal Identity Without Thought Experiments* (Oxford: Oxford University Press, 1988).

3   Adolf Trendelenberg, "A Contribution to the History of the Word Person: A Posthumous Treatise By Adolf Trendelenberg," trans. Carl H. Haessler, *The Monist* 20 (1910): 338 and 342. But see also Arthur C. Danto, "Persons," *Encyclopaedia of Philosophy*, ed. Paul Edwards (New York: Macmillan, 1967), 6: 110-14. There is an exact cognate, *purusa*, in Sanskrit with all the ambiguity of our contemporary term "person."

4   Trendlenberg, *A Contribution*, p. 336.

5   Ross, *Aristotle*, pp. 240-41.

6   Samuel E. Stumpf, *Socrates to Sartre: A History of Philosophy*, 4th ed. (New York: McGraw-Hill, 1988), p. 11.

7   See, for instance, Milton C. Nahm, ed., *Selections from Early Greek Philosophy* (New York: Appleton, Century, Crofts, 1947), p. 91.

8   Erich Fromm and Ramón Xirau, *The Nature of Man* (New York: Collier, 1968), p. 44.

9   Heraclitus, in ibid., p. 43.

10   Stumpf, *Socrates to Sartre*, p. 13.

11   Roger Trigg, *Ideas of Human Nature* (Oxford: Basil Blackwell, 1988), p. 6.

12   Stumpf, *Socrates to Sartre*, p. 13.

13   Since I wrote this, I have heard of someone setting up in a mall and doing fairly well.

14   Stumpf, *Socrates to Sartre*, p. 32.

15   The following discussion is my way of reading Plato's *Republic* through the filter of my interest in persons. See Plato, *The Collected Dialogues*, ed. Edith Hamilton and Huntington Cairns (Princeton, NJ: Princeton University Press, 1961).

16   Wilkes, *Real People*, pp. 201-209.

[17] Ibid., p. 209.

[18] See Plato's dialogue *Parmenides*, in *The Collected Dialogues*, ed. Edith Hamilton and Huntington Cairns (Princeton, NJ: Princeton University Press, 1961).

[19] Aristotle, *De Anima*, in *The Basic Works of Aristotle*, ed. Richard McKeon (New York: Random House, 1941), pp. 535-606.

[20] Wilkes, *Real People*, p. 210.

[21] Ibid., p. 212.

[22] Aristotle, *De Anima*, iii 9 pp. 432a22ff. See Wilkes, *Real People*, p. 210.

[23] Trigg, *Ideas of Human Nature*, pp. 23-25.

[24] Ibid., pp. 25-28.

[25] Plato, *Republic*, 5, p. 456b.

[26] Aristotle, *De Anima*, p. 412b17.

[27] Trendelenberg, "A Contribution," p. 343.

[28] Stumpf, *Socrates to Sartre*, p. 119.

[29] Fromm and Xirau, *The Nature of Man*, p. 69.

[30] Stumpf, *Socrates to Sartre*, p. 129.

[31] Trendelenberg, "A Contribution," pp. 346 and 348.

[32] Stumpf, *Socrates to Sartre*, p. 129.

Notes to Chapter Four

[1] Samuel E. Stumpf, *Socrates to Sartre: A History of Philosophy*, 4th ed. (New York: McGraw-Hill, 1988), p. 135.

[2] Plato, *Republic*, 5, p. 456b.

[3] Stumpf, *Socrates to Sartre*, p. 170.

[4] Ibid., p. 171.

[5] Roger Trigg, *Ideas of Human Nature* (Oxford: Basil Blackwell, 1988), p. 40.

[6] Leslie Stevenson, *Seven Theories of Human Nature*, 2d ed. (Oxford: Oxford University Press, 1987), p. 45.

[7] Trigg, *Ideas of Human Nature*, p. 53.

[8] Ibid., p. 42.

[9] Ibid., p. 46.

[10] Erich Fromm and Ramón Xirau, *The Nature of Man* (New York: Collier, 1968), pp. 103-105.

[11] Adolf Trendelenberg, "A Contribution to the History of the Word Person: A Posthumous Treatise By Adolf Trendelenberg," trans. Carl H. Haessler, *The Monist* 20 (1910): 336-63, p. 352.

[12] Ibid., pp. 351-53.

[13] Ibid., p. 354.

Notes to Chapter Five

[1] Samuel E. Stumpf, *Socrates to Sartre: A History of Philosophy*, 4th ed. (New York: McGraw-Hill, 1988), p. 215.

[2] Erich Fromm and Ramón Xirau, *The Nature of Man* (New York: Collier, 1968), p. 108.

[3] Stumpf, *Socrates to Sartre*, p. 20.

[4] Fromm and Xirau, *The Nature of Man*, pp. 103-105.

[5] Stumpf, *Socrates to Sartre*, p. 214.

[6] Michel de Montaigne, *Apology for Raymond Sebond*, in Fromm and Xirau, *The Nature of Man*, p. 133.

[7] Stumpf, *Socrates to Sartre*, p. 218.

[8] Leonard Cohen, "Stories of the Street" (New York: Stranger Music, 1967).

[9] Stumpf, *Socrates to Sartre*, p. 227.

[10] René Descartes, *Discourse on Method*, trans. John Veitch, in *The Rationalists* (Garden City, NY: Dolphin Books, 1960), part iv, p. 63.

[11] René Descartes, *Meditations*, in *The Rationalists*, Meditation 2, p. 42.

[12] Descartes, *Discourse on Method*, in *The Rationalists*, part 4, p. 63.

[13] Peter Unger, *Identity Consciousness and Value* (Oxford: Oxford University Press, 1990), p. 15.

[14] Stumpf, *Socrates to Sartre*, p. 247.

[15] Descartes, *Meditations*, in *The Rationalists*, Meditation 1, pp. 115-17.

[16] Stumpf, *Socrates to Sartre*, p. 252.

[17] Fromm and Xirau, *The Nature of Man*, p. 140.

[18] Stumpf, *Socrates to Sartre*, pp. 249-53.

[19] Harold W. Noonan, *Personal Identity* (London: Routledge, 1989), p. 30.

[20] Derek Parfit, *Reasons and Persons* (Oxford: Oxford University Press, 1986, originally published 1984; reprinted [with corrections, new as paperback] 1985).

[21] Thomas Nagel, *The View from Nowhere* (Oxford: Oxford University Press, 1986).

[22] Noonan, *Personal Identity*, p. 30.

[23] John Locke, *An Essay Concerning Human Understanding*, II, xxvii.14. See also Noonan, *Personal Identity*, p. 33.

[24] Kathleen Wilkes, *Real People: Personal Identity Without Thought Experiments* (Oxford: Oxford University Press, 1988), pp. 169-71.

[25] Noonan, *Personal Identity*, p. 48.

[26] Stumpf, *Socrates to Sartre*, p. 269.

[27] John Perry, "The Problem of Personal Identity," in *Personal Identity* (Berkeley: University of California Press, 1975), p. 21.

[28] Locke, *An Essay Concerning Human Understanding*, II, xxvii.

[29] Noonan, *Personal Identity*, p. 53.

[30] Locke, *An Essay Concerning Human Understanding*, II, xxvii.20.

[31] Noonan, *Personal Identity*, p. 54.

[32] Locke, *An Essay Concerning Human Understanding*, II, xxvii. 6.

[33] Gary Wedeking, "Locke's Metaphysics of Personal Identity," *History of Philosophy Quarterly* 4 (January 1987): 17-31, p. 17. Professor Wedeking tells me he does not accept the persons-as-modes interpretation of Locke.

[34] Locke himself uses this way out in a related matter. See *Essay* II, xxvii.13.

Notes to Chapter Six

[1] George Berkeley, "Three Dialogues Between Hylas and Philonous," in *Berkeley: Essay, Principles, Dialogues with Selections from Other Writings*, ed. Mary W. Calkins .(New York: Charles Scribner's Sons, 1937).

[2] Harold W. Noonan, *Personal Identity* (London: Routledge, 1989), pp. 63-64.

[3] G.W. Leibniz, *New Essays on Human Understanding*, trans. and ed. Peter Remnant and Jonathan Bennett (Cambridge: Cambridge University Press, 1981).

[4] Ralph Walker, "Leibniz's Philosophy of Mind," in *The Oxford Companion to the Mind*, ed. Richard Gregory (Oxford: Oxford University Press, 1987), p. 433.

[5] Noonan, *Personal Identity*, p. 62.

[6] Walker, *Leibniz' Philosophy*, p. 433.

[7] Noonan, *Personal Identity*, p. 62.

[8] Ibid., p. 61.

9 Kathleen Wilkes, *Real People: Personal Identity Without Thought Experiments* (Oxford: Oxford University Press, 1988), p. 105.

10 Noonan, *Personal Identity*, pp. 63-64.

11 Warren Bourgeois, "The Identity of Indiscernibles" (doctoral thesis, University of California, Irvine, 1979), chap. 1.

12 Noonan, *Personal Identity*, p. 65.

13 Bourgeois, "The Identity of Indiscernibles," pp. 13-17.

14 John Perry, "The Problem of Personal Identity," in *Personal Identity* (Berkeley: University of California Press, 1975), p. 15.

15 Noonan, *Personal Identity*, pp. 66-67.

16 David Hume, *A Treatise of Human Nature*, ed. L. A. Selby-Bigge (Oxford: Oxford University Press, 1973), Book I, Part IV, section vi, p. 251.

Notes to Chapter Seven

1 Samuel E. Stumpf, *Socrates to Sartre: A History of Philosophy*, 4th ed. (New York: McGraw-Hill, 1988), p. 293.

2 Immanuel Kant, *Groundwork of the Metaphysic of Morals*, trans. H.J. Paton (New York: Harper & Row, 1964), pp. 32-33.

3 Immanuel Kant, *Critique of Pure Reason*, trans. Norman Kemp Smith (New York: St. Martin's Press, 1965), p. 342 A363.

4 S. Korner, *Kant* (Harmondsworth, England: Pelican Books, 1955), p. 67.

5 Kant, *Critique of Pure Reason*, pp. 469-79 B568-B586.

6 Stumpf, *Socrates to Sartre*, pp. 299-319.

7 Kant, *Groundwork of the Metaphysic of Morals*, p. 22.

8 Korner, *Kant*, p. 165.

9 Stumpf, *Socrates to Sartre*, p. 328.

10 G.W.F. Hegel, *The Phenomenology of Mind*, trans. J.B. Baillie (New York: Harper Colophon Books, 1967), p. 133.

11 Stumpf, *Socrates to Sartre*, p. 333.

12 G.W.F. Hegel, *The Philosophy of History*, trans. J. Sibree (New York: Dover Publications, 1956), p. 70.

13 Stumpf, *Socrates to Sartre*, p. 337.

14 Walter Kaufmann, *Hegel: A Reinterpretation* (Notre Dame: University of Notre Dame Press, 1965), p. 250.

15 Hegel, *The Philosophy of History*, p. 56.

16 Richard L. Gregory, "Hegel," in *The Oxford Companion to the Mind*, ed. Richard L. Gregory (Oxford: Oxford University Press, 1987), p. 308.

17 Stumpf, *Socrates to Sartre*, p. 341.

18 Vincent Barry, *Philosophy: A Text With Readings* (Belmont, CA: Wadsworth, 1980), p. 159.

19 Peter Singer, *Practical Ethics* (Cambridge: Cambridge University Press, 1979), pp. 49-50.

20 Roger Trigg, *Ideas of Human Nature: An Historical Introduction* (Oxford: Basil Blackwell, 1988), pp. 108-109.

21 Karl Marx, quoted in Leslie Stevenson, *Seven Theories of Human Nature*, 2nd ed. (Oxford: Oxford University Press, 1987), p. 62.

22 Barry, *Philosophy*, p. 49.

23 Stumpf, *Socrates to Sartre*, p. 442.

24 Barry, *Philosophy*, p. 198.

25 Stumpf, *Socrates to Sartre*, p. 479.

26 Alasdair MacIntyre, "Existentialism," in *The Encyclopedia of Philosophy* (London: Macmillan and New York: The Free Press, 1967), Vol. 3, pp. 147-54, p. 148.

27 Thomas Nagel, *Mortal Questions* (Cambridge: Cambridge University Press, 1979), p. 15.

28 Stumpf, *Socrates to Sartre*, p. 389.

29 Barry, *Philosophy*, p. 396.

30 Stumpf, *Socrates to Sartre*, p. 422.

31 Murray G. Murphey, "Peirce, Charles Sanders," in *The Encyclopedia of Philosophy* (London: Macmillan and New York: The Free Press, 1967), 6: 70-78, pp. 73-74.

32 Stumpf, *Socrates to Sartre*, p. 420.

33 William James, "The Will to Believe," an address to the Philosophical Club of Yale and Brown Universities, first published in *New World* (1896).

34 John Dewey, "The Nature of Moral Philosophy," in *The Moral Writings of John Dewey*, ed. James Gounlock (New York: Hafner Press, 1976), pp. 1-22.

35 William James, *Pragmatism and Other Essays* (New York: Washington Square Press, 1963), p. 193.

Notes to Chapter Eight

1 Samuel E. Stumpf, *Socrates to Sartre: A History of Philosophy*, 4th ed. (New York: McGraw-Hill, 1988), p. 397.

2 T.A. Goudge, "Bergson, Henri," in *The Encyclopedia of Philosophy* (London: Macmillan and New York: The Free Press, 1967), 2: 287-94, pp. 288, 295.

3 Stumpf, *Socrates to Sartre*, p. 404.

4 Alfred North Whitehead, *Process and Reality* (New York: Free Press, 1969), p. 39.

5 Stumpf, *Socrates to Sartre*, p. 404.

6 Ibid., p. 408.

7 Alfred North Whitehead, *Symbolism: Its Meaning and Effect* (New York: G.P. Putnam's Sons, 1959), p. 20.

8 David Berlinski, *Philosophy: The Cutting Edge* (Port Washington, NY: Alfred Publishing, 1976), p. xi.

9 Leslie Stevenson, *Seven Theories of Human Nature*, 2d ed (Oxford: Oxford University Press, 1987), p. 99.

10 Stumpf, *Socrates to Sartre*, p. 486.

11 Edmund Husserl, *Ideas: General Introduction to Pure Phenomenology* (London: Collier Macmillan, 1962), pp. 37-42.

12 Stumpf, *Socrates to Sartre*, p. 491.

13 Georges Thines, "Husserl," in *The Oxford Companion to the Mind*, ed. Richard L. Gregory (Oxford: Oxford University Press, 1987), pp. 326-27.

14 Husserl, *Ideas*, p. 161.

15 Stumpf, *Socrates to Sartre*, p. 499.

16 Ibid., p. 500.

17 Martin Heidegger, *Being and Time* (New York: Harper & Row, 1962), pp. 78-90.

18 Victor Farias, *Heidegger and Nazism* (Philadelphia: Temple University Press, 1990).

19 Jean-Paul Sartre, *Existentialism and Humanism*, trans. Philip Mairet (London: Methuen, 1949), p. 85.

20 Ibid., p. 85.

21 Leslie Stevenson, *Seven Theories of Human Nature*, 2d ed (Oxford: Oxford University Press, 1987), p. 109.

22 Jean-Paul Sartre, *Being and Nothingness: A Phenomenological Essay on Ontology*, trans. Hazel E. Barnes (New York: Washington Square Press, 1966).

23 Stevenson, *Seven Theories*, pp. 100-101.

24 Ibid., pp. 101-102.

25 Richard Rorty, *Contingency, Irony, and Solidarity* (Cambridge: Cambridge University Press), 1989, p. 44.

Notes to Chapter Nine

1 Samuel E. Stumpf, *Socrates to Sartre: A History of Philosophy*, 4th ed. (New York: McGraw-Hill, 1988), p. 446.

2 Bertrand Russell, *An Outline of Philosophy* (London: George Allen and Unwin, 1970), p. 312.

3 Ibid., p. 83.

4 Ibid., p. 387.

5 Bertrand Russell, *An Inquiry into Meaning and Truth* (Baltimore, MD: Penguin Books, 1962), p. 93.

6 Bertrand Russell, *Human Knowledge: Its Scope and Limits* (London: George Allen and Unwin, 1948), p. 247.

7 Bertrand Russell, *The Problems of Philosophy* (Oxford: Oxford University Press, 1959), p. 4.

8 David F. Pears, "Russell's Philosophy of Mind: Dualism," in *The Oxford Companion to the Mind*, ed. Richard L. Gregory (Oxford: Oxford University Press, 1987), pp. 688-90, p. 689.

9 Willard V. Quine, "Russell's Ontological Development," in *Essays on Bertrand Russell*, ed. E.D. Klemke (Chicago: University of Illinois Press, 1970), pp. 3-14, pp. 12-13.

10 David F. Pears, "Russell's Philosophy of Mind: Neutral Monism," in *The Oxford Companion to the Mind*, ed. Richard L. Gregory (Oxford: Oxford University Press, 1987), pp. 690-91, p. 690.

11 Quine, "Russell's Ontological Development," p. 14.

12 Pears, "Russell's Philosophy of Mind: Neutral Monism," p. 690.

13 Bertrand Russell, "Science and Ethics," in *Philosophy: Paradox and Discovery*, ed. Arthur J. Minton (New York: McGraw-Hill, 1976), p. 229.

14 Bertrand Russell, quoted in Charles W. Morris, *Six Theories of Mind* (Chicago: University. of Chicago Press, 1932), p. 136.

15 Russell, *Inquiry into Meaning and Truth*, p. 322.

16 Ludwig Wittgenstein, *Tractatus Logico-Philosophicus*, trans. D.F. Pears and B.F. MacGuinness (London: Routledge and Keagan Paul, 1961), 6.54.

17 Russell, *Inquiry into Meaning and Truth*, p. 322.

18 In the introduction to Wittgenstein, *Tractatus*, p. ix.

19 Wittgenstein, *Tractatus*, 5.631-5.632.

20 Ludwig Wittgenstein, *Philosophical Investigations*, trans. G.E.M. Anscombe (Oxford: Basil Blackwell, 1976).

21 Ludwig Wittgenstein, *The Blue and Brown Books* (New York: Harper Colophon Books, 1958).

22 Ludwig Wittgenstein, *Philosophical Remarks*, ed. Rush Rhees, trans. Raymond Hargreaves and Roger White (Oxford: Basil Blackwell, 1975), pp. 88-89.

23 Wittgenstein, *Blue Book*, pp. 61-62.

24 Wittgenstein, *Philosophical Investigations*, 404b.

25 Kathleen Wilkes, *Real People: Personal Identity Without Thought Experiments* (Oxford: Oxford University Press, 1988).

[26] John Passmore, "Logical Positivism," in *The Encyclopedia of Philosophy* (London: Macmillan and New York: The Free Press, 1967), 5: 52-57, p. 52.

[27] Gilbert Ryle, *The Concept of Mind* (Harmondsworth, Middlesex: Penguin Books, 1963).

Notes to Chapter Ten

[1] P.F. Strawson, *Individuals: An Essay in Descriptive Metaphysics* (London: Methuen, 1959).

[2] Kathleen Wilkes, *Real People: Personal Identity Without Thought Experiments* (Oxford: Oxford University Press, 1988).

[3] Strawson, *Individuals*, pp. 90-94.

[4] Ludwig Wittgenstein, *Tractatus Logico-Philosophicus*, trans. D.F. Pears and B.F. MacGuinness (London: Routledge and Keagan Paul, 1961), p. 74, paragraph 7.

[5] Strawson, *Individuals*, p. 99.

[6] Thomas Hobbes, *Leviathan* (London: J.M. Dent and Sons, 1914).

[7] Strawson, *Individuals*, pp. 113-15.

[8] Wilkes, *Real People*, pp. 200-209.

[9] Strawson, *Individuals*, p. 115.

[10] Alfred J. Ayer, "The Concept of a Person," in *The Concept of a Person and Other Essays* (London: Macmillan, 1963), pp. 82-128, p. 82.

[11] Strawson, *Individuals*, p. 94.

[12] Ayer, "The Concept of a Person," p. 117.

[13] Willard V. Quine, "Two Dogmas of Empiricism," in *From a Logical Point of View: Logico-philosophical Essays* (New York: Harper & Row, 1953), pp. 20-46. See also Samuel E. Stumpf, *Socrates to Sartre: A History of Philosophy*, 4th ed. (New York: McGraw-Hill, 1988), pp. 458-59.

[14] Willard V. Quine, *The Roots of Reference: The Paul Carus Lectures* (Lasalle, IL: Open Court, 1973), p. 9.

[15] Antony Flew (editorial consultant), *A Dictionary of Philosophy* (London: Pan Books, 1979), p. 250.

[16] Quine, *The Roots of Reference*, p. 35.

[17] Willard V. Quine, "Identity, Ostension and Hypostasis," in *From a Logical Point of View*, pp. 65-69, p. 65.

[18] Harold W. Noonan, *Personal Identity* (London: Routledge, 1989), p. 107.

[19] Willard V. Quine, *Theories and Things* (Cambridge, MA: Harvard University Press, 1981), p. 12.

[20] Ibid. See also Noonan, *Personal Identity*, p. 107.

[21] Strawson, *Individuals*, pp. 132-33.

Notes to Chapter Eleven

[1] David Wiggins, *Identity and Spatio-temporal Continuity* (Oxford: Basil Blackwell, 1967). See also *Sameness and Substance* (Oxford: Basil Blackwell, 1980).

[2] Wiggins, *Sameness*, p. 183.

[3] Wiggins, *Identity*, p. 47.

[4] Wiggins, *Sameness*, p. 187.

[5] Wiggins, *Identity*, p. 41.

[6] Aristotle, quoted in Wiggins, *Identity* p. 47.

[7] Wiggins, *Identity*, pp. 47-48.

[8] Wiggins, *Sameness*, pp. 151-53.

9 Depending on what one counts as synthetic, this can be done now. It is medically feasible to take an ovum from an aborted fetus and fertilize it with sperm preserved from a dead male human being. The fertilized ovum can then be implanted in a woman's womb and brought to term. The resulting infant may grow to be an adult.

10 Bernard Williams, *Ethics and the Limits of Philosophy* (Cambridge, MA: Harvard University Press, 1985), p. 114.

11 Bernard Williams, "Personal Identity and Individuation," in *Problems of the Self* (Cambridge: Cambridge University Press, 1973), pp. 1-18, p. 1.

12 Kathleen Wilkes, *Real People: Personal Identity Without Thought Experiments* (Oxford: Oxford University Press, 1988), pp. 185-86.

13 Williams, "Personal Identity and Individuation," p. 17, n. 9.

14 Charles Rycroft, "Dissociation Of The Personality," in *The Oxford Companion to the Mind*, ed. Richard L. Gregory (Oxford: Oxford University Press, 1987), pp. 197-98, p. 197.

15 Williams, "Personal Identity and Individuation," p. 18.

16 Bernard Williams, "Are Persons Bodies?" in *Problems of the Self*, pp. 64-81, pp. 64-78.

17 Williams, *Ethics and the Limits of Philosophy*, p. 114.

18 Williams, "Are Persons Bodies?" p. 76.

Notes to Chapter Twelve

1 Robert Nozick, *Philosophical Explanations* (Cambridge, MA: Harvard University Press, 1981), p. 114.

2 Nozick conceives of the continuer and predecessor relations as quite different from equivalence relations which must be symmetric, reflexive, and transitive. These relations have none of those properties.

3 Ibid., p. 42. See also Derek Parfit, *Reasons and Persons* (Oxford: Oxford University Press, 1986, originally published 1984; reprinted [with corrections, new as paperback] 1985), pp. 200-201.

4 Nozick, *Philosophical Explanations*, p. 107.

Notes to Chapter Thirteen

1 Derek Parfit, *Reasons and Persons* (Oxford: Oxford University Press, 1986, originally published 1984; reprinted [with corrections, new as paperback] 1985), p. 217.

2 Perhaps what Parfit says can be compared to the following mathematical convention: a set has members, but we cannot say that a set is its members; a set, moreover, is distinct from its members, but cannot exist separately from them. Experiences, on this way of thinking, are just members of a set including physical events, character, and other items. It is the set which is the person. We could, however, describe the things in the set without unifying them, by convention, in such sets and calling them "persons."

3 Briefly put, Parfit wants personal identity to be a transitive relation.

4 Derek Parfit, "Personal Identity," *The Philosophical Review* 80, 1 (January 1971), reprinted in *Personal Identity*, ed. John Perry (Berkeley: University of California Press, 1975), pp. 199-226, p. 208.

5 Parfit, *Reasons and Persons*, p. 206.

6 See above, chapter six.

7 Parfit, *Reasons and Persons*, p. 206.

8 John Perry, "The Importance of Being Identical," in *The Identities of Persons*, ed. Amelie O. Rorty (Berkeley: University of California Press, 1976), pp. 67-90, p. 84.

9 Parfit, *Reasons and Persons* p. 241.

[10] P. Strawson, *Individuals: An Essay in Descriptive Metaphysics* (London: Methuen, 1959), p. 133.

[11] Derek Parfit, *Reasons and Persons* (Oxford: Oxford University Press, 1986, originally published 1984; reprinted [with corrections, new as paperback] 1985), p. 247.

[12] Colwyn Trevarthen, "Split Brain and the Mind," in *The Oxford Companion to the Mind*, ed. Richard L. Gregory (Oxford: Oxford University Press, 1987), pp. 741-46, p. 746.

[13] Parfit, *Reasons and Persons*, p. 217.

[14] Kathleen Wilkes, *Real People* (Oxford: Oxford University Press, 1988), chap. 5.

[15] Comparing the works cited for Wilkes and Parfit will show that Wilkes successfully deflates other attempts by Parfit to use real-world examples as exotic examples of division paralleling the teletransportation case.

Notes to Chapter Fourteen

[1] Thomas Nagel, *The View from Nowhere* (Oxford: Oxford University Press, 1986), p. 3.

[2] Charles W. Morris, *Six Theories of Mind* (Chicago: University of Chicago Press, 1932), p. 245.

[3] Nagel, *View*, p. 28.

[4] Hilary Putnam, *Representation and Reality* (Cambridge, MA: MIT Press, 1989), p. xi.

[5] Nagel, *View*, p. 27.

[6] See, for example, David Lewis, "Survival and Identity," and John Perry, "The Importance of Being Identical," in *The Identities of Persons*, ed. Amelie O. Rorty (Berkeley: University of California Press, 1976), pp. 17-40 and pp. 67-90 respectively.

[7] Nagel, *View*, p. 17.

[8] Abraham Kaplan, *The Conduct of Inquiry: Methodology for Behavioural Science* (New York: Chandler Publishing, 1964), p. 11.

[9] Nagel, *View*, pp. 49-50.

[10] Harold W. Noonan, *Personal Identity* (London: Routledge, 1989), p. 16.

[11] Nagel, *View*, p. 44.

[12] Ibid., p. 46. See also Saul A. Kripke, *Naming and Necessity* (Cambridge, MA: Harvard University Press, 1972), p. 155n.

[13] Nagel, *View*, p. 46.

[14] Bernard Williams, "Personal Identity And Individuation," in *Problems of the Self* (Cambridge: Cambridge University Press, 1973), p. 14.

[15] Nagel, *View*, p. 66.

[16] Thomas Nagel, "The Absurd," in *Mortal Questions* (Cambridge: Cambridge University Press, 1979), pp. 11-23.

Notes to Chapter Fifteen

[1] Michael Carrithers, Steven Collins, and Steven Lukes, eds., *The Category of the Person: Anthropology, Philosophy, History* (Cambridge: Cambridge University Press, 1985), p. 13.

[2] Clifford Geertz, *Local Knowledge: Essays in Interpretive Anthropology* (New York: Basic Books, 1983), p. 59.

[3] Kathleen Wilkes, *Real People: Personal Identity Without Thought Experiments* (Oxford: Clarendon Press, 1988), p. 170.

[4] See chapter eleven.

[5] David Wiggins, *Sameness and Substance* (Oxford: Basil Blackwell, 1980), p. 160.

6 Gauche as it is to explain a joke, I must say for those of my readers who are not trained in philosophy that G.E. Moore was a British philosopher who championed common sense.

7 See above, chapter ten

8 See above, chapter eight.

9 Aristotle, *Nicomachean Ethics*, trans. W.D. Ross (Oxford: Oxford University Press), 1925.

10 Adolf Trendelenberg, "A Contribution to the History of the Word Person: A Posthumous Treatise By Adolf Trendelenberg," trans. Carl H. Haessler, *The Monist* 20 (1910): 336-63.

11 William James, "The Will to Believe," an Address to the Philosophical Club of Yale and Brown Universities, in *Reason and Responsibility*, ed. J. Feinberg (Belmont, CA: Wadsworth, 1989), pp. 91-98; first published in *New World*, 1896.

12 Blaise Pascal, *Penseés: Notes on Religion and Other Subjects*, ed. Louis Lafuma, trans. John Warrington (London: J.M. Dent and Sons, 1960).

Notes to Chapter Sixteen

1 Derek Parfit, *Reasons and Persons* (Oxford: Oxford University Press, 1986, originally published 1984; reprinted [with corrections, new as paperback] 1985), pp. 254ff.

2 Kathleen Wilkes, *Real People: Personal Identity Without Thought Experiments* (Oxford: Clarendon Press, 1988), pp. 38-39 and passim.

3 See above, chapter fifteen.

4 Jonathan Glover, *I: The Philosophy and Psychology of Personal Identity* (London: Penguin Books, 1988), p. 65.

5 W.D. Ross, *The Right and the Good* (Oxford: Clarendon Press, 1930), p. 141.

6 See the discussion of Steven G. Smith's concept of spirit in chapter two, above.

7 See above, chapter twelve.

8 Wilkes, *Real People*, p. 210.

9 Adolf Trendelenberg, "A Contribution to the History of the Word Person: A Posthu-mous Treatise By Adolf Trendelenberg," trans. Carl H. Haessler, The Monist 20 (1910): 338.

10 Wilkes, *Real People*, p. 213.

11 See above, chapter eleven.

12 Wilkes, *Real People*, p. 210.

13 Parfit, *Reasons and Persons*, pp. 206, 216.

14 Wilkes, *Real People*, p. 105.

15 Note that a fetus is not a person on this view but may have special worth because of the potential to become a person.

16 Trendelenberg, "A Contribution."

17 David Wiggins, *Sameness and Substance* (Oxford: Basil Blackwell, 1980), p. 187. See also chapter eleven, above.

18 See chapter fifteen, above.

19 Trendelenberg, "A Contribution," p. 356.

20 Ibid., p. 223.

Notes to Chapter Seventeen

1 John Rawls, *A Theory of Justice* (Cambridge, MA: Harvard University Press, 1971). Rawls intends to deal only with large social questions, not interpersonal moral matters, so he might disagree with the positions I take on the basis of social-contract theory. Indeed, even my positions on social questions may depart from his, though my survey owes a great debt to Rawls.

2 Peter Singer, *Practical Ethics* (Cambridge: Cambridge University Press, 1979), pp. 128-30.

3 Jane English, "Abortion and the Concept of a Person," *The Canadian Journal of Philosophy* 5, 2 (October 1970); reprinted in *Biomedical Ethics*, ed. T.A. Mappes and J.S. Zembaty (New York: McGraw-Hill, 1986), pp. 479-80. English disagrees with my theses about the importance of the concept of a person, but we concur on the importance of the social contract and of sympathy.

4 English, "Abortion."

5 For an interesting discussion of the concept of the differences between future interests and full rights, see Herbert Morris, "Persons and Punishment," *The Monist* 52, 4 (October 1968),

6 Southwestern India is an example in favour of this thesis, as are most developed nations.

7 Robert E. Goodin, "Ethical Principles for Environmental Protection," in *Contemporary Moral Issues*, ed. Wesley Cragg, 3rd ed. (Toronto: McGraw-Hill Ryerson, 1992), pp. 323-35.

8 A *locus classicus* of this move is Bernard Williams, *Morality: An Introduction to Ethics* (New York: Harper & Row, 1972), pp. 20-26.

9 Utilitarians try to maximize utility as the way of doing what is morally right. Utility is pleasure for the hedonistic utilitarians. Act utilitarians judge each action individually, while rule utilitarians follow a set of rules which they believe will maximize utility.

10 Sheila and George Grant, "Abortion and Rights, " in Cragg, *Contemporary Moral Issues*, pp. 68-74, p. 70.

11 D. Schlitz, *The Gambler*, Elektra/Asylum Records, ASCAP, 1980.

Bibliography

Aristotle, *De Anima*. In *The Basic Works of Aristotle*. Edited by Richard McKeon, pp. 535-606. New York: Random House, 1941.

_____. *Nicomachean Ethics*. Translated by W.D. Ross. Oxford: Oxford University Press, 1925.

Asch, Solomon. "The Psychology of Relativism." In *Social Psychology*. Englewood Cliffs, NJ: Prentice Hall, 1952. Reprinted in *Philosophy: Paradox and Discovery*. Edited by Arthur J. Minton, pp. 215-22. New York: McGraw-Hill, 1976.

Ayer, A.J. "The Concept of a Person." In *The Concept of a Person and Other Essays*. London: Macmillan, 1963.

Barry, Vincent. *Philosophy: A Text With Readings*. Belmont, CA: Wadsworth, 1980.

Berkeley, George. "Three Dialogues Between Hylas and Philonous." In *Berkeley: Essay, Principles, Dialogues with Selections from Other Writings*. Edited by Mary W. Calkins. New York: Charles Scribner's Sons, 1937.

Berlinski, David. *Philosophy: The Cutting Edge*. Port Washington, NY: Alfred Publishing, 1976.

Black, Max. "The Identity of Indiscernibles." *Mind* NS 61 (1952): 153-64.

Bourgeois, Warren. "The Identity of Indiscernibles." Doctoral thesis, University of California, Irvine, 1979.

Carrithers, Michael; Steven Collins, and Steven Lukes, eds. *The Category of the Person: Anthropology, Philosophy, History*. Cambridge: Cambridge University Press, 1985.

Churchland, Patricia S. and Paul M. "Could a Machine Think?" *Scientific American* (January 1990), pp. 32-37.

Danto, Arthur C. "Persons." In *The Encyclopedia of Philosophy*. Vol. 6, pp. 110-14. London: Macmillan and New York: The Free Press, 1967.

Dennett, Daniel C. *The Intentional Stance*. Cambridge, MA: MIT Press, 1989.

Descartes, René. *Discourse on Method*. Translated by John Veitch. In *The Rationalists*. Garden City, NY: Dolphin Books, 1960.

_____. *Meditations*. Translated by John Veitch. In *The Rationalists*. Garden City, NY: Dolphin Books, 1960.

Deutsch, Eliot. *Personhood, Creativity, and Freedom*. Honolulu: University of Hawaii Press, 1982.

Dewey, John. "The Nature of Moral Philosophy." In *The Moral Writings of John Dewey*. Edited by James Gounlock. New York: Hafner Press, 1976.

English, Jane. "Abortion and the Concept of a Person." *The Canadian Journal of Philosophy* 5, 2 (October 1970). Reprinted in *Biomedical Ethics*. Edited by T.A. Mappes and J.S. Zembaty, pp. 479-80. New York: McGraw-Hill, 1986.

Farias, Victor. *Heidegger and Nazism*. Philadelphia: Temple University Press, 1990.

Findlay, J.N. *Values and Intentions*. New York: George Allen and Unwin, 1961.

Flew, Antony, editorial consultant. *A Dictionary of Philosophy.* London: Pan Books, 1979.

Frankfurt, Harry G. *The Importance of What We Care About.* Cambridge: Cambridge University Press, 1988.

Fromm, Erich, and Ramón Xirau. *The Nature of Man.* New York: Collier, 1968.

Geertz, Clifford. *Local Knowledge: Essays in Interpretive Anthropology.* New York: Basic Books, 1983.

Glover, Jonathan. *I: The Philosophy and Psychology of Personal Identity.* London: Penguin Books, 1988.

Goodin, Robert E. "Ethical Principles for Environmental Protection." In *Contemporary Moral Issues.* Edited by Wesley Cragg, pp. 323-35. 3rd ed. Toronto: McGraw-Hill Ryerson, 1992.

Goudge, T.A. "Bergson, Henri." In *The Encyclopedia of Philosophy.* Vol. 3, pp. 287-94. London: Macmillan and New York: The Free Press, 1967.

Grant, Sheila and George. "Abortion and Rights." In *Contemporary Moral Issues.* Edited by Wesley Cragg, pp. 68-74. 3rd ed. Toronto: McGraw-Hill Ryerson, 1992.

Gregory, Richard L. "Hegel." In *The Oxford Companion to the Mind.* Edited by Richard L. Gregory. Oxford: Oxford University Press, 1987.

Hegel, G.W.F. *The Phenomenology of Mind.* Translated by J.B. Baillie. New York: Harper Colophon Books, 1967.

Heidegger, Martin. *Being and Time.* New York: Harper & Row, 1962.

Hobbes, Thomas. *Leviathan.* London: J.M. Dent and Sons, 1914.

Hume, David. *A Treatise of Human Nature.* Edited by Selby-Bigge. Oxford: Oxford University Press, 1973.

Husserl, Edmund. *Ideas: General Introduction to Pure Phenomenology.* London: Collier Macmillan, 1962.

James, William. "The Will to Believe." An Address to the Philosophical Club of Yale and Brown Universities. In *Reason and Responsibility.* Edited by J. Feinberg, pp. 91-98. Belmont, CA: Wadsworth, 1989. First published in *New World* (1896).

_____. *Pragmatism and Other Essays.* New York: Washington Square Press, 1963.

Kant, Immanuel. *Groundwork of the Metaphysic of Morals.* Translated by H.J. Paton. New York: Harper & Row, 1964.

_____. *Critique of Pure Reason.* Translated by Norman Kemp Smith. New York: St. Martin's Press, 1965.

Kaplan, Abraham. *The Conduct of Inquiry: Methodology for Behavioural Science.* New York: Chandler Publishing, 1964.

Kaufmann, Walter. *Hegel: A Reinterpretation.* Notre Dame: University of Notre Dame Press, 1965.

Korner, S. *Kant.* Harmondsworth, England: Pelican Books, 1955.

Kripke, Saul. A. *Naming and Necessity.* Cambridge, MA: Harvard University Press, 1972.

Leibniz, G.W. *New Essays on Human Understanding.* Translated and edited by Peter Remnant and Jonathan Bennett. Cambridge: Cambridge University Press, 1981.

Lewis, David. "Survival and Identity." In *The Identities of Persons*. Edited by Amelie O. Rorty, pp. 17-40. Berkeley: University of California Press, 1976.

Locke, John. *An Essay Concerning Human Understanding*. London: J.M. Dent and Sons, 1961.

MacIntyre, Alasdair. "Existentialism." In *The Encyclopedia of Philosophy*. Vol. 3, pp. 147-54. London: Macmillan and New York: The Free Press, 1967.

Minton, Arthur J. *Philosophy: Paradox and Discovery*. New York: McGraw-Hill, 1976.

Montaigne, Michel de. *Apology for Raymond Sebond*. In Fromm and Xirau, *The Nature of Man*.

Moore, G.E. *Principia Ethica*. Cambridge: Cambridge University Press, 1971.

Morris, Charles W. *Six Theories of Mind*. Chicago: University of Chicago Press, 1932.

Morris, Herbert. "Persons and Punishment." *The Monist* 52, 4 (October 1968). Reprinted in Joel Feinberg, *Philosophy of Law*. 2d ed. Belmont CA: Wadsworth, 1975.

Morton, Adam. "Why There Is No Concept of the Person." In *The Person and the Human Mind: Issues in Ancient and Modern Philosophy*. Edited by Christopher Gill, pp. 39-68. Oxford: Clarendon Press, 1990.

Murphey, Murray G. "Peirce, Charles Sanders." In *The Encyclopedia of Philosophy*. Vol. 6, pp. 70-78. London: Macmillan and New York: The Free Press, 1967.

Nagel, Thomas. "Brain Bisection and the Unity of Consciousness." In *Personal Identity*. Edited by John Perry, pp. 227-46. Berkeley, CA: University of California Press, 1975.

_____. *Mortal Questions*. Cambridge: Cambridge University Press, 1979.

_____. "The Absurd." In *Mortal Questions*. Cambridge: Cambridge University Press, 1979, pp. 11-23.

_____. *The View from Nowhere*. Oxford: Oxford University Press, 1986.

Nahm, Milton C. *Selections from Early Greek Philosophy*. New York: Appleton, Century, Crofts, 1947.

Noonan, Harold W. *Personal Identity*. London: Routledge, 1989.

Nozick, Robert. *Philosophical Explanations*. Cambridge, MA: Harvard University Press, 1981.

Parfit, Derek. "Personal Identity." *The Philosophical Review* 80, 1 (January 1971). Reprinted in *Personal Identity*. Edited by John Perry, pp. 199-226. Berkeley: University of California Press, 1975.

_____. *Reasons and Persons*. Oxford: Oxford University Press, 1986. Originally published 1984. Reprinted [with corrections, new as paperback] 1985.

Pascal, Blaise. *Penseés: Notes on Religion and Other Subjects*. Edited by Louis Lafuma. Translated by John Warrington. London: J.M. Dent and Sons, 1960.

Passmore, John. "Logical Positivism." In *The Encyclopedia of Philosophy*. Vol. 5, pp. 52-57. London: Macmillan and New York: The Free Press, 1967.

Pears, David F. "Russell's Philosophy of Mind: Dualism." In *The Oxford Companion to the Mind*. Edited by Richard L. Gregory, pp. 688-90. Oxford: Oxford University Press, 1987.

_____. "Russell's Philosophy of Mind: Neutral Monism." In *The Oxford Companion to the Mind*. Edited by Richard L. Gregory, pp. 690-91. Oxford: Oxford University Press, 1987.

Perry, John. "The Problem of Personal Identity." In *Personal Identity*. Berkeley: University of California Press, 1975.

_____. "The Importance of Being Identical." In *The Identities of Persons*. Edited by Amelie O. Rorty. Berkeley: University of California Press, 1976.

Plato. *The Collected Dialogues*. Edited by Edith Hamilton and Huntington Cairns. Princeton, NJ: Princeton University Press, 1961.

Puccetti, R. "Brain Bisection and Personal Identity." *British Journal for the Philosophy of Science* 24: 339-55.

Putnam, Hilary. *Representation and Reality*. Cambridge, MA: MIT Press, 1989.

Quine, Willard V. "Two Dogmas of Empiricism." In *From a Logical Point of View: Logico-philosophical Essays*, pp. 20-46. New York: Harper & Row, 1953.

_____. "Identity, Ostension and Hypostasis." In *From a Logical Point of View: Logico-philosophical Essays*, pp. 65-69. New York: Harper & Row, 1953.

_____. "Russell's Ontological Development." In *Essays on Bertrand Russell*. Edited by E.D. Klemke, pp. 3-14. Chicago: University of Illinois Press, 1970.

_____. *The Roots of Reference: The Paul Carus Lectures*. Lasalle, IL: Open Court Publishing, 1973.

_____. *Theories and Things*. Cambridge, MA: Harvard University Press, 1981.

Rawls, John. *A Theory of Justice*. Cambridge, MA: Harvard University Press, 1971.

Rorty, Amelie Oksenberg, ed. *The Identities of Persons*. Berkeley: University of California Press, 1976.

_____. "A Literary Postscript: Characters, Persons, Selves and Individuals." In *The Identities of Persons*, pp. 301-24. Berkeley: University of California Press, 1976.

_____. "Persons and Persona." In *The Person and the Human Mind: Issues in Ancient and Modern Philosophy*. Edited by Christopher Gill, pp. 21-38. Oxford: Clarendon Press, 1990.

Rorty, Richard. *Contingency, Irony, and Solidarity*. Cambridge: Cambridge University Press, 1989.

Ross, David. *Aristotle*. London: Methuen, 1949.

Ross, W.D. *The Right and the Good*. Oxford: Oxford University Press, 1930.

Russell, Bertrand. *Human Knowledge: Its Scope and Limits*. London: George Allen and Unwin, 1948.

_____. *The Problems of Philosophy*. Oxford: Oxford University Press, 1959.

_____. *An Inquiry Into Meaning and Truth*. Baltimore, MD: Penguin Books, 1962.

_____. *An Outline of Philosophy*. London: George Allen and Unwin, 1970.

_____. "Science and Ethics." In *Philosophy: Paradox and Discovery*. Edited by Arthur J. Minton. New York: McGraw-Hill, 1976.

Rycroft, Charles. "Dissociation of the Personality." In *The Oxford Companion to the Mind*. Edited by Richard L. Gregory, pp. 197-98. Oxford: Oxford University Press, 1987.

Ryle, Gilbert. *The Concept of Mind*. Harmondsworth, Middlesex: Penguin Books, 1963.

Sartre, Jean-Paul. *Existentialism and Humanism*. Translated by Philip Mairet. London: Methuen, 1949.

_____. *Being and Nothingness: A Phenomenological Essay on Ontology*. Translated by Hazel E. Barnes. New York: Washington Square Press, 1966.

Schlitz, D. *The Gambler*. Elektra/Asylum Records, ASCAP, 1980.

Singer, Peter. *Practical Ethics*. Cambridge: Cambridge University Press, 1979.

Smith, Steven G. *The Concept of the Spiritual: An Essay in First Philosophy*. Philadelphia: Temple University Press, 1988.

Stevenson, Leslie. *Seven Theories of Human Nature*. 2nd ed. Oxford: Oxford University Press, 1987.

Stone, Jim. "Parfit and the Buddha: Why There Are No People." *Philosophy and Phenomenological Research* 68, 3 (March 1988): 519-32.

Strawson, P.F. *Individuals: An Essay in Descriptive Metaphysics*. London: Methuen, 1959.

Stumpf, Samuel E. *Socrates to Sartre: A History of Philosophy*, 4th ed. New York: McGraw-Hill, 1988.

Thines, Georges. "Husserl." In *The Oxford Companion to the Mind*. Edited by Richard L. Gregory, pp. 326-27. Oxford: Oxford University Press, 1987.

Tolstoï, Lyof N. *Life*. London: Walter Scott, 1889.

Trendelenberg, Adolf. "A Contribution to the History of the Word Person: A Posthumous Treatise by Adolf Trendelenberg." Translated by Carl H. Haessler, *Monist* 20 (1910): 336-63.

Trevarthen, Colwyn. "Split Brain and the Mind." In *The Oxford Companion to the Mind*. Edited by Richard L. Gregory, pp. 741-46. Oxford: Oxford University Press, 1987.

Trigg, Roger. *Ideas of Human Nature*. Oxford: Basil Blackwell, 1988.

Unger, Peter. *Identity Consciousness and Value*. Oxford: Oxford University Press, 1990.

Walker, Ralph. "Leibniz's Philosophy of Mind." In *The Oxford Companion to the Mind*. Edited by Richard Gregory, p. 433. Oxford: Oxford University Press, 1987.

Wedeking, Gary. "Locke's Metaphysics of Personal Identity." *History of Philosophy Quarterly* 4 (January 1987): 17-31.

Whitehead, Alfred North. *Symbolism: Its Meaning and Effect*. New York: G. P. Putnam's Sons, 1959.

_____. *Process and Reality*. New York: Free Press, 1969.

Wiggins, David. *Identity and Spatio-temporal Continuity*. Oxford: Basil Blackwell, 1967.

_____. *Sameness and Substance*. Oxford: Basil Blackwell, 1980.

Wilkes, Kathleen. *Real People: Personal Identity Without Thought Experiments*. Oxford: Oxford University Press, 1988.

Williams, Bernard. *Morality: An Introduction to Ethics*. New York: Harper & Row, 1972.

_____. "Personal Identity And Individuation." In *Problems of the Self*, pp. 1-18. Cambridge: Cambridge University Press, 1973.

_____ "Are Persons Bodies?" In *Problems of the Self*, pp. 64-81. Cambridge: Cambridge University Press, 1973.

_____. *Ethics and the Limits of Philosophy*. Cambridge, MA: Harvard University Press, 1985.

Wittgenstein, Ludwig. *The Blue and Brown Books*. New York: Harper Colophon Books, 1958.

_____. *Tractatus Logico-Philosophicus*. Translated by D.F. Pears and B.F. MacGuinness. London: Routledge and Keagan Paul, 1961.

_____. *Philosophical Remarks*. Edited by Rush Rhees. Translated by Raymond Hargreaves and Roger White. Oxford: Basil Blackwell, 1975.

_____. *Philosophical Investigations*. Translated by G.E.M. Anscombe. Oxford: Basil Blackwell, 1976.

Index

333